WHAT GOES ON

WHAT GOES ON

THE BEATLES, THEIR MUSIC, AND THEIR TIME

Walter Everett and Tim Riley

OXFORD
UNIVERSITY PRESS

OXFORD
UNIVERSITY PRESS

Oxford University Press is a department of the University of Oxford. It furthers
the University's objective of excellence in research, scholarship, and education
by publishing worldwide. Oxford is a registered trade mark of Oxford University
Press in the UK and certain other countries.

Published in the United States of America by Oxford University Press
198 Madison Avenue, New York, NY 10016, United States of America.

Library of Congress Cataloging-in-Publication Data
Names: Everett, Walter, 1954– author. | Riley, Tim, 1960– author.
Title: What goes on : the Beatles, their music, and their time /
Walter Everett and Tim Riley.
Description: New York, NY : Oxford University Press, [2019] |
Includes bibliographical references and index.
Identifiers: LCCN 2018045545 | ISBN 9780190213176 (pbk. : alk. paper) |
ISBN 9780190949877 (hardcover : alk. paper)
Subjects: LCSH: Beatles—Criticism and interpretation. |
Rock music—England—1961–1970—History and criticism.
Classification: LCC ML421.B4 E92 2019 | DDC 782.42166092/2—dc23
LC record available at https://lccn.loc.gov/2018045545

9 8 7 6 5 4 3 2 1

Paperback printed by Sheridan Books, Inc., United States of America
Hardback printed by Bridgeport National Bindery, Inc., United States of America

CONTENTS

PREFACE

In today's world, popular music styles, their means of distribution, and their listenerships grow increasingly fragmented. It's hard to imagine any musical artist releasing a new collection of songs once—let alone twice—every year. But consider such a schedule, with each new record meeting a clamor of intense critical support and sales that dominate those of all others until that artist's own next record came due. That's what the Beatles were to the 1960s. Their twelve full albums, twenty-two singles, and thirteen extended-play discs—all 215 original EMI tracks (plus solo releases and various assorted ephemera) recorded in a stretch of just under seven years—led and mirrored the rapidly changing social developments taking place in a newly global ecology. For the '60s, the Beatles were *What Goes On*.

At this writing, nearly all of the songs recorded by the Beatles have had their fifty-year anniversary. Still, it seems that all college students know the names and sounds of at least a few Beatles songs, some know dozens, and younger kids too know the records as handed down from multiple older generations. Everyone knows music that was influenced in one way or another by this British foursome, because they changed the popular music industry in terms of songwriting, performing, recording and marketing procedures, the role of personal and filmed appearances in the shaping of a musical career, and the very legitimacy of pop as art.

The authors have taught college courses on the music of the Beatles in a wide range of schools and to a diverse span of student constituencies since the summer of 1981. Over the years, our various courses have hosted students of journalism, of the history of the alternative press, of cultural and media studies, of music criticism and various other professional music disciplines at the undergraduate and graduate level. In addition, we've given talks on the Beatles at dozens of universities and public audiences such as library gatherings, scholarly conferences, and radio and television broadcasts. We've written on the Beatles for academic music journals, general-interest book readers, podcast listeners, and blog subscribers. With a growing number of college courses devoted to the Beatles for students of varied disciplines we became aware of the need for a textbook that would cover the band's music in a thorough way, teaching the elements of music from the ground up, and contextualizing it in an understanding of the times in which it was produced. The '60s were, after all, the most explosive decade for popular music of the twentieth century. The

Beatles' accomplishment as leaders of this movement ties together with the larger culture of arts, intellectual development, and historical events.

This book and its accompanying online materials combine to introduce readers—particularly those with an instructor's classroom guidance—to the Beatles' story and to how they redefined pop music, reworking the early rock 'n' roll of Elvis Presley, Little Richard, Buddy Holly, Chuck Berry, Carl Perkins, the Everly Brothers, the Coasters, and Carole King, along with a wide range of other materials from realms that had never before been considered as related to pop culture, such as the Western classical string quartet, North Indian ragas, the European avant-garde, and East Asian philosophy. To fully appreciate their art requires some background in the basics of musical structure, so one important goal of this book is to introduce the concepts of musical form, instrumentation, harmonic structure, melodic patterns, and rhythmic devices. But even students with a strong background in music fundamentals and those who consider themselves experts on the Beatles can learn much in these pages; we seek not only to describe the content of the Beatles' music but also to offer interpretations and, by extension, to help all listeners develop strategies from our examples for creating their own interpretations. The art of listening involves the growth of a very personal and creative relationship with the potential meanings behind these and any other songs. Beatle John Lennon and his artistic inspiration Yoko Ono particularly believed that music was unfinished until the listener had a chance to develop his or her own understanding of it; they even released two albums called *Unfinished Music* to this end, while John also brought this attitude to his Beatle projects, whether requiring the deciphering of puns or challenging listeners to conjure many intertextual musical, literary, and cultural references.

We believe any college instructor, whether their interest lies in cultural and media studies, textual analysis, music performance or education, musicology, composition, or music theory, will find a ready pathway to their desired objective through *What Goes On*. This book and online materials offer a wealth of approaches to guide a semester-long college course in the music of the Beatles and their cultural context, with varying avenues traversing alternative levels of depth. Some readers will wish to concentrate on the band's historical development and its relation to world events, which become increasingly relevant as the story progresses. Some will be more interested in enriching their understanding of the historical record by immersing themselves in the musical discussion. Still others who possess some experience in focused listening can push further into exclusively musical matters. We leave it to the instructor to review our offerings and select the most appropriate tack for any given environmental conditions.

What Goes On, then, comprises four basic streams of approaches:

1. Narrative history: A biographical treatment of the band's story, highlighting the four major themes of their catalog and times: race, class, generational conflict, and gender relationships and stereotypes. Each chapter closes with discussion questions and selections for further reading. Those pursuing research papers will find leads in the more comprehensive book-ending bibliography.

2. Song essays (embedded chronologically within chapters): Deep-focus analyses of particular tracks, highlighting the artistic tensions between form and content, technology and imagination, mechanics and meaning. Song charts that follow each essay illustrate significant structural signposts for attention to detail. The essays vary in depth in the

ways they rely on a student's background in technical matters, so as to reach the widest range of readers and to suggest the breadth of the Beatles' appeal.

3. Online video tutorials: Full definitions and a thorough overview of musical concepts and instrumental details as related to the Beatles' music, from rhythmic patterns to harmonic tropes, with full demonstrations on piano, guitars, vocals, bass, and drums. You will wish to use external speakers, headphones, or earbuds to focus your listening, particularly as laptops and smaller devices are unable to reproduce bass frequencies. And screens sized 13″ diagonally or larger are recommended for viewing the animated graphics and titles. While the videos themselves can be lengthy, they are divided into short chapters, which may be assigned individually by the timings given in the note below, "About the Companion Website."

4. Interactive Listening Guides (online, iOs app, and DVD): Animated illustrations of track details to accompany close listening. Just cue up the recording from any source (CD, streaming platform, or YouTube) at 0:00 and start when directed by the guide.

A selected Beatles bibliography opens up the expansive critical and scholarly literature for further research. One could easily devote a lifetime to just reading the best of the best about these musicians, which brings to mind a catchphrase heard since the band broke up in early 1970: *Beatles forever!*

A note on chord designations: Some readers (particularly those who play guitar) may wonder at the use of Roman-numeral designations (e.g., IV), rather than root/color labels (e.g., Dm) as chord symbols. The latter system indicates where the individual harmonies sound, whereas the former indicates chordal relationships (harmonic function) with or without reference to any particular key. This decision was made for a number of reasons: chiefly, it is in the chord relationships, not the chords themselves, that Beatle songs are of primary interest. But also, some songs lie "in the cracks": "Strawberry Fields Forever," for instance, sounds neither in B♭ major nor in A major but in between. In other cases, songs may be widely available in more than one key, depending on the speed with which mastering took place: thus, mono and stereo mixes for "She's Leaving Home" are in different keys—neither is the "true" tonal center. In many other cases, the sounding key is not the key in which the Beatles performed their songs; "I'm Only Sleeping" sounds in E♭ minor in all releases, although the Beatles played it in E minor and the tape was then slowed down. From *Rubber Soul* through *Abbey Road*, the Beatles often used capos, and so any performance-aimed designation of chord by root would best include notes about performance practice that would lie beyond this book's purview. ⏵ Primers on chord construction can be found in Videos 1.3, 1.5, and 1.6.

Walter Everett, Ann Arbor
Tim Riley, Boston
April, 2019

PROLOGUE

WHO WERE THE BEATLES?

Who were the Beatles? John Lennon, Paul McCartney, George Harrison, and Ringo Starr formed the rock band from Liverpool, England, who recorded world-renowned albums and singles from 1962 through 1969. They sang and played instruments, but most importantly created the words and music for nearly all of the more than two hundred songs they recorded, bringing more and more imagination to each project. Their combined vocals, guitars, drums, keyboards, and much more brought pop songwriting, performance, and recording techniques to new heights that made them the most musically and culturally influential rock band in history. John, Paul, George, and Ringo brought the world together through music, style, attitudes, and dreams; their story has been told innumerable times from a variety of angles. This book covers the facts of their lives and work, interprets their musical message through the varied poetic meanings within their songs, and relates their story to the larger cultural history of their vibrant and turbulent times. We address a wide general audience, from inquisitive college students to the curious music listener, and anyone who wishes to learn more about that volatile decade, the 1960s.

Who were the Beatles? They asked themselves that question constantly, as when assuming such a confounding group name (echoing the Crickets, the band backing their 1950s' idol Buddy Holly). They posed coyly as "Sgt. Pepper's Lonely Hearts Club Band" (see Photo 0.1) when releasing that landmark album by that title in 1967, hoping that adopting a fictitious collective alter ego might free their creativity. With every project, they dropped previous trademarks and devised new delights. Through all this furious creativity, releasing two albums and other radio hits most years, the Beatles fundamentally changed what it means to be a pop musician. They especially created new kinds of studio-based compositions in five final projects released over a three-year period after they stopped touring in 1966. Their image changed from that of a studied, well-dressed quartet in the public eye to the casual appearance of unrecognizable recluses as they dropped a managed compliance to espouse a free expression of will. Their lyrics matured from covering aspects of boy-girl romance to questioning their own perspectives, those of their fans and critics,

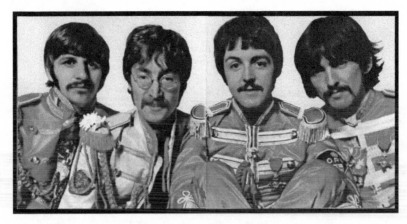

PHOTO 0.1. Michael Cooper's portrait of the Beatles, March 30,1967. Inside gatefold cover of *Sgt. Pepper's Lonely Hearts Club Band* LP (released in UK June 1, 1967). *Left to right*: Ringo Starr, John Lennon, Paul McCartney, George Harrison.

and the nature of fame, the modern era, and life itself. Their music grew from an embrace of pop conventions to the creation of imaginative, original sounds and patterns on a symphonic scale.

Liverpudlians John Lennon, Paul McCartney, George Harrison, and then-drummer Pete Best exuded energy, charm, and humor in surviving in a war-ravaged seaport, then winning over first their inexperienced manager Brian Epstein in November 1961 and next their skeptical record producer George Martin in June 1962. Then, with Ringo Starr replacing Best on drums, their charisma clicked anew, allowing them to win over a hostile American press in February 1964, any of the world's remaining holdouts with their brazen musical film *A Hard Day's Night* in July 1964, and music's intelligentsia with such radically original works as *Revolver* (1966) and *Sgt. Pepper's Lonely Hearts Club Band* (1967). All four personalities were examined and stereotyped as to which one was the most artistically imaginative, which led the development of musical craft, which possessed a spiritual calm, and which acted as an everyman to keep the band rooted: the thinker, the entertainer, the quiet anti-materialist, and the humble. Initially, their charge intensified in hit record after hit record, rechanneling their key influences into a compelling new sound: the liberated physicality and visceral vocals of Elvis Presley; the lascivious yelps and stage antics of Little Richard; the downhome sweetness of the Everly Brothers; the phallic, bluesy electric guitar strut and stick-in-your-eye glint of Chuck Berry; the charmingly logical rush of songwriter Carole King; and the reliance of Berry, Buddy Holly, and Carl Perkins upon original material, their own clever words, melodies, rhythms, chords, and guitar stylings. Despite borrowing from such precursors in 1963 to attain the biggest-selling UK record to date with "She Loves You," the Beatles adjusted their sound with more subtle shadings in 1964 ("I'm a Loser"), expanded their palette with instruments from around the world and from throughout musical history in 1965 ("Yesterday," "Norwegian Wood," "Girl"), experimented with altered states of consciousness in 1966 ("She Said, She Said," "Tomorrow Never Knows," "Rain," "Got to Get You Into My Life"), harvested radical new colors and shifts of orientation in 1967 ("Lucy in the Sky with Diamonds," "A Day in the Life"), abstracted a dreamscape of the band's unconscious in 1968 ("Revolution 9"), and finally returned to casual rock 'n' roll ("One after 909") and polished group performance ("Come Together") by their final sessions in 1969. The band's musical legacy extends well beyond its 1970 breakup, continuing into the twenty-first century through such far-flung artists as Danger Mouse, Radiohead, TV on the Radio, Sam [née Leslie Ann] Phillips, the Black Keys, Fountains of Wayne, and Wilco. Hyperbole has long since become a cliché in articulating the Beatles' accomplishments, but even in today's digital recording studios, their work is invoked in reverential tones. As rock stars, they assumed a rarefied status previously reserved for movie icons.

The Beatles' mark on the larger culture has been similarly profound. Like Elvis Presley, the band extended rock's key themes of race, class, youth, and gender. The postwar rise of the teenager in the 1950s led to a youthful embrace of hopeful heroes rejected by world-weary parents. When the Beatles established a beachhead on American shores in 1964, elders proclaimed their sound "noise" and their long hair alarming, articulating a generation gap between "establishment" tastes and free-spirited youth. They and the "British Invasion" that followed brought to a mesmerized world a galvanizing beat boom, smart contemporary dress that renewed London as a fashion mecca, and an all-out rejection of racial and gender inequalities, authoritarianism, and the religions and wars symbolic of the "establishment." The Beatles refused to play to racially segregated American audiences in 1964, sang for love and understanding in 1966 and 1967 and for peace in 1969, and started a trend of rock stars taking social stands and branding charities. Above all, the Beatles led their listeners to question assumptions and pursue creative individual identities. As successive generations encounter their music, many of these same values hold true. Being British, the Beatles retranslated many American musical tensions to create a new, universal approach to pop sound. Largely through the Beatles' popularity, rock 'n' roll ceased to be a distinctly American style. As early as 1965, the world's two most important rock bands—the Beatles and the Rolling Stones—came from the United Kingdom. This transformation of rock 'n' roll into what we now commonly call rock signifies the larger coming-of-age story their music relates, from teenage romantic and sexual experience to the concrete-hard foundation of young adulthood and beyond. This story arc—from youth to maturity—remains one of the Beatles' most important contributions to their diverse global audience.

ABOUT THE COMPANION WEBSITE

www.oup.com/us/whatgoeson

Oxford University Press has created a website to accompany *What Goes On: The Beatles, Their Music, and Their Time*. A timeline of the Beatles' lives and work, contextualized with relevant world events; video demonstrations of musical topics; a series of interactive listening guides that pinpoint events within a representative selection of Beatle songs; and a listing of recordings to have influenced the Beatles up to the point of their worldwide fame may be found there. We encourage the reader to take advantage of these additional resources, but please note that bass frequencies do not reproduce well on many devices including laptop computers. Earbuds or, better, over-the-ear headphones or external speakers are recommended for full audio streaming. Videos available online are indicated in the text with Oxford's ▶ symbol.

All materials are available without password protection. Appendix 1, our listing of recordings to influence the Beatles, and Appendix 2, our timeline of events, are presented as PDF files that may be freely downloaded.

The eleven videos may be viewed in their entirety or in individual chapters that may be accessed separately according to the following guide of timing cues in the videos' progress. (Currently, videos cannot be accessed by search engines such as those included with browsers including Firefox, Safari, etc., but only with their URL addresses, given below. The URLs are also given at the book's Oxford website, as live links, or for copy-and-paste convenience.)

Video 1.1 Beatle Records on Vinyl
http://youtu.be/StK_Wv5QPk4
   1:13 Vinyl formats
   3:27 Record packaging
   6:23 Running order
   7:40 Audio reproduction
   9:48 Some vinyl highlights: singles and EPs
   13:40 Some vinyl highlights: LPs

Video 1.2 Rhythm, Part 1
http://youtu.be/3UvJvSJRMrA
    1:30 Tempo
    3:10 Harmonic rhythm
    5:35 Accent and meter
    7:49, 25:57 Downbeat
    8:39 Upbeat
    8:50 Syncopation
    9:21, 27:12 Backbeat
    9:56 Offbeat
    12:34 The bass drum
    12:57 The snare drum
    13:08, 28:10 The hi-hat
    14:52 Dotted pattern on bass drum
    16:35 12/8 meter
    18:03 Pre-Beatles use of the drum set
    29:29 The surf backbeat
    31:17 The shuffle
    33:18 Phrase rhythm
    35:44 Stop time

Video 1.3 Form, Part 1
http://youtu.be/lv1dHWLg_Rw
    4:19 Twelve-bar blues
    5:40 Basics of major scale and harmony
    18:35, 24:49 The refrain
    21:02 The period
    24:07 The verse
    25:19 Bar form
    26:37 Strophic form
    27:13 The chorus
    29:12 The bridge
    30:00 The retransition
    31:07 Open phrase group
    37:59 The instrumental break

Video 1.4 Melody, Part 1
http://youtu.be/XY__57yCviI
    2:57 The chromatic scale
    3:53 The major scale
    10:38 The minor pentatonic scale
    12:29 The tumbling strain
    13:01 The 0–2–5 "blues" trichord

Video 1.5 Harmony, Part 1

http://youtu.be/yWaDafGaLoU

    0:18 Interval sizes

    2:08 The triad

    4:08 The major triad

    4:11 The minor triad

    8:54 Register

    9:12 Voicing

    9:30 Doubling

    14:30 The bass as harmonic support

    20:55 Power chords

Video 1.6 Harmony, Part 2

http://youtu.be/fuGQp_6oT8U

    0:30 Roots and scale degrees

    1:54 Harmonic function

    2:09 Tonic triad (I)

    2:32 Dominant triad (V)

    4:43 Authentic cadence

    5:03 Dominant preparation: IV and ii

    8:50 Half cadence

    11:38 Plagal cadence

    12:43 Deceptive cadence

    15:07 Circle of fifths

    19:25 Major triads on minor-pentatonic scale

Video 1.7 Arrangement, Part 1

http://youtu.be/kdSv39J22HE

    0:50 The doubled bass line

    2:42 The tattoo

    5:30 Solo vocals

    6:05 Paul's solo vocals

    7:20 John's solo vocals

    8:07 George's solo vocals

    8:23 Ringo's solo vocals

    9:01 John and Paul singing in unison

    9:44 Paul's descant lines

    11:06 John and Paul doubling at the octave

    11:27 Parallel thirds

    12:53 John's lower harmony vocal

Video 2.2 Form, Part 2

http://youtu.be/hzS5QpY8wkg

    0:46 SRDC form

    11:41 The introduction

18:37 The coda

23:17 The one-more-time cadence

Video 2.3 Rhythm, Part 2

http://youtu.be/Fbq43W-Jndw

1:08 The tom-toms

2:33 Cross-sticking

5:39 Ringo's bass drum

7:48 Pete Best's snare work

8:43 Ringo's snare work

9:10 The drum roll

10:12 Ringo's cymbal work

12:04 Ringo's use of the hi-hat

16:55 Ringo's changing drum style through 1963

17:54 Ringo's raver mode

Video 2.6 Arrangement, Part 2

http://youtu.be/fCoc0bATJ_Q

0:44 Multiphonics

1:45 Falsetto

2:42 Florid ornamentation: the melisma

3:35 The mordent

4:45, 5:30 Parallel motion

4:58, 6:35 Similar motion

5:08, 7:17 Contrary motion

5:13, 8:01 Oblique motion

5:40 Parallel fourths

8:46 The countermelody

9:20 Backing vocals

Video 3.1 Rhythm, Part 3

http://youtu.be/36j6CXO8QEM

1:09 The slow introduction

2:00 The fermata (the caesura)

3:03 The *son clave* rhythm

7:10 The triplet

11:01 Ringo's use of syncopation

13:06 Ringo's snare fills

14:01 Ringo's tom-tom fills

14:40 Ringo as "the left-handed right-handed drummer"

19:05 The flam

19:38 The floor tom-tom

20:32 Ringo's use of the crash cymbal

A selection of twenty-one Beatle recordings, most of which are covered in the text's boxed essays, are detailed through moving timelines grouped into early, middle, and late songs, available at the URLs given below. Each cues for starting while playing (as on iTunes) or streaming (as from Spotify) the Beatles' audio recordings.

(* indicates corresponding song essay box)

EARLY

https://timrileyauthor.com/what-goes-on-beatles-textbook/listening-guide-i/

- ▶*"I Saw Her Standing There"
- ▶*"There's a Place"
- ▶*"All I've Got to Do"
- ▶*"Not a Second Time"
- ▶*"She Loves You"
- ▶*"If I Fell"
- ▶*"I Should Have Known Better"

MIDDLE

https://timrileyauthor.com/what-goes-on-beatles-textbook/listening-guide-ii/

- ▶*"We Can Work It Out"
- ▶*"Ticket to Ride"
- ▶*"Doctor Robert"
- ▶*"Paperback Writer"
- ▶*"Strawberry Fields Forever"
- ▶*"Penny Lane"
- ▶*"A Day in the Life"

LATE

https://timrileyauthor.com/what-goes-on-beatles-textbook/listening-guide-iii/

- ▶*"Dear Prudence"
- ▶*"Everybody's Got Something to Hide Except Me and My Monkey"
- ▶"Happiness Is a Warm Gun"
- ▶*"Don't Let Me Down"
- ▶*"I've Got a Feeling"
- ▶*"Two of Us"
- ▶"I Want You (She's So Heavy)"

WHAT GOES ON

INTRODUCTION

Revolt into Sound: Race, Class, Generation Divide, and Gender Dominate Pre-Beatles Rock 'n' Roll

JOHN LENNON DISCOVERS ROCK 'N' ROLL

As a sixteen-year-old at the Quarry Bank School in Liverpool, the future Beatle John Lennon often skipped out at lunch to gather at friends' homes for cigarettes, hot chocolate, and potato crisps while listening to records. One of these mates, Michael Hill, had just visited Holland on a school trip in the spring of 1956 and found a 78 rpm record by a mysterious character named Little Richard. He knew he had to play it for Lennon. It was called "Long Tall Sally" (see Photo 0.2), and he assured Lennon it was "better than Elvis," a declaration too galling to be true during a season when Presley bestrode the galaxy like a colossus with major hits like "Heartbreak Hotel" (see Photo 0.3) and "Hound Dog." Hill remembers the moment vividly:

> I rarely remember him losing his composure, but that day he dropped his guard completely. . . . He was clearly stunned at what he heard. He didn't want to be convinced that Little Richard was better than Elvis. We played it over and over again, and I must say it was one of the few times any of us ever saw Lennon completely lose his tough veneer. (Riley 2011, 55)

All his whooping and blaring made Little Richard sound as if he was trying detonate Hill's old family phonograph from within, and the hysteria temporarily stunned Lennon's typically macho

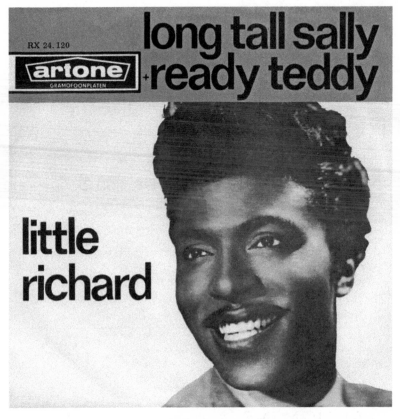

PHOTO 0.2. Little Richard, "Long Tall Sally" 45 (originally released in US, March 1956), as reissued in the Netherlands in 1963.

facade. This particular record also counted as a futuristic rarity: Although Presley had become a household name in Britain by then, Little Richard didn't score his first UK hit until a year later. And since the BBC didn't yet program any rock 'n' roll, fans had to catch their favorite performers on TV or tune in to Radio Luxembourg beamed from the European continent late Sunday nights. Lennon remembered this moment and talked about it for years afterward: "When I heard it, it was so great I couldn't speak. . . . How could they be happening in my life, both of them?" Lennon would soon discover, upon meeting his future partner, Paul McCartney, that Elvis Presley and Little Richard were to be shared musical heroes.

When one of Lennon's friends pointed out that Little Richard was African American (this term was not used in the 1950s; in fact, Lennon's friend used the N-word in referring to Richard), Lennon's response betrayed his naiveté, even as the music thundered something vast and unknowable in his young mind. "I didn't know Negroes sang," he said. To his inexperienced ears, the gulf between white and black was so basic that they might as well live in separate realities—which to a great extent, they did.

"Thank you, God," he told himself, relieved that Presley and Little Richard had somehow come along at the same point to make sense of his troubled adolescence. The sound proclaimed how much room there was for both rock characters—and more. Within weeks, Lennon had formed a

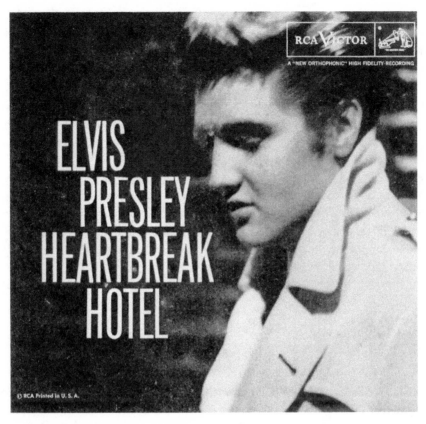

PHOTO 0.3. Elvis Presley, "Heartbreak Hotel" / "I Was the One" 45 (released in US January 27, 1956).

band, the Quarry Men. He began singing the American folk and rock songs that had made such a huge impact on his British ears.

A BRITISH RESPONSE TO AMERICAN THEMES

To understand the pre-Beatles era in rock history involves several imaginative leaps: How differently would we hear Elvis Presley or Little Richard today had the Beatles not come along? (Can one understand modern cinema without Charlie Chaplin or Alfred Hitchcock?) Part of the Beatles' accomplishment was to seem inevitable, but several cultural planets had to align to determine how they came upon their style, mastered it, and began retooling it toward their own ends. The Beatles both consolidated and built upon their predecessors. Understanding this larger context deepens the way we hear the band's conversation with rock history.

To begin with, these young British musicians, the first generation to grow up with rock 'n' roll on the radio, listened with different ears than Americans did. To Lennon's ear, rock 'n' roll sounded like "working class" music, suggesting how thoroughly it was embraced among less affluent and anti-establishment listeners. After all, in 1960, blacks made up barely 2 percent of the UK population, and ethnic prejudice had ugly contours, chiefly expressed in anti-Semitism and working-class resentment. In addition, the British economy strained under massive war debt throughout the

1950s. Goods and services were far scarcer than in America, which made the Hollywood fantasy of American life seem that much more magical and out of reach. In America, the surface world of the 1950s spelled exuberant materialism; in economic terms, in the United Kingdom, those yearning for America's '50s had to wait for London's Swinging '60s.

Comprising four distinct personalities, the Beatles amplified all these rock 'n' roll values, enlarging some while leaving others behind. Indeed, early on, the band's sheer musicianship stole attention from how stridently they avoided sounding "black" (especially compared to their closest rivals, the Rolling Stones). Ironically, they largely sidestepped the issue of race in their catalog.

The Beatles' impact on rock history proves so vast that most of the world, including America, now hears a lot of this early music through Beatle ears. As they ascended the stepladder of performing and recording in the early 1960s, the band mastered much of this early rock repertoire as a primary library of moods and effects. To understand where the Beatles' sounds came from and the tradition they wanted to join, we need to put into context what Lennon heard on that day in 1956.

ELVIS PRESLEY AND OTHER FIRST-GENERATION ROCKERS

Elvis Presley's breakout success as an unlikely Memphis singer who stormed the southern and then national pop charts during 1955–1956 magnifies other social forces. In fact, many argue that rock's early history traces the civil rights era in creative terms. Several cultural signs pointed toward greater integration long before 1954's *Brown v. Board of Education* decision, which integrated public schools (by law if not in practice). Jackie Robinson joined the Brooklyn Dodgers in 1947, becoming the first black player on a major-league baseball team. President Truman integrated the military with an executive order in 1948. Just weeks before Presley cut his first single, "That's All Right (Mama)," on June 17, 1954, Robinson had his best day ever at the plate, hitting two home runs and two doubles. The following season, his Dodgers beat the Yankees in the 1955 World Series. But Robinson's success sparked a racist backlash, and he was the target of hate mail and angry outbursts from white crowds wherever he went. Similar threats attended later African American public figures like the Rev. Dr. Martin Luther King, Jr., and heavyweight champion Muhammad Ali.

In Lennon and McCartney's Liverpool, of course, racial tensions had nowhere near the same fever pitch. A polyglot seaport with the oldest Chinatown in Europe, the town greeted ethnic minorities at a relatively modest rate. Blacks mingled with whites as a matter of course, and with no ancestral slavery (although historically Liverpool as a shipping center had a huge role in the global slave trade), the wildness in black music symbolized a more exotic status than that of "oppressed minority." Derry Wilkie (né Derek Davis) of Derry and the Seniors was a black man from Liverpool's poor Toxteth district who just happened to front a white band. Few in that early Merseyside scene took much notice of the racial mix. Wilkie's Seniors would earn status in later years as one of the first Liverpool beat bands to visit Hamburg, pioneering the route that would later catapult the Beatles to fame. (In fact, Britain as a whole would continue to have more of an open mind to African American music than Americans themselves would: for example, Ike and Tina Turner's rock-oriented "River Deep Mountain High," a barrier-breaking post-R&B record produced by the legendary Phil Spector and released in May 1966 that never got higher than no. 88 on *Billboard*'s singles chart in the United States but was a no. 3 smash in the United Kingdom.)

By the end of 1955, RCA Records bought out Presley's contract with the small Memphis label Sun Records for the unprecedented sum of $40,000 (about $376,000 in 2019 dollars). Presley rose as pop's answer to Hollywood's Marlon Brando or James Dean: a new figure who appealed to younger audiences with larger-than-life daring and zeal. Presley's cardboard acting in a number of B-grade films became a yardstick for how little Hollywood knew how to take advantage of such eccentricities and how the old showbiz scaffolds creaked in support of such novel talent.

To the Beatles over in Liverpool, Presley's music counted for far more than any other aspect of his persona, commercial projects, or social significance. For them, Elvis was a wildly ambitious singer whose country, gospel, R&B, and rock singles delivered something fresh, colorful, and cunning. In rock scholarship, several schools of thought have sprung up: many still value Presley's blues-oriented Sun sides—like his debut recording "That's All Right" and "Mystery Train"—above everything else he ever did, including his influential RCA singles, staples such as "Hound Dog," "Love Me Tender" from his debut film, and "Blue Suede Shoes."

When Lennon met his future songwriting collaborator Paul McCartney in July 1957, their first moments of bonding included shared rapture over records by Presley, Little Richard, and Eddie Cochran. McCartney remembers the first time a school friend introduced him to Presley, also in 1956, when RCA began releasing his material in the United Kingdom: "Somebody pulled out a music paper, and there was an advert for 'Heartbreak Hotel.' Elvis looked so great: 'That's him, that's him—the Messiah has arrived!' Then when we heard the song, there was the proof" (*Beatles Anthology* 2000, 21). As Lennon and McCartney studied their hero and learned to play their instruments, they adopted a lot of this early rock 'n' roll material into their repertoire, including "Heartbreak Hotel" and "Blue Suede Shoes" and Presley's early Sun tracks such as "That's All Right" and "I Forgot to Remember to Forget." Lennon's eccentric mother, Julia, even named her cat after Elvis. One of the Beatles' earliest aspirations was to be "bigger than Elvis," which was as ridiculously hopeful as it was prophetic. As history shows, they became bigger in commercial, aesthetic and cultural terms.

Less than a decade later, the Beatles became universal symbols of the teen explosion forged by Presley, Little Richard, Carl Perkins, Jerry Lee Lewis, Chuck Berry, Buddy Holly, the Everly Brothers, and the Coasters. Much of Presley's preteen audience came of age as the '60s counterculture: listeners who were ten to twelve years old in 1956 turned eighteen to twenty in 1964 and caught the Beatles throughout their college years, just as the civil rights movement evolved into student protests against both the nuclear threats posed by the amorphous Cold War and the very real tragedy of the growing Vietnam War. (The Cold War was based in the West's fear of the global spread of Soviet-based communism, marked by the Iron Curtain that divided postwar Western Europe from Soviet-bloc states—centered on the division of Germany itself; the Soviet Union engineering an atomic bomb in 1949, thus beginning the US/Soviet arms race; China's turning "red" the same year; the Korean War of 1950–1953; the start of the Vietnam War in 1955, with the first (noncombat) American troops arriving there in 1961; the Soviet crushing of the Hungarian Revolution in 1956; the space race as spurred on by the Soviet launch of the satellite Sputnik in 1957; and Castro's 1959 revolution in

Cuba.) For the first time in American life, teens were becoming a separate, defined part of the culture: As they had their own spending money, they were a market, and as a market they were listened to and catered to. To the young Beatles, Elvis signaled this shift.

The future Beatles, white northern Brits, crossed some of these same cultural boundaries by adopting this music as their own. The translation between cultures became a key feature of how their sound transfixed America in early 1964. Where some (mostly older) Americans recoiled in a moral panic at the style's metaphorical race mixing, British youths heard the style more as class comeuppance, the working stiff's rebuke of centuries of aristocracy. If Presley's white interpretations of the blues introduced race as an American musical issue, the Beatles universalized the new style by emphasizing attention to class, generations, and gender. (▶ The twelve-bar blues as a musical form is covered in Video 1.3.)

THE FIRST GENERATION OF ROCKERS

Elvis Presley kicked down the door for a parade of new talent that comprises rock 'n' roll's first generation. The Beatles saw themselves as successors to this tradition, and they faithfully covered songs by Presley and his peers as a way of joining in. In a stretch of just over fifteen months, between Presley's first Sun single, released in July 1954, and his RCA contract, signed in November 1955, Elvis, his producer Sam Phillips, and Sun Studios quickly became synonymous with the new style, first called "rockabilly" after its mix of black rocking and rolling and white hillbilly country sounds. Sun attracted young talent like a magnet: soon Phillips recorded a diverse crew of hitmakers, including Roy Orbison ("Ooby-Dooby"), Jerry Lee Lewis ("Great Balls of Fire"), Carl Perkins ("Blue Suede Shoes"), and Johnny Cash ("Teenage Queen"). Phillips added what he called a "slap-back echo" to the sound by using a delayed tape signal to simulate a booming environment. All of these artists played off differing aspects of rock's major themes, sprinkling different colors into the mix, emphasizing different polarities of feeling, and casting off more and more complicated moods. If the primary value of Presley's accomplishment lay in individuality, these and many others figures brought their own idiosyncrasies, their own flash and swagger, enlarging the style's meanings and renewing its ideas.

Meanwhile, not too far from Memphis, in St. Louis, a former hairdresser named Chuck Berry began churning out first-person teenage soap operas in song, even though by the time he scored his first 1955 hit, "Maybelline," Berry was nearing thirty. In a succession of numbers built around the same three chords that sounded both freshly minted and utterly familiar, including "Roll Over Beethoven" (1956) (see Photo 0.4), "Rock and Roll Music" (1957), and "Johnny B. Goode" (1958), Berry wrote his own material, a black man chasing a white teenage audience. In Chuck Berry's songs, teenage experience dominated storylines—like the school stress of "Almost Grown"—and young listeners embraced him as one of their own, even across the racial divide. John Lennon especially adored Berry's driving verbal rhythms, clever wordplay, and dynamic tales. Lennon told one of his friends that he particularly liked the protagonist of "Johnny B. Goode" as his namesake: he heard himself as one of Berry's heroes. Long after the Beatles recorded their own performances of Berry tunes, Lennon eventually met and worked with Berry in 1969 and again in 1972.

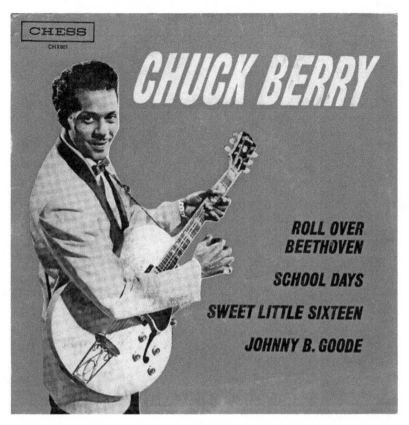

PHOTO 0.4. Chuck Berry, *Roll Over Beethoven* EP for Chess (originally released in US May 1956), as reissued in Australia in 1964.

From Lubbock, Texas, came Buddy Holly, who wrote disarming songs like "Peggy Sue" and "Words of Love" (1957). Visually, Holly looked nerdy, with thick glasses and a thin, wiry body; however, he also had an intense musical energy, which was complemented by his Fender Stratocaster guitar, carrying a newly introduced, space-age design. At least as important to the Beatles, Holly led his own band, the Crickets (see Photo 0.5). Lennon and McCartney latched onto this idea of a stable group that produced its own original material with electric lead and rhythm guitars, bass, and drums. Holly's act became a model for them in ways it had never been for Presley, Berry, Little Richard, and Jerry Lee Lewis, who all performed with varying backup players: all Holly's Crickets sang backup, and his electric guitar exuded futuristic cool against the stand-up acoustic bass. A new paradigm emerged: the self-contained unit, with singer, songwriter, lead and rhythm guitar, bass, and drum players all performing in studio, onstage, and over the airwaves as a compact ensemble. Holly also embodied an important link to country styles, not least because he most resembled the typically groomed country singer in his relatively chaste presentation. But he also sang Berry songs ("Brown-Eyed Handsome Man") with a mesmerizing glint and indulged in peculiar vocal hiccups that were oddly enchanting. Finally, Holly became an important technical maverick by following the lead of Les Paul in overdubbing his own voice on songs and tinkering with electronic echo. Holly enjoyed greater success in the United Kingdom than in his

PHOTO 0.5. The Crickets, *The Chirping Crickets* LP (released in US November 27, 1957). Buddy Holly is third from left.

native America, something that has continued to today. After many alternatives, the Beatles ultimately named themselves as successors to the Crickets.

These performers expanded the terms of Presley's breakthrough, creating new intrigues and harnessing new contradictions. Little Richard's outrageous bouffant unraveled as he screamed "Long Tall Sally," footnoting his skin color to the glory of his mane, making him a peacock more wily than threatening. (Few at the time took note of the gay signifiers in his act; after all, even the unquestionably heteronormative Elvis wore pink suits and eyeliner.) "Sally" became a staple of McCartney's repertoire, long serving as the Beatles' concert closer. And Carl Perkins concocted an indelible rock 'n' roll image with "Blue Suede Shoes," expressing the scorn of a lowlife who prizes style above everything else. Elvis scooped up the song as an emblem, his cover version eclipsing Perkins's prior recording in popularity when the song's composer was injured in a car accident and sidelined from promoting the song. Admiring Perkins as an innovative guitarist, the Beatles performed several of his numbers, notably with George Harrison singing "Everybody's Trying to Be My Baby" and John Lennon—and then Ringo Starr—doing "Honey Don't." Vocal arrangements that inspired the Beatles were provided by the Everly Brothers (see Photo 0.6), who blended a lead vocal with an upper descant harmony in "Wake Up Little Susie" (about a

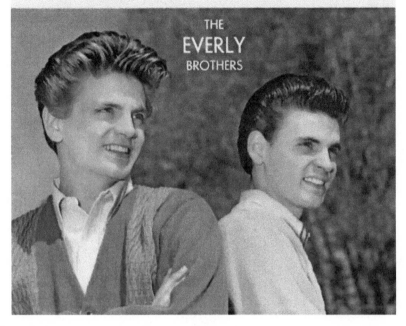

PHOTO 0.6. The Everly Brothers, "Lucille" / "So Sad (To Watch Good Love Go Bad)" 45 (released in US August 1960).

teen rushing his date home to Mom and Dad after sleeping with her), and the Coasters (see Photo 0.7), whose tenor Billy Guy would provide the calling lead vocal against the gospel-derived concerted response of his groupmates in then-humorous, now-creepy stalking tomcat songs like "Searchin'," "Young Blood," and "Three Cool Cats."

From these unruly beginnings, young listeners found confirmation in, and attraction to, a sound that adults feared and scorned. The adult world, in its moral panic, conspired against it as if to blunt early rock careers. There were simply no rock roadmaps yet, so traditional show business paths imposed themselves for lack of more appropriate alternatives. Presley baffled Hollywood, to the point where his movies work as a neutered, abstract parallel world to his earthy recordings, as though celluloid could project him only as half alive. Then the army drafted him right at the height of his fame in 1958. Being a good mama's boy and true-blue American, he suspended his career to serve as a private in the peacetime army in Friedberg, Germany. John Lennon later said, "Elvis died when he went into the army" (Booth 2000, 51). Just as devastating for rock's early history was Perkins's 1956 car accident; Little Richard kept finding religion and renouncing sinful secular music, taking to the pulpit, then relapsing; Jerry Lee Lewis took his thirteen-year-old cousin for his third bride, with the ensuing notoriety ending his pop career in 1958; and Buddy Holly died in an airplane crash at age twenty-two in early 1959.

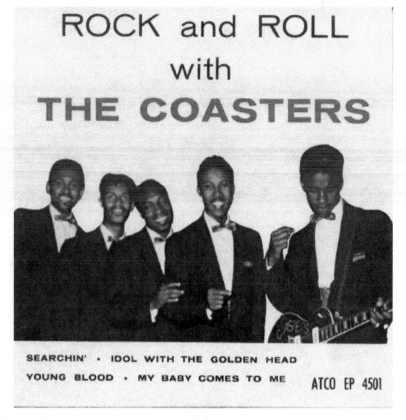

ROCK and ROLL
with
THE COASTERS

SEARCHIN' · IDOL WITH THE GOLDEN HEAD
YOUNG BLOOD · MY BABY COMES TO ME   ATCO EP 4501

PHOTO 0.7. The Coasters, *Rock and Roll with the Coasters* EP (released in US 1958). Billy Guy is fourth from left.

Conspiracy theorists believe that adult authorities officially targeted early rock performers. Much of this backlash was seated in racism—even when the artists themselves were white, their open embrace of black style served as an allegory for racial mixing, and a threat to the dominant white culture. Nowhere was this more fraught than where tinged with sex. As bell hooks writes,

> Undoubtedly, sexuality has been the site of many a black male's fall from grace. Irrespective of class, status, income, or level of education, for many black men sexuality remains the place where dysfunctional behavior first rears its ugly head. This is in part because of the convergence of racist sexist thinking about the black body, which has always projected onto the black body a hypersexuality. The history of the black male body begins in the United States with projections, with the imposition onto that body of white racist pornographic sexual fantasies. Central to this fantasy is the idea of the black male rapist. (hooks 2004, 67)

In late 1959, Chuck Berry was arrested for violating the Mann Act by transporting a fourteen-year-old Apache waitress across state lines, which many understood as code for a black man seducing a minor. After contesting his first trial, he served eighteen months in prison (1962–1963). While he had a few hits following his jail time—notably "No Particular Place to Go," "You Never Can Tell," and "The Promised Land"—Berry's career got a temporary sales bump on behalf of the Beatles, but he faded into an oldies act soon after. All of this only reinforced Berry's, and all of rock's, early subversive image.

It's also likely that economics played a role in the harsh reaction to rock 'n' roll. Most of the established, white-produced, popular music of the early 1950s was distributed and promoted by a small handful of "major" record companies operating coast-to-coast, whereas African American R&B was issued by numerous small, independent companies. The sudden mass popularity of black music crossing over to formerly white-controlled recording, broadcasting and sales threatened the majors' financial stranglehold on a huge market.

The Beatles latched onto many of rock 'n' roll's side currents to illuminate its history as a whole. When they first appeared on the British charts at the end of 1962 with "Love Me Do," listeners heard a distinctly old-fashioned R&B groove, unlike any from previous British performers, in their sound. However, the song should be compared with the then-current chart toppers: Johnny Leyton's "Johnny Remember Me," Shirley Bassey's "Reach for the Stars," and the Shadows' "Kon-Tiki"; none of these was remotely like the Beatles' raw first single. Very few British groups preceding the Beatles contained singers, guitars, bass, and drums. Ignoring these British hitmakers, the Beatles adored rockabilly, a cappella doo-wop, the vocal phrasing of the Everlys, early Motown soul, the Brill Building writers Gerry Goffin and Carole King, the "girl groups," and novelty acts such as the Coasters. In short, the explosive energies released by Presley and his peers created an ocean of sounds for young musicians to draw from, and the Beatles proved giddy historians of the style's many offshoots.

THE BEATLES ON THE BBC

The early Beatles spent several grinding stints as nightclub performers in the red-light district of Hamburg, Germany, between 1960 and 1962, playing everything they knew to fill their sets and learning how to put their music across as a thrilling live ensemble. They even made early recordings there backing a singer named Tony Sheridan as the Beat Brothers, but nothing much came of them.

As part of their early British touring circuit, in late 1962 the Beatles began making regular appearances on BBC Radio's "light programs" like *Saturday Club* that were aimed at younger listeners (see Photo 0.8). For many of these shows, they played songs from their generous live set list, which included covers of numbers by the early, first-generation rockers they admired. These performances survive on more than a dozen CDs' worth of broadcast material, much of which has been traded among collectors since the early '70s. The Beatles have released four hours' worth of this vast archive in two double-CD sets, *Live at the BBC* (1995) and *On Air: Live at the BBC Volume 2* (2013). The rival nine-CD set from Italy's underground Great Dane label, *The Complete BBC Sessions* (a 1993 bootleg), lasts well over ten hours, much of this devoted to repeated performances of favorites that allow later listeners to eavesdrop on how the Beatles' arrangements of a song changed slightly over the years. As old tapings of original broadcasts have continued to emerge, the BBC material has expanded to fill thirteen CDs, speed-corrected on

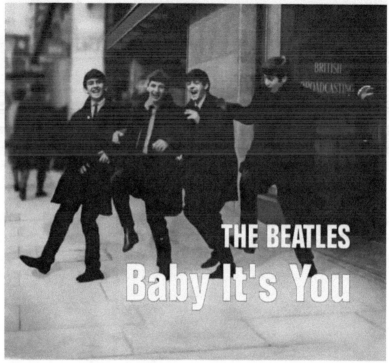

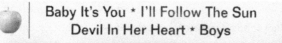

PHOTO 0.8. Dezo Hoffman photo of the Beatles outside London's "Paris" BBC studio on April 4, 1963. *Baby It's You* maxi-CD single (released in US March 23, 1995).

underground labels such as Purple Chick and Hobnail. These recordings provide a vivid picture of the Beatles becoming the Beatles.

Unlike American commercial radio stations, the British Broadcasting Corporation saw itself as a curator, educating its audience about all forms of "classical" culture, be it music, theatre, or literature. For the longest time, it simply did not broadcast rock 'n' roll, and when it did, it almost seemed embarrassed by it.

American rock stars Bill Haley, Elvis Presley, Eddie Cochran, and Gene Vincent grew popular in Britain through broadcasts from Radio Luxembourg. Broadcasting in English from the tiny European nation, the station was designed to challenge the monopoly the BBC had on domestic radio programming. Unlike the BBC, Radio Luxembourg relied on advertising income to stay on the air, so it catered to listeners' tastes rather than the stuffy standards set by the BBC. Songs by Fats Domino, Little Richard, Jerry Lee Lewis, Phil and Don Everly, Carl Perkins, and Buddy Holly all vaulted straight into early Beatles set lists. Only in 1962 did the "official" British media channels even deign to put pop music on the air; then, the BBC featured the Beatles on Saturday mornings as a sop to the teenage audience. Many of their fans might have been hearing Little Richard and Gene Vincent numbers for the first time through these Beatle interpretations. The BBC itself never considered this material worthy enough to archive outside of a few transcription discs; most surviving tapes of the Beatles' early BBC performances have been gathered (even for the official 1995 and 2013 releases) from enthusiastic listeners who recorded the shows off of their home radios.

To our ears, these tracks provide a vivid map of both rock history and the Beatles' embryonic style. They trace Lennon and McCartney's distinct vocal development, the seeds of their songwriting partnership, and the way these four instrumentalists learned to play off one another's strengths to create an unparalleled ensemble. Paradoxically, the BBC sessions also show how the Beatles elevated the idea of covering other peoples' songs into an act of self-definition, a glossary of their own taste and aspirations, an index of their influences, and the impulse to absorb, imitate, and expand on their models. Live and unvarnished, this early period documents the Beatles' early persona and holds up as well as what they later crafted in the studio.

By now it's axiomatic that the Beatles had exceptional taste. But at the time, the material on *Live at the BBC* constituted a radical picture of early rock history, if only because the Beatles were among the first to frame it. The Beatles performed at least nineteen songs made popular by Presley, more than those associated with any other artist. Paul McCartney copies most of Elvis's vocal mannerisms, and George Harrison recreates all of Elvis's first guitarist Scotty Moore's bent blue notes when the Beatles perform "That's All Right (Mama)" for one of their early appearances on BBC Radio. As part of a generous and combustible live act, this material seeded early Beatle-composed gems such as "From Me to You" and "She Loves You," which made even obscure covers like "The Honeymoon Song (Bound by Love)" sound all the richer. The string of songs they considered "standards"—culminating in the girl-group literature written by the Carole King–Gerry Goffin team—taught them about formal structure: the roles of introductions and smooth transitions between verses; the value of repetition in refrains and choruses; the tension contained in bridge-ending retransitions; and the means of building momentum and bringing numbers to satisfying conclusions. (⏵ Formal designations such as refrain, chorus, bridge, and retransition are discussed in Video 1.3.) A closer listen to this BBC material helps us hear the music on several distinct levels: performance, material, formal structure, and arrangements. We can then note how the Beatles' later interest in production and poetic concept would complete the package essential to all of rock history.

UNDERSTANDING THE BEATLES'
BBC RECORDINGS

Performance. The Beatles drew on their favorite recordings to hone their playing, ensemble, and vocal skills. They imitated the records they loved, mastering new chords, fills, and hooks to bring this material to life. These numbers reveal how much they already heard in, and identified with, rock's early history. Lennon's swelling vocal frustration in the bridge of "To Know Her Is to Love Her," which teeters on the edge of threat, predicts the pent-up revenge in their own later "I'll Get You" and "Another Girl." In the only Everly Brothers cover they ever released, "So How Come (No One Loves Me)," they show just how much promise the Lennon-McCartney vocal duets held (such as in the last verse of "All My Loving"). And "I'll Be On My Way," an early Lennon-McCartney ditty, sounds like the Everlys singing Buddy Holly. Gathered together on *Live at the BBC*, this material presents a picture of how the Beatles defined their rock style as a mixture of rhythm and blues (Arthur Alexander), catchy guitar riffs (Chuck Berry), campy belters (Little Richard), and film soundtrack numbers ("The Honeymoon Song"). There are also more covers of country songs than we might expect: the Harrison-sung Carl Perkins number "Everybody's Trying to Be My Baby," Buddy Holly's "Crying, Waiting, Hoping," and an early Lennon-McCartney duet on Perkins's "Sure to Fall."

Material. On another level, this early rock 'n' roll repertoire fueled the Beatles' quest to become great songwriters and to compose their own original songs. This ambition led to ingenious theft. Take their affection for the so-called "girl groups," which by 1961–1963 ranked as highly as the earlier records by Elvis Presley or Buddy Holly. They started by completely reimagining the gender roles in songs by the Shirelles and the Cookies. Manhandling Little Eva's "Keep Your Hands off My Baby," Lennon bites into the original possessive girl talk and transforms it into insecure macho menace. In the Shirelles' "Baby It's You" (by Goffin-King) (see Photo 0.9), instead of portraying a woman pleading to a man, he reverses the emotional tone from one of shivering feminine dependence to shuddering male vulnerability. When they get to the second verse ("You should hear what they say about you"), Paul and George chirp "cheat-cheat," which lends the original Shirelles' gesture an early twinge of Lennon paranoia. Sung by men, the "sha-la-las" lilting behind the lead vocal turn precociously liberated and subversive. On the one hand, they adored this material so much

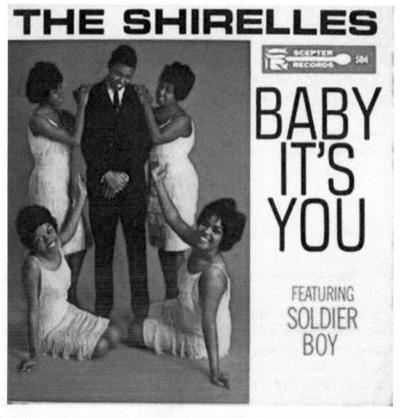

PHOTO 0.9. The Shirelles, *Baby It's You* LP (released in US 1962). The male model is not a member of this famous girl group!

that they toughened its pulse without worrying about the unexplained reversed gender roles; on another level, their affection for it completely transforms gender, responding to girl-group queries as a boy band intent on joining in. Remarkably, in a homophobic age when gays were completely marginalized, no one thought twice when Ringo sang romantically about "Boys." This gesture also displayed an eagerness to celebrate material produced and consumed primarily by females.

These favored rock traits dramatized their conflicting ideas about rock 'n' roll, and how the Beatles pounced on new themes based on their own experience. McCartney idolized Little Richard's unhinged attack and the comic perversity animating his screams, along with Presley's ruthless sincerity in addressing women. Lennon admired Chuck Berry's tight narratives and heard an emotional directness in Berry's candid swagger to counter Richard's showmanship. They didn't merely imitate specific signature sounds from these recordings. For example, many '60s rockers, most notably the Beach Boys, adopted Berry's signature guitar figures from "Johnny B. Goode" and "Roll Over Beethoven" as musical tropes that echo throughout the classic rock catalog the same way Led Zeppelin and rappers alike would later invoke James Brown.

The larger conversation between black America and working-class Liverpool can be heard through John Lennon singing "Johnny B. Goode." To Lennon, the song's hero isn't as freighted with the racial baggage that Chuck Berry slyly concealed (many contemporary listeners heard "country boy" as code for "colored boy"). Some hear this epic fable as Presley's shadow biography, or a fantasy of Berry's own life story. To Lennon, "Johnny B. Goode" was an all-inclusive statement: lurking inside these enviable American heroes with their rock 'n' roll soundtrack, there lay a universal impulse toward flight, fantasy, and recognition. British rock hopefuls, especially Liverpudlians, strongly identified with how much noise American black musicians had to make to get noticed—never mind respected—in the pop music world. Berry's sound—simplicity fraught with potential—had enough openings for a Brit like Lennon to identify with, apply to his own contempt for middle-class strictures, and sing back to Americans as his own. Traces of Berry's vocal melodies of oft-repeated pitches that would thereby accent his poetry can be heard in Lennon's personal pleas, as in "Help!" At the time of its release, "Johnny B. Goode" signaled how much the Beatles already heard themselves in this sound, and how far rock 'n' roll might carry them from the parochial (northern, working-class) prejudices more "sophisticated" Londoners held against them. Even before he began writing his own songs, Lennon made claims to being Berry's best vocal interpreter, although Mick Jagger would also revitalize Berry as lead singer of the Rolling Stones (with whom he would borrow and boost the work of Chicago bluesmen like Willie Dixon and Howlin' Wolf, and of other African Americans such as Tina Turner).

McCartney's path veers off into whooping triumph, dizzying showmanship, and unhinged yet wholesome sexuality. Where Lennon heard humor, verbal gymnastics, and point-of-view tricks in Chuck Berry's writing, McCartney heard pure ecstatic release in Little Richard's "Long Tall Sally" and "Lucille," coy humor in Presley's "That's All Right (Mama)," and nothing but fun in the Jodimars' "Clarabella" and Chan Romero's "The Hippy Hippy Shake." McCartney's impressive vocal yammer on these songs traces how much the Lennon-McCartney partnership remained steeped in the most basic rock 'n' roll.

Formal structure and arrangements. As they developed their playing and writing, another creative thread emerged: the manner in which verses, refrains, bridges, openings, closings, and transitions elevated and amplified a song's character. When they covered the Isley Brothers' version of "Twist and Shout" (originally penned by Bert Berns for the Top Notes), they completely reimagined the song's instrumentation. The Isleys adopted strings and brass and approached the tune with a gentleman's tact, the only way a black act could get over with white audiences with such suggestive content in its day. The Beatles funneled the Isleys' elaborate brass instrumentation down into guitars, bass, and drums to give the song an urgent, primal thrust. (In the 1950s, electric guitars would typically take over the melodic and rhythmic roles previously taken by trumpets and saxophones.) They heard the song simmering beneath the Isleys' fancy arrangement and remade it in their own image. With its totemic vocal climaxes, climbing with every repeat until it runs out of juice at the end, "Twist and Shout" emerged as their ensemble signature, but only after they test-drove many alternatives.

And like good music historians, the Beatles drew on tunes that predate rock 'n' roll. This has nurtured a debate rock 'n' roll has had with history ever since: Should it embrace the craft and formal rigor of its pre-rock parents, or break completely and launch its own manifestos cleansed of pedigree? Roughly speaking for the Beatles, McCartney adopts such outmoded styles as supper club, vaudeville and Broadway classics, and Lennon dismisses them. But even this characterization oversimplifies the great strides the Beatles made as rock shouted down Tin Pan Alley. Where Lennon seemed to sing about himself, McCartney always seemed to be playing a character. These jarring contrasts—from breathtaking excitement to jittery self-scrutiny to music hall sentimentality—sum up the inclusive Beatle embrace. Add a streak of country and rockabilly (something they're not famous for but plenty adept at), and you have the early recipe for their daunting stylistic range. George Harrison makes the perfect awkward narrator of the predatory Leiber-Stoller-Pomus song, "Young Blood," one of several vocal-ensemble Coasters pieces covered by the young Beatles. (The bluesy melodic phrase ending on ♭7 that George sings in "yellow ribbon in her *hair*" would later turn up throughout his own 1965 Beatles song "I Need You" (as at "and never leave *you*"), as well as phrase endings in his later "If I Needed Someone," "Love You To," "Only a Northern Song," "Within You Without You," and "The Inner Light.") Harrison also shines in his sheepish Presley cover, "I Forgot to Remember to Forget"; his earliest choices of material often verge on the "novelty" genre, either for such wordplay in "I Forgot to Remember" and "Roll Over Beethoven," the silliness of "Three Cool Cats" and "The Sheik of Araby," or the hiccups of "A Picture of You" and "Crying, Waiting, Hoping." Such playfulness flowers particularly in Lennon's eventual titles such as "A Hard Day's Night" and "Eight Days a Week."

Most of the BBC songs sharpen assumptions we might already have from the Beatles' catalog—except for those about Ringo. *Live at the BBC* should forever clear Ringo's reputation as the luckiest man in rock (for replacing the band's previous workaday drummer on the eve of their rapid rise to stardom) and position him as one of the most underrated musicians of all time. Ringo was as important to the Beatles' success as their vocals, guitar lines, themes, or arrangements. Early on, he was breaking himself in as the Beatles' locomotive, and on each of these tracks, as well as on the wild live Hamburg sets recorded in the last days of 1962, he proves crucial to the developing Beatle sound. Acutely attuned to the nuances in Lennon and McCartney's songs as they began pouring out, Ringo combined a controlled rhythmic drive with a keen sensitivity to each number's overall shape and hidden detail. He developed into a songwriter's answered prayer. Underrated because they are often as invisible as wallpaper, his early drum parts meld into songs as neatly as the composed retransitions and rhythm guitar fixtures do. As a drummer, Ringo never plays to the spotlight; he frames every number with the perfect touch. That he disappears utterly into certain numbers (like "I Want to Hold Your Hand" and "You Won't See Me") only adds to his mystique.

Listen to "Thank You Girl," done in front of a live audience in June 1963, not long after it was released as the B-side to "From Me to You." As the band finds its groove and leans into one of its early songwriting peaks, Ringo tugs back just slightly where lesser drummers would push; he clinches for tautness instead of shoving ahead (you can even hear Ringo steady the others' energies on the intro). This withheld energy adds an extra stream of tension to the sound. In song after song, Ringo yanks the reins against the band's momentum, creating a backlog of energy that swells hard against his imposing rhythmic drive. On the heels of "Some Other Guy," from the same live spot, this toughened version of "Thank You Girl" streaks past its more charming studio A-side counterpart. And when Ringo takes his breaks on the live sprints through "Ticket to Ride" in May 1965, nothing he does simply repeats what he had already recorded brilliantly. Not only is each verse-closing drum break varied; he alters each one subtly from version to version, deliberately dragging his fills behind the bar. His anticipations are often simply onrushing silences (just after the brief post-bridge guitar solos) that pack even more tension than his fleet and syncopated, irresistible double-stick flams. (⏵ Drummer Billy Harrington discusses and demonstrates Ringo's equipment and technique in Videos 1.2, 2.3, and 3.1.)

FROM PERFORMANCE TO PRODUCTION AND POETIC CONCEPT

From this foundation (performance, material, arrangements), the Beatles went on to master the new studio techniques then emerging from the two-track units that produced their first records to four-track machines in 1963 and eight-track taping in 1968. At every step, the manner of recording (adjusting timbres, adding overdubs, employing echo and reverb, bouncing tracks from one generation of tape to a second, and reversing tape to play backward) influenced their sound as no productions had before. By *Revolver* in 1966, their mastery of studio technique becomes an important force in their artistry: songs become both performed arrangements of material and meticulously crafted mixes, to the point where it's impossible to separate the recorded product from the music and lyrics, especially when the sound itself emerges as uncanny, impossible to create on acoustic and electric instruments alone. The ultimate version of a Beatles song is the track itself, not simply words performed with music.

For their final feat, the Beatles soared high above the pop album to create something greater than the sum of its parts, a sequence that goes deeper than a well-thought-out series of songs laid across two sides of a vinyl LP. At least by late 1965's *Rubber Soul*, and in some instances before, Beatles albums became conceptual in how they flowed from one song to the next, in how the listening experience divulged meanings it wouldn't otherwise if the songs had been in a different, less meaningful equilibrium. By 1967's *Pepper*, this conceptual prowess became overt, but it had been brewing for at least five years.

The BBC tapes carry an immediate, direct, and unselfconscious snapshot of the Beatles becoming the Beatles, a sense of how alive rock could be in the moment before the world caught on to what these four voracious fans were up to. Playing this music promised more than a primer in rock history; it dramatized how much rock music had to teach. Not only had rock 'n' roll reached across the Atlantic and seized the imaginations of British teens, it had taught two promising young songwriters how to compose, and by the time of its final crystallization in August 1962 led three self-taught guitarists and a replacement (!) drummer to create a single four-limbed voice—in other words, how to fashion a band. Lennon-McCartney heard early rock as an opening chapter and not a self-enclosed world; their admiration for Presley and his colleagues exploded their creative ambitions; and their mastering this early catalog turned into a platform for playful experimentation.

POINTS FOR DISCUSSION

1. What roles are played by Chuck Berry, Buddy Holly, Little Richard, Carl Perkins, Jerry Lee Lewis, the "girl groups," and Motown's roster in early rock music and the Beatles' development?
2. How does the generation gap express itself in the 1950s and 1960s?
3. What musical gestures do the Beatles make to signal their affinity for prior rock history?
4. Name three distinct layers of the musical taxonomy explained in this chapter.

FURTHER READING

Braun, Michael. *Love Me Do: The Beatles' Progress*. Harmondsworth, UK: Penguin, 1964.

Frith, Simon, and Howard Horne. *Art into Pop*. London: Methuen, 1972.

Guralnick, Peter. *Last Train to Memphis: The Rise of Elvis Presley*. New York: Little, Brown, 1994.

Halberstam, David. *The Fifties*. New York: Ballantine, 1994.

hooks, bell. *We Real Cool: Black Men and Masculinity*. London: Routledge, 2004.

Laing, Dave. *Buddy Holly*. New York: Collier, 1972.

Miller, Jim, ed. *The Rolling Stone Illustrated History of Rock and Roll*. New York: Random House, 1972.

Oldham, Andrew Loog. *Stoned: A Memoir of London in the 1960s*. New York: St. Martin's, 2001.

Riley, Tim. *Lennon: The Man, the Myth, the Music—The Definitive Life*. New York: Hyperion, 2011.

Sandbrook, Dominic. *Never Had It So Good: A History of Britain from Suez to the Beatles*. London: Little, Brown, 2006.

Wills, Garry. *John Wayne's America*. New York: Simon & Schuster, 1997.

CHAPTER 1

THE QUARRY MEN (1940–1960)

A PREHISTORY

To understand how the Beatles changed the world, we need to look first at their backgrounds—what their childhood worlds were like, what sort of environment shaped their attitudes, what economies drove the production of popular music, and what kind of music soundtracked their adolescence. The Beatles were war babies, all born between July 1940 and February 1943, at the height of a worldwide conflict staged at the dawn of the atomic age, when the threat of a nuclear holocaust lingered not as metaphor but horrifying reality, triggering a decades-long period that engulfed Western civilization in fears of instant global destruction and pleas for peace and understanding. The Beatles came to symbolize the many tensions between members of the "baby boom" generation and their parents, who had lived through the Depression and World War II.

On the mouth of the Mersey River, their city, Liverpool, hosted a crucial port—after London, the second largest in England—built on the triangle of the slave trade: in the eighteenth and early nineteenth centuries, Liverpool's great ships carried Africans from their homes to the United States, and brought back slave-picked American cotton to be worked and sold in textile centers like Liverpool and Manchester. The Merseyside cotton industry thrived until decline set in during the first years of the twentieth century, by which time textile production became much more localized in the American South. Approaching this time, Liverpool also peaked in its acceptance of penniless refugees from Ireland, spurring labor unrest and civil strife in a shrinking economy. John Lennon, Paul McCartney, and George Harrison all had deep Irish roots, their immigrant forebears settling in the 'Pool's Everton and Wavertree districts and bringing with them a high regard for singing amongst family, friends, and coworkers. Both Lennon and McCartney had late-nineteenth-century ancestors living on Scotland Road in Everton, also the home to the Rotunda Theatre, where Scotch-Irish minstrelsy was enjoyed weekly.

By the early 1940s, Liverpool's decay nurtured tough "Scousers" who dodged Nazi bombing raids that killed four thousand Liverpudlians and laughed at their own misery, fostering a growing comic-centered entertainment trade. Many years later, John Lennon mocked Hitler from the stage (especially in Hamburg, Germany); at such times, the Beatles' direct connection to the tyrant felt palpable. (While not as out of control onstage as the guitar-smashing Pete Townshend or guitar-burning Jimi Hendrix would be by the mid-to-late '60s, Lennon displayed antisocial behavior by mocking those with speech impediments and impaired mobility, flaunting the dark side of his wide-ranging humor at the height of the Beatles' fame, a time when ableism was the accepted norm.) Although the European war ended in May 1945, the strict rationing of foods, clothing, fuel, and other consumer goods (and a strong black market in the ports) continued for another nine years in England. Military conscription did not end until 1960, with British soldiers embattled in the Far East, Africa, and the eastern Mediterranean throughout the 1950s. While Eisenhower America enjoyed a postwar boom, an austere Britain rationed sugar until 1953 and meat until 1954.

The shipping companies employed Alfred Lennon, John's father, on merchant and cruise ships, taking him away from John's mother, Julia, for months and years at a time, with John replaying Alf's own youth as an orphan himself. The cotton brokers employed James McCartney, Paul's father, as a salesman. Paul's mother, Mary, worked as a state-supported midwife until her death from breast cancer in 1956, which threw the family into financial and emotional straits. The McCartneys nurtured musical genes: Paul's grandfather played tuba in a municipal band; his father Jim led a dance-hall ragtime band in the 1920s and created his own tunes on the piano at home ever after, one of which, "Walking in the Park with Eloise," was recorded by Paul with Nashville players in 1974. As Paul recalled in the booklet that accompanied his 1989 world tour, Jim would say, "Learn the piano, you'll always get invited to parties" (McCartney 1989, 39). A clownish Alf Lennon sang to his fellow shipmates, and the free-spirited Julia entertained friends on the banjolele, an inexpensive hybrid instrument with a banjo body and ukulele neck, its four strings easily mastered by beginners. The banjolele was immensely popular in the United Kingdom through the 1940s, largely through the comedic entertaining of Lancashire film star George Formby (see Photo 1.1) (whose act was imitated in 1995 at the end of the Beatles' "Free as a Bird" video). Formby would wink through rakish double entendres, surely caught with glee by the young Beatles; listen, for example, to his 1939 film song "I Can Tell It by My Horoscope." John's mum Julia taught the youngster to play the banjolele, and Paul learned it from his cousin Bett.

As the cotton trade imploded, other industries—notably vehicle assembly and chemical production—grew in midcentury Liverpool, alongside newly constructed modest row houses in Speke, a riverside flatland south of the city. Paul's family lived here (until they moved to Allerton, closer to the city center, in 1955), as did that of George Harrison (until 1963). Neither of George's parents seemed particularly musical, though their gramophone purred to Bing Crosby, Hoagy Carmichael, Glenn Miller, and Jimmie Rodgers. George's dad encouraged him to take up the guitar; as soon as John and Paul heard the red-blooded Elvis Presley in 1956, their parents' music sounded somewhat artificial.

"The gramophone" was what Brits called the record player, as it is known in the United States. This motor-driven machine spun a record, a flat disc onto which a musical recording had been imprinted in a long groove that ran from the outside edge in a spiral to the middle, with a label

PHOTO 1.1. George Formby, *Ukulele Man No. 1* EP (released in UK 1995).

in the center. (▶ Vinyl records, their formats, packaging, and means of audio reproduction, are covered in Video 1.1.) A stylus (or "needle") rested in the groove, a magnetic cartridge converted the vibrations into disturbances in an electric supply, and an amplifier processed the current to drive loudspeakers. Records came in different sizes and ran at different speeds; ten-inch discs played at seventy-eight revolutions per minute (rpm) and had one song per side. In the 1950s, this format was gradually replaced by seven-inch 45 rpm singles. ("Singles" had one song per side, but only the "A-side" was marketed as a hit and plugged on the radio. Newly released singles cost anywhere between fifty cents and a dollar each.) Twelve-inch discs ran at 33 1/3 rpm and typically carried five to seven songs per side, each song being two or three minutes long. These "long-players" (LPs), or "albums," cost about five times as much as a single and appealed more to adults with their lengthier repertoire. In the United Kingdom, another in-between format found favor: extended-play seven-inch singles (EPs), which had two songs per side and typically featured songs taken from the LPs, whereas (in the United Kingdom, unlike the United States) singles would not. Until the Beatles came along, best-selling albums mostly carried classical pieces or Broadway shows, but rock 'n' roll stars such as Elvis Presley also sold albums, although in much smaller quantities than singles.

Singles and EPs also played from jukeboxes, large coin-fed record players found in bars and soda stands that contained fifty or so discs, any title of which could be chosen by a customer.

Seven-inch pop records remained monophonic until 1968, playing a single channel (instead of two-channel stereo), whereas by the late 1950s in the United States (somewhat later in the United Kingdom) albums saw publication in both stereophonic and monophonic sound. The Beatles' studio ingenuity advanced stereo programming, the era's leading technological musical innovation: instead of tracing a single signal in the vinyl's groove, the needle now tracked two channels that brought wondrous new effects like separation and depth, requiring dedicated playback equipment. In the early Beatles era, artists typically released one or two albums and three or four singles per year, and the popularity of records was measured by sales and airplay posted in charts of from thirty to two hundred discs, varying by single/album format and by chart publisher, updated weekly in trade magazines such as *Billboard* in the United States and the *New Musical Express* in the United Kingdom, among others.

To illustrate the nature of dual-channel stereo, Figure 1.1 shows the waveforms of the two stereo signals in the first six-plus seconds of the CD mix of the Beatles' "Drive My Car" (a track on the 1965 album *Rubber Soul*). Here, the channel that's heard as left is shown above the channel heard as right. An initial second of silence is broken (find "1.1" along the upper scale) by the entry of the lead guitar on the right; the bass guitar enters on the left at 2.3 seconds, the drums on the left at 4.3, and the vocals on the right at 5.7.

The Beatles applied their ingenuity to all these formats, both in conception and in their jackets' graphic design. From early on, they were determined not to wind up like Elvis, producing an LP with a couple of hits dominating side 1 and "filler" to flesh out the remainder. Each Beatles single and album came to market thoughtfully conceived as either a radio song or an album track, and sometimes both. As the industry progressed from mono 45s toward stereo and LPs, the Beatles' own material advanced this technical progression, making it an aesthetically-driven change. The Beatles' innovations in the cohesion of album content in works like *Rubber Soul* (1965) and *Revolver* (1966) led the industry into new vistas, although their lead was followed in fits and starts, especially in that American releases did not faithfully carry the same songs as did the British originals. This caused confusion in the American market until *Sgt. Pepper's Lonely Hearts Club Band* appeared in June 1967, at which point the British and American album sequences were finally correlated.

Although material made famous by Elvis Presley, Chuck Berry, Carl Perkins, Jerry Lee Lewis, Little Richard, Eddie Cochran, Gene Vincent, and the Everly Brothers would

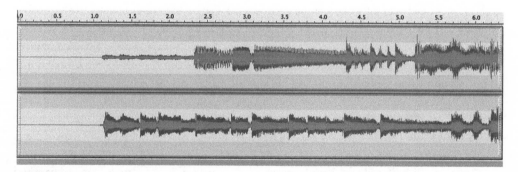

FIGURE 1.1. Waveshapes of the opening seconds of "Drive My Car."

eventually form the proto-Beatles' repertoire, American rock 'n' roll was hardly known in the United Kingdom until Elvis broke there in May 1956. Already by January 1956, Liverpool youth were smitten by another form of popular music that spun off the jazz world, called "skiffle." This amateur style, played on homemade washboards and washtub or tea-chest basses with banjos and acoustic guitars, presented songs from the rural blues tradition of the 1930s, often related to manual labor or railroad adventure, such as Lead Belly's "Rock Island Line." Lonnie Donegan (see Photo 1.2) popularized the style in Britain, followed by the Vipers and Chas McDevitt and Nancy Whiskey. One or two vocalists typically hollered lines over the simplest of chord changes; Donegan's televised performance (ca. 1955) of "Mr. Froggy" (accompanied by the singer's simple cowboy chords on acoustic guitar, plus jazz-based brushed drums and stand-up bass) is typically available online. (▶ Basic aspects of chord construction are covered in Video 1.5.) Because of skiffle's inexpensive instrumentation and simple musical skill set, skiffle bands erupted all over Britain, literally hundreds within Liverpool alone. One band that used the sound as a launch pad for rock 'n' roll came from the Merseyside suburbs of Woolton and Allerton: the Quarry Men, led in late 1956 by their founder, John Lennon.

PHOTO 1.2. Lonnie Donegan, *Hit Parade, Volume 3* EP (released in UK October 1957).

THE QUARRY MEN

Not only did young John Winston Lennon (b. October 9, 1940) have an absent father, but his flighty mother, Julia, was found unfit by the Liverpool County Council, so he was raised by his strict aunt Mimi and her gentle husband, George Smith, in a pleasant semi-detached home with a good-sized back yard in the suburban hills of Woolton. Uncle George gave John emotional support—and a harmonica to quench his thirst for music—but he died suddenly at age fifty-two in June 1955. The eccentric Julia soon reentered the teenage boy's life, sharing her rock records and teaching him how to play some of Elvis's songs on the banjolele and then the cheap Gallatone acoustic guitar she bought for him. She, too, died young and suddenly, fatally run over by an off-duty policeman right near John's Menlove Avenue home, in July 1958. Julia's death haunted John the rest of his life and figured in his son Julian's name, his contemplative 1968 Beatles song "Julia," and his solo career's "Mother."

Even before Julia's death uprooted him, John had disciplinary problems from boyhood. A constant cut-up in school, Lennon always demanded the attention his absent parents never provided. His inventive turn of mind resonated with the dream world and wordplay of Lewis Carroll and the gobbledygook double-talk of Stanley Unwin. He adored the absurdist humor of the Goons, who had a top-five hit in 1956 called "I'm Walking Backward for Christmas." He also displayed talent in the visual arts and drew scathing cartoons for a notebook he called "The Daily Howl," loaded with punning satire on teachers, vicars, and British pomposity in general. These sources find their greatest flowering in Lennon's books *In His Own Write* and *A Spaniard in the Works* (1964 and 1965, respectively), his sublime 1967 songs "Lucy in the Sky with Diamonds" and "I Am the Walrus," and 1968's mock-conspiratorial "Glass Onion." Largely because of Lennon, crypto-speak became an important part of Beatle lore. For instance, one running joke through several 1963 episodes of the BBC Radio series *Saturday Club* had to do with a mysterious "Harry and his box." When asked to explain, in a show taped on June 24, 1963 (and broadcast five days later), John clarified in his best evocation of Stanley Unwin: "The truth about Harry's box is, a ferry pardon, often the parky walkthrough, don't we?" George also cultivated such linguistic peculiarities, and Ringo's language naturally turned in odd locutions; all this foolishness was somewhat beneath Paul, it seems, whose wordplay would manifest in somewhat earnest song lyrics.

Lennon advanced on the guitar, even though he mistuned it, trying to duplicate the stringing of Julia's banjolele. He gathered his mates into a skiffle group sarcastically named for their Quarry Bank High School, in turn named for the huge excavated hills of Woolton, which provided the stone for the city's architectural pride, the world's largest Anglican cathedral. Best friend Pete Shotton scratched out a rhythm on the washboard, Rod Davis played banjo, Colin Hanton worked a small drum set, and Eric Griffiths joined John with a second acoustic guitar. Various figures came and went with a tea-chest bass, one being Len Garry, who added a second vocal part to John's. This was the six-man group that played at a fair at St Peter's Church, Woolton, on July 6, 1957, where they were seen by Paul McCartney, who was invited by ex-tea-chest player Ivan Vaughan. They played mostly skiffle hits, "Cumberland Gap" (England's no. 1 hit for Lonnie Donegan in May 1957), "Railroad Bill" (also recorded by Donegan), "Maggie May" (a Liverpool folk ballad about a mythical sex worker, released in a recording by the Vipers in March 1957), and "Putting on the Style" (a 1920s country song recorded by Donegan), but they also included Elvis's old Sun recording "Baby Let's Play House" and the Del-Vikings' "Come Go with Me." This last song was an American hit in May 1957; though not very popular in England, it happened to be the first record Paul had ever bought. Paul loved John's style—his command of the group and the way he made up gibberish when he didn't know the words. Meeting with John after the performance, the two had a lot to talk about. Paul played "Long Tall Sally" on the church hall piano and showed off on the guitar with Eddie Cochran's "Twenty Flight Rock"—and then dutifully wrote down all the lyrics. He also retuned John's guitar.

Incredibly, a friend of John's brought a tape recorder to the Woolton church fair, and we have recordings of parts of two songs played on the day that John met Paul: three fragments of "Putting on the Style" and a half minute of "Baby Let's Play House." The poor-sounding tapes, which can be heard on file-sharing sites online, preserved John Lennon's remarkable voice, already piercingly direct and freighted with emotion.

The family of James Paul McCartney (b. June 18, 1942) moved from homes north of the city (in Everton) to several far south of the city (in Speke) before settling in Allerton, steps from Calderstones Park, which separated Paul's house from John's. Perhaps Paul's mother's death cemented something of an emotional detachment from his surroundings, distinctly in contrast to John's more desperate acting out. Paul found emotional nourishment in the stage lights, donning a persona subject to mass appreciation, somewhat more superficial than Lennon's confessional mode. It was John who would bare his soul in self-portraits such as "I'm A Loser," "You've Got to Hide Your Love Away," and "Strawberry Fields Forever" and Paul who would tickle his listeners with music-hall turns such as "When I'm Sixty-Four" (a song Paul began writing as a teen and completed in late 1966, months after his father turned that age). For John, vaudevillian stances seemed ripe for irony, as in his 1971 country rag "Crippled Inside," which many take as a slam against his now estranged former partner.

But Paul took his music seriously in a completely different way. He sang in a boys' choir in St Barnabas in nearby Penny Lane and was photographed in a handbell group in the Liverpool Cathedral a few weeks before his eleventh birthday. Building his vocal-harmony and piano skills under his father's wing, Paul traded a trumpet his dad had given him for a guitar soon after hearing Presley and Donegan. Paul started writing his own three-chord songs with "I Lost My Little Girl," tied to the grief over losing his mother Mary, mentioned in his later ballad for the Beatles' "Let It Be." In the early summer of 1957, Paul saw The Girl Can't Help It, which featured Eddie Cochran performing "Twenty Flight Rock," Gene Vincent doing "Be-Bop-a-Lula" (see Photo 1.3), and three songs by Little Richard. Paul was particularly enamored of the flamboyant garb and falsetto shrieks in Richard's "Long Tall Sally," a top-five record in the United Kingdom in March and April 1957. (▶ Regarding the falsetto, see Video 2.6.) It became one of the first songs he sang after joining the Quarry Men that October and was the Beatles' rousing concert closer in 1964–1965. Once Paul joined the Quarry Men, he and John constituted the front line, all others functioning as their backing group. Unlike most pop acts, it never occurred to them to pick a single "lead" front man; they always traded vocals and frequently duetted. Paul likely also caught the 1956 film Don't Knock the Rock, because he imitates Little Richard's backwards tumble on the line "He ducked back in the alley" onstage, swinging his arms while holding his bass, visible just after George's guitar solo in the February 1964 Washington Coliseum show. Seeing Paul in this performance, one can easily imagine how wildly the thirteen-year-old got "Long Tall Sally" across while standing on his school desk, screaming his way through the tune on the last day of the 1956–57 school year.

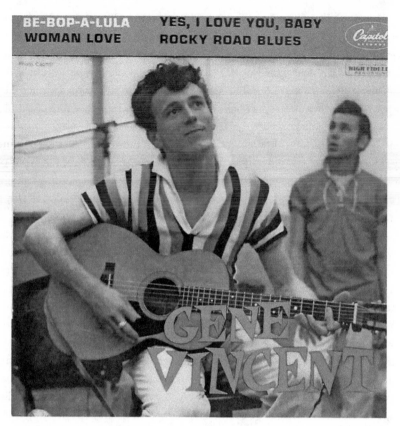

BE-BOP-A-LULA   YES, I LOVE YOU, BABY
WOMAN LOVE   ROCKY ROAD BLUES

PHOTO 1.3. Gene Vincent, *Be-Bop-a-Lula* EP (as reissued in France in 1961).

As Paul befriended John, he reconsidered the talents of another friend, a better guitarist than either John or himself. George Harrison (b. February 25, 1943) was a bus driver's son known to Paul as a Speke neighbor (George having moved there in 1949 from Wavertree, just north of Penny Lane) and then, after Paul moved to Allerton, as a rider on the same bus to the Penny Lane transfer station. George learned the note-bending lead part for Bill Justis's "Raunchy," a top 20 instrumental hit in the United Kingdom through the first three months of 1958, and Paul coaxed George to demonstrate it as an audition with John. This impressed Lennon, who made George a member that March. These three teens, with their acoustic guitars (John still with his Gallatone; Paul with a second guitar, a Zenith; and George with his Höfner President), formed the fast core of the Quarry Men.

BECOMING THE BEATLES: "IN SPITE OF ALL THE DANGER"

The group's name quickly lost its relevance, however. In the fall of 1957, John moved on from Quarry Bank High School to the Liverpool College of Art, where he attracted a new group of friends and discovered beat poetry. A number of new group names were tried out; recent re-search by Mark Lewisohn has uncovered the name "Japage 3," which condenses John's, Paul's, and George's names, in that order, and indicates them as the group's key members (Lewisohn 2013, 201). Along with occasional sidemen (Ken Brown on guitar, John "Duff" Lowe on piano, either Colin Hanton or Paul's brother Mike on drums) or none at all, the proto-Beatles played small venues—street fairs, private social clubs, and dance halls—exclusively in greater Liverpool into the spring of 1960, plus two late 1959 auditions in large cinemas for TV appearances that didn't pan out, the second of which took them to nearby Manchester.

On July 12, 1958, just three days before Julia Lennon's death, Lennon, McCartney, Harrison, Hanton, and Lowe took their gear to Kensington Street in the city center, where Percy Phillips ran a rudimentary home recording studio. The group taped Buddy Holly's no. 1 hit from the previous year credited to the Crickets, "That'll Be the Day," plus McCartney's own Elvis-inspired song, "In Spite of All the Danger," with Lennon singing lead on both numbers. Phillips pressed both songs that day on a ten-inch shellac disc, and they later appeared in edited form on the 1995 release *The Beatles Anthology 1*. Buddy Holly, like Carl Perkins and Chuck Berry, wrote his own material; this inspired John and Paul, who identified with these figures as *writers* and began to compose frag-mentary songs of their own.

Paul's "In Spite of All the Danger" demonstrates how the Beatles modeled their first compositions on songs by others that they admired. Years later, Mark Lewisohn interviewed the composer about "In Spite of All the Danger," about which he said, "It's very similar to an Elvis song. It's me doing an Elvis." Lewisohn asked Paul if there was a particular song that served as his model; the Beatle responded rather coyly (probably not wishing to set off a copyright-infringement claim), "Yeah, but I'm a bit loathe to say which! . . . It was one I'd heard at scout camp when I was younger and I'd loved it. And when I came to write the first couple of songs at the age of about 14 that was one of them" (Lewisohn 1988, 7). The musical ear can determine that McCartney took several salient ideas from Elvis's "Tryin' to Get to You" (written by Rose Marie McCoy and Charles Singleton) (see Photo 1.4) to create a tensile song of his own that would com-bine a number of structural features that would eventually make blockbusters out of their more assured 1963 singles. The excitement that Paul takes from Elvis results from a simple yet profound blend of harmonic power, rhythmic tension, and temporal placement in the song's structure. We need to examine each of these functions to understand how their interaction stamps the song as a raw exercise of some basic tools that would soon be used to establish them as world-dominating songwriters and performers.

Elvis recorded "Tryin' to Get to You" in July 1955, in Sun Studios in Memphis. Sun did not release the record, but four months after Sam Phillips sold Elvis's contract to RCA in November 1955, the new company put out the long-playing record *Elvis Presley*, which included Sun's taping. RCA released "Tryin'" as a non-charting single in the United States only in mid-1956, and it was later a hit in the United Kingdom, where its popularity peaked at no. 16 in November 1957. We know Paul was at scout camp several weeks after his fifteenth birthday, in late July and early August 1957. Perhaps he heard the song on Radio Luxembourg at about the time of the British single re-lease, learned it on guitar when he got home from camp, taught it to the Quarry Men soon after he joined them that October, and kept returning it to the Beatles' set lists through early 1962.

In "Tryin' to Get to You," Elvis's voice is accompanied by Scotty Moore's electric lead guitar (given a roomy slap-back echo), Bill Black's upright acoustic bass, Johnny Bernero's drums, and

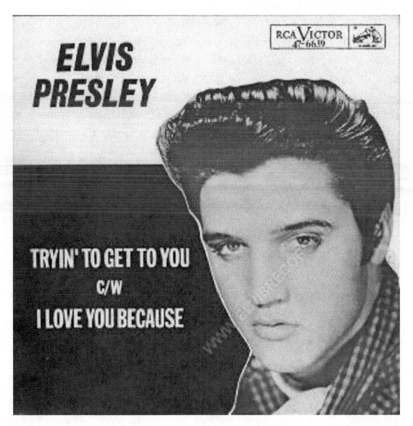

PHOTO 1.4. Elvis Presley, "Tryin' to Get to You" / "I Love You Because" 45 (released in US August 31, 1956).

a piano possibly played by Elvis himself. Most notable in the rhythm is the *shuffle* pattern in the cymbal, played throughout but most easily picked out during the instrumental break, 1:16–1:34. (▶ Rhythmic terms such as "shuffle," "backbeat," "accent," and "tempo" are covered in Video 1.2.) This was a typical rockabilly underpinning, and it provides most of the song with a repetitive short-long, short-long ("ba-bump . . . , ba-bump . . ."—a poet's iambic meter) accompaniment that accentuates the vocal's jauntiness. The shuffle rhythm is heard on every metrically strong beat (the first and third beat of every bar), alternating with strong *backbeats* on the snare, which *accent* every weak beat (two and four in each bar). The shuffle and backbeat combine for a loping yet cocky quality. The most noticeable difference between Elvis's and McCartney's songs lies in their *tempos*: "Tryin'" moves quickly, whereas "Danger" has a slower feel, often seeming to drag. While the Quarry Men's drums (played by Colin Hanton) can't be heard clearly except for a random bass-drum foundation that occasionally accents the backbeat, the Elvis-like shuffle is most pronounced in John Lennon's lead vocal and the chords strummed on John's and Paul's acoustic guitars and banged on the piano by John "Duff" Lowe, most prominently at 2:19–2:25. The pre-Beatles do not play a bass line, but Harrison seems to play his lead lines for the intro, solo, and ending on an amplified acoustic guitar. Each song's moment of greatest rhythmic tension occurs when all instrumentalists and backing vocalists suddenly break the shuffle/backbeat pattern by stopping dead, putting the spotlight on the solo singer at a point of particular formal anticipation. This point requires a bit of explanation, so we'll turn next to the song's formal design.

A song's form is based on the relationships among related and contrasting phrases, and among related and contrasting sections. Repeating material creates a sense of familiarity; varying material suggests change, progress, or novelty; and contrasting material connotes a change of perspective or contradiction. These relationships play out in the large scale, when verses (sections with recurring music but differing sets of lyrics), a refrain (a line within a verse whose music and lyric both recur), and bridges (contrasting material that usually builds to the tense retransitional anticipation of a returning verse) are played off against one another.

On a smaller scale, musical phrases can be joined to form sentence-like constructions. All of these structures—sentences, verses, refrains, and bridges—are present in both of these songs. (▶ Formal designations—such as verse, refrain, bridge, retransition, and instrumental break—are covered in Video 1.3.) Table 1.1 provides "roadmaps" of each song's large-scale form.

Both have comparable content in this regard, although Presley's model has different lyrics for each verse, whereas McCartney repeats his first two sets. Precise consideration of large-scale form is impeded at this level by the fact that two undocumented sections—likely a repeated verse and a second bridge—have been edited out of the Quarry Men recording for the 1995 *Anthology* release.

The surface-level sentences, however, remain telling. The musical sentence combines four phrases in what we call "SRDC" form: a statement, a restatement (a repetition of the opening idea with new words and perhaps a slight musical variation), a departure (featuring strongly varied material, sometimes in repeated fragments), and a conclusion. (▶ SRDC form is demonstrated in Video 2.2.) In "Tryin'," the opening S-gesture sets the eight-syllable lyric "I've been traveling over mountains." This is then varied in a seven-syllable R-line: "Even through the valleys too."

TABLE 1.1. Formal sections within "Tryin' to Get to You" and "In Spite of All the Danger."

"TRYIN' TO GET TO YOU":

(0:02–0:19)	Verse 1 with refrain
(0:20–0:39)	Verse 2 with refrain
(0:39–0:56)	Bridge 1 with retransition
(0:57–1:14)	Verse 3 with refrain
(1:15–1:34)	Instrumental break
(1:34–1:52)	Verse 4 with refrain
(1:53–2:10)	Bridge 2 with retransition
(2:11–2:30)	Verse 5 with refrain

"IN SPITE OF ALL THE DANGER":

(0:00–0:06)	Intro
(0:06–0:29)	Verse 1 with refrain
(0:29–0:50)	Verse 2 with refrain
(0:51–1:13)	Bridge with retransition
(1:13–1:36)	Verse 1 with refrain
(1:36–2:09)	Instrumental break
(2:10–2:29)	Verse 2 with refrain
(2:29–2:43)	Verse extension

TABLE 1.2. SRDC phrase structures and rhyme schemes in "Tryin' to Get to You" and "In Spite of All the Danger."

"TRYIN' TO GET TO YOU":		
VERSE:	S-, R-gestures (4 bars)	D-, C-gestures (refrain)(4 bars)
VERSE 1	mountains, even through the valleys TOO	<u>day</u>–<u>way</u> . . . get to YOU
VERSE 2	letter, where you said you love me TRUE	<u>day</u>–<u>way</u> . . . get to YOU
"IN SPITE OF ALL THE DANGER":		
VERSE:	S-, R-gestures (4 bars)	D-, C-gestures (refrain)(4 bars)
VERSE 1	Danger, . . . may BE	<u>you</u>–<u>to</u> . . . true to ME
VERSE 2	Heartache, . . . cause ME	<u>you</u>–<u>to</u> . . . true to ME

(The S- and R-gestures combine for a four-bar length, but the listener must wait until the start of the word "mountains" to begin counting; the prior words "I've been traveling over . . ." have an anticipatory effect.) So each verse begins with an anticipatory introduction that initially seems to hold the phrase back, presents a first phrase that is then truncated (eight syllables followed by seven) and then, in the departure gesture, continues with a fragment that repeats ("I've been traveling night and day," "I've been running all the way"), all suggesting a chase that becomes breathless as it quickens—all totally appropriate for the bird-dog lyrics. The departure-conclusion portion becomes the song's refrain, because its lyrics (which end with the title) are the same in each verse. Table 1.2 summarizes these points; the uppercase and underscored markings indicate the lyrics' interpenetrative, interior rhyme scheme, which emphasizes the fragmentary nature of the D-gesture, which in turn is also highlighted by dynamic ornamentation in Elvis's vocal: even an excited yodel breaks through (as at 0:09–0:14). As seen in the table's second half, all of these formal relationships are borrowed in the McCartney song, which substitutes an ardent pledge of fidelity for Elvis's excited chase.

Consideration of the song's harmony proves the influence of one song upon another. For each verse of both songs, the entire S–R portion is made on the *I chord* but ends with inflections of its flatted seventh; the two fragments of the D phrase appear on IV and then on V; and the phrases conclude on tonic, I.[1] The sped-up *harmonic rhythm* in the motion from IV to V within the D-gesture heightens the tension of the sense of anticipation we've noted in "Tryin'" and the ardency of Lennon's passion in "Danger." (▶ Harmonic rhythm is defined in Video 1.2; the I, IV, and V chord functions are discussed and demonstrated in Video 1.6.)

Comparison of the songs' bridges also betrays McCartney's borrowing: both have the chordal pattern IV–I–IV–V, sustaining each chord for two bars and increasing the tension of the retransitional V through *stop time* (▶ see Video 1.2). This is the technique whereby the singer is on his own, without support, his passion bursting through improvisatory ornamentation (Presley's *melisma* on "thi-i-i-i-ing" at 0:53–0:56; Lennon's "knockin' at your door" at 1:09–1:14) while

1. In case the above observations are not enough to convince the reader of the dependency of "In Spite of All the Danger" upon "Tryin' to Get to You," it must be noted that the third verse of the Elvis number includes the words "in spite of all."

instrumentalists can only stand back, gaping at the emotional outpouring of pure song. (▶ The melisma is covered in Video 2.6.) Such a moment at the end of each bridge section—ripe with anticipation of the verse to follow—will ride the crests of 1963 Beatlemania through falsetto "oohs" (in the retransitions of "From Me to You," "She Loves You," and "I Want to Hold Your Hand") and other emotion-filled syllables (in "This Boy": "till he's seen you cry-hy-hy-hy"). Elvis's retransition is heightened geometrically by Scotty Moore's bluesy lead licks, which clash against the vocal; Harrison cannot seem to pull this off, but at least Lennon carries off McCartney's lyrics about knocking at the door with enough suggestion of sexual energy to give the otherwise unadventurous setting an anticipatory hint of the drama to come. This song bridges Elvis Presley's earliest recordings for Sun Records and the peak of Beatlemania tension in "I Want to Hold Your Hand."

EARLY PAYING GIGS

The Beatles' most important venue of these years was the Casbah Club, which opened in August 1959, in a basement below a large home in the eastern Liverpool suburb of West Derby. Under the management of Casbah-owner Mona Best, the Quarry Men served as the house band for the club's hundreds of teenage members for weekends through that October, at which point a disagreement ended the relationship for some time. In these last months of the 1950s, the group enhanced their repertoire by learning more and more material, performing more than two hundred songs made famous by Elvis Presley, Chuck Berry, Buddy Holly, Little Richard, Gene Vincent, Carl Perkins, Jerry Lee Lewis, Lonnie Donegan, Larry Williams, Fats Domino, Duane Eddy, the Coasters, Eddie Cochran, the Everly Brothers, and others. Appendix 1 lists the core repertoire that influenced the Beatles in their early years, either as source material for their own performance or songs that had a direct bearing on their composition. Song titles and artists appear with the dates the recordings first charted in both the United States and the United Kingdom, along with peak chart position.

Notably, all of these artists were American. Britain came late to the rock 'n' roll party. Top among the few were the London-based Shadows (see Photo 1.5), admired by the Beatles for their futuristic Fender electric guitars. Like the Crickets, the Shadows' foursome employed an electric lead guitar (played by Buddy Holly with the Crickets and Hank Marvin with the Shadows), often featuring notes bent by the vibrato or "whammy" bar (see the Shadows' 1960 miming of "Apache," in which Marvin uses the technique at 0:56 and 1:02). The lead guitar was backed by the band's rhythm section: one electric rhythm guitar, drums, and bass (electric Fender bass for the Shadows, acoustic string bass for the Crickets), altogether the same onstage lineup that crystallized for the Beatles in the spring of 1961. And that took shape more than a year before the Beatles' personnel attained final form, when Ringo Starr joined John, Paul, and George to become their drummer in August 1962. The Quarry Men went electric when George bought a used Höfner Club 40 in 1958, and John and Paul followed, so that by June 1960 all three owned electric guitars. In these years, although the electric guitar style suddenly made famous by Memphis-bred rock 'n' roll acts was largely unknown in England, a closely related style based on the electric blues of Chicago was developing in London under the encouragement of club owner Alexis Korner; the Rolling Stones were the first major band to emerge from this scene.

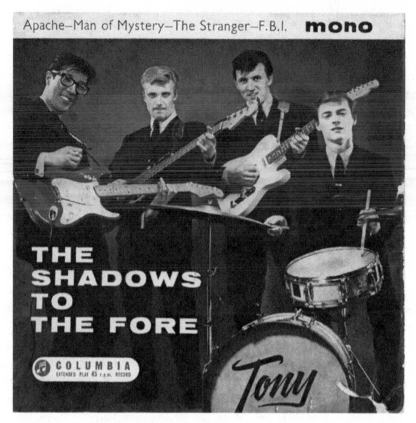

PHOTO 1.5. The Shadows, *Shadows to the Fore* EP (released in UK May 1961). Hank Marvin is at far left.

At art school, John befriended a promising expressionist painter named Stu Sutcliffe. Sutcliffe worshipped Presley, so despite his limited musical skills, he became a Quarry Man. All he had to do was buy a bass guitar, which he did with the proceeds from the prominent sale of a painting. Although he was a member of the band from January 1960 through the first weeks of 1961, Stu never gained competence as a singer or player. A fair impression of his unskilled playing can be heard in forty-eight minutes of performing he did among the total eighty-five minutes on three tapes of the evolving Quarry Men around April 1960, recorded at Paul's Allerton home, some with Paul's brother Mike on drums. A number of aimless blues set in relief a few well-developed Lennon-McCartney compositions, "Hello Little Girl," "I'll Follow the Sun," "One after 909," "You'll Be Mine," and "Cayenne" among them, plus competent covers of Eddie Cochran's "Hallelujah! I Love Her So," Fats Domino's "I'll Always Be in Love with You," Carl Perkins's "Matchbox," Gene Vincent's "Wildcat," Duane Eddy's "Movin' 'n' Groovin'," and others. On the late 1964 album *Beatles for Sale*, "I'll Follow the Sun" has a slow and steady tempo; in 1960, it had a jaunty rhythm redolent of the music-hall style of Jim McCartney. "One after 909" also returns to later Beatle sessions; it was passed over for "From Me to You" as the group's third single in March 1963, and it then reappeared as the fondest of memories at the January 1969 "rooftop" concert, heard on the *Let It Be* album. While the poor-quality 1960 tapes can make for difficult listening, they capture a fascinating snapshot of a band starting to assert itself as a musically creative force.

The group approached its now-familiar name by late March 1960, as documented in a letter Stu wrote that month. Thinking of the Crickets as a pun (cricket was quite a popular sport throughout Britain and its colonies), Sutcliffe suggested "the Beatals" in reference to beat poetry and beat music (as electric rock 'n' roll was being called in Liverpool) as well as cricket-like insects. The ultimate spelling came that May, when the Silver Beatles were advertised for one appearance, and June saw the "Silver" dropped. John later explained the name in a story he contributed to the premiere July 6, 1961, issue of *Mersey Beat*, Liverpool's journal of beat-music happenings published through 1964: "Ugh, Beatles, how did the name arrive? So we will tell you. It came in a vision—a man appeared on a flaming pie and said unto them 'From this day on you are Beatles with an "A"'" (Harry 1977, 17). The story was commissioned by *Mersey Beat*'s editor, Bill Harry, a friend of John's from art college, who added the title "Being a Short Diversion on the Dubious Origins of Beatles."

Despite not having a regular drummer, the Beatles made a favorable impression on a national impresario, Larry Parnes, in a May 1960 audition (see Photo 1.6), and this was repaid with a week-long tour (May 20–28) of small towns in northern Scotland (mostly between Inverness and Aberdeen) as the backing group for Johnny Gentle (né John Askew), who also went by the

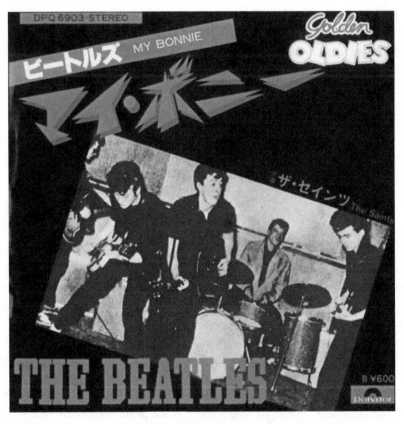

PHOTO 1.6. The Beatles, auditioning for Larry Parnes on May 10, 1960. *Left to right*: Stu Sutcliffe, bass; John Lennon, guitar; Paul McCartney, guitar; Johnny Hutchinson, drummer sitting in; George Harrison, guitar. Photo appears on "My Bonnie" / "The Saints" 45 (as reissued in Japan, September 1, 1977).

name Darren Young. The week passed dreadfully—the unsuccessful Gentle had a weak voice, their knockabout amplifiers were inadequate, the pay was lousy, and a car accident knocked out the front teeth of temporary drummer Tommy Moore. But they played to appreciative crowds and felt like celebrities, signing autographs, three with stage names: Paul Ramon, Carl Harrison, and Stu de Stael. The earliest surviving set list from a Beatles performance comes from Liverpool's rowdy Grosvenor Ballroom, where the Beatles played every Saturday night in June and July. The list contains only those songs sung by Paul, solo or with John:

Eddie Cochran's "Hallelujah! I Love Her So"
Elvis Presley's "That's All Right (Mama)"
Elvis Presley's "Stuck on You"
Little Richard's "Tutti-Frutti"
Little Richard's "Long Tall Sally"
Ray Charles's "What'd I Say"
Emile Ford's "Red Sails in the Sunset"
Jerry Lee Lewis's "Whole Lotta Shakin' Goin' On"
Elvis Presley's "Mean Woman Blues"
Elvis Presley's "I Don't Care if the Sun Don't Shine"
Carl Perkins's "Honey Don't"
The Jodimars' "Clarabella"
Chuck Berry's "Little Queenie"
The Everly Brothers' "Cathy's Clown"
"One after 909" (Lennon-McCartney)
Buddy Holly's "Words of Love"
Elvis Presley's "I'll Never Let You Go (Little Darlin')"
The Everly Brothers' "I Wonder If I Care As Much"
Carl Perkins's "Sure to Fall"

The page also lists five other songs under consideration: Little Richard's "Rip It Up," Charlie Gracie's "Fabulous," Gene Vincent's "Lotta Lovin'," Little Richard's "Kansas City," and Little Richard's "Jenny Jenny."

By mid-1960, Liverpool heaved with electric beat bands. The Bluegenes, Derry and the Seniors, Gerry and the Pacemakers, Cass and the Cassanovas, King Size Taylor and the Dominoes, and the city's most popular group—Rory Storm and the Hurricanes—led the pack. Each played a mix of standards from decades before (such as the Gershwins' "It Ain't Necessarily So") and current rock 'n' roll hits (such as "The Hippy Hippy Shake"). To stand out from each other, they looked for obscure songs no one else played—another impetus for the Beatles to write original songs. Rory Storm's group brought rock music to the Cavern Club, an underground venue in the heart of Liverpool in May 1960; previously the Cavern hosted jazz only. The city's best rock drummer kept the Hurricanes' beat swift and lively: Ringo Starr (né Richard Starkey on July 7, 1940). Ringo spent his youth in and out of hospitals for peritonitis and pneumonia, once for a ten-month period. In addition, his parents divorced when he was about five years old, uncommon enough then to earn the term "broken home." To keep the hospital patients occupied, nurses passed around percussion instruments, and in 1954 young Richie discovered he loved the drum as well as the

Texas-style blues of Lightnin' Hopkins and yodeling cowboys such as Hank Snow and Gene Autry. He carried his lone big bass drum to family parties for sing-alongs, and by 1958 he had a proper kit and played in several bands before landing with Rory Storm. With the Hurricanes, Ringo took the microphone for "Ringo Starrtime" once each set, at which point he came out from behind the drums, sometimes donning a guitar, to sing the Hollywood Argyles' "Alley-Oop" or the Shirelles' number "Boys," the latter destined to become his first vocal on a Beatles record.

By 1960, various local figures helped the Beatles find work. Most prominent among them was Allan Williams, a center-city club owner who had hosted the Larry Parnes audition in May 1960. In late July, Williams drove the Beatles to London to meet Bruno Koschmider, who sought British beat groups to attract audiences to his seedy clubs in the red-light district on the Grosse Freiheit of Hamburg, West Germany. At this time, Germany was divided politically into East and West by the Iron Curtain, which separated communist rule to the east and democratic rule to the west (although the Berlin Wall didn't enforce this division with barbed wire and guns until 1961).

In the late 1950s and early '60s, German popular music swelled with an innocuous syrupy form of kitsch called *Schlager*, often German-language reworkings of pop hits originating elsewhere. Among the most popular examples at the start of the Beatles' Hamburg apprenticeship were Lale Andersen's "Ein Schiff wird kommen" (compare "Never on Sunday") and the Trio Kalenka's "Vier Schimmel, ein Wagen" (compare "Wheels"). Listen to the singing of Nana Mouskouri, Gerhard Wendland, Peter Kraus, Conny Froböß, or Gus Backus and imagine the Beatles waiting in the wings—it's incongruous. Rough-and-tumble sailors and young residents preferred the far more raucous American rock 'n' roll, and Koschmider discovered through Derry and the Seniors that British bands, particularly those forming in Liverpool, could provide it. He hired the Beatles to play the Indra Club beginning on August 17, 1960, but they needed a drummer. Just days before they departed, Pete Best (son of Mona Best, owner of the Casbah) took the job, and he stayed with the group for two full years. Saying goodbye to their families and girlfriends (John's Cynthia Powell and Paul's Dot Rhone), John, Paul, George, Pete, and Stu left for three months of club playing in Germany.

At the Indra and Koschmider's other club, the Kaiserkeller, the Beatles logged some five hundred hours onstage in Hamburg between August 17 and November 30. Here they learned their craft—not only adding lots of new repertoire but tightening their ensemble and discovering how to put over their music with dynamic personalities. "Mach Schau!" ("Make a show!") was Koschmider's demand, and they responded with antics and shtick to fit the goofball lyrics and wayward beat. In his book about mastery, *Outliers: The Story of Success*, Malcolm Gladwell refers to this period as the band's "10,000 hours" onstage as a necessary apprenticeship toward building a repertoire and conceiving an audience, but it took several generations to be recognized as such. Living in squalor, making no money, the band eked by, buoyed by some fast new friends with an ear for excitement and artistic flair: the photographer Astrid Kirchherr (who produced several series of important images of the Beatles soon after meeting them; see Photo 1.7), the fashion-conscious Jürgen Vollmer (responsible for the "Beatles haircut"), and the illustrator Klaus Voormann (who created the cover for *Revolver* and later collaborated with three solo ex-Beatles as bassist).

Another friend was guitarist and singer Tony Sheridan, a Londoner playing down the street at the Top Ten Club. To the Beatles, he became "the Teacher," as he tutored them on guitar, showing them many new techniques. They occasionally snuck away to serve as Sheridan's backup band, a violation of their contract for the Kaiserkeller. Furious, Koschmider fired the Beatles and had

PHOTO 1.7. The Beatles, as photographed at a Hamburg fairground by Astrid Kirchherr in the Autumn of 1960. Pete Best is nearly cropped out at the left, and Stu Sutcliffe is completely removed from the right for this release of "Ain't She Sweet" / "Cry for a Shadow" 45 (as reissued in Japan, September 1, 1977).

most of them deported over a minor fire in their living quarters and George's underage status, as he was not yet eighteen and was violating a minors' curfew. They trudged back to Liverpool that December, all except for Stu, who left the group to continue both his painting in Hamburg and his romance with girlfriend Astrid until returning home in late February. Rekindling their Freiheit spirits back home, the band made a spectacular appearance at the Litherland Town Hall, just north of Liverpool, on December 27, 1960. Advertised as "Direct from Hamburg," the Beatles were mistaken for Germans by the unfamiliar crowd. Honed and toughened into a tight, entertaining squad, they roared forth like nothing their hometown audience had ever heard, and John, Paul, George, and Pete (plus one Chas Newby filling in on bass) rocketed from anonymity to the top of Liverpool's scene.

POINTS FOR DISCUSSION

1. How did their upbringing in the environment of postwar Liverpool contribute to the Beatles' tough exterior and senses of humor?

2. What economic and musical roles were played by American race relations?
3. How was popular music marketed in the early rock 'n' roll era?
4. What were some early rock 'n' roll stars emulated by the Beatles? What songs by others did they cover? Choose some titles from the list in Appendix 1 and describe some aspects of these songs.
5. What instruments did the Quarry Men play?
6. Why did skiffle prove so popular in Britain?
7. Name some ways the Beatles were influenced musically by Elvis Presley.
8. Describe some of the differences in John Lennon's and Paul McCartney's musical personalities.
9. What were the first Liverpool-area performance venues for the Quarry Men and Beatles? How was Hamburg significant to their musical development?
10. Provide an outline of the phrases and chords (in Roman numerals) of a standard twelve-bar blues.
11. Define a shuffle rhythm and name a Beatle recording that features this pattern.
12. Define from text: single, LP, shuffle, backbeat, verse, refrain, bridge, chorus, SRDC.
13. ⓥ Define from videos: tempo (Video 1.2), syncopation (1.2), stop time (1.2), surf backbeat (1.2), tumbling strain (1.4), cadences (1.6), tattoo (1.7), descant (1.7).

FURTHER READING

The Beatles. *The Beatles Anthology*. San Francisco: Chronicle Books, 2000.

Best, Roag. *The Beatles: The True Beginnings*. With Pete Best and Rory Best. New York: Thomas Dunne Books/ St. Martin's Press, 2003.

Brocken, Michael. *Other Voices: Hidden Histories of Liverpool's Popular Music Scenes, 1930's–1970's*. Surrey, UK: Ashgate, 2010.

Du Noyer, Paul. *Liverpool: Wondrous Place—Music from Cavern to Cream*. London: Virgin, 2002.

Frith, Simon, et al. *The History of Live Music in Britain*, vol. 1, *1950–1967: From Dance Hall to the 100 Club*. London: Ashgate, 2013.

Garry, Len. *John, Paul and Me: Before the Beatles: The True Story of the Very Early Days*. Toronto: CG Publishing, 1997.

Gentle, Johnny, and Ian Forsyth. *Johnny Gentle and The Beatles: First Ever Tour, Scotland 1960*. Runcorn, UK: Merseyrock, 1998.

Gladwell, Malcolm. *Outliers: The Story of Success*. New York: Little, Brown, 2008.

Gottfridsson, Hans Olof. *The Beatles from Cavern to Star-Club: The Illustrated Chronicle, Discography and Price Guide 1957–1962*. Stockholm: Premium Publishing, 1997.

Guralnick, Peter. *Last Train to Memphis: The Rise of Elvis Presley*. New York: Little, Brown, 1994.

Harry, Bill. *Mersey Beat: The Beginnings of the Beatles*. London: Quick Fox, 1977.

Hyde, Francis E. *Liverpool and the Mersey: An Economic History of a Port, 1700–1970*. Newton Abbot, UK: David & Charles, 1971.

Lewisohn, Mark. *The Beatles: Recording Sessions; The Official Abbey Road Studio Session Notes, 1962–1970*. London: Harmony, 1988.

Lewisohn, Mark. *The Complete Beatles Chronicle*. New York: Harmony, 1992.

Lewisohn, Mark. *Tune In: All These Years*, vol. 1. New York: Crown Archetype, 2013.

McKinney, Devin. *Magic Circles: The Beatles in Dream and History*. Cambridge, MA: Harvard University Press, 2003.

Pawlowski, Gareth L. *How They Became the Beatles: A Definitive History of the Early Years, 1960–1964*. New York: E. P. Dutton, 1989.

Sutcliffe, Pauline. *Stuart Sutcliffe: The Beatles' Shadow and His Lonely Hearts Club*. With Douglas Thompson. London: Sidgwick & Jackson, 2001.

CHAPTER 2

THE PETE BEST ERA (1961–1962)

The year 1961 saw the Beatles log hundreds of hours onstage in both Liverpool and Hamburg. The band worked constantly, with gigs nearly every day, often both afternoons and evenings. This experience led them to learn many new songs, develop stronger and more varied guitar techniques and ensemble skills, and nurture a strong rapport with their listeners for a loyal and growing fan base. Before the August 1960 standing job at Hamburg's Indra Club, the group had been aimless, taking what came along. Their 1961 successes gave them a strong musical foundation and a purpose—a reason to work their fingers sore. By the end of the year, the Beatles had a recognizable persona, a talent focused on musical creativity, a manager who would take them to lasting world fame in two years' time, and the release of their first single, "Love Me Do." In 1962, their performing skills tightened, their new record producer, George Martin, helped them arrange their earliest song drafts into viable hits, and they finished their apprenticeships as a bar band playing covers in the top clubs of each of their two home port cities, poised to spread their own original sound throughout England.

While the Beatles concentrated on honing their craft, building an audience, and beginning their recording career with EMI, the world noted advances in space exploration, with both the Soviet Union and the United States sending men into earth orbit (Yuri Gagarin and John Glenn, respective firsts) and launching fully functional communications satellites, most notably Telstar 1 in 1962. A movement to protect the earth, now dominated by mankind as never before, was given a strong impetus by Rachel Carson's 1962 publication of *Silent Spring*, a shocking indictment of chemical companies that misinformed the public about the toxic effects of pesticides. In the same year, the United Nations condemned South Africa's racist apartheid policies, calling for a universal boycott; while apartheid had officially existed since 1948 (and de facto—if not de jure—segregation persisted in much of the United States), outrage grew especially upon the state's 1960 massacre of sixty-nine unarmed black demonstrators in Sharpeville, a township just south of Johannesburg. It is difficult to know the direct mark these and other world events had on the

Beatles and their circle, because of a lack of such information, but also because once under management starting at the end of 1961, the group was advised not to speak out on difficult or controversial topics, a stance that would begin eroding only in 1965.

1961–1962 Original releases (British unless specified otherwise):
Single: "My Bonnie" / "The Saints" (rel. in Ger. in Oct. 1961)
EP: *My Bonnie* (rel. in Ger. in Sept. 1961)

Side 1:	Side 2:
"My Bonnie"	"Cry for a Shadow"
"Why"	"The Saints"

Single: "Love Me Do" / "P.S. I Love You" (rel. Oct. 5, 1962)
EP: *Ya Ya* (rel. in Ger. in Oct. 1962)

Side 1:	Side 2:
["Ya Ya" Part 1]	"Sweet Georgia Brown"
["Ya Ya" Part 2]	["Skinny Minny"]

THE CAVERN, "MY BONNIE," AND BRIAN EPSTEIN

The Beatles (now a quartet, without Stu) continued to play small-pay bookings in dance halls throughout the Merseyside area following their triumph in Litherland in the last days of 1960. They returned to Mona Best's Casbah on New Year's Eve after a fourteen-month absence. Mona was one of a number of friends and opportunists who would promote the band, finding them local one-off gigs in one dive or another. Neil Aspinall, the father of Mona's third son, who was thus Pete's half-brother, became the group's regular roadie, ferrying their gear from the Best home above the Casbah to performance locations, a role he continued to the end of the group's stage career. (Much later, he would become the head of the Beatles' company, Apple.)

In January 1958, the Quarry Men had played the Cavern Club, a brickwork cellar on narrow Mathew Street in the heart of Liverpool. Playing skiffle and rock 'n' roll numbers, they quickly wore out their welcome, as the club's dues-paying jazz aficionados had no interest in the emerging rock style. By the band's next Cavern appearance in February 1961, ownership of the club and the status of electric rock music had both changed (Rory Storm and the Hurricanes having opened the way), and they played to an appreciative Cavern crowd. More popular than any other Liverpool attractions, the Beatles became the Cavern's house band at noontime and evening sessions alike, with about 290 appearances there in 1961 and '62 and—as a favor—three more scattered across 1963. At the Cavern, a dank one-time fruit cellar, patrons would have a Coke and a smoke, sit in rows, and dance both to records spun by the witty DJ Bob Wooler and to bands that covered the top hits.

At first, Stu's vacancy on the bass was filled by Chas Newby, but he left the group in the first weeks of 1961, requiring Paul to take up the instrument. This move quickly had a profound impact on the group's sound—already by May (the time of the first recordings we have of bassist McCartney), Paul had mastered the instrument in ways Stu Sutcliffe never did, and by late 1965 he had completely reimagined the instrument's role in the rock ensemble. Originally, the bass provided a simple rhythmic support for the most elementary aspects of harmony, but McCartney began to make it sing with a fluent, melodic voice creating lush counterpoint with the vocal and instrumental lines above. (⊙ The bass line as harmonic support is introduced in Video 1.5.)

For five hundred hours in the months of April–June 1961, the Beatles stomped the stage in their nightly Top Ten Club residency alongside and often backing Tony Sheridan in Hamburg—Harrison had reached legal age, and the band rose in the local scene's hierarchy. In addition to being an accomplished rocking guitarist, Sheridan possessed a reasonable voice, often in nonchalant imitation of Presley. By this time, the King had finished a two-year army hitch and made his first disappointing comeback with a repertoire of weak film soundtracks beginning with *G.I. Blues*, released in October 1960. Elvis had been stationed in Germany, and the film included "Wooden Heart," a simple traditional oom-pah march for accordion with several verses sung in German. It was a perfect example of the *Schlager* ("hit songs") music that the Beatles mowed down with their hard rock 'n' roll. "Wooden Heart" was a no. 1 hit in both Germany and England but was not even released as a single in America until 1964. Despite its corny nature—or maybe because of it—the Beatles covered the song and other continental crowd-pleasers, with McCartney singing Marlene Dietrich's "Falling in Love Again (Can't Help It)" (from the 1930 film *The Blue Angel*) and "Besame Mucho" (an English-language version of the Mexican hit from the 1940s, as performed by the Coasters), and Harrison leading Joe Brown's hokey arrangement of the 1921 number "The Sheik of Araby."

In addition to such staples and more rigorous rock 'n' roll ("Red Hot," "Leave My Kitten Alone," "Road Runner"), the most influential songs the Beatles adopted in the first months of 1961 came from the Brill Building "song factory" along a stretch of Broadway near Times Square, where songwriting teams like Gerry Goffin and Carole King created "Will You Love Me Tomorrow" and "Boys" for the Shirelles, "Keep Your Hands off My Baby" and "The Loco-Motion" for Little Eva, and "Chains" for the Cookies; Jerry Lieber and Mike Stoller, who wrote "Searchin'," "Young Blood," and "Three Cool Cats" for the Coasters and "Stand By Me" for Ben E. King; and Doc Pomus and Mort Shuman, who together produced "Save the Last Dance for Me" for the Drifters and "(Marie's the Name) His Latest Flame" for Elvis Presley. These songs and many others of similar lineage made their way to the Beatles' 1961 set lists. Even though they addressed teenage themes, these numbers featured professionally crafted, strongly contrasting sections: the verses sported clever lyrics, the choruses brought recurring slang catchphrases for "hooks," and the bridges often digressed to foreign tonal areas leading into strong retransitions back to the home key. For the early efforts of the Lennon-McCartney songwriting team, these simple yet pliable structures worked like templates.

Tony Sheridan recorded for German hit producer Bert Kaempfert, and he tapped the Beatles as his backing group to make their first commercial recordings for Polydor on May 22–23, 1961 (see Photo 2.1). (It was not done in a studio—the tapings were made on the stage of a local school auditorium.) McCartney had recently purchased his viol-shaped Höfner electric bass, likely in the same Hamburg shop in which John had found his Rickenbacker the previous November. These two guitars—John's Rickenbacker and Paul's Höfner—along with the Gretsch Country Gentleman and Ludwig black oyster pearl drum set that George and Ringo, respectively, would acquire in May 1963—became iconic as central features of the Beatles' look in the first wave of their world domination. At the time of these recordings, George still played a poor Czech guitar, but he upgraded in late July '61 to a fine American-made Gretsch, a 1957 Duo Jet. Pete Best's drumming

PHOTO 2.1. Tony Sheridan and the Beat Brothers, *My Bonnie* LP (as released in West Germany, April 1962).

on the Sheridan tracks sounds quite unusual—there is no bass drum or toms; only a snare is evident, with infrequent accents on hi-hat and suspended cymbal. As their own cheap and run-down amplifiers were not useable for recording, the Beatles played on amps supplied by Kaempfert, who was a composer and conductor in his own right; he had arranged the instrumental accompaniment for Presley's "Wooden Heart" a year before, which appeared after his own huge international hit "Wonderland by Night" (1960).

In addition to a number of Sheridan's most popular titles, Kaempfert chose two featuring the Beatles alone: the instrumental "Cry for a Shadow," composed by John and George as they worked over ideas inspired by the Shadows, and Lennon's raunchy vocal in a rocked-up rendition of "Ain't She Sweet," the conspiratorially sexist Tin Pan Alley standard from 1927. In "Shadow," George bends blue notes by manipulating the whammy bar while playing John's Rickenbacker; in "Sweet," John embellishes his expressive vocal with fast mordents (at "you," 0:09) and throws away word endings with immediate changes of dynamics ("direction," 0:30). (▶ Mordents are demonstrated in Video 2.6.) Sheridan contributed his own song, "Why" (on which we hear only Sheridan's vocal and guitar supported by bass and light snare), and led the Beatles through a handful of his other stage favorites, his solo guitar leading nearly all performances. Of greatest importance was their reworking of the old folk song "My Bonnie (Lies over the Ocean)"—this would be chosen as the single, released in

October. Kaempfert knew that his customers liked well-known tunes, and he had Sheridan introduce the song with a traditional, slow, triple-time German verse before breaking into a hard quadruple rock beat featuring Lennon's boogie technique beneath the English lyrics, sure to get everyone dancing. (In an alternate edit, Tony sings the intro in English.) In fact, one version of the record's sleeve carried the description "TWIST" very prominently, to cash in on Chubby Checker's 1960 dance craze. All of this passed for knowing charm in this era, but the screams that call forth Sheridan's twelve-bar guitar solo (and a bit of McCartney's already nimble walking bass) are the record's only elements to carry forth into the Beatles' own repertoire. In a similar vein, the Beatles also performed "Beautiful Dreamer" at this time, not in the traditional waltz-like triple meter, but with a hard-rocking backbeat. (▶ The concepts of meter and accent are illustrated in Video 1.2.)

"My Bonnie," crediting Sheridan's accompanists only as "The Beat Brothers," was a minor hit in Germany and reached no. 33 for the month of February 1962, mainly on the strength of Hamburg's fans of Sheridan and the Beatles. Although slight, the single represented a huge career stride. Decades before the internet made it easy to instantly make a recording available worldwide and on demand, most talented musicians struggled to secure club dates and concert performances, achieve recording contracts, and attain radio airplay and television appearances carried live and then lost for ages, to be reheard at a later time only in the rarest of cases. Most of this had to be handled through established booking managers, club owners, concert promoters, record producers, and radio programming executives, none of whom would be interested in unknown artists without a guaranteed return on investment.

The year of 1961 continued with the Beatles alternating daily gigs at the Cavern with ones at other clubs around Liverpool. By November, when they headlined "Operation Big Beat" at the Tower Ballroom across the Mersey in New Brighton, they received top billing above the city's other groups: Rory Storm and the Hurricanes, Gerry and the Pacemakers, the Remo Four, and King-Size Taylor and the Dominoes. This was major recognition, but still merely local. One promoter, Sam Leach, booked them in Aldershot in the south of England on December 9, thinking its location near London would generate press interest and be a stepping stone to the big time. Unfortunately, miscommunication prevented any interest in the event beyond that of the paltry and unfazed audience of only eighteen locals.

With the drive for recognition going nowhere, fortune arrived in November 1961 in the person of Brian Epstein. The manager of a family-owned record shop, North End Music Stores (NEMS), Brian had perfected music merchandising, presenting his wares with album covers stapled across the ceiling. His simple and original inventory system let him know immediately when he needed to reorder hit singles. This led to a wildly successful record shop: always having on hand the disc a customer wanted, but not being left holding too many copies after a song's popularity had faded. Brian gladly took special-order requests and followed Bill Harry's *Mersey Beat* (to which he contributed a column) and other tips and trade sheets about local musical trends. (Jazz devotees appreciated that Epstein carried the complete Blue Note label catalog.) Brian's success with promotion at NEMS marked a sharply positive turn in his own life, as his early interest in dress designing had been discouraged by his father, a denial that was followed by failures in the military and as a student at the Royal Academy of Dramatic Art. Most of his problems stemmed from the tightrope he walked between his public persona and his private life as a closeted gay man. Although a prominent businessman, he constantly dodged legal scrapes at a time when gay sex was not only considered immoral but prosecuted as criminal, with blackmail always a threat.

John, Paul, George, and Pete frequented NEMS in the city center, but Brian would not have recognized them other than as part of the stream of teenagers who auditioned records in his shop's listening booths. In late October, a customer asked Brian for a copy of "My Bonnie" by Liverpool's own Beatles. Curious and excited by the idea of successful local talent, Brian could find out nothing about the record (by this point released only on the Continent), but he located the Beatles at the Cavern, where he met them on November 9, the day before the triumphant "Operation Big Beat." At the Cavern, Brian caught the Beatles virus; intoxicated by their free-and-easy stage banter, he sensed the audience's adoration and their own gangbuster charm. (Perhaps Epstein heard Lennon introduce "Shimmy Shimmy" as "Shitty Shitty" or sing the words "A Waste of Money" in backing Paul's smarmy spotlight "A Taste of Honey.") He left to try to locate two hundred copies of "My Bonnie" as a first step toward a stronger business alliance.

Epstein began inquiring about their management, and found out they had none. Allan Williams, who had arranged their first Hamburg job, told Brian, "Don't touch them with a fucking bargepole; they will let you down," because the Beatles had refused to send Williams any agent's fee when they began finding their own work. Epstein contacted Polydor in Germany to arrange the release of "My Bonnie" in the United Kingdom, which took place on January 5, 1962. Brian scheduled publicity photos in the studio of Albert Marrion for December (see Photo 2.2)

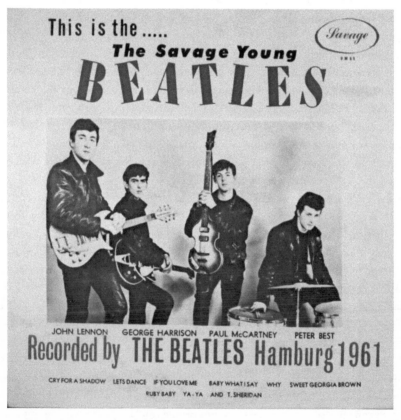

PHOTO 2.2. Albert Marrion's portrait of the Beatles, December 17, 1961. *The Savage Young Beatles* LP (released in US mid-1964).

and a recording audition in London with Decca for New Year's Day. These early Epstein accomplishments—contrasted with Sam Leach's disappointing failure in Aldershot—convinced the Beatles that he could advance their career, and so the band signed a management agreement in January. Brian began to push hard for a London-based record contract and live appearances on both radio and television.

RECORDING FOR EMI: GEORGE MARTIN

The entire space above the front-page fold in the January 4, 1962, issue of *Mersey Beat* consisted of the headline "Beatles Top Poll!" and a Marrion photograph of the group posing in matching leathers with their instruments. The Beatles were in fact the top rock 'n' roll attraction in the city but were still unknown outside of it. The same could practically be said of rock 'n' roll itself: only a few rare bands featured electric guitars in London in January 1962. Aside from the Shadows, there was Johnny Kidd and the Pirates, whose "Shakin' All Over" unleashed fierce, percolating arpeggios alongside a quivering vibrato bar from guitarist Joe Moretti, all of which the Beatles soon emulated in softer form in their own "Ask Me Why." The lesser-known Joe Brown and His Bruvvers (an idol of George Harrison's) had three top 10 hits in the United Kingdom in 1962–1963, but Shane Fenton and the Fentones (soon to be the Beatles' stable mates on Parlophone Records) cracked the top 20 with only one record, which peaked at no. 19. Other London electric guitar acts steered toward novelty in the purely instrumental work by the John Barry Seven (which included the highly regarded session guitarist Vic Flick), Johnny and the Hurricanes, and Rhet Stoller. Outside of Liverpool, music that featured electric guitarists who sang while playing was practically unknown; Cliff Richard notably didn't play, while his Shadows didn't sing. But uniquely on Merseyside, beat music modeled itself on American guitarist-singers Presley, Perkins, Berry, and Holly.

The Decca audition produced mixed results. The Beatles ran through fifteen of their most popular numbers but could not convince Decca that they had any future; "Groups with guitars are on the way out," they were famously told. On the plus side, they left town with a tape that Brian proceeded to play for representatives of the country's largest record companies, but EMI, Decca, and Pye all declined. Brian learned he might have more convenient acetate discs pressed from his tape at EMI's His Master's Voice outlet on Oxford Street in London. There, in early February, disc cutter Jim Foy showed interest in the tape's three Lennon-McCartney originals, particularly Paul's "Like Dreamers Do," and he introduced Brian to Sid Colman of the publication house Ardmore and Beechwood, who purchased song rights for resale. Publishers like Colman routinely sold sheet music and helped arrange for recording and airplay in return for a large share of songwriting royalties.

Colman had a good working relationship with producer George Martin, the head of Parlophone Records, and he arranged for the Beatles to receive a hearing there (despite the fact that Parlophone was a subsidiary of EMI, which had already turned them down). Decca had the Shadows, Martin's Parlophone partner Ron Richards had the Fentones, and Martin also wanted a rock group that could appeal to teens and make hit records. Martin liked some aspects of the Beatles' tape but wondered, given the British conventions of the time, which of the three singers should be promoted as the sole leader. (John and the Beatles? Paul and the Beatles?) Listening to the Decca performance of "Till There Was You," most producers would have overlooked the relative sophistication of Harrison's guitar playing and imagined the track overlaid with soaring strings, trilling flutes, and perhaps even a reverb-laden choir such as the Mike Sammes Singers, a frequent backing group. Martin had more progressive ears than most of his peers, more imagination, and less interest in fluff. The most successful record he had produced to that point was a 1920s-style dance-band knockoff called "You're Driving Me Crazy" by the Temperance Seven, which hit no. 1 in May 1961. Martin also had more familiarity with northern tastes—he had regularly taped dozens of pipe-band reels, jigs, and marches in Edinburgh and Aberdeen and discovered the satirical troupe Beyond the Fringe at the Edinburgh Festival. He soon scouted Liverpool's Cavern as a potential setting for a live Beatles LP. (It proved too noisy and so was never attempted.)

Having produced Peter Sellers's comedy records and recognizing the auditioning group's sense of humor, he gambled on the Beatles as a potential novelty act with an unclear musical talent and signed the group in May for a June recording session. Martin's recordings with Beyond the Fringe and with Sellers's Goons (whom Lennon had loved as a child), along with the novelty effects he had achieved with tape manipulation, show his leaning toward the unexpected, unconventional, offbeat, and incongruously funny. All this endeared him to the Beatles long before they would appreciate what Martin could contribute to their music. In addition to his ear for song structure, Martin possessed training as an oboist and orchestrator; by 1965, his classical background would come in handy in recording revolutionary pop records. In turn, the young group's charm, wit, and sponge-like capacities bowled him over when they convened at the EMI Studios on June 6.

At this point, the group had traveled abroad for the first of its three 1962 residencies in Hamburg (April 13–May 31, November 1–14, and December 18–31) and had been conscripted once again by Bert Kaempfert to record with Tony Sheridan, this time taping "Sweet Georgia Brown" and one other undocumented number in May. Announcement of the Parlophone recording session reached them by telegram. The year played out in Liverpool and Hamburg stage shows, adding a small handful of ballrooms in Wales and southern England over the second half. This period also saw their first radio and television appearances, singing Roy Orbison's "Dream Baby (How Long Must I Dream)," Chuck Berry's "Memphis," and the Marvelettes' "Please Mr. Postman" on BBC Radio in March (see Photo 2.3); the Coasters' "Besame Mucho," Joe Brown's "A Picture of You," and their own "Ask Me Why" in June; covering Richie Barrett's "Some Other Guy" and a medley of Little Richard's "Kansas City" and "Hey-Hey-Hey-Hey!" at the Cavern in August for telecast in November; and promoting the release of their own first EMI record, "Love Me Do" backed with "P.S. I Love You," plus Lenny Welch's "A Taste of Honey" and the Isley Brothers' "Twist and Shout," on both radio and television that October–December. Brian Epstein's diligent promotion brought the Beatles to the cusp of national attention by the end of 1962, with their first no. 1 record in the can and awaiting release.

The June session at EMI enabled producers Martin and Ron Richards to get to know the new performers, but nothing fruitful came from the day's work. Engineers had to devise a workaround to get a good bass sound from Paul, as his amplifier (powering a homemade speaker cabinet wired by a chum) created too much distortion. They taped "Ask Me Why" and "Besame Mucho" along with "Love Me Do" and "P.S. I Love You," the two songs that ultimately comprised the Beatles' first EMI single (when re-recorded in September). Martin was concerned with the arrangement, tempo, and structure; for "Love Me Do," he asked Paul to sing a phrase he'd never sung before, as

PHOTO 2.3. The Marvelettes, "Forever" / "Please Mr. Postman" 45 (originally released in US August 21, 1961), as reissued in the Netherlands in 1965.

John was trying to sing the line even though it interrupted his harmonica solo. (By next February, Martin would consider a two-step process: (1) record the guitars, drums, and voices as a basic track, and then (2) superimpose the harmonica on top of that work, but before that, a completely live performance—as if done onstage—was apparently the desire.) More worrisome was Best's drumming, which sped up and slowed down during "Love Me Do." Martin told Epstein that the Beatles could continue to use Pete onstage, but he would have to hire a professional drummer for recording. The pop world made common use of recording-session drummers, as well as other instrumentalists and backing singers, and Martin would not have considered this matter consequential. To John, Paul, and George, on the other hand, this critique compounded the moody Pete's ill fit with the band's otherwise outgoing personalities. Two weeks before they were to record again in September, they had Epstein fire Best and replace him with Ringo Starr.

Ringo, star of one of Liverpool's top bands in his own right, knew John, Paul, and George well. He'd even taken Pete's place with them onstage on occasion in Hamburg, and swiftly found a musical rapport. Along with Johnny Hutchinson of the Big Three, Starr had earned a reputation as one of the two best drummers in Liverpool. And his style trounced that of his predecessor: From what his recordings tell us, Best added an ersatz razzamatazz to the Beatles' tone with his rapid snare subdivisions. Ringo, on the other hand, provided a stronger foundation with an emphatic rock backbeat—his heavy snare conveyed a bedrock energy, and his propulsive tom-tom fills—unknown in Best's playing—shot euphoric shivers through the sound. He had an innate gift for tempo and placement. Although his cymbal work was not showcased in the Beatles' first recordings, it would begin revolutionizing rock music by late 1963. Ringo joined the Beatles on August 18, 1962, converting their rhythmic backbone from that of a mere dance band to one of a punchy rock group.

The Beatles returned to EMI on September 4, 1962, for their first successful studio session. Martin, still skeptical of Lennon and McCartney's songwriting ambitions, had given them a demo recording of a new song by pop craftsman Mitch Murray called "How Do You Do It" and instructed them to rehearse it as their debut single. The Beatles dutifully learned the song and recorded a reasonable performance but convinced Martin by degrees of enthusiasm to reconsider their own original material. Thus, the Beatles' first singles, beginning with the Everly Brothers–derived "Love Me Do" and "P.S. I Love You," greeted their listeners as originals, a stance they held with religious conviction. Their second single, recorded on November 26, featured a version of John's new song "Please Please Me." When Martin first heard the song in September, it ran rather slow and increased in pitch to a fever-blown falsetto climax, the operatic Roy Orbison echoing through reminders of Elvis's growl. Martin suggested the group pick up the tempo, which brought new intensity to John's melodic arch and bluesy chords. They re-recorded "Ask Me Why" for the B-side. "How Do You Do It," now a castoff, got handed to Gerry and the Pacemakers, one of a number of Liverpool acts that Epstein would sign and bring to stardom following his success with the Beatles, for a no. 1 hit. Whereas the Beatles scuttled "How Do You Do It," they borrowed its unusual three-chord progression, G–C♯ diminished–D, for the introduction of "P.S. I Love You."

It wasn't only the tempo and structure of "Please Please Me" that got Martin's attention. With the September 4 B-side, "P.S. I Love You," Ringo's attempt at simultaneously playing drums and maracas struck Martin as amateurish, reigniting the concern that had led to Best's ouster. (▶) The components of drum sets and the playing techniques of Pete and Ringo are demonstrated in Videos 1.2 and 2.3.) The next recording session on September 11 found drummer Andy White powering the group—with Ringo relegated to the tambourine—in cutting a new version of "Love Me Do" (which appears on the Beatles' first album, whereas Ringo's recording was used on the single) and one of "P.S. I Love You." All the Beatles fretted openly over this treatment of Ringo, and Martin never hired a substitute Beatle again.

"Ask Me Why" possessed an anomalous formal structure, partly due to its naive charm, a quality also found in Paul's rambling "Like Dreamers Do," a song known only from the Decca audition. Most pop songs were in verse-chorus form, alternating changing verses and repeated choruses with a possible bridge, or reducing the proportions of the chorus to fixed refrains that lay within the confines of otherwise variable verses, often in an overall SRDC (statement—restatement—departure—conclusion) relationship. In "Ask Me Why," however, functions and orderings of passages are quite ambiguous; a best interpretation of the large-scale structure might be [0:00–0:02] Introduction–[0:02–0:24] Verse 1 with 1st ending–[0:25–0:48] Verse 2 with 2nd ending–[0:49–1:02] Bridge–[1:03–1:13] Chorus–[1:14–1:36] Verse 1 with 1st ending–[1:36–1:48] Chorus *with 2nd ending* (!)–[1:48–2:01] Bridge–[2:02+] Chorus and *Coda*. (▶ Aspects of the introduction, coda, and the "one more time" cadence are covered in Video 2.2.) At a lower level, the verse contains three phrases (unusual outside of a blues verse, but championed by the Beatles, as in the verses of "I Want to Hold Your Hand"); this *a–a'–b* verse structure is interrupted after its first phrase by the "tattoo," the guitar line that served as the song's introduction. This tattoo will reappear in each verse, and also after the first (but not the second) chorus, recalling the song's introduction most clearly. At the surface level of each phrase, proportional lengths are quite asymmetric: the two-bar intro is followed by a verse with phrases of 4 + 4 + 5 (!) bars; each verse maintains this pattern. The (second) ending of the second verse (at 0:47) acts as a smooth transition into the bridge. Each bridge has a standard 4 + 4 (c–c') pattern. Each of the first two choruses is a single six-bar phrase (with d material, derived from the a melody of the verse), but the third chorus/coda combination is of a 5 + 2 + 2 arrangement. This coda is of the "one more time" type (also to be reused in "Hold Your Hand"), repeating the final thought but coming to a cold ending rather than fading out. It is singularly odd to save the first chorus until after the bridge, and then present a second bridge following a chorus.

Also, note the verse's unusual rhyme scheme: the a phrase ends in "want to know," the a' phrase rhymes this with "goes to show" and then raises that immediately with "that I know"; the final b phrase ends with "be blue," which rhymes only with the openings (!) of both a and a': "I love you" and "And it's true." Although the singer is happily in love, he is confused—bewildered—by his surprising new feelings, all conveyed in the flashing uproar of his wildly haphazard sensations.

Two other batches of recordings remain from late 1962: a Cavern Club rehearsal dating from around October, featuring an early group run-through of a new original number, "I Saw Her Standing There" (this song without much participation from Harrison, who may have been hearing it for the first time; it's also notable for Lennon's playing harmonica but no driving guitar rhythm), and several sets from the Star-Club recorded with a single microphone between Christmas and New Year's. While many live recordings by the Beatles remain from their broadcast performances and their touring dates, these Star-Club tapes show best the Beatles' intimate relationship with an audience that still numbered in the hundreds. Joking back and forth, taking requests, and teasing barmaids were as big a part of their act as the songs this behavior helped put across. Embedding this nonchalance into their sound allowed them to glide through their musical homestretch.

The decision to release singles of original material represents a huge distinctive marker, not only because their own catalog of original songs was then small, but also for the immense implications it had for their future. No one then could have predicted how Lennon and McCartney would bloom into the century's top songwriters. Performing more than three hundred songs composed by others had made them popular. It's widely noted that among the last cover material learned by the Beatles were the "girl group" songs of the Shirelles, Donays, and Cookies and the Motown products of Barrett Strong, the Marvelettes, and the Miracles, along with other African American singer-songwriters such as Arthur Alexander. More rarely discussed are the ways that aspects of this music—and all music they heard before and after their signing with EMI—show up re-engineered in their own original compositions.

This brings us to another important feature of how the Beatles elevated the rock 'n' roll style. Formal classical musicians like Bert Kaempfert and George Martin learned in a written tradition, where sounds were notated on musical staves and music passed between generations by manuscript more than by sound recording. The advance of recordings and the continuing popularity of the phonograph as a home furniture staple disrupted this process. Through recordings, pop musicians began to learn music the way the Beatles themselves did: by ear, or in what's called an "aural" tradition. Instead of learning to read and write music along an established path that typically includes conventional repertoire, learning by ear became a new way to absorb and internalize musical principles. And keep in mind that there was no resource like the internet for looking up chord changes or lyrics. Folk musicians had played by ear for centuries, alongside the more formal academic traditions that grew out of the Western classical tradition, and it was the ear, rather than the eye, that guided the creators of blues, country, and then rock 'n' roll.

In the world the Beatles grew up in, these remained two distinct avenues of thought: the high culture of Bach, Beethoven, and Brahms regarded as more elite and specialized and the popular idiom of Woody Guthrie, skiffle, and rock 'n' roll viewed as more "common," as a lower form of music-making. One of the Beatles' key accomplishments lies in how they eventually reconciled these two worlds, making rock 'n' roll so elaborate and thoughtful that it drew listeners from the "high" art classical crowd, and working alongside classical soloists in Britain to earn their respect.

From today's vantage point, with the band's catalog continuing to win over new listeners at a fifty-year remove, it's clear that the Beatles conceived and produced music on as high a level as any jazz virtuoso or classical player in the twentieth century, despite a middling grade of wizardry as instrumentalists. But at the time, rock suffered from the perception that it was a lowbrow form, a junky, disposable style that wouldn't last into the next decade.

The Beatles had size-ten ears. They learned dozens of songs by playing along with records, but they didn't own recordings of all the hundreds of songs they learned. Before their apprenticeship was over, they could sing and play a tune after hearing it a few times in a broadcast from Luxembourg, on a German jukebox, or in Epstein's record store, no matter how new and complex a texture it may have in relation to everything learned before. Musicians can learn so many songs so quickly and thoroughly only if they have already deeply assimilated many aspects of song structure, poetic practice, and melodic/harmonic voicing and function. Over the course of their entire career, Lennon and McCartney's songs rapidly progressed to an unmatched degree: the Beatles had honed an ability to hear a new musical idea from any source across the globe and instinctively integrate it alongside the musical ideas they had already mastered. Their unique mix of talent, hard work, curiosity, confidence, ambition, and enjoyment of each other and what they accomplished together took them to the heights of music history. Now that we have considered what got them to this point—particularly in songs created by others—we turn to what they would produce as composers and performers under their own name.

"Please Please Me"

Recorded November 26, 1962, for the second EMI A-side

—treating simple aspects of the song's instrumental and vocal arrangement, its use of particular major scale degrees, and its formal structure (including the SRDC pattern).

When the Beatles first brought this song in to play for George Martin at EMI Studios in the summer of 1962, they were desperate to record their own material but knew on some level they weren't quite ready. Captivating silences aside, "Love Me Do" was fairly humdrum. Martin may have gone ahead with it as much to encourage them as anything else. Perhaps he was distracted by the question of the drummer, calling in studio hand Andy White on September 11, even after hearing Ringo play on September 4, 1962.

No earlier slow recordings remain, but Lennon and McCartney spoke of "Please Please Me" as something they wrote with Roy Orbison in mind: a medium-tempo weeper, a platform for vocal melodrama. Martin suggested they speed it up. And when they returned to EMI on November 26, not only did the new tempo fix whatever problem Martin heard in it, but the result bowled him over. After getting the track on tape, he reportedly leaned forward toward his control room mic to tell them, "You've just made your first number one" (Lewisohn 1988, 23). This story seems both apocryphal and self-serving: lots of producers say this to lots of groups; few say it to groups who will dominate the charts, and culture, for the rest of their careers. The miracle spins out into how far his early encouragement went, and how acceptance and unthinkable fame sparked by this song propelled their songwriting muse.

"Please Please Me" resumes and expands on all the high spirits of "Love Me Do" while boosting all levels of musical development. Booming guitars and keening harmonica introduce a ripened vocal arrangement, where Lennon and McCartney duet on interwoven lines of unison and harmony. Marching stepwise down a *major scale*, they start singing in *unison* before splitting off into McCartney's upper pedal point and Lennon's descending steps for the melody, *parallel* lines dividing into oblique, geometric patterns. (▶ The major scale is covered in Videos 1.3 and 1.4; matters of voicing in unison and parallel are demonstrated in Videos 1.7 and 2.6.) The ending, sustaining the word "you" over changing chords, will become an idea reworked for the endings of "From Me to You" and "She Loves You" and the introduction to "Help!" Paul's last two vocal pitches, a very high sustained B to G♯, are scavenged from his ending to the Decca audition number "Love of the Loved."

At the end of each R-gesture, a full stop (as at 0:19) trips a guitar arpeggio that sets up the rave-up to the title refrain ("Come on . . . come on . . . come on . . . come on . . ."), which Lennon sings with developing entreaties, and the splashy title line spills forth as McCartney takes a giant vocal leap up to the second "please." (Compare the rising "come on" phrase in "Please Please Me" with the similarly boiling-over phrase "'cause I want a girl to call my own," in Bobby Darin's "Dream Lover" (1959). Not only are the phrases related on their own merits in the climax-approaching contour of the lead vocal and the interjected two-word choral responses, but they each occur as the D-phrase within an SRDC structure in their respective verse-refrain passages.) Pert drum fills patch verses up with bridges (at 1:01), where McCartney and Harrison shadow Lennon's lead. The bridge swells to a Lennon falsetto vocal leap on "you" (at 1:13), before a brief splurge of three-part harmonies (at 1:14, "Whoa yeah"). The beat keeps whooshing past while vocals smooth over the top of the sound: the track elevates words and music to a realm where arrangement augments both, where different pieces of a song fit together in both sympathy and contrast. The convincing fit of matching parts is especially fine, considering the jumble of elements brought together: jazzy guitar octaves, smart Everlys vocal harmony, blue Perkins chords, borrowed Darin arrangement, and stratospheric Orbison register, and that's just in the verse/refrain passage.

All this activity frames straight talk about sex maneuvers in an era when explicit talk of positions and reciprocation remained socially unmentionable. (Today, it's hard to comprehend the strict codes that still repressed public expressions of sexuality in 1960s' culture, despite trends in relaxed mores that had pushed against these boundaries in recordings, film, and literature since the 1920s.) The cascading vocal attacks in "Please Please Me" convey a breathless anticipation, the fevered unbuttoning of desire that accompanies young physical intimacy—the same kind of rough yet inspired musicality on display here. Still, the singer remembers his polite "please."

CUE	SECTION	HARMONY	DETAIL
0:00	Introductory tattoo	I	
0:06	Verse 1: S-gesture	I–IV–I→III–IV–V	PM/JL duet
0:14	Verse 1: R-gesture	I–IV–I	
0:19	Transition		GH guitar
0:21	Verse 1: D-gesture	IV–ii–vi–IV	JL lead (PM/GH bkg)
0:27	Verse 1: C-gesture (refrain)	I–IV–V–I	
0:31	Tattoo repeats (harmonica)	I–IV–V	
0:34	Verse 2		
1:01	Transition	I	drum fill
1:02	Bridge	IV–V–I–IV–V–I–IV–V	
1:15	Tattoo repeats as retransition (harmonica)	I–IV–V	
1:19	Verse 1		
1:44	Refrain: repeat twice		
1:50	Closing cadence	I→III (!)→VI (!)–V–I	

POINTS FOR DISCUSSION

1. Describe the differences between music's "written" and "aural" traditions.
2. How did Brian Epstein work to advance the Beatles' career in the first half of 1962?
3. What British electric guitarists were recording before the Beatles?
4. Why did the Beatles fire Pete Best and hire Ringo Starr? Discuss some aspects of Ringo's playing, as covered in the videos for this chapter.
5. Describe some elements from other writers' songs that influenced Lennon-McCartney's approach.
6. Why was it so important for the Beatles to record their own original material?
7. What possible reason would John Lennon have had for stating that the Beatles' career as a band ended with their last Star-Club performances in 1962?
8. How did the Beatles' performing and recording in Hamburg prepare them for a meeting with EMI producer George Martin?
9. Name some aspects of George Martin's background that made him ideally suited to produce the Beatles.

10. What are some musical qualities of the Beatles' first A-sides?
11. ▶ Define, after viewing Video 2.6: falsetto; melisma; parallel, similar, contrary, and oblique motion.

FURTHER READING

Epstein, Brian. *A Cellarful Of Noise*. New York: Doubleday, 1964.

Geller, Debbie. *In My Life: The Brian Epstein Story*. New York: St. Martin's, 2000.

Martin, George. *All You Need Is Ears*. With Jeremy Hornsby. New York: St. Martin's, 1979.

Oldham, Andrew Loog. *Stoned: A Memoir of London in the 1960s*. New York: St. Martin's, 2001.

Sutcliffe, Pauline. *Stuart Sutcliffe: The Beatles' Shadow and His Lonely Hearts Club*. With Douglas Thompson. London: Sidgwick & Jackson, 2001.

Taylor, Alistair. *With the Beatles*. London: John Blake, 2003.

Thompson, Gordon. *Please Please Me: Sixties British Pop, Inside Out*. New York: Oxford University Press, 2008.

CHAPTER 3

RUNAWAY TRAIN

British Beatlemania (1963)

Beatlemania, experienced in cascading waves, exploded across Britain throughout 1963. *Please Please Me* quickly topped the album charts after its March release, held the top slot into the fall, and turned the Beatles into headliners on a Roy Orbison package tour. A dizzy hysteria surrounded their performances; London became their center of operations; and Epstein began planning their United States campaign for the following February. Several key steps to fame and influence lay ahead of them in 1964 and beyond, but before then, the Beatles zoomed from obscurity to ubiquitous cultural force in a matter of months.

Their huge success had both logical and intangible features, although when asked in a February 7, 1964, press conference what it was about their music that excited people so much, Lennon quipped, "If we knew, we'd form another group and be managers." They routinely won over cynical reporters with agile wit. As the Beatles became better known, four distinct personalities emerged, so their act showcased individual characters as well as group identity. To the conformist mindset of that era, they looked quite unusual; in defiance of the military-issue crew cuts worn by all men and boys, they grew their hair long, with androgynous-looking bangs reaching the eyebrows that no one could have imagined as fashionable. By March 1962, Epstein dressed them in tailored suits aligned with mod style and had them do polite, from-the-waist bows after every song, which styled their swaggering musicianship in a crisp frame.

As Lennon and McCartney became prolific and outstanding songwriters, their music amplified this bold visual image: clothed in conventional pop melody and song forms, Beatle records bristled with a new electricity from the lead guitar's rhythm-and-blues riffs of bent notes and Chuck Berry–like slides, falsetto Little Richard "woos" over dissonant chords and propulsive drum fills, and harmonizing vocals that spoke directly to their listeners, emphasizing personal pronouns for one-to-one communication. Altogether, the music harnessed a tantalizing balance of power, harmony, passion, and tightly focused control. The many stage shows and press interviews that brought the Beatles to national prominence by mid-1963 schooled them in how to leave their audiences breathless. By the first weeks of 1964, they were primed to make the strongest impression on America—the world's biggest pop market, which they both craved and feared.

Their UK success also paralleled a worrisome, yet at the same time tiresome, sex scandal carried out by the secretary of state for war, John Profumo, with nineteen-year-old Christine Keeler, who was also having sex with a Soviet spy. The fallout forced Prime Minister Harold MacMillan to resign in October 1963. At the same time, the 1960 shooting down of CIA spy Francis Gary Powers, who was flying in Soviet airspace, had stoked a new American fascination with secret-agent intrigue. This set the stage for the Stateside popularity of the James Bond, Secret Service Agent 007, spy novels and blockbuster films, beginning with *Dr. No* in 1962, contextualizing American interest in the Profumo scandal as part of an early-sixties absorption in exciting British popular culture. To a greater degree than Britain's suffering in the wake of MacMillan's humiliation, the United States was brought to a standstill by the shocking assassination of President Kennedy in late November. Many sociologists believe these political hangovers left Britain and then America more open to Beatlemania's color, eccentricity, zeal, and promise.

Others cite the tremendous bulge in the numbers of baby boomers, a generation of children born beginning just after World War II, who were then entering adolescence. The numbers stagger the mind: between 1946 and 1960, the birth rate escalated at an unprecedented pace, peaking between 1957 and 1961. From 1950 to 1970, America's population ballooned from 150 to 200 million in a single generation. Not only were Western youth growing in numbers, but their women were acquiring new independence with the advent of oral contraceptives in 1960 followed by the publications of Helen Gurley Brown's *Sex and the Single Girl* (1962) and Betty Friedan's *The Feminine Mystique* (1963), all of which set in motion the second wave of feminism. At the same time, young people in America were protesting war in ever-growing numbers throughout 1963—a year when a new international nuclear test-ban treaty was signed and Martin Luther King, Jr., gave the rousing "I Have a Dream" speech to an August 1963 gathering of a quarter million at Washington, DC's Lincoln Memorial—despite a white supremacist's assassination of civil-rights leader Medgar Evers only two months earlier. Combine this youth dynamic with the fading luster of the elites and their sometimes backward institutions, and you have the perfect cultural cocktail for a pop explosion that mirrored in music the manifold changes wrought throughout Western society over the coming few years.

1963 British releases:
Single: "Please Please Me" / "Ask Me Why" (rel. Jan. 11)
LP: *Please Please Me* (rel. Mar. 22)

Side 1:	Side 2:
"I Saw Her Standing There"	"Love Me Do"
"Misery"	"P.S. I Love You"
"Anna (Go to Him)"	"Baby It's You"
"Chains"	"Do You Want to Know a Secret"
"Boys"	"A Taste of Honey"
"Ask Me Why"	"There's a Place"
"Please Please Me"	"Twist and Shout"

Single: "From Me to You" / "Thank You Girl" (rel. Apr. 12)
Single: "She Loves You" / "I'll Get You" (rel. Aug. 23)
LP: *With the Beatles* (rel. Nov. 22)

Side 1:	Side 2:
"It Won't Be Long"	"Roll Over Beethoven"
"All I've Got to Do"	"Hold Me Tight"
"All My Loving"	"You Really Got a Hold on Me"
"Don't Bother Me"	"I Wanna Be Your Man"
"Little Child"	"Devil in Her Heart"
"Till There Was You"	"Not a Second Time"
"Please Mr. Postman"	"Money (That's What I Want)"

Single: "I Want to Hold Your Hand" / "This Boy" (rel. Nov. 29)

THE RISE TO NATIONAL PROMINENCE: *PLEASE PLEASE ME*

These factors can make the Beatles' career seem divinely timed. January of 1963 began with four dates in snow-covered northern Scotland, leading to a television appearance in Glasgow on the eighth. Such bookings continued with rapidly improving venues. Already on the thirteenth, the Beatles mimed "Please Please Me," their dynamic new A-side released two days prior, for a national television audience of loyal viewing teens. The group's growing professionalism finds expression in the evolution of Ringo's bass drum head: his crudely applied name is seen in January in Glasgow; this is covered by a sash with the new "bug-with-antennae" logo (designed by Paul) as televised from Teddington in February and April, and previous identifiers are finally replaced by the ultimate sleek and strong drop-T logo as broadcast in Birmingham in June, on the iconic black oyster pearl Ludwig drum set, then just a month old. Drumming moored the Beatles' power.

Brian Matthew, host of the BBC's radio program *Saturday Club*, introduced the band not only nationally but across four continents; when the Beatles taped five songs for the show on January 22, Matthew introduced "Love Me Do" thus: "At the moment the majority of the Beatles' fans are in their hometown of Liverpool, and I have a very strong suspicion it won't be long before they're all over the country." By March 6, BBC broadcasts captured girls screaming in anticipation of the Beatles' performance, and by April 18 at the Royal Albert Hall, the bedlam carried right through the songs themselves. "People here [are] twisting all over the Albert Hall," a surprised radio reporter comments. It may be hard to appreciate now just how shocking such a thing would have been in a venue that—outside of the summer pops season, called the Proms—had seen only the quietest audiences for its routine classical orchestral, choral, ballet and opera performances.

The best description of early Beatles performances comes from one of Epstein's publicists, Andrew Loog Oldham, who went on to manage the Rolling Stones:

> The Beatles were fast becoming a national treasure, each new single replacing the previous one as the national anthem. . . . At the Granada Theatre in Bedford, I stood at the back of the stalls beside Brian Epstein, who'd been slightly apprehensive about the lukewarm reactions his boys had been getting "down south." This night, though, there was a tangible sense of mad hysteria rising all over the theatre, and with the arrival of the Beatles on-stage it rose to a frenzy and took on a life of its own.
>
> The kids broke *all* the backstage windows. It was pandemonium. Onstage, you could not hear the Beatles for the roar of the crowd, and the roar I heard was the roar of the whole world. You can hear something without seeing it, in the same way as you can have an experience that is beyond anything you've had before. You don't have to be clever, you only have to be a member of the public. The noise that night hit me emotionally, like a blow to the chest. The audience that evening expressed something beyond repressed adolescent sexuality. The noise they made was the sound of the future. Even though I hadn't seen the world, I heard the whole world screaming. The power of the Beatles touched and changed minds and bodies all over the world. I didn't *see* it—I heard and felt it. When I looked at Brian, he had the same lump in his throat and tear in his eye as I. (Oldham 2001, 182–183)

Still covering hits made famous by others, the Beatles added a few new girl-group songs ("Keep Your Hands off My Baby," "Chains") and R&B numbers ("You've Really Got a Hold on Me," "A Shot of Rhythm and Blues") to their early-1963 set lists. (The Beatles were drawn primarily to the vocal arrangements in the girl-group and R&B songs, which originally did not typically feature guitars.) But success primed their original efforts as well. In preparation for a tour of the nation's theaters behind celebrity singer Helen Shapiro, John wrote "Misery" for her, hoping she would showcase it on stage and through recording. Her manager rejected it—its melancholy words did not fit her bouncy, upbeat image, and so it passed to another tour mate, Kenny Lynch, instead. Again, Matthew provides some context during the Beatles performance of six songs for *Saturday Club* on March 16, suggesting the group has already exerted cultural influence as he and John introduce "Misery":

MATTHEW: Now, apart from establishing a sort of fashion in hairstyles, clothes, music, and everything else, you write songs as well, don't you?

LENNON, *laughing*: Oh, is that what we do? . . . We do write songs.

MATTHEW: And haven't you written one for Kenny Lynch?

LENNON: Kenny Lynch, yes, I don't know when it's out.

MATTHEW: It's out now. Why didn't you keep it for yourself? It's a great number.

LENNON: Well, you know, he's a friend of ours, Kenny. We met him on the Helen Shapiro tour.

MATTHEW: I see. But you do, you sing this number yourselves?
LENNON: We've done it on our [*strong emphasis, flogging ironically*] LP.
MATTHEW, *imitating John's tone*: Out next week.
LENNON, *laughing*: Yes.

Toward the end of the tour, on February 28, John and Paul wrote "From Me to You" for their third single. But more momentous was February 11, the full day booked at EMI's Studio No. 2 for the recording of the Beatles' first long-playing album, the one John had pitched to *Saturday Club* listeners. Dubbed *Please Please Me* for its hit single, which topped some national sales charts by the first week of March, the album suggests with its song sequence a stage set list, with ten new recordings performed live in the studio, with minimal overdubs, all sandwiched by the four songs comprising their first two singles.

EMI's engineers had to perform some workarounds with the novices' tatty equipment. John's guitar breaks up at several points in "Chains" (at 1:03–1:15 and elsewhere) due to a poor connection, and Paul's bass amp produced a buzzing sound requiring a replacement speaker pulled from the studio's echo chamber. The months of April and May would mark the purchase of new gear, necessitated by a full-time touring schedule playing houses as large as ten thousand for the *New Musical Express* Poll-Winner's All-Star Concert on April 21, Paul obtaining a state-of-the-art Vox bass amp in late March, George buying his Gretsch Country Gentleman in early May, and Ringo taking delivery of his Ludwigs on May 12. But aside from the Gibson acoustic-electrics purchased for the September '62 recording sessions, the Beatles' first album memorializes the gear they'd had since 1960 and '61.

The morning session captured two Lennon-McCartney originals, "There's a Place" and "I Saw Her Standing There," both of which required numerous takes to get right. Then, the Beatles rehearsed straight through their first break instead of having lunch. Richard Langham, an engineer on the session, says that when Martin and crew returned to the studio at 2:00, the Beatles had not stopped practicing for the afternoon's work, which comprised "A Taste of Honey," "Do You Want to Know a Secret," "Misery," and overdubs of handclaps, harmonica, and second vocals (Paul's "trick" duet in "Honey"). After dinner, an attempt at "Hold Me Tight" failed, so they turned to five well-honed cover songs, "Anna (Go to Him)," "Boys," "Chains," "Baby It's You," and finally, after ten at night, "Twist and Shout," none of which required more than four takes or any overdubs, the first performance judged best in two cases. To get a sense of why John, Paul, and George regarded Ringo as the best drummer in Liverpool, compare his work in "Baby It's You" with that on the Shirelles' model recording; Ringo improves the tempo to perfection, and his supple placement, always in the pocket, brings every moment of the song to life. Recorded onto two-track tape, the album needed little in the way of postproduction (Martin added keyboard parts to "Misery" and "Baby It's You," doubling and thereby beefing up Harrison's guitar parts in those songs, on February 20) and appeared in stores on March 22. On the strength of a no. 1 hit single and exposure through radio, television, and national tour dates, *Please Please Me* (see Photo 3.1) reached no. 1 in its fifth week on *Melody Maker*'s album chart, where it stayed lodged for an unprecedented thirty-week run before being knocked off by the group's second album, *With the Beatles*, in November. Between May 4, 1963, and February 6, 1965, the Beatles held the no. 1 album spot for eighty-two of ninety-three weeks.

PHOTO 3.1. The Beatles, photographed by Angus McBean on March 5, 1963. *Please Please Me* LP (released in UK first in mono March 22, 1963, and in stereo the following month).

The Beatles' session for their next single, "From Me to You" and "Thank You Girl" (plus an outtake of "One after 909") recorded on March 5, came right before a second theater tour through the rest of the month, with Tommy Roe and Chris Montez quickly knocked out of top billing by the Beatles, now crowd favorites and overwhelming national stars. Audiences heard the Beatles play their hits plus a few covers. National radio and television programs as well as nightly ballroom and theater gigs throughout the country now showcased the Beatles, and a third national tour, in which they edged out megastar Roy Orbison for headliner status (because "From Me to You" topped the singles chart for seven weeks), took them from mid-May into mid-June. "You can't measure success," Lennon would later say, "but if you could, then the minute I knew we'd been successful was when Roy Orbison asked us if he could record two of our songs" (Beatles 2000, 94).

Owing to this phenomenal stardom, the BBC contracted for a new nationally networked radio series, *Pop Go the Beatles,* providing an audience of millions in May through September as the Beatles played their hits (plus dozens of the R&B covers frequently requested in their Hamburg and Liverpool club days) and cracked wise with other personalities. The Beatles had become their home country's darlings.

"I Saw Her Standing There"

Recorded February 11, 1963, for _Please Please Me_

> —_showing how the Beatles copped Chuck Berry with a driving groove . . . and added their own harmonic surprise._

George Bernard Shaw once wrote, "We recognize originals at first by their influences." Chuck Berry soared in the Beatles' imaginations as one of the great early rockers, and while Lennon sang most of his songs in Beatles' sets (including "Too Much Monkey Business," "I'm Talking about You," and "Memphis, Tennessee"), McCartney handled "Little Queenie," and Harrison took "Roll Over Beethoven." Like countless guitar bands in this era, the Beatles launched Berry songs as testing grounds, exercises in getting a beat to float on air, and deliver rollicking excitement as a show staple. Berry was twenty-eight when he put out "Maybelline" in 1955, so his identification with teen pleasure takes on added emphasis when you consider the first-person candor of his narratives. He didn't write about how he remembered teenage experience; he describes how teenagers felt walking through everyday life, dealing with school and parents and romance and fate. The verbal immediacy of Berry's songs gives them force, pluck, and drive; as mere words and rhythm they resemble raps; pitches are repeated so much they're sometimes almost irrelevant. "Johnny B. Goode" tells the story of rock 'n' roll in capsule form: young country talent earns fame and fortune in the city by playing guitar to the rhythms of the train. Other songs celebrated teen scenarios as matter-of-fact realities: "Almost Grown," "No Particular Place to Go," and "Sweet Little Sixteen."

As writers, Lennon and McCartney took the next logical step: writing their own Chuck Berry–style "standard," a cornerstone of original material that matched and extended Berry's delight with suggestive words. This became a common trope among rock bands who placed themselves in the same tradition: think of Led Zeppelin's "Rock 'n' Roll," (1971), the Rolling Stones' "It's Only Rock 'n Roll" (1973), or the Who's "Long Live Rock" (1974), pillars of the style that celebrate its depth and longevity. The Beatles have several such Berry homages, including 1968's "Back in the U.S.S.R." (which angles off the Beach Boys' "Surfin' U.S.A.," rebounds into Ray Charles's "Georgia on My Mind," and boomerangs back to Berry's "Back in the U.S.A."), and 1969's "Come Together" (which spins its opening lines from Berry's "You Can't Catch Me" out into hippie esoterica). Later, Lennon combines his adoration for Chuck Berry with his newfound home, in "New York City" (1972). (Lennon performed "Johnny B. Goode" with Chuck Berry on the _Mike Douglas Show_ in 1971, in a segment that can be found online.)

In "I Saw Her Standing There," the opening McCartney count-off (which Martin edits onto this take) is part charm, part insolence. It's not just a musician's cue, it's the pull crank that turns the engine over, the flag that starts a tantalizing race (more than a few heard it as "One, two three, FUCK!"). And his bravado in merely announcing the tempo tips you off to its torque. Jazzers used to call this "swing," the way a slight delay in the rhythm could pull listeners more deeply into the beat, to connect on a physical as well as mental level. Rockers do the same thing at a quicker pace, updating the backbeat (on 2 and 4) into something dirtier, less seductive than propulsive. (Later on, Bruce Springsteen takes this count-in conceit over the cliff into delirium when he summons the band back in after the break in "Born to Run," or at the top of "Bobby Jean.") A driving rhythm is underlined by the boys' handclaps, superimposed on top of the recording of their instruments and vocals.

Now consider all this history, all this ambition to link yourself up with your hero's work and place the song as the lead track on your debut album—the first thing many listeners might hear from you, your first utterance in a medium nobody takes seriously. As an act, the Beatles resemble the unknown actor who shows up late in the movie, steals the scene from the big-shot Hollywood star, and arrives home from the premiere to find the phone ringing off the hook.

Even before McCartney starts singing, the opening bars convey just how much fun these players find together, how confident they feel in the sound with one another, how much they all lift one another up; the scene is set with a bass ostinato stolen from Berry's "I'm Talking about You." Lennon's syncopated rhythm guitar pattern resembles their cover of "The Hippy Hippy Shake." Every inanity in the lyric only hints at the joy impelling them forward. Scholar Ian Hammond points out how the words "I'll never dance with another" and the melody to which they're set echoes the familiar "When the Saints Go Marching In" ("I want to be in that number") (Everett 2001, 384n131), but turns immediately by hitting a harmonic accent on the word "Oh!" (which lands on an unexpected ♭VI chord, first at 0:24). It's the only use of this chord in the song's harmonic scheme, a flare and a giddy revelation. By then the song has muscle and grind, and the harmonized "oh" that follows, an instant signature returning as "ooh!" in "From Me to You" and "She Loves You," sounds less coy than determined, as if the dance, the song itself, has already carried them way past flirtation into the headiest idea: their bombastic romance with rock history, and their own romantic notions of where they might fit in it. The Beatles also know how to take the edge off, concealing the hard ardor of their excitement when the out-of-control V chord that would normally end the bridge (at the falsetto-shrieked "mi-hine") is pulled back to more gentlemanly composure in the IV at 1:08.

CUE	SECTION	HARMONY	DETAIL
0:00	Intro	I7	
0:07	Verse1: phrase 1	I–IV–I–V	PM lead vocal
0:20	Verse 1: refrain	I–I7–IV→VI–I–V–I	L-M duet
0:31	Verse 2: phrase 1	Repeats V1	
0:43	Verse 2: refrain		
0:54	Bridge 1	IV–V–IV	L-M duet
1:10	Verse 3: phrase 1	Repeats V1	
1:22	Verse 3: refrain		
1:34	Guitar solo	I–V–I–IV–I–V–I	Varied verse
1:57	Bridge 2		
2:13	Verse 3: phrase 1	Repeats V1	
2:25	Verse 3: refrain and coda		

"There's a Place"

Recorded February 11, 1963, for *Please Please Me*

> *—noting well-placed silences and other rhythmic tricks, plus more on ensemble and melodic scale-degree relationships, now in portrayal of the inner sanctum of John Lennon's mind.*

Everywhere on the Beatles' debut album you hear immersion in pop history, soaring creativity, and high spirits that transcend craft. Opening with a Chuck Berry–style original, "I Saw Her Standing There," counts as audacious; closing with "Twist and Shout," which streaks past original (the familiar Isley Brothers' cover hit) overfills the promise. Imagine a Dutch baseball team routing the Mantle-Maris Yankees in an exhibition game. That's how the enormous American audience felt when it first heard the Beatles perform rock 'n' roll in early 1964: aghast.

Saving your best original song for the penultimate number on side two of your first album—lighting the fuse that ignites "Twist and Shout"—announces an ambition as big as Elvis Presley's. "There's a Place" carries a new promise for the style, not just through its craft but through the fever behind the notes, the impulse to restore its majesty without nostalgia, as if Elvis never entered the army and Carl Perkins's car never crashed. The track combines the best elements of their songwriting and arranging so far for a heady new concoction: the harmonica from "Please Please Me" and "Love Me Do," the alternation of harmony vocals and unison singing from "Misery" and "I Saw Her Standing There," and an ensemble kick that strides with a vast, irresistible confidence. This sound still rings out as boundless; the music smiles with a brash, impulsive grin that overwhelms technique. And yet every detail makes the story bigger; each nuance harbors meaning.

Lennon and McCartney songs play with stop-time silence so commandingly in many early singles (each time the title hook comes around in "Love Me Do"; the chorus endings in "She Loves You" at 1:11 and 1:50, building to a final *caesura*, with a *fermata* (⊙ See Video 3.1) at 2:03–2:06); perhaps they learned it from sizzling pauses that shook up the background vocals in "Money": "that's . . . what's I want," or the stop-time verses in Chuck Berry's "Too Much Monkey Business."

In the opening moments of "There's a Place," Lennon's harmonica doubles Harrison's lead guitar riff, which guides them into the medium tempo on a dissonance (a long D♯ over the E chord) that's left dangling, then repeated, but then—silence. In that silence—just enough to make you blink—the anticipation springs from the quiet, not the harmonica: now the whole song teeters on a precipice, and gives Lennon and McCartney's determined cheer a tantalizing suspense. Their inwardly pointing unaccompanied duet hovers briefly ("There . . ." at 0:06) before diving headlong back into the band's communal groove with two sharp *upbeats* ("is a" before "place" at 0:08–0:09). (⊙ Upbeats and downbeats are discussed in Video 1.2; the triplet is demonstrated in Video 3.1.) Once the two lead singers land on the word "place," the song has both motion and momentum, a sense of arrival inseparable from its ongoing pulse. As they pump the triplet transition into the second half of the verse ("And it's my mind" at 0:21), they yank back at the forward melodic thrust to extend its tension. McCartney soars up as Lennon tugs down on two held notes ("mind" at 0:22–0:23 and "time" at 0:25–0:27), and the inimitable Beatles sound emerges: two individuals swerving, glancing, and soaring; two substantial egos and personalities sparring with each other in ecstatic struggle, before landing in unison on another perilous (minor) perch ("When I'm al-one" at 0:29). (This deceptive cadence on vi fulfills the strong unresolved hints from melodic sixth scale degrees the harmonica has landed on twice in the introduction; the growth of sixth scale degree from melodic aside to harmonic goal is a major thread in "Do You Want to Know a Secret," "She Loves You," "I Should Have Known Better," and others.)

While Lennon and McCartney found many ways to express their independence within the band setting, this early peak has the best aspects of voices in tandem, gnawing at the same melody to see who can twist it where it most wants to go, and where it might take them together. When Harrison joins them in bridges and final refrains into the fadeout (at 1:34), the three voices combine to erase all worry and doubt from the song's keening tensions; the *octaves* sung by Paul and George at "Don't you know that it's so" take advantage of the pure consonance of that interval to portray trustworthiness. (▶Vocal octave doubling is demonstrated in Video 1.7.) Astute listeners could tell: here was an act whose material was perfectly pitched by its ensemble and vocal breaks; as long as they were singing about feelings lifted this high, they made mere ambition seem small-minded. Even when listeners were consciously unaware of what caused the sensation, they intuitively sensed the mastery behind it.

CUE	SECTION	HARMONY	DETAIL
0:00	Intro	IM7–IV–IM7–IV	harmonica doubling guitar octaves
0:06	Verse 1: phrase 1	I–IV–I–IV–I–vi–V7	L–M duet
0:21	Verse 1: phrase 2	iii–IV–I–IV–vi	L–M contrary motion
0:31	Verse 2: phrase 1	I–IV–I–IV	
0:47	Pre-bridge	IV–V	Alternate cadence
0:54	Bridge	vi–II–I–III	Repeated
1:08	Verse 1: phrase 1		
1:24	Verse 1: phrase 2		
1:33	Outro	I–IV–I–IV	2-part harmony vocals

GROWTH AS MUSICIANS

Meanwhile, Britain developed a strong taste for Liverpool's beat music, and Gerry and the Pacemakers, Billy J. Kramer and the Dakotas, the Remo Four, the Searchers, the Undertakers, the Swinging Blue Jeans, the Fourmost, and Cilla Black, several of whom recorded hits with remaindered Lennon-McCartney compositions, were topping the national charts and heard everywhere. (Kramer's recording of John's song "Bad to Me" reached no. 1 in August; Liverpool acts accounted for the no. 1 spot in 32 of the weekly 1963 *NME* charts.)

Elsewhere, taste grew for electric music based on grittier American R&B and classic blues. In April of 1963 the Beatles heard the Rolling Stones playing in London, and George Harrison recommended them to Dick Rowe of Decca Records, which—realizing their error in not signing the Beatles—released the Stones' first single in June (a cover of Buddy Holly's hit "Not Fade Away") to modest success; their second record, "I Wanna Be Your Man," came from a famous scene where John and Paul finished writing the number right in front of the incredulous Stones, thereby inspiring Mick Jagger and Keith Richards to begin composing their own material. Soon, in addition to Liverpool acts, R&B-influenced electric pop groups from all over England swarmed the charts: the Hollies, Wayne Fontana and the Mindbenders, and Herman's Hermits from Manchester; the Animals from Newcastle-upon-Tyne; the Zombies, the Kinks, the Who, the Yardbirds, the Honeycombs, the Dave Clark Five, and Manfred Mann from London and its suburbs; the Spencer Davis Group from Birmingham; and the Troggs from Andover. These bands would soon ride the Beatles' coattails to America in 1964–1966 as the "British Invasion."

The Beatles' exuberant next (fourth) single, "She Loves You," cemented their domination over all other British musical acts and was the all-time best-selling record in the United Kingdom until 1977, when Paul McCartney's "Mull of Kintyre" became the first 45 rpm record to sell two million copies in Britain. "She Loves You" occupied the no. 1 slot for four weeks beginning September 14, and then—after sitting at no. 2 or no. 3 for seven weeks—returned to the top of the charts for November 30 and December 7, until "I Want to Hold Your Hand" toppled it and reigned as no. 1 for five weeks itself. As they did with "From Me to You," Lennon and McCartney wrote "She Loves You" together in the week before the July 1 recording session; it combines melodic elements of songs by Bobby Vee and Bobby Rydell, plus harmonizing on the Little Richard–inspired falsetto "woos" that had become their own trademark and suggestions of guitar licks from Chuck Berry's blues and Duane Eddy's rockabilly, all framed by concentrated tension in the introduction and coda. For the B-side, the Beatles recorded "I'll Get You," planned for the A-side until a better item, "She Loves You," came along. This song's bridge borrows from the chorus of another Goffin/King song, "Don't Ever Change," written for the Crickets. The smash hit that introduced the Beatles to the United States, "I Want to Hold Your Hand," consolidated the dynamic features of the three previous singles, and then the group would make a radical turn in the first recordings of 1964.

"She Loves You"

Recorded July 1, 1963, for the fourth EMI A-side

—in which Lennon and McCartney offer sophisticated chord changes and a mixture of major, minor, and pentatonic modes, and both Harrison and Starr assert imaginative independence, in an intense portrayal of a blending of joy and pain.

"She Loves You" is likely the early Beatles' most tensile display of supercharged energy, a combination of melodic, registral, harmonic, rhythmic, timbral, and formal precision. This dynamic quality, a goal of the 1963 A-sides, would not often be sought in 1964–1967, but would be recaptured in more diffuse ways in several "throwback" structures in 1968–1969. McCartney has said that the song was inspired by a Bobby Rydell hit; he was referring to "Forget Him," which has a melodic contour and series of chords—particularly the use of iii and a poignant progression from vi through II7 to ii°6/5—clearly borrowed by the Beatles. The sharp *chromaticism* with ♯2—then the deflating borrowing of the minor mode's ♭6—of these chords underlines both the ecstasy and pain of the lyrics, and points to the song's deep jouissance. (⏵ The chromatic and minor scales are covered in Video 1.4; the value of register is introduced in Video 1.5.) Mention should also be made of Bobby Vee's "Take Good Care of My Baby," covered by the Beatles in 1961–1962, the bridge of which opens with similar melodic scale degrees (particularly in the sustained treatment of 7) and chords as heard in "She Loves You." The progression in the Vee bridge is the offset doo-wop, IV–V–I–vi, later adapted in the bridges of "I Want to Hold Your Hand," "I Should Have Known Better," and many other—principally Lennon—Beatle songs.

"She Loves You" was the first recording made with both George's new Gretsch Country Gentleman guitar and Ringo's first Ludwig set; otherwise, John strums his amplified Gibson J-160, and Paul alternates roots and fifths on the Höfner bass in dotted rhythm. (⏵ The dotted pattern is demonstrated in Video 1.1.) George switches pickups eight times through the course of the song, dampening the subversively *minor-pentatonic* Chuck Berry–like sliding *tattoos* (as at 0:11–0:12) and the final Duane Eddy–like bends on the low E string (1:52–1:53) by playing these through the dark neck pickup and highlighting a vi chord with rhythmically emphasized slow strums on G—F♯—E *octaves* (as at 0:29–0:31) that echo "yeah, yeah, yeah" through the bright bridge pickup. (⏵ The minor-pentatonic scale is discussed in Video 1.4; voicing in octave doublings is covered in Video 1.5.) George also takes advantage of the Gretsch's unusual mute switch, as when alternating soft and loud versions of the G—F♯—E motto (compare 0:26–0:28 and 0:29–0:31). John and Paul take lead and descant vocal lines, respectively, climaxing with a two-part falsetto train-whistle "woo" just as each refrain moves to the chorus (a rare combination of refrain and chorus—two strong passages—in a single song), with George reinforcing vocal parts here and there. The emphases created by both vocal falsetto and the Gretsch's bridge pickup make the highest register a locus for locking together textural and formal events. For his part, Ringo opens the song with an unusual floor-tom alert, creates a sense of urgency with constantly sizzling beat divisions on open hi-hat through verses, responds to the "woos" by unleashing rough-and-tumble fills, and powers choruses with strong syncopated flams.

A closer look at this song's original chordal relationships reveals even more creativity. First, although the song lies in G major, it opens with an ambiguous E-minor chord, vi, setting an uncertain context for the scene. (⏵ Major and minor triads are compared in Video 1.5.) Then, when the bold II7 chord does not move to V (as it would have been expected to do in all pre-Beatles repertoire) but instead resigns into a plagal IV, the Beatles announce the Lydian II♯ chord that will mark "Eight Days a Week,"

"Yesterday," "You Won't See Me," "She's Leaving Home," and many other numbers as quintessential Lennon-McCartney creations. The IV leads nicely into a cadential I for the sustaining "yeah," but this plagal resolution is blurred when George sings a non-triadic sixth scale degree against John's fifth directly below, and Paul's first above, creating an added-sixth chord that remains a trademark for a year or so. This combination of first and sixth scale degrees ties together all chords heard thus far, as these are the two tones common to all of them, but, more importantly, sets up a battle between the optimistic G major ("glad") and its shadow, E minor ("bad"), through the course of the song. We've already noted the important emphasis given G and E in the G—F♯—E motto; it's also the core of the song's very first three vocal notes, the (025) *blues trichord*, D—E—G, which are the same as the last three sung pitches—all together in the final chord. (▶ The blues trichord is explained in Video 1.4.) These same three pitches are also the ones that call forth the first refrain (2:24–2:26), made more powerful by the insistently repeated notes (the repeated D on "she said she") that begin it, and the suddenly intense syncopation occurring for the first time in bass and drums (0:26). The strong motivic contrast between first and sixth scale degrees had been discovered in "Do You Want to Know a Secret" and would be mined again in "This Boy," "I Should Have Known Better," and "And I Love Her."

For the ultimate in drawing out tension, an authentic V–I release does not occur before 1:11–1:14, ending the eighth formal element identified in the chart below, directly following the chorus's tense II–ii°6/5 display. In its final appearance, this moment expands for full appreciation by the one-more-time closing technique, 1:48–2:06, with the final V7 sustained by a caesura so powerful it would not be repeated before "Happiness Is a Warm Gun" (1968) (and then again by Lennon's "(Just Like) Starting Over" (1980)). The concentrated one-more-time repetitions of "yeah, yeah, yeah" bring reharmonizations of the repeated melodic fragment a step beyond that which had closed "From Me to You."

Amazingly, after it seems that John and Paul's vocal octave on I (2:05–2:07) has brought things to a "glad" and perfect close, the coda finds a way to distill the tension further, by telescoping both vi and II7 chords into a simultaneous sonority (2:09–2:12), and then allow it to dissipate in one final, long-held chord comprising the "glad"/"bad" added-sixth blues-trichord combination, complex and longing yet fully consonant. In two minutes and eighteen seconds, the Beatles bring to full boil a harmonic lobscouse of a joyous major mode (that depends as much on diminished ii° and minor iii and vi chords as it does on major I, IV, and V), chromaticism and mode mixture, and minor-pentatonic guitar riffs. "She Loves You" may be the only early Lennon–McCartney song that makes "I Want to Hold Your Hand" seem tame in comparison.

CUE	SECTION	HARMONY	DETAIL
0:00	Introduction	vi–II7–IV–Iadd6	Variation of chorus material
0:11	Tattoo	I	Chuck Berry reference
0:13	Verse 1: *a*	I–vi–iii–V7	
0:19	Verse 1: *a*	I–vi–iii–V7	

CUE	SECTION	HARMONY	DETAIL
0:25	Verse 1: *b* (Refrain)	I–vi–iiø6/5–V7	
0:36	Tattoo	V7	(minor pentatonic)
0:38	Verse 2		
1:03	Chorus	vi–II7–iiø6/5–V7–I	
1:13	Tattoo	I	(minor pentatonic)
1:16	Verse 3		
1:41	Chorus		Expanded; ending with caesura at 2:02–2:05
2:05	Coda	I–viadd#6–IV–Iadd6	

WITH THE BEATLES AND "I WANT TO HOLD YOUR HAND"

Among the key accomplishments in the Beatles' story is the way they adapted so quickly to fame and how fame itself fueled their creativity. They taped their second album, *With the Beatles*, on stray dates squeezed in amid fall 1963's hectic touring schedule. Where *Please Please Me* sounded raw, almost like a snapshot of their live stage set, *With the Beatles* pulled the Beatles' sound into a more professional class of recording. The material held clues to an emerging musical intelligence: seven new Lennon-McCartney songs, a first composition by George Harrison, and covers of three songs with heavy backing vocals taken from Motown Records ("Please Mr. Postman," "You've Really Got a Hold on Me," and "Money (That's What I Want)"), George's guitar vehicle "Roll Over Beethoven" (a Berry favorite), "Devil in Her Heart" (taken from the B-side of a very obscure R&B track by the Donays), and "Till There Was You" (in a Latin arrangement calling for bongos and nylon-string classical guitar). There are still strong hints of derived songwriting evident in the original songs, but the Beatles are now drawing from themselves as much as from their forebears: note, for example how the SRDC structure of the "Hold Me Tight" verse includes a responsorial vocal arrangement in its departure gesture—"so hold" ("HOLD!") "me tight" ("ME TIGHT!")—based largely on that of "Please Please Me"—"come on" ("COME ON!"), etc. Recall that "Hold Me Tight" was attempted in the February EMI session, the first studio gathering after "Please Please Me" was taped. Such formulaic crutches largely disappear by 1964.

Some of the recordings, along with "I Want to Hold Your Hand," deployed the newer four-track tape machines, allowing engineers to capture a basic performance with drums and bass on one track, guitars on another, and vocals on a third, reserving the fourth track for overdubs of another guitar part, additional vocals, harmonica, hand percussion and hand claps, or keyboards from producer George Martin. The same procedure snowballed through the Beatles' recording career, allowing for more complexity from additional layers of effects by copying all four filled tracks onto a reduction in a second and sometimes a third generation of tape to make room for more and more ideas. Before long, the end product captured not so much a concert experience but an artwork embedded in the recording itself, rendering a live performance of certain tracks a meager simulacrum if not beside the point. By 1966, the Beatles would tour the world to support

Revolver without performing any of its songs onstage; their career shifted from that of a top live act into a premier "studio" act, a brand new category of musician that sprang organically from the original material Lennon and McCartney wrote specifically for the studio. This change that began in 1963 ultimately led to major shifts in rock styles, particularly with the development of psychedelic progressive rock after 1966; as recorded music no longer had to present the sound of live performance, it could stray further from reality altogether.

"All I've Got to Do"

Recorded September 11, 1963, for *With the Beatles*

—an exploration of the narrator's attitude as colored by shifting syncopations and major/minor mood swings.

All pop songs contain an imagined speaker and audience, a singer ("I") who tells a story to an implied listener ("you"). Both these imaginings flow from a real author, the song's composer, who may or may not inhabit a fictional persona.

These factors come into play when considering "authorial voice" in Beatles songs even before contemplating how the Lennon-McCartney partnership breaks down. Does the singer address a secondary imaginary subject or the listener directly? How do so many of these early Beatles songs deploy the emphatic personal pronouns with such intimate candor? In a harmonized melody, do two voices split from single consciousness into different layers of a single author's psyche?

Lennon's lead vocal in "All I've Got to Do" drips with irony: his lyrics express confidence; his delivery broods with insecurity. His words boast of boundless confidence in the sturdiness of love; his vocal leaks torment. In the opening moments, that questioning guitar arpeggio of an augmented triad plus added ninth and eleventh undermines the singer's opening statement: "Whenever I / I want to kiss you, yeah." And the band's stop-and-start rhythms, yoked by Ringo Starr's tight syncopations, frame the singer's resolve in uneasy, shifting patterns (forecasting similar strategies in "Any Time at All" and "In My Life").

In verses, the singer starts on a minor chord ("Whenever I") and swerves toward major ("I want to kiss you, yeah"). (The lead melody and, when harmonized, the descant part, are drawn fully from the E major-pentatonic scale, E-F♯-G♯-B-C♯, despite augmented and minor colors for a subtle modal intrigue in the vocal interaction with guitars.) In the bridges, this pattern reverses, from major ("And the same goes for me . . .") to minor ("I'll be here yes I will"). This tension between major and minor conveys the uneasy mood vexing the singer, where his fervor rides on currents of dismay and insecurity (and resembles the following year's "No Reply," wherein he will try to convince himself of his own resolve during bridges). Other songs that deploy this major-minor tension between contrasting song sections include "I'll Be Back," "Can't Buy Me Love," "I Should Have Known Better," "Things We Said Today," "Girl," "Wait," and "Fixing a Hole."

With so many tight spaces, so many falling vocal lines trailing off into exasperation, so much withheld tension vying for release in the bridges, the ensemble sustains the singer as he fights for air (0:48, and again at 1:28 when Lennon skids right off the melody as the others carry him). There's a crimped, desperate quality to this track that carries a dark emotional quandary, where no amount of rallying can puncture the mood. Note how each bridge closes with a declaration of major tonic-chord confidence (at 0:59 and repeated for emphasis at 1:39) and then dissolves right back into the stop-and-start hedging of verses. Finally, all the constriction and denial leaves the listener with the sense that none of the clever harmonic manipulations and concluding reassurances ("You just gotta call on me") can scratch the song's itch.

CUE	SECTION	HARMONY	DETAIL
0:00	Caesura chord	I+ add 9, 11	Guitar arpeggio
0:03	Verse 1 (11 bars)	vi–I–vi–ii–iv–I	JL solo vocal
0:09	Refrain		PM descant
0:15	(continued Verse 1)		Drums surf backbeat (▶ see Video 1.2)
0:25	Verse 2		
0:47	Bridge 1	IV–vi–IV–I–IV–I	JL lead, PM/GH bkg vocals
1:05	Verse 3		
1:27	Bridge 2		JL with heightened pitch
1:43	Repeat closing line	IV–I	"One-more-time" plagal cad.
1:48	Coda	vi–I–vi–I	JL solo vocal; fadeout

"Not a Second Time"

Recorded September 11, 1963, for *With the Beatles*

—*Producer George Martin adds a bass-register piano part to color John Lennon's sullen, almost menacing, reflection of the album's somber cover portrait.*

For all the piano the Beatles make use of on their second album ("Please Mr. Postman," "Money," "You've Really Got a Hold on Me"), you would still never mistake them for anything but a guitar band. "Roll Over Beethoven" opens side two with that terrifically earnest Harrison guitar solo, quickly trounced by Ringo's steamroller groove, and "Till There Was You" combines cheeseball flamenco with an arty classical feel, which they soon return to with all sincerity in "And I Love Her." By contrast, "Not a Second Time" forges a texture deemphasizing guitars in favor of vocals, drums patterns, and vocal support.

In this track's shifty plot line, Lennon has again fallen too hard for a woman who intrigues him yet plays one too many games. After what can only have been a torrid fling, she dumps him, but she returns to tempt him again, and Lennon summons every ounce of courage to admit weakness, then turn her down. Naturally, this refusal comes draped in every shade of apology, regret, compulsion, attraction, revulsion, self-loathing, admiration, fondness, timidity, and gloating he can muster, and you don't believe a word of it—the subtitle might as well be "You win again." But his refusal carries these emotions around as if in triumph, so his rejection carries more weight, more candor, and more sheer passion than anything this lover might have expected. He plays this trump card so emphatically it's startling, both protesting too much and gaining strength from his tirade.

Martin's piano shadings (0:45–1:02) add thickly mannered mascara to Lennon's worried vocal mystique—the cheesy contrast (reminiscent of the producer's bolstering of Harrison's guitar lines with celeste in "Baby It's You") makes Lennon sound even more intense. The number works as an afterthought to "You've Really Got a Hold on Me," as if Lennon doesn't just cover Smokey Robinson but concocts a whole new soliloquy about the situation. Did he realize how hung up he was on this woman when he writhed in loneliness, or only when she came back and he couldn't bear to drag himself through it all over again? Does it matter? Like the piano line in "Misery," the texture has an expiration date of about six months, best consumed by 1964, and its dated hangover signals something crucial about the brevity of this romance: sticky sweet yet yesterday's news.

CUE	SECTION	HARMONY	DETAIL
0:00	Verse 1: Statement (7 bars)	I–vi–I–vi–V–I–V	Piano, gtrs, bass
0:07			Drums enter
0:13	Verse 1: Restatement (7 bars)	I–vi–I–vi–V–ii7–V	Cadence varied
0:26	Verse 1: Departure (4 bars)	ii–iii7–I–vi	
0:33	Verse 1: Conclusion (6 bars)	ii–iii–V7–vi	Refrain
0:43	Drum break		
0:45	Piano solo	ii7–iii7–I–vi–ii–iii–V–vi	Based on D–C gestures
1:02	Drum break		
1:04	Verse 1: SRDC–drum break		
1:50	Outro on refrain	I–vi–I–vi	

"I Want to Hold Your Hand"

Recorded October 17, 1963, for the fifth EMI A-side

—The tension of American Beatlemania as propelled by a song's bridge that begins in romantic relaxation and culminates in a building and venting of cliff-edge libido, all portrayed with expressive chord choices, melodic emphases of dynamic scale degrees, and offbeat cymbal crashes. The new four-track recording procedure is deconstructed here in fine detail.

For most Americans, the opening sequence of "I Want to Hold Your Hand" sketched a thrilling embrace. When commentators talk of how Beatlemania rescued America from its grief for Kennedy, assassinated less than four months previously, this is the sound they invoke. Kennedy's death left a gaping hole in the cultural heart, not just that someone so young and powerful could be lost so instantly but that so many dreams and images of America's future, invested in his persona, might also be erased. The Beatles stepped into this uncertainty with pluck: as Brits, they had suffered through a perilous war on their own shores, endured the privations of war debt and food rationing far longer than Americans ever appreciated, and strode into their own sunny future with something more imaginative than commercial largesse. With leisure products flooding the teenage market, it had never occurred to American youth (or their parents) that something might be missing. The Beatles filled up a hole nobody even knew was there. That young Brits had done it through a distinctly American musical style, rock 'n' roll, a nationalistic impulse as primal as baseball and hot dogs, only made the argument that much more decisive.

It's hard to separate the clashing chords that open "I Want to Hold Your Hand" with the Beatlemania craze that went viral in early 1964. It seemed as if the Beatles hit American shores completely formed, without the running leaps of "Love Me Do" and "Please Please Me," or the breakout triumph of "She Loves You," earlier formative benchmarks that led to their British preeminence during the summer of 1963. These previous tracks didn't strike US ears until later in the spring of 1964, when they drowned the charts to form a top 5 hit blockade in April, unleashing the opening wave of the British Invasion, rock's second generation after Elvis Presley.

Scholars hear "Hand" as part of a larger mosaic of songs that trace a developing arc from "Love Me Do" through "From Me to You," "She Loves You" and the entire second album they recorded between constant gigs in the fall of 1963, which includes new originals "It Won't Be Long," "All I've Got to Do," and "Not a Second Time," laying the groundwork for the all-original score for *A Hard Day's Night*. "Hand" also benefits from a technology upgrade: from two-track recorders to the four-track machines that dominated their work into 1968. This enhanced fidelity gives the playing a determined, juicy punch, like lightning against a dark sky. It allowed John and Paul to reinforce their most arresting moments by double-tracking key words here and there. Combining precision with force positions this song's sexual conquest into a contest between ardent anticipation and triumphant release.

For the beguiling introduction, they pound out two opening chords in emphatically displaced ensemble kicks as if gaining quickly on some urgent ultimatum. Critic Jonathan Gould's description tackles this sequence: "It begins with a rapid buildup of harshly syncopated accents over a grinding rhythm guitar—once, twice, three times—as if the song itself were shuddering to life on a cold January morning" (Gould 2007, 214). The leap comes as the vocals land on the fifth scale degree with the word I ("Oh yeah . . . I" at 0:08), and the song unfurls. As an opening, it rivals "I Saw Her Standing There," spooling up energy for release just when you can't stand the expectation any longer. The cadence of the first phrase, "I think you'll under-*stand*," recalls the second line of "I Saw Her Standing There" ("You know . . . what I *mean*"), leaving the most explicit tease unspoken, in that universal teenage language of suggestion minus detail (for who knows, perhaps they will get even further than they expect).

But where that earlier song lingered on its tonic as a way of setting its tone, "I Want to Hold Your Hand" toys with alternate harmonies, and its tonic becomes apparent in retrospect (the two introductory chords alternate between IV and V, but they don't sound relative to I until the verse starts). This simple yet wily gesture keeps the listener off balance and signals a growing awareness of how songs can function like puzzles, pointing the ear in wayward directions to set up delayed gratifications. (Other examples of this introductory harmonic maneuver include "Hold Me Tight," "The Word," and "Dig a Pony.") This brief harmonic riddle masks another layer of poetic tension: the coquettish lyrics atop the band's aggressive torque. Where Lennon and McCartney sing as young prom dates picking up their girl, the energy rising up around them flies apart every which way. It's as if they make small talk with the parents while giving their date come-to-bed eyes.

The track swells with tension: momentum that gallops through verses and their refrains counters the tension that's withheld in the bridges. It lurches between coyness and grit, musical wisdom and romantic naiveté, precision and fluidity, brash ensemble playing beneath a calculated vocal duet. Ambiguous harmonies meet emphatic flirtation, especially on that word "under-*stand*" (at 0:13) which lands on a strangely distant seventh scale degree (atop an ambiguous, thirdless III/iii chord: major or minor?) and gets left hanging: a delirious suggestion dropped in the middle of conversation, but gapingly unresolved. It finds an answer in the corresponding leap on "hand" six bars later (on scale degrees 3 and 7 and, at 0:20), a titillation metaphorically fulfilled, a fondle before a kiss. Within a combustible 2'27", all this detail—handclaps draping vocal swerves, trickster harmonies atop a card-shark's drums—carried the sound of a new, irresistible future. The III/iii moment is recaptured in a new context in the song's thrilling "one more time" ending, brought home with the slow reins-pulling triplets on the final word, "hand."

And these lyrics seem ripe for projection, for reading more into them than they seem capable of bearing. Dylan heard the bridge's retransition back to the verse as "I get high, I get high," when the text scans "I can't hide, I can't hide." But who's to say he heard it "wrong"? The sound approximates adolescent hormones at full tilt; the band hugs its curves and digs into every *offbeat*, four moving as one cutting a swath of pleasure through impatience, elderly prudishness, and ambitions suddenly inflated beyond reason. (▶ The syncopated offbeat is defined in Video 1.2.)

The bridge opens with a relaxed minor triad on the fifth scale degree, just as did "From Me to You," and continues with what might be understood as an offset doo-wop progression—the standard I–vi–IV–V or its closely related alternate, I–vi–ii–V appearing with its third and fourth chords rotated to appear before the first two: IV–V–I–vi (or ii–V–I–vi). Both rotations appear in "Hand": IV–V–I–vi in the title refrain, and ii–V–I–vi to open the bridge. These progressions become a standard go-to place of comfort for

Lennon; it's the closest to a "normal" harmonic move in "Strawberry Fields Forever," for instance. But just as the bridge of "From Me to You" took the listener to a whole new world, that of "Hand" opens with this offset doo-wop pattern not in the home key of G but in the key of C, removing F♯ from play and thus relaxing the proceedings. When the bridges ease off the forward thrust for a laid-back timbre (at 0:51 and 1:33), they bring both comfort and relief, accenting the resolve of the verses while promising an intimacy such pleasure can harness. This contrast—made most manifest when "I can't hide, I can't hide" boils over with V harmony, falsetto shrieks and suddenly interrupted phrase lengths of 4 + 3 + 4 bars—made the Beatles sound both aggressive and tender, zealous and contingent. And the control it dramatized in musical terms only made their whole approach seem cocky beyond measure, master musicians manipulating deeply felt desires. Where the parents heard sincerity, daughters heard lusty promise.

Finally, "Hand" holds status as one of the great early Lennon-McCartney duets. They sing the entire song together, breaking from unison into harmony only at the most expressive points: Lennon's double-tracked octave leap into falsetto on the first title line (at 0:20, on that tantalizing iii5 chord), spreading out into glorious thirds to wind down on the third phrase, and finally joining together for unison at the close. Two sets of triplets (when the final title line gets sung over the last IV–I cadence), borrowed from the last chorus of Buddy Holly's "That'll Be the Day," gently pump the brakes on a track that might otherwise glide off happily into a slipstream of wonder.

The Beatles were less a cultural import than adopted sons, fast friends rousing their tribe (almost anyone within earshot) with songs that sprang straight from some collective dream life, a mass Jungian unconscious, instantly creating its own possibilities, contexts for new realities, reviving unselfconsciously dormant spirits. "I Want to Hold Your Hand" carries this promise still, and it makes the Beatles seem eternally new, young icons who channel mystic chords of memory and transformation.

"I Want to Hold Your Hand" captured the sound of the future calling out from the rooftops, shouting down the past and packing too many promises about how much fun there was to be had, how fellowship might provide a path toward individuality, and how everybody's coming-of-age story might sound when shared on an unprecedented scale. If "This Boy" was a love letter to doo-wop, "I Want to Hold Your Hand" sounded like an answer to the Shirelles' "Will You Love Me Tomorrow?" where the Beatles respond, "You have to ask?"

CUE	SECTION	HARMONY	DETAIL
0:00	Intro	IV–V, IV–V, IV–V . . .V7	syncopated guitars
0:07	Verse 1: a	I–V–vi–iii5	PM/JL vocal duet
0:14	verse 1 :a'	I–V–vi–iii5	
0:22	Verse 1: b (refrain)	IV–V–I–vi–IV–V–I	offset doo-wop
0:28	Verse 2 with refrain		
0:51	Bridge	(ii7–V7–I–vi–ii7–V7–I of IV)	offset doo-wop
1:02	Retransition	IV–V, IV–V, IV–V8–7 (echoes intro)	expanding vocal harmonies

CUE	SECTION	HARMONY	DETAIL
1:10	Verse 3 with refrain		
1:33	Bridge 2		
1:45	Retransition		
1:53	Verse 3 with refrain		
2:14	Deceptive cadence	IV–V7–iii7/5 (!)	
2:16	final cadence	IV–V7–IV–I	triplets on plagal IV

Because so many varied mixes exist of "I Want to Hold Your Hand," it is possible to recreate with precision the song's likely recording procedure.[1] It appears that three tracks of tape were filled with the basic live performance, the remaining fourth track was given a number of overdubs, and then this entire tape had to be mixed and copied to three tracks of a second tape to accommodate one final overdub. Although a second generation of pre-master tape was not desirable, due to the buildup of noise that results from the analog-on-mylar recording medium, it had been necessary in a fair amount of previous two-track recording and so must have been deemed admissible with the advent of four-track work. Here is the likely content of the two working tapes from October 17, 1963:

First Generation:

Track 1 (live): Ringo's Ludwig drums, Paul's Höfner bass, and John's highly compressed Rickenbacker 325 (on the rhythm guitar's *power-chord* boogie part) (▶ The power chord is demonstrated in Video 1.5.)

Track 2 (live): George's new Rickenbacker 425 (for lead guitar)

Track 3 (live): John's lead vocal, Paul's descant vocal (the two mostly singing in unison but split for refrains and the second bridge)

Track 4 (overdubs, possibly recorded in sections): John's and Paul's handclaps at 0:07–0:18, 0:30–0:40, 1:12–1:22, and 1:54–2:09; John's and Paul's reinforcing vocals on the word "hand" at 0:20–0:22, 0:42–0:44, 1:24–1:26 and 2:07–2:09; John's second bridge vocal "and when I touch you . . . I can't hide" and Paul's falsetto "woo" at 1:34–1:56; and George's additional lead guitar for the coda triplets.

1. Aside from the since-released fragmentary takes 1, 2 and 9, the complete performance of take 17 (all recorded on October 17, 1963) was mixed to mono for the single on October 21, was given two different stereo mixes (on October 21, 1963, and November 7, 1966), was given new German-language vocals, handclaps, and a new guitar part in overdubs made in Paris in January 1964, and then was treated to three digital 5.1 surround-sound mixes (for the *Anthology, Love,* and *Rock Band* projects). It is possible to remove all sources mixed to center in the stereo mixes (with the OOPs process), and all stems from the surround-sound mixes may be heard in isolation, yielding further hints as to the identity of the contents of the original working tapes and masters. Thanks to Andrew Lubman for a valuable conversation on the 425 guitar used by Harrison in this day's work.

BEATLEMANIA OFFICIALLY RECOGNIZED

The remainder of 1963 played out with ever more momentous concerts, BBC appearances, and the recording of their second LP in July–September (see Photo 3.02) and fifth single in October, establishing a schedule of two LPs and several singles per year. One highlight was the filming of a half-hour documentary, *The Mersey Sound*, at the end of August, featuring *Mersey Beat* editor Bill Harry discussing the professionalization of Liverpool bands, Brian Epstein recounting his life with the Beatles, interviews with the four band members on their clothing and their fans throwing jelly babies at them on stage, and several performances showing audiences howling for their heroes. This all drew national attention to the immense talent issuing from economically depressed Liverpool when broadcast nationwide in October and November. On October 13, the Beatles headlined a variety of acts for the country's most popular television program, *Val Parnell's Sunday Night at the London Palladium*. The crowds outside the theater had grown so wild that the British press dubbed it "Beatlemania." Fifteen hundred screaming fans met the group on its return to London's Heathrow Airport on October 31 from a weeklong Swedish tour, attracting attention even in American news reports.

On November 4, the Beatles played a command performance for the Queen Mother and Princess Margaret at the Prince of Wales Theatre, the highest honor bestowed on any entertainment act. As usual, the four songs they played were punctuated by stage banter. The Beatles typically asked the audience to clap their hands and stomp their feet for their wild closing number "Twist and Shout." On this occasion, John Lennon wished to break the apprehension caused by the stark mix of royal formality and direct, unselfconscious expression, so he announced with a grin, "For our last number I'd like to ask your help. For the people in the cheaper seats, clap your hands . . . and the rest of you, if you'd just rattle your jewelry." As a proud Liverpudlian, with deep-seated class resentments and a lifelong antipathy toward the monarchy, Lennon had actually threatened to Brian that he was going to say "rattle your *fuckin'* jewelry." Perhaps he realized an obscenity at such a moment might halt their momentum, or perhaps he had been bluffing, aiming to get under Brian's skin. This widely quoted Lennon quip only made him more popular. For many

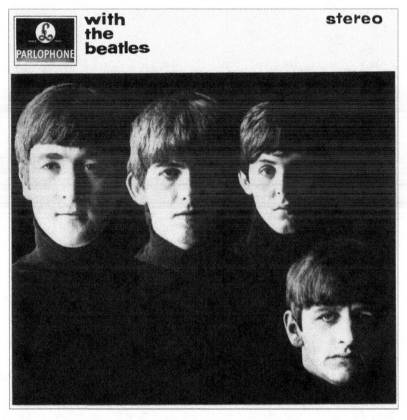

PHOTO 3.2. The Beatles, photographed by Robert Freeman in mid-August, 1963. *With the Beatles* LP (released in UK November 22, 1963).

younger fans, Lennon's derision was clear enough. Just as with the motivations residing within "Please Please Me" and "I Want to Hold Your Hand," primal urges were coated in a polite veneer.

The Beatles' move from Liverpool to London permitted Paul more time with the actress Jane Asher, his soon-to-be fiancée, whom he'd met in April. Other Beatles would find apartments, but Paul chose to live in the Ashers' home. Jane's brother Peter was given several McCartney songs for his duo, Peter and Gordon, which took Paul's "A World Without Love" to no. 1 in both the United Kingdom and the United States in April–June 1964. Jane's mother was a professional oboist (in fact, she had been George Martin's teacher at the Guildhall School of Music and Drama on that instrument), and the cultural tone set in her household had a profound influence on McCartney's sense of style. McCartney composed on the family's Ramsden upright. In January 1967 in this house, McCartney heard David Mason play piccolo trumpet in a televised performance of Bach's Second Brandenburg Concerto, and he knew right then he wanted Mason to play it on "Penny Lane."

The Beatles performed in Liverpool on only ten more nights in 1963 after February, including two last dates at the Cavern, three nights at the Odeon Cinema, and four at the Empire Theatre, where they would also play their last two concerts in Liverpool in the Decembers of 1964 and '65. With plans to visit the United States and Australia in 1964, they were poised in the wings of the world's stage. If Andrew Loog Oldham had described Beatlemania's sound in early 1963 as the future screaming, by year's end, the future had arrived.

POINTS FOR DISCUSSION

1. Beatlemania had "both logical and intangible features." Name three examples of each.
2. Discuss the growth of the Beatles' professionalism in 1963.
3. How does Lennon's quip at the Royal Command Performance illustrate the generation gap? Class consciousness?
4. What significance did BBC Radio hold for the Beatles' career and their legacy?
5. How did Merseybeat differ from other musical trends at the time? Choose a British Invasion group other than the Beatles and investigate their music.
6. Discuss the influence of the sudden rush of fame on Lennon and McCartney's songwriting.
7. How did recording a song in 1963 both replicate and differ from performing it on stage?
8. Name a Beatles song that has a powerful retransition. What factors contribute to this?
9. Choose a Beatle song recorded before 1964 through which you can discuss ways in which the Beatles brought new rhythmic, melodic, harmonic, formal, and timbral ideas into rock music.

FURTHER READING

Babiuk, Andy. *Beatles Gear: All the Fab Four's Instruments, From Stage to Studio*, rev. ed. San Francisco: Backbeat, 2015.

Braun, Michael. *Love Me Do: The Beatles' Progress*. London: Penguin, 1964.

Gould, Jonathan. *Can't Buy Me Love: The Beatles in the Sixties*. New York: Harmony, 2007.

Howlett, Kevin. *The Beatles: The BBC Archives—1962–1970*. New York: Harper Design, 2013.

Keeler, Christine. *The Truth at Last*. New York: Picador, 2002.

Kehew, Brian, and Kevin Ryan. *Recording the Beatles: The Studio Equipment and Techniques Used to Create Their Classic Albums*. Houston: Curvebender, 2006.

Kessler, Jude Southerland. *She Loves You*, vol. 3, *The John Lennon Series*. Monroe, LA: On the Rock, 2013.

Melly, George. *Revolt into Style: The Pop Arts in Britain*. London: Faber & Faber, 2013.

Oldham, Andrew Loog. *Stoned: A Memoir of London in the 1960s*. New York: St. Martin's, 2001.

Winn, John C. *Way Beyond Compare: The Beatles' Recorded Legacy*, vol. 1, *1957–1965*. New York: Three Rivers, 2008.

CHAPTER 4

INSTANT COMBUSTION

World Embrace (1964)

STORMING THE STATES

At one point in "She Loves You," on the *Ed Sullivan Show* appearance on February 9, 1964, just after delivering a line from some dreamy reverie, John catches George's eye for a second. The instant broad smile that George returns to John shows it has sunk in: they've gotten the same hysterical welcome in the States they'd left behind in England. As the third song performed live before New York's screaming audience in the CBS theater studio for the Sunday-night variety show, televised to at least seventy-three million, the song closed a set that blindsided America. "All My Loving" and "Till There Was You" had gone over well, and their confidence surged as they finished with their biggest British hit. The United States represented the world's largest and most influential market, the cradle of rock 'n' roll, and their ultimate conquest. The Beatles, seducing a cynical press and catatonic TV host, arrived on American shores with trepidation and left as victors. Photos 4.1 and 4.2 show the Beatles onstage during their first American appearances.

Although fueled by Beatlemania's fumes in Britain, the band faced major hurdles. British acts had mostly foundered in the States: Cliff Richard had flopped; the only British records to reach no. 1 in America during the early rock era were a spiritual and two instrumentals—Laurie London's "He's Got the Whole World in His Hands" (1958), Acker Bilk's "Stranger on the Shore" (1962), and the Tornados' "Telstar" (1962). The Beatles had just come off an eighteen-day residency in

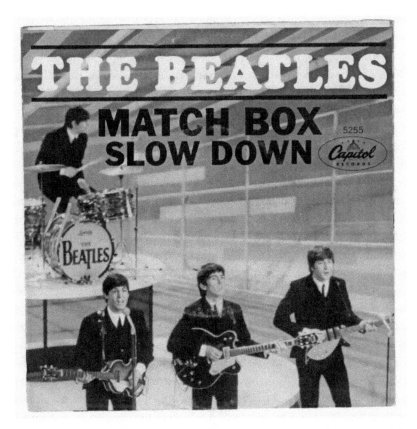

PHOTO 4.1. The Beatles on Ed Sullivan's stage, February 9, 1964. "Matchbox" / "Slow Down" 45 (released in US August 24, 1964).

PHOTO 4.2. The Beatles in Washington, DC, February 11, 1964. Inside gatefold cover of *Beatles for Sale* LP (released in UK June 1, 1967).

Paris playing to unfazed French crowds. In signing a group photo on the flight from London to New York, McCartney drew an arrow from his autograph to his face, suggesting he believed that he would not be remembered once the Beatles returned to the United Kingdom. When the plane landed at Kennedy Airport, however, three thousand fans met the Beatles, stoked by near-constant New York radio airplay of their British catalog. Capitol Records, the American branch of their record company, EMI, had blanketed the States with a $50,000 campaign touting their phenomenal success in the United Kingdom, promoting "I Want to Hold Your Hand" and the companion LP, *Meet the Beatles!*, with a merchandising blitz of buttons, stickers, and Beatle wigs.

"Hand" saw a rush release on December 26 after radio stations in major markets had begun playing imported discs, and Capitol cobbled together the *Meet the Beatles!* album from nine *With the Beatles* songs, the current hit single, and its two B-sides: "This Boy" in the United Kingdom and "I Saw Her Standing There" in the United States. This blanket radio exposure, combined with their flamboyant mop-top appearance, lively demeanor with the press, and a phenomenal *Ed Sullivan Show* appearance, stirred public rapture. During their New York visit, teenagers lined the streets around the Plaza Hotel in midtown Manhattan to sing "We love you Beatles, oh yes we do, we love you Beatles, and we'll be true." In what seemed like a lightning bolt, the Sullivan sets seared the four Beatles' likenesses deeply upon a new generation. Young men began growing their hair out; teens collected Beatles bubble gum cards, Beatle wigs, and every other scrap of Beatle memorabilia they could find.

In addition, the Beatles included a musical-comedy number, "Till There Was You" from Meredith Willson's *The Music Man*, in their Ed Sullivan appearance, breaking with the typical rock 'n' roll approach. This conventional score had entered American consciousness through a three-year run on Broadway and a hit 1962 film. Aimed at parents, this song sent a confounding signal: if rock 'n' roll's resurgent style broke all Tin Pan Alley rules like moderate tempos, family values, and lush sincerity, why include a number that genuflected to all three principles? On one level, it linked the style up with a larger historical continuum and showed the Beatles' grander ambitions to appeal across generational lines, even as they focused on the teenage experience. On another level, the number reassured skeptics that rock 'n' roll arose from familiar styles.

For all the ramifications of the Kennedy assassination, the growing gap between freedom-loving teens and the dominant authority of parents and teachers, as well as tensions from racial oppression and an international cold war, the Beatles' breakthrough held a lasting effect for a musical enlightenment that proved more than merely distracting social entertainment. "This isn't show business," Lennon told Michael Braun in 1963. "This is something else" (Braun 1964, 52). The screaming and audience sing-alongs, peaking in ecstasy with Paul's Little Richard falsetto, crowned a year-long crescendo of popularity. The songs had such robust energy that kids who once balked at practicing for piano lessons suddenly took up guitars and drums in droves. Several transformative elements motivated this: the Beatles' strikingly original combination of pretty melodic turns with searing blues references, propulsive rhythms, and unusual harmonic changes, all topped off with delirious vocal harmonies. The new single, Paul's "Can't Buy Me Love," had more infectious energy knit around a tight twelve-bar blues—like the raving "Some fun tonight" coda to "Long Tall Sally" and the ending of "I Wanna Be Your Man"—and John came right back with his own twelve-bar fuse of jealous lust with "You Can't Do That" (which appeared as the B-side of "Can't Buy"). The Beatles made the wild and blue "Long Tall Sally" into a concert mainstay in the States even before they'd recorded it at EMI. Vee Jay and Swan, small record companies that had leased the rights to release the Beatles' music in America the previous year, quickly reissued the discs that had initially failed to sell, flooding an insatiable market in advance of the Sullivan show. By late March, the Beatles dominated national record sales as well as the radio as never witnessed before or since; the April 4, 1964, *Billboard* "Hot 100" chart looked like this:

No. 1 "Can't Buy Me Love" (Capitol, beginning a five-week run at the top)
No. 2 "Twist and Shout" (Tollie, a new and short-lived Vee Jay subsidiary)
No. 3 "She Loves You" (Swan, following two weeks at no. 1)
No. 4 "I Want to Hold Your Hand" (Capitol, following seven weeks at no. 1)
No. 5 "Please Please Me" (Vee Jay)

The Beatles sat atop the US singles surveys for fourteen weeks; also on the April 4 chart, other Beatle records held positions no. 31, no. 41, no. 46, no. 58, no. 65, no. 68, and no. 79, with the Dave Clark Five, the Searchers, and the Swinging Blue Jeans already invading the top 30 with British product. The album chart of May 2 sported three Beatle albums among the top four.

The excited fascination with which Americans greeted the Beatles was largely, but not entirely, a Caucasian phenomenon. Everyone could celebrate the brash beauty of African American Cassius Clay, a gold-medalist boxer in the 1960 Rome Olympics who upset world heavyweight champion Sonny Liston in Miami in 1964 (where Clay crossed paths with the Beatles for a stunning photo-op) and the commanding Bahamian voice and marquee allure of Sidney Poitier, who in 1964 became the first African American awarded the best-actor Oscar, for *Lilies of the Field*. But now in this year, whites as well as American blacks (then known politely as "negroes") came to know first-hand the state-supported terrorism that led to the murder of three civil-rights workers (two of whom were white northerners) in Mississippi, the same state in which Medgar Evers was brutally murdered. Martin Luther King, Jr., had famously intoned a year before, "I have a dream that one day even the state of Mississippi, a state sweltering with the heat of injustice, sweltering with the heat of oppression, will be transformed into an oasis of freedom and justice." Despite being continuously hounded by the FBI as well as vilified and threatened by racist groups, King was instrumental in having racial segregation in schools and other discriminatory acts outlawed by the Civil Rights Act, signed by President Lyndon Johnson in July 1964, three months before King would be awarded the Nobel Peace Prize. Still, these seemed like small steps just weeks after Nelson Mandela was sentenced to life in prison, an ocean away, on charges of conspiring to overthrow the state of South Africa. Upon his release in 1990, Mandela would negotiate the end of apartheid in a country that would elect him president in 1994.

From the American perspective, rock 'n' roll had waned in popularity since Little Richard entered the ministry in 1957, Jerry Lee Lewis succumbed to scandal in 1958, Buddy Holly died in a 1959 plane crash, Elvis Presley was inducted into the military, and Chuck Berry was incarcerated in 1962. Merseybeat felt like a stylistic sea change from what had been popular in the States. Bland songs aimed at adults like Bobby Vinton's "There! I've Said It Again" and the Singing Nun's "Dominique" outsold teen favorites like the Kingsmen's "Louie Louie," the Beach Boys' "Be True to Your School" and "In My Room," and the Ronettes' "Baby I Love You," let alone African American product from Motown like Martha and the Vandellas' "Quicksand" and Marvin Gaye's "Can I Get a Witness." The Beatles pushed other styles out of the way even as they borrowed much of their spirit and salient qualities: the folk of Peter, Paul, and Mary; the garage rock of the Trashmen; the street harmony of the Four Seasons; the soul of Sam Cooke; the torch songs of Brenda Lee; the surf music of the Rip Chords; the hot-rod sound of Jan and Dean; the dance craze of Chubby Checker's "The Twist"; the soft jazz of Al Hirt; the Broadway numbers of Barbra Streisand; the orchestral instrumentals of Henry Mancini; the mariachi style of Herb Alpert; the R&B of Ray Charles; the country and western of Lefty Frizzell; and, most symbolically, an innocuous new release from Elvis Presley ("Viva Las Vegas"): all these held on to the chart's lower rungs in the weeks of the Beatles' reign. Tribute records like Donna Lynn's "My Boyfriend Got a Beatle Haircut," the Swans' "The Boy with the Beatle Hair," and the Four Preps' "A Letter to the Beatles" made the band's presence inescapable.

The new appetite for electric music in America began to create "rock" out of rock 'n' roll, with the first important homegrown example after surf music coming from folksinger Bob Dylan (b. May 24, 1941). The Beatles listened obsessively to Dylan's second record, *Freewheelin'*, in Paris in January 1964, and soon channeled his psychological approach to lyrics by that August with Lennon's moody "I'm a Loser." They communed with him over marijuana a few days later in New York. All this time, Dylan played a folkie in the Woody Guthrie tradition; his albums pled for common-sense responses to racial hatred and nuclear threats with simple acoustic guitar and harmonica accompaniment. His voice, however, gnawed through expectations about "prettiness" and pop smoothness. Only twenty-two when he recorded *Freewheelin'* (see Photo 4.3), he sounded far wiser than his years even as he expressed generational self-consciousness in songs like "A Hard Rain's Gonna Fall," "Talkin' World War III Blues," and "Oxford Town," which referred explicitly to slain civil rights activists. When he shocked the folk establishment by recording half of his fifth album, *Bringing It All Back Home* (released in March 1965), with electric-instrument settings of poetry emphasizing personal experience rather than social causes, then by plugging in his Stratocaster at the July 1965 Newport Folk Festival, Dylan merely punctuated what the Beatles and the harder Stones, Who, Kinks, Animals, and Yardbirds had suggested: rock music would outgrow mere teenage consciousness.

1964 Original Releases (British unless specified otherwise):
Single: "Komm, Gib Mir Deine Hand" / "Sie Liebt Dich" (rel. in Germany Jan. 29)
Single: "Sweet Georgia Brown" / "Nobody's Child" (rel. Jan. 31)
Single: "Can't Buy Me Love" / "You Can't Do That" (rel. Mar. 20)
Single: "Ain't She Sweet" / "Take Out Some Insurance on Me, Baby" (rel. May 29)
EP: *Long Tall Sally* (rel. June 19)

Side 1:	Side 2:
"Long Tall Sally"	"Slow Down"
"I Call Your Name"	"Matchbox"

LP: *A Hard Day's Night* (rel. July 10)

Side 1: Songs from the film *A Hard Day's Night*	Side 2:
"A Hard Day's Night"	"Any Time at All"
"I Should Have Known Better"	"I'll Cry Instead"
"If I Fell"	"Things We Said Today"
"I'm Happy Just to Dance with You"	"When I Get Home"
"And I Love Her"	"You Can't Do That"
"Tell Me Why"	"I'll Be Back"
"Can't Buy Me Love"	

PHOTO 4.3. Bob Dylan, *Freewheelin'* LP (released in US May 27, 1963).

Single: "A Hard Day's Night" / "Things We Said Today" (rel. July 10)
Single: "I Feel Fine" / "She's a Woman" (rel. Nov. 23)
LP: *Beatles for Sale* (rel. Dec. 4)

Side One:
"No Reply"
"I'm a Loser"
"Baby's in Black"
"Rock and Roll Music"
"I'll Follow the Sun"
"Mr. Moonlight"
"Kansas City" / "Hey-Hey-Hey-Hey!"

Side Two:
"Eight Days a Week"
"Words of Love"
"Honey Don't"
"Every Little Thing"
"I Don't Want to Spoil the Party"
"What You're Doing"
"Everybody's Trying to Be My Baby"

A HARD DAY'S NIGHT

After the *Ed Sullivan Show* and a closed-circuit televised concert in Washington, DC, the Beatles spent a week in Miami performing a second *Sullivan* show, where George practiced on a new Rickenbacker electric twelve-string guitar presented to him by its manufacturer before leaving New York. This model helped launch the new genre of folk-rock when Roger McGuinn of the Byrds saw its appearance throughout the Beatles' first feature film, *A Hard Day's Night*, and began to paint Dylan songs like "All I Really Want to Do" and "Mr. Tambourine Man" with an electric twelve-string jangle. The movie recreates a claustrophobic day in their life preparing for a fictional televised concert, featuring a handful of new songs, a frothy script by Liverpool playwright Alun Owen, and visually vibrant direction by an American, Richard Lester. Replacing the working title *Beatlemania*, the eventual lead track derived from a Ringo Starr non sequitur, which Lester proposed to the Beatles on April 15. Lennon took the bait and wrote the title song around the phrase that night, and the group recorded it the next day. (Lennon's haste is betrayed in his apparent borrowing of poetic text and chord progression from the bridge [1:00+] of the Crystals' 1963 hit, "He's Sure the Boy I Love," for his own contrasting section.) The film, released to theaters around the world in July, featured their new single, "Can't Buy Me Love," a big departure from all previous work in featuring a solo McCartney vocal and a verse mapping out their first twelve-bar blues, signaling a frequent and more deeply structural inclusion of blues material into their writing, which continued into 1966.

The film's opening sequence featured the band sharing a first-class cabin with an elderly upper-crust businessman, complete with bowler hat. This establishment stand-in looks visibly perturbed by the band's long hair and takes issue with their having the window open and listening to pop radio. "I ride this train twice a week," he proclaims, as if rendering a verdict. "We have rights too," Ringo calmly responds. Lennon pretends to snort something from his coke bottle. "Give us a kiss," he says, pressing into the man's face. "I won the war for your sort," the oldster finally grumbles. "I bet you're sorry you won," Ringo instantly shoots back.

This scene fixed the Beatles in their audience's mind as young, imperturbable iconoclasts who could care less what the older generation made of their looks and attitudes. Most Americans missed the class tension at play, which would have stood out for British audiences: a big piece of this man's grievance comes from sharing a first-class cabin with four working-class ruffians (even though they wear suits): he's insulted to even share the same space with these secondary citizens; for people like him, their youth only underscores their lower-class status. At the start of this film's essay on all things establishment that the Beatles openly defy—old-fashioned showbiz propriety, a patronizing manager and TV director—this openly contemptuous scene depicting outdated class strictures pivots the new game off the old. (The irony, of course, is that Paul's grandfather, played by UK television star Wilfrid Brambell, gets some of the best lines and carries the most rebellious flag. He even calls policemen "paid assassins." Rock critic Lester Bangs famously wrote: "Fuck the Beatles! It's BLATANTLY OBVIOUS that the most rock-and-roll human being in the whole movie is the fucking grandfather! That wily old slime of Paul's! He had more energy than the four moptops put together! Plus the spirit! He was a true anarchist!" (Bangs 1988, 325)).

The film's first "performance," "I Should Have Known Better," also showcased the group's mystique, the thrills they brought to simple gestures. Given a treatment unlike any prior pop-movie sequence, the song plays out as a fantasy, continuing the previous scene's surreal tone announced by their incongruously running along outside the moving train compartment. As the Beatles play cards in a storage car, their instruments suddenly appear in their hands; as the song comes to a close, they disappear once again. Throughout the narrative, cast and crew manipulate and mock film conventions such as lip-synching and instrumental miming (watch Lennon's mocking lips at the start of "If I Fell," trying to get Ringo to break character and laugh), and the viewer wonders, in the context of the story: Are they or are they not really playing instruments and singing? The cultivation of the imagination is front and center, and this absurdist black-and-white fantasy foreshadows full-blown psychedelia. In a typically shocked expression of the movie's virtues, critic Andrew Sarris called it a "brilliant crystallization of such diverse cultural particles as the pop movie, rock 'n' roll, *cinéma vérité*, the *nouvelle vague*, free cinema, the affectedly hand-held camera, frenzied cutting, the cult of the sexless sub-adolescent, the semi-documentary, and studied spontaneity" (Sarris 2006, 56–57).

A Hard Day's Night, the Beatles' first extended project with all-original songs, documents the growing variety of influences in the Lennon-McCartney palette; Lennon in particular reaches an early creative peak. "If I Fell" shows John with a new level of introspection and complex harmony, and Paul and John's vocal duet gains a new expressive intricacy. In "I'm Happy Just to Dance with You," John's rhythm guitar figures turn kaleidoscopic. In the bridge of "I Should Have Known Better," John verges on the drama of an Italianate aria, but it's spiced with a touch of the blues. The ballad "And I Love Her" takes Paul's melodic construction to a new level of complexity as George's lead guitar ideas (on a nylon-string flamenco instrument) drive the song's stylistic novelty. The same song explores radical tonal relationships, opening off-tonic, ambivalent as to whether E major or C♯ minor is the key center, and then jolted up a half step just before the nylon-string solo to fluctuate between D minor and F major, only to end surprisingly on D major. George Martin described John's title song as "instant combustion," saying of the sustained dissonant chord that opens the song, film, and album: "It sort of set the whole tone for the song and for the whole film, because we knew that what was going to follow was going to be dramatic, wonderful, funny, exciting." The haste with which Lennon wrote the song is evident in the easily reworked borrowing of the bridge idea from the Crystals' "He's Sure the Boy I Love": the bridge in each song opens with the unusual iii chord for the idea of everything being right when the singer is held tight. "I'll Cry Instead," cut from the film but appearing on the album, was a rockabilly number John sings in the vein of Elvis's "I'm Gonna Sit Right Down and Cry (Over You)" or Johnny Burnette's "Lonesome Tears in My Eyes."

In between *A Hard Day's Night* shoots, the Beatles appeared four times on British television, miming to their records, and in a feature program, *Around the Beatles*. They also had numerous other appearances in these busy months, including Lennon's presence at a Foyle's literary luncheon in honor of his first book, *In His Own Write*. In their first UK stage shows after the American mini-tour, they closed April with a poll-winner's concert for ten thousand at Wembley's Empire Pool and Sports Arena and then two dates in Scotland. Fans camped out overnight for tickets in Edinburgh. A year earlier, they could still be heard at the Cavern Club in Liverpool; now, Epstein filled their schedule with the best concert halls and media. May won them an overdue vacation before a regrouping for June studio work to complete the *Hard Day's Night* album (pictured as Photo 4.4), with six new Lennon-McCartney songs to complement the seven from the film.

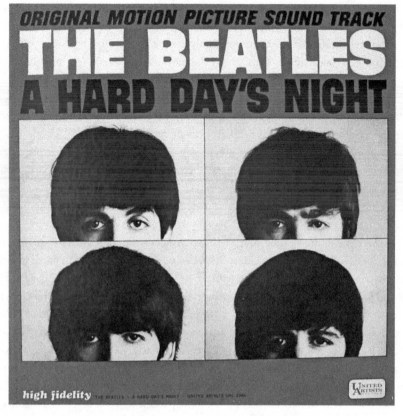

PHOTO 4.4. The Beatles in March–April 1964, *A Hard Day's Night* LP (released in US June 26, 1964).

"I Should Have Known Better"

Recorded February 26, 1964, for *A Hard Day's Night*

—whereby a close examination of melodic patterning reveals the gloriously fulfilled promise of new love.

Some Beatles love songs convey layered intelligence and poetic feel for love's slippery contrasts: happy lyrics sit atop brooding music ("All I've Got to Do"), or downcast words work off upbeat settings ("All My Loving"). Another romantic flavor pushes through as a tonic to any and all misgivings: breezy emotional joyrides that feed off their own melodic euphoria ("I Want to Hold Your Hand," "Little Child," "Eight Days A Week," "One after 909"). "I Should Have Known Better" turns into carnal triumph (Meltzer 1988, 106) for an intoxicating surge of feeling, trumping all conflict and doubt.

A zesty Lennon vocal blankets the track's many nuances. The first layer of tension lies in how Lennon's solo vocal doesn't rely on any support from Harrison or McCartney (no harmonizing, no backing vocals), and the group dynamics stay invisible but palpable: Lennon couldn't have sung this victoriously standing on anybody else's shoulders. It's the same rapport they give McCartney singing "Can't Buy Me Love" and the verses of "All My Loving," where the instrumental ensemble bathes everything with warm group ensemble. Underneath Lennon's blues harp lies an acoustic cushion, relaxed and buoyant, a bedding of feathers for his elongated vowels ("I—— should have known better"). The multiple sonic smirks across these early tracks help define the early Beatles' sound: cascading in waves of resilient cheerfulness, they all seem to land in some better place. Even though the lead singer stands alone, nobody would mistake any of these numbers for "solo" turns; they remain group efforts from top to bottom. (This song also shares an affinity with Lennon's *Imagine* number "Oh! Yoko!," where the harmonica trails off into the fadeout in blissful frenzy.)

The deceptively simple narrative straddles several realms: the early phase of a relationship; the rush of passion, euphoria, and mystery before "love" has been officially declared; and the arrogance of a lover who submits to feeling while boasting victory, or patriarchal ownership. In the Beatles' time, this macho arrogance symbolized an idealized form of romance for both partners, even though in retrospect we tend to view it as unbalanced, and "ownership" as entitled, even abusive. The poetry here overwhelms this antiquated view of women. This posing culminates a year later in "Run for Your Life," later reorienting itself toward an emerging feminism during mid- and late-period songs.

The number also celebrates the very earliest moments of a relationship, an emotional pink cloud that sends young lovers adrift in pleasure. The bridge doesn't shift rhythmic gears but slows surely into a half-time feel, framed by Harrison's guitar chimings (at 0:40 and 2:01), which convey a delicately contrasting uncertainty amid all the devotion. And beneath the bridge's relative minor mode (0:40 and 2:01) a humility looms, yielding through the idyllic falsettos (1:00 and 2:21), a key early Lennon trait that elevates his considerable bluster: in this song, "I'll Be Back," and "Not a Second Time," and even "She Loves You," he admits to past shortfalls. Bouncing back into verses with inimitable "whoa-oh-I" and "So-whoa-I" from each bridge implants the kind of sparkle that give early Beatle songs their glint: the wide-eyed innocent nonsense that elevates, instead of cheapens, everything around it, the joyous whoops they (most often led by Paul) insert around instrumental passages, and the way even the "Hey hey hey"s in this song vaguely echo the "yeah yeah yeah"s from "She Loves You." And the closing passage carries a virtuoso touch: the way Lennon floats a new melody (a manic play on the original "hey hey hey" pitches) into the fadeout (at 2:29), repeating the phrase as if somehow everything up to this point had built up to it, boasts fathomless creativity: there are plenty more melodies where this came from, he suggests as the song glides off into silence.

In its exploration of the sixth degree of the major scale, "I Should Have Known Better" presents a simple idea that develops in depth, showing an atypical discipline in John's harnessing of his tonal imagination. First (at the word "should" at 0:09), Lennon sings the sixth degree as an unassuming upper neighbor to 5 as he had regularly played in his guitar's boogie formations. But 6 takes on a life of its own by brazenly not returning to 5 at the end of a phrase ("you," at 0:12), then enriching its role when 6 is fleshed out, becoming a root with the minor vi chord's support at "do" (0:16). To find its way into the bridge, 6 then pushes through 7 (at 0:38, just as suggested subliminally in the 5–6–7–6–5 harp intro and then all-knowingly in the vocal outro). The sixth degree then attains a fantasy-inspired glory when vi acts as a fully tonicized area for the first two phrases of the bridge, in one of Lennon's most beautiful tunes ever, before acquiescing to its clichéd doo-wop-based service of the tonic G major for a return to reality in the bridge's second half. The falsetto that culminates Lennon's arpeggiating melisma on "mine" (0:59–1:02), highlights a nostalgic last glimpse of the minor vi chord that is swallowed up by that final doo-wop progression. The high falsetto pitch on "mine" is a natural third scale degree that rectifies the beautifully blue flatted third scale degree sighed just before, "oh" (0:53–0:54), that had itself followed a luxuriating Holly-like melisma on "too-hoo-hoo-ho-oo-hoo" (0:51–0:53).

Yes, he should have realized so many things before (and that "Pride can hurt you too," as the addressee was advised in "She Loves You"), but the track persuades you that even his insecurities push an otherwise delicious naiveté toward insight, updating Buddy Holly's intuitive wisdom into a soaring Lennon-McCartney theme.

CUE	SECTION	HARMONY	DETAIL
0:00	Intro	I–V–I–V	harmonica
0:07	Verse 1	I–V–I–V–vi–IV–V–I	JL lead vocal
0:24	Verse 2	I–V–I–V–vi–IV–V7/vi	
0:40	Bridge 1: phrase 1	vi–IV–I–V7/vi	tonicizing vi
0:47	Bridge 1: phrase 2	vi–I–V7/IV	tonicizing IV
0:54	Bridge 1: phrase 3	IV–V7–I–vi	offset doo-wop
1:01	Bridge 1: phrase 4	IV–V7–I	doo-wop cadence
1:08	Verse 3		based on Verse 1
1:28	Guitar solo		based on Verse 1
1:45	Verse 2		
2:01	Bridge 2		
2:30	Outro	I–V–I–V	fadeout

"If I Fell"

Recorded February 27, 1964, for *A Hard Day's Night*

—working through an authorship mystery in Lennon and McCartney's most celebrated vocal duet, conveying the poetic text's caution based in the pain of the past.

The Lennon and McCartney songwriting partnership presents intriguing emotional riddles. Early on, we think they collaborated quite closely, each contributing lines and sections to each other's song drafts. But even then, they had an unusual arrangement: they agreed to share legal and financial credit even if only one had composed a majority of, or even a complete, song. This gave them each great freedom to work alone or together, and help one another with simple fragments or fully formed drafts. As they develop throughout their career, you can hear them growing apart both in terms of subject matter and in the way their distinctive duets give way to vocal solos. The late vocal duets carry distinctly different creative moods than their earlier, closer harmonies.

Only they know who contributed what to which songs, but the guiding principle judging authorship stems from who sings lead. "Strawberry Fields Forever" has a Lennon lead with no vocal harmonies from others, typical for the middle period. It's the kind of song McCartney could never have penned. In fact, a week after Lennon presented it to his partner, McCartney came back with his answer: "Penny Lane," in which he sang lead with no harmonizing.

With early Lennon-McCartney songs, scholars still dissect which strands belong to which partner, often futilely. In hindsight, we hear "If I Fell" as the first in a string of Lennon confessionals that includes "I'm a Loser," "Help!," "You've Got to Hide Your Love Away," "Norwegian Wood," "Julia," "Because," and "Don't Let Me Down." "If I Fell" poses the ultimate example of this authorship riddle: Lennon sings lead only on the introduction, the number's harmonically deceptive eight-bar soliloquy. (One ♭II chord, a triadic jazzy tritone substitution for the local dominant, first helps tonicize the leading tone and in a second phrase is reinterpreted as the tonic itself.) When the verse begins, it slips into perpetual duet: "If I give my heart to you" (at 0:18–24) sung in harmony (McCartney leading on the upper line, Lennon on a lower harmony part), and "I must be sure" (at 0:25–27) in unison (same notes sung by both singers). Should we presume to call this song a closer collaboration than, say, "All My Loving," where McCartney sings lead through most of the song with only faint backup vocals from Lennon and Harrison in the chorus (and a double-tracked descant addition to the final verse)? Perhaps. (In surviving demo tapes of "If I Fell," Lennon takes the upper vocal melody in verses, and the lower line in bridges, so at least as far as these vocals go, their collaboration involved working out vocal parts as part of the composition.) These authorial questions frame the song's larger subject: the free-fall insecurity of leaping headlong into an affair.

This duet from 1964's *A Hard Day's Night* soundtrack traces poetic threads of the Lennon-McCartney partnership expressed as both promise and peril. Lennon sings the preamble, teetering between commitment and reluctance, and the song spins out indecision through intricate vocal lines.[1] For the verses, McCartney's upper line ducks and glides with geometric lyricism. Each individual line would have made a sturdy melody on its own, although the upper part is tonally more often goal-directed; combined, they trace a poetry of uncertainty.

The lyrics describe love's oscillating, intemperate swells, seeking comfort and reassurance where only risk abides. The narrator describes wanting to make a commitment to his new lover while recounting the humiliation of his lingering broken heart from a previous romance. This confounds the typical romantic narrative, wherein

---

1. For more technical discussions of this harmonic scheme, see Everett 2001, 229–233, and Riley 1988, 102–104.

a suitor pledges devotion while praising and flattering his subject. In this song, the singer can barely contain his hurt (regularly invoked by the mixture-induced minor iv chord, first in Harrison's twelve-string turnaround at 0:38, later coloring both the bridge and coda) while considering a new commitment. The appeal to the subject stems mainly from the singer's candor: you should know I'm still hurting from a recent breakup; can you reassure me that you won't jilt me too?

In a mistake that hardcore Beatles fans cherish, McCartney actually chokes on a high note on the word "vain" during the second bridge (1:44). In the mono mix, this mistake was "corrected" with the previously performed true note spliced in (1:11). But in the lower-priority stereo mix, this crack remains as sung, only intensifying the song's sentiment: the emotional pitch of the song actually brings the suitor to a breaking point while expressing fear that his love might be "in vain," all for nothing.

Was a ballad ever so fluid yet tough-minded? Would two harmonizing writers ever sound as timidly poised?

CUE	SECTION	HARMONY	DETAIL
0:00	Intro: phrase 1	ii→III!–I–vi, all of a tonicized VII	JL unison vocal
0:09	Intro: phrase 2	ii→III!, both of VII, –ii7–V7	JL unison vocal
0:18	Verse 1: phrase 1	I–ii–iii–iii°–ii7–V	PM/JL duet
0:27	Verse 1: phrase 2	I–ii–iii–iii°–ii7–V–I	PM/JL duet
0:28	HC turnaround	iv–V	GH 12-string mode mixture
0:40	Verse 2	I–ii–iii–iii°–ii7–V	
0:59	Bridge 1	V9/IV–IV–iv–I–V7	duet
1:13	Verse 3		based on Verse 2
1:32	Bridge 2	V9/IV–IV–iv–I–V7	
1:45	Verse 3		
2:11	Coda	I–iv–I	Guitar echoes vocal

"Things We Said Today"

Recorded June 3, 1964, for *A Hard Day's Night*

—a title placing today in the past, with McCartney's audacious contrast of a moody minor-mode verse/refrain and a perky major-mode bridge.

McCartney's early ballads have a guileless irony, as if they sprang complete from some ambitious whim. This medium-tempo love ballad casts a dark undertow, similar to that of "And I Love Her" in the way promissory lyrics join with foreboding melody. This track gets fleshed out with more ambitious production, demonstrating how eager the Beatles were to integrate technical features into their arrangements: the tone of the bridge comes on so strong, turns so thick, that it could almost be wedged in from another number. The singer, who has been speaking intimately with his lover, begins addressing a completely different audience to boast about his magical good luck. With an invisible pirouette, he returns to his lamenting verse, as if an outburst interrupts steady eye contact.

The mood here might be called anticipatory retrospection, by which adolescents picture their future selves with immense feeling. McCartney's protagonist looks back fondly on an epic romance that has lasted decades, pinning his hopes to feelings that run so deep, seem so permanent, that life hinges on their profundity.

The major contrast in this song comes from its galloping acoustic pickups into overcast (minor) verses leavened by intense, presumptive bridges (in major) that swell up like unconscious surges and course through smirking chord patterns (I–IV7–II7–V7–I) only to resume the minor mode with an effective single-chord switch (whereby a gloomy ♭II7 appears as a tritone substitute for V—McCartney invoking the "If I Fell" intro?). In this effortless yet unworldly way, the singer seems nostalgic for the future, the ways in which he can memorialize his love in some distant sentimental haze— not the way people look back on their affections so much as the way old songs sound antiquated when depicting bygone courting rituals. With McCartney, he ties an almost gothic tone in verses to a driving beat in bridges as if welding courtly resolve with sexual heat. The result still sounds daringly incongruous, but the contrast reeks of ambition stretching form.

CUE	SECTION	HARMONY	DETAIL
0:00	Intro tattoo	i	Acoustic guitars
0:03	Verse 1: S, R	i–v7–i (four times)	McCartney solo lead, double-tracked
0:17	Verse 1: D	♭III→♭III9→VI→II (!)	PM adds descant part
0:25	Verse 1: C	i–v7–i	McCartney solo lead, double-tracked
0:30	Tattoo		
0:33	Verse 2: SRDC		
0:58	Bridge 1	I–IV7–II7–V7, I–IV7–II7–♭II7 (!)	Drums push forward
1:15	Verse 3: SRDC		
1:41	Bridge 2		
1:57	Verse 3		
2:23	Coda		Outro recalls tattoo

"I'll Be Back"

Recorded June 1, 1964, for *A Hard Day's Night*

—an album closer that combines the loss referred to tentatively in "If I Fell" with the brash confidence of the "Things We Said Today" bridge.

The first two Beatles albums came crashing closed with covers ("Twist and Shout" and then "Money"). To finish off their third album's first all-original sequence, they step back from stage-driven impulses for a romantic quandary.

Many of the early Beatles tracks teem with "I," "you," and "me," almost as if they're diagraming how many different ways personal pronouns can be twisted. (Do these identifiers, and the way Lennon would frequently mash up his pronouns in live performance—as when he frequently mixes up "that boy" with the title of "This Boy"— anticipate the confusion of identity in the opening line of "I Am the Walrus"?) Many note how songs like "From Me to You" and "She Loves You" guide the listener through a variety of songwriting tricks, from addressing the lover directly ("If I Fell") to using the pronoun as a metaphor for their love affair with rock history ("I Want to Hold Your Hand," "I Should Have Known Better").

In "I'll Be Back," Lennon and McCartney reverse the narrative of "Not a Second Time" to promise that even after the subject has hurt the singer as much as she has, he'll be back, and they both know it. After he runs away from her, he assumes she'll want him back but he gets a "big surprise," presumably because she's moved on. The song confronts this reckoning: he has to choose his words carefully, persuade his ex that he's learned the necessary lessons to reunite. The "oh-ohs" at the end of each bridge give the song the gentlest rhythmic and melodic hook, wary yet insistent, coloring the storyline with uncertainty. The major-mode colorings of the bridge's vi, ii and IV chords and the vocalized C♯s—rather than the home-key minor mode's sonorities—seems to betray the false hope that drives the confessional, always revealed by the major mode that lies underneath the dejected surface. In the end, Lennon repeatedly vacillates between major hope and minor despair.

Innovation arrives in the form of two distinct bridges between verses (Bridge 1a at 0:26, Bridge 2 at 1:03, Bridge 1b at 1:44), as if the singer's thought process spins forward without making much headway. The structure builds from vocal pairing: duets in the verses (Lennon on lead, McCartney on descant), Lennon solos (double-tracked) in each bridge.

CUE	SECTION	HARMONY	DETAIL
0:00	Intro	I	Acoustic guitars
0:04	Verse 1	i (!)–VII–VIM7–V–I	PM/JL duet; repeated lament bass
0:26	Bridge 1a	vi–ii–V–IV–V–IV–V	JL double-tracked
0:40	Verse 2		duet; repeated

CUE	SECTION	HARMONY	DETAIL
1:03	Bridge 2	ii–iii–vi–II7–IV–V–IV–V	JL double-tracked; nylon-string countermelody (▶ See Video 2.6)
1:22	Verse 2		duet
1:44	Bridge 1b		JL double-tracked
1:58	Verse 1		duet; repeat not taken
2:06	Outro	I–i–I–i	Major-minor oscillation

"I Call Your Name"

Recorded March 1, 1964, for the EP *Long Tall Sally*

—more cowbell? An examination of chromatic harmony (with three different triads built on the sixth scale degree!) that parallels the multifaceted nature of John Lennon's ego.

Many early Beatles recordings whiz past on sheer momentum, bounding surges of energy that smother boredom with restlessness. Every so often, a single detail enlivens the whole, shining up its surroundings with surprising glints, in ways something more dramatic might obscure. The cowbell in "I Call Your Name" is such a gesture. Lennon would later boast about working in a "ska" middle section at 1:10 for the guitar solo ("deliberate and self-conscious," Lennon 1981, 92; see also Riley 1988, 96), but it's the same sort of shuffle that had been inserted into contrasting middle sections since Carl Perkins's "Sure to Fall (In Love with You)" and "Lend Me Your Comb," Tony Sheridan's "Why (Can't You Love Me Again)," "Red Sails in the Sunset," and "A Taste of Honey."

The verse structure recalls the chromatic circle-of-fifths "Rhythm" changes of "Sweet Georgia Brown": it starts on I, moves to a major VI in the second line (on "there"), resolves as an applied dominant to supertonic, II7 (on "blame"), and then to the dominant, V7. The bridge (IV–vi–II→♭VI7–V7) swaps out the defiant major VI for a more reconciled minor vi (for the admission of helpless ignorance, "I don't know who can") before passing through the deflating ♭VI7 on its way back to V7 (which anticipates a similar move in "Day Tripper"). The melody trades short bursts that build toward self-exposing melismas ("ma-ya-ake it," "ma—an,"), and all the parry and thrust gets kicked in syncopated bursts near the end during the fadeout as Lennon repeats the title line, every kick landing just before the bar, blurring anticipation with frustration.

CUE	SECTION	HARMONY	DETAIL
0:00	intro	II7–V7–I–V7	GH 12-string guitar
0:07	Verse 1: antecedent	I–VI7–II7–V7	JL double-tracked
0:24	Verse 1: consequent	I–VI7–II7–IV–iv–I	JL double-tracked

CUE	SECTION	HARMONY	DETAIL
0:21	Bridge	IV7–vi–II7→VI7–V7	
0:55	Verse 2: consequent		
1:11	Guitar solo	based on Verse consequent	shuffle
1:24	Bridge		
1:41	Verse 2: consequent		
1:54	Outro	I7–IV7–I7–IV7	Repeat into fadeout

WORLD TOUR AND FURTHER RECORDING: *BEATLES FOR SALE*

Before 1964, artists had toured, on rare occasion extensively. But the Beatles' hyper-popularity pushed them into huge venues, inventing the major-attraction large-arena rock concert tour long before amplifiers could produce decent sound for such halls. The crowds in these 1964 dates ranged from 3,600 to 32,000. Following June theater appearances in Denmark and Holland—notable for Ringo's temporary replacement by Jimmie Nicol due to a tonsillectomy—the Beatles flew to Hong Kong and Australia, where a street crowd estimated at 300,000 to 350,000 engulfed their Adelaide hotel. In Australia and New Zealand, where they played twenty-six shows in under three weeks, the Beatles developed a half-hour set repeated night after night to huge audiences. Their equipment was inadequate, and they could not be heard above the screaming (and fainting) throngs, let alone hear themselves. This set list greeted these houses:

"Twist and Shout"
"I Want to Hold Your Hand"
"I Saw Her Standing There"
"You Can't Do That"
"All My Loving"
"I Wanna Be Your Man" (Ringo's solo vocal)
"She Loves You"
"Till There Was You"
"Roll Over Beethoven" (George's solo vocal)
"Can't Buy Me Love"
"This Boy"
"Long Tall Sally"

In August and September, the Beatles toured the United States and Canada, playing thirty-two shows in twenty-four cities. Transported from airports in helicopters or ambulances, enduring painful transit in unpadded metal vans, the month proved grueling even for the Beatles' road-warrior spirits. In Montreal, security protected Ringo in the face of a death threat; in Cleveland, police shoved

George aside when fans rushed the stage. Stewards constantly flushed enterprising young girls from hotel closets and bathrooms before occupation by Beatles. Supported by the Bill Black Combo, the Righteous Brothers, the Exciters, and Jackie DeShannon, the Beatles updated their set list to perform:

"Twist and Shout" or "I Saw Her Standing There," or (in Kansas City) "Kansas City" / "Hey-Hey-Hey-Hey!"
"You Can't Do That"
"All My Loving"
"She Loves You"
"Things We Said Today"
"Roll Over Beethoven" (George's solo vocal)
"Can't Buy Me Love"
"If I Fell"
"I Want to Hold Your Hand"
"Boys" (Ringo's solo vocal)
"A Hard Day's Night"
"Long Tall Sally" or "Twist and Shout"

Highlights of the tour included meeting Fats Domino in New Orleans and Elvis Presley in Los Angeles. The Kansas City show was booked upon the Beatles' arrival in the States on what was originally to be a day off—they turned down offers of $50,000 and $100,000, finally accepting a record fee of $150,000. Hucksters did brisk business selling one-square-inch cutouts from the sheets the Beatles had slept on in various hotels, as well as the carpets upon which they'd walked. Unlike most previous shows, many concerts were locally broadcast and thus preserved by home tapers, to be bootlegged for black-market sale in the 1970s and beyond. The Hollywood Bowl show was professionally recorded by nearby Capitol Records; though this show was deemed for years to be too marred by crowd noise, parts of it and its repeat in 1965 were nevertheless released in 1977 as *The Beatles at the Hollywood Bowl*.

Of most lasting import, the Beatles took a leadership role standing up for civil rights when they discovered their show at the Gator Bowl in Jacksonville was to have segregated seating. Lennon demanded, "We never play to segregated audiences and we aren't going to start now. I'd sooner lose our appearance money." Over the course of a few weeks as the tour went on, Jacksonville acceded to the Beatles' demand. To prevent such an issue in the future, the group's 1965 contracts stipulated that the Beatles "not be required to perform in front of a segregated audience." Such stands taken in the sports and entertainment industries, along with rock 'n' roll's mix of black and white styles, advanced social changes that were afoot beyond the anti-discrimination Civil Rights Act of 1964. Lyndon Johnson won the presidency in a landslide that November in large part for passing that bill, which helped him expand Franklin D. Roosevelt's New Deal legacy into his own Great Society.

Beatle records became so iconic that they set off a new trend: blacks covering white music. Although there were few African Americans seen among Beatlemania's crowds, they became an important segment of their record-buying audience. And black soul singers especially began covering Lennon-McCartney material: Ella Fitzgerald sang "Can't Buy Me Love" and the Supremes appropriated "You Can't Do That" in 1964, Otis Redding slayed "Day Tripper" in 1966, Wilson Pickett performed "Hey Jude" in 1968, and Stevie Wonder recorded "We Can Work It Out" in 1970. Booker T. & the M.G.'s, the house band at Stax, created instrumental versions of nearly the

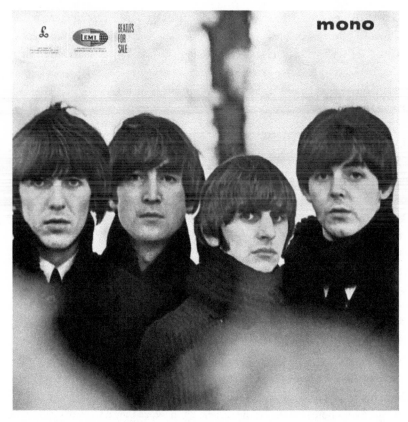

PHOTO 4.5. The Beatles in Autumn 1964, photographed by Robert Freeman. *Beatles for Sale* LP (released in UK December 4, 1964).

entire *Abbey Road* album, as *McLemore Avenue*—in 1970. If the real world hadn't integrated yet, rock 'n' roll held aloft an ideal of racial harmony for all to hear. Just as Johnson approached the November election, Martin Luther King, Jr., a key leader of the civil rights movement, accepted the Nobel Peace Prize in Stockholm. The US government, in the person of FBI's J. Edgar Hoover, stepped up its slander and illegal wiretapping of King. It was easy to tell which side the Beatles were on. All this encouraged the Beatles' increasing candor when speaking about social matters, most importantly manifest in John Lennon's later devotion to world peace.

The Beatles' fourth album, *Beatles for Sale* (see Photo 4.5), was recorded in the fall of 1964. Often called a tired effort due to the subdued expressions of the four in its jacket photo and its return to reliance on songs written by others, a more nuanced understanding holds clues to their larger ambitions. Despite their composing prowess, the Beatles still loved their cover-song heritage; "Twist and Shout" and "Long Tall Sally" each continued to serve as concert closers until McCartney penned his own Little Richard-styled raver, "I'm Down," for 1965 appearances. (▶ The raver mode is demonstrated in Video 2.3.) *Sale* included Buddy Holly's "Words of Love," an oldie that re-entered the group's repertoire in July 1963, soon after George acquired the Gretsch guitar that when fed through his Vox amp gave him a brighter tone, perhaps reminding him of Holly's Stratocaster. The Beatles enjoyed a studio visit from Carl Perkins in June 1964, and their homage continued with George singing Perkins's "Everybody's Trying to Be My Baby" (drenched in a slap-back echo in tribute to Sam Phillips's Sun Records sound) in lieu of a song of his own, and Ringo taking Perkins's "Honey Don't," a song John had sung onstage and for the BBC. Lennon's white-hot streak through Chuck Berry's "Rock and Roll Music" countered his feverishly oddball "Mr. Moonlight." Paul's belting of the Little Richard medley "Kansas City" / "Hey-Hey-Hey-Hey!" resurrected at the last-minute for the hastily added Missouri concert, was also taped for the album. It's only in retrospect, with future Beatle records containing almost exclusively original content, that critics noted the number of borrowed songs on *Beatles for Sale*; between this album and the final project, *Abbey Road*, only four more covers appeared alongside 142 more original songs.

The year 1963 had seen them sweep Britain; 1964's schedule took them to America twice, provided for an all-original soundtrack to their first film, and prompted still another holiday product that fall. The summer touring schedule wore them down, but they did not take time off. Back in January '64, three weeks holed up in the George V hotel in Paris had given them space to complete their soundtrack songs; another month's vacation in May afforded them time to write the remainder of the *Hard Day's Night* album. Ten new Lennon-McCartney songs appeared with the fall single and album, although both "Baby's in Black" and "I'll Follow the Sun" were actually among the first songs John and Paul had written together. The new songs highlight innovative introductions (bass-to-acoustic guitar feedback in "I Feel Fine," backbeat chords in "She's a Woman" that are only understood as occupying weak beats when the rhythm section enters late, and an intriguing fade-in to "Eight Days a Week"), new sounds in an acoustic twelve-string in "I'm a Loser" (and a new use of the harmonica, ending the track just as Dylan often did), timpani along with the piano's deep register in "Every Little Thing," and growing reliance upon their own harmonic ideas (such as the subtonic ♭VII chord of the "I'm a Loser" verse and the chorus of "Every Little Thing," the Lydian II♯ chord of the "Eight Days a Week" verse, and the changing chords over an unchanging bass pedal, as in the "Eight Days" intro) that would find many uses in the album and become hallmarks of rock style. A new textural idea appears with the brief bass-drums duet at the end of "What You're Doing," used only once more, a year and a half later going into the coda of "Rain."

Beatles for Sale continued to nurture an interest in the blues patterns begun with "Can't Buy Me Love." Heard against the bright, high-register emphases in the 1963 hits, the Beatles had matured by late 1964; they were worldly as much as world-weary, and with "No Reply," "I'm a Loser," "Baby's in Black," and "I Don't Want to Spoil the Party" explored negative thoughts and feelings alongside buoyant charmers like "I Feel Fine" and "Eight Days a Week." Such a broadening range of approaches marked this year's work as a first step in a continuing search for new horizons.

POINTS FOR DISCUSSION

1. How was the Beatles' UK catalog mined in leading to their American chart dominance in the spring of 1964? Can you discover what twelve Beatle songs occupied *Billboard's* April 4, 1964, "Hot 100" chart?

2. Consult Appendix 1 and discuss some ways that the Beatles were opening up new sounds not heard in prior music. Find lists of songs popular in the United States in 1963; listen to a few and describe how the Beatles' music of that year would have sounded fresh in comparison.

3.   Name some ways the Beatles' personalities shone through *A Hard Day's Night*, cementing their bond with their new global audience.
4.   Describe class-based tensions as portrayed in scenes from *A Hard Day's Night*.
5.   What can you infer from the Beatles' set lists during this first phase of their world tours?
6.   How does Bob Dylan's *Freewheelin'*, an acoustic folk album, begin to influence Lennon and McCartney's writing? What other British and American rock artists were pushing into new territory in 1964?
7.   What are some of the Beatles' new musical directions in 1964?
8.   What is the significance of black artists covering Lennon-McCartney songs?
9.   How did the Beatles' serious social consciousness first manifest itself in 1964?
10.   Name a Beatles song that has a powerful introduction. What factors contribute to this?
11.   How is the *phrase rhythm* of the verses of "Every Little Thing" organized? (▶ Phrase rhythm is defined in Video 1.2.)
12.   Can you hear the "Hard Day's Night" chord (♭VII9/5) in the introduction of "I Don't Want to Spoil the Party"? Can you hear it borrowed by Bruce Springsteen midway through his "Born to Run"? Where in "Spoil" or "Eight Days a Week" does II♯ move to IV, an idea introduced in "She Loves You"?
13.   Is the middle section of "Can't Buy Me Love" best considered a bridge or a chorus? The middle section of "Eight Days a Week"? Defend your decision.

FURTHER READING

Babiuk, Andy. *Beatles Gear: All the Fab Four's Instruments, From Stage to Studio*, rev. ed. San Francisco: Backbeat, 2015.

Bangs, Lester, and Greil Marcus, eds. *Psychotic Reactions and Carburetor Dung*. New York: Alfred A. Knopf, 1988.

Braun, Michael. *Love Me Do: The Beatles' Progress*. London: Penguin, 1964.

Gunderson, Chuck. *Some Fun Tonight! The Backstage Story of How the Beatles Rocked America: The Historic Tours of 1964–1966*. San Diego: Gunderson Media, 2014.

Kane, Larry. *Ticket to Ride: Inside The Beatles' 1964 and 1965 Tours That Changed the World*. Philadelphia: Running Press, 2003.

Kirchherr, Astrid, and Max Scheller. *Yesterday: The Beatles Once Upon a Time*. New York: Vendome, 2007.

Lennon, John. *The Writings of John Lennon: In His Own Write / A Spaniard in the Works*. New York: Simon & Schuster, 1981.

Marsh, Dave. *The Beatles' Second Album: Rock of Ages*. Emmaus, PA: Rodale, 2007.

Melly, George. *Revolt into Style: The Pop Arts in Britain*. London: Faber & Faber, 2013.

Meltzer, Richard. *The Aesthetics of Rock*. New York: Da Capo, 1988.

Sarris, Andrew. "Bravo Beatles!" *Village Voice*, August 27, 1964. Reprinted in June Skinner Sawyers, ed., *Read the Beatles* (New York: Penguin, 2006).

Spizer, Bruce. *The Beatles Are Coming: The Birth of Beatlemania in America*. New Orleans: 498 Productions, 2003.

Sussman, Al. *Changin' Times: November 22, 1963–March 1, 1964—101 Days That Shaped a Generation*. Chicago: Parading Press, 2013.

CHAPTER 5

REPEAT WITH A TWIST (1965)

Young gods of teens the world over, the Beatles seemed outwardly to continue to toy with rock style as though it were a plaything, and fame a distraction. As late as 1963, rock 'n' roll had been pronounced dead before the Beatles performed an emergency rescue; now they symbolized its future. But their career quickly underscored the outmoded market pressures that kept them touring and recording at a breakneck pace, as if any lull might doom their fortune. If conquering America in early 1964 gave Beatlemania an adoring global audience, they solidified their group persona with an all-original third album, toured relentlessly, and posted a somewhat fatigued fourth LP for the holiday market. Now, in 1965's third year of Beatlemania, they confronted the liabilities of world domination: no rock act had ever been this big before, and few thought it would last. How best to sustain their popularity while pushing their music forward? As this larger question came into view, they soldiered on through a repeat cycle of 1964's pop machinery: single and album, movie, tour, single and album.

Peers joined in all the chaotic adulation, and began to compete with them directly for critical acclaim and the no. 1 slot: Bob Dylan's first electric ventures (including "Like a Rolling Stone"; see Photo 5.1), the Rolling Stones' early peaks ("(Can't Get No) Satisfaction" and "Get Off of My Cloud"), several defining Motown numbers ("My Girl" from the Temptations, "Stop! In the Name of Love" from the Supremes, and "I Can't Help Myself (Sugar Pie, Honey Bunch)" from

PHOTO 5.1. Bob Dylan, photographed by Daniel Kramer. *Bringing It All Back Home* LP (released in US March 22, 1965). Note the lens distortion, a possible harbinger of the *Rubber Soul* cover.

the Four Tops), exotic new sounds from the Byrds ("Mr. Tambourine Man" and "Turn! Turn! Turn!"), and continuing stiff competition from the Beach Boys ("Don't Worry Baby" and "Help Me, Rhonda"). The aesthetic challenge came from innovating within this increasingly outworn series of pop formulas while coping with complicated tour dynamics: unruly crowds, obsolete technology, and the growing awareness that theirs might not be a flash-in-the-pan career. (Everyone, the Beatles included, put stock in the premise behind the relentless press question "What are you going to do when the bubble bursts?") While the Beatles may seem they were treading water at times in 1965, just keeping up with the world's insatiable demands, a closer look shows one important twist: great strides toward the unmistakable revolution to come in 1966.

1965 Original Releases (British unless specified otherwise):
Single: "Ticket to Ride" / "Yes It Is" (rel. Apr. 9)
Single: "Help!" / "I'm Down" (rel. July 23)
LP: *Beatles VI* (rel. US, June 14)

Side 1:	Side 2:
"Kansas City" / "Hey-Hey-Hey-Hey!"	"What You're Doing"
"Eight Days a Week"	"Yes It Is"
"You Like Me Too Much"	"Dizzy Miss Lizzie"
"Bad Boy"	"Tell Me What You See"

"I Don't Want to Spoil the Party"   "Every Little Thing"
"Words of Love"

LP: *Help!* (rel. Aug. 6)

Side 1: Songs from the film *Help!*   Side 2:
"Help!"   "Act Naturally"
"The Night Before"   "It's Only Love"
"You've Got to Hide Your Love Away"   "You Like Me Too Much"
"I Need You"   "Tell Me What You See"
"Another Girl"   "I've Just Seen a Face"
"You're Going to Lose That Girl"   "Yesterday"
"Ticket to Ride"   "Dizzy Miss Lizzie"

Single: "We Can Work It Out" / "Day Tripper" (rel. Dec. 3)
LP: *Rubber Soul* (rel. Dec. 3)

Side 1:   Side 2:
"Drive My Car"   "What Goes On?"
"Norwegian Wood (This Bird Has Flown)"   "Girl"
"You Won't See Me"   "I'm Looking through You"
"Nowhere Man"   "In My Life"
"Think for Yourself"   "Wait"
"The Word"   "If I Needed Someone"
"Michelle"   "Run for Your Life"

THE BEATLES AND THE CHANGING GLOBAL CULTURE OF 1965

The career growth outlined in this chapter collides with agonizing cultural upheavals. Literary critic David Wyatt notes how 1964's Civil Rights Act and 1965's Voting Rights Act led to new expectations for an end to American segregation. Five days after Congress passed that second watershed law in August 1965, the Watts neighborhood of Los Angeles erupted with violence, killing thirty-four and causing millions of dollars in property damage. This followed smaller riots in Harlem and Philadelphia the previous summer. Over the next several years, these uprisings grew in size and ferocity in many US cities. A frightening new question came into view: "How is it that as things became truly better, they also became so dramatically worse?" Wyatt asks (2014, 120). In practical terms, American racism was too deeply engrained for mere laws to apply a quick fix. The civil rights movement that had earned significant moral victories with nonviolent marches in the South was now faced with violent counter-reactions in the North, as cities like Chicago, Detroit, Washington, DC, and Newark all saw protests around entrenched unemployment, poverty, and police brutality. In February, Malcolm X, a black rival to Martin Luther King who championed equality "by any means necessary" including defensive violence, fell publicly to bullets prior to a New York City speech, portending further violence yet to come.

Standard Hollywood fare clung to Broadway musicals and Tin Pan Alley formulas, as if youth culture and racial divides didn't exist: the Academy Awards honored *My Fair Lady* as best picture and Rex Harrison as best actor. The spring of 1965 brought *The Sound of Music*, a Rodgers and Hammerstein musical starring the virginal Julie Andrews, with an all-white cast and a sentimental Tin Pan Alley score that never so much as glanced at rock (never mind sex). The following year, it won the Oscar for Best Picture. While the Beatles won their first Grammy, for Best Performance by a Vocal Group ("A Hard Day's Night"), jazz titan Louis Armstrong's overtly sentimental "Hello, Dolly" took home Song of the Year. On television, the western series *Bonanza* entered its eighth season, and other TV hits included *The Man from U.N.C.L.E.* and *The Munsters*. When mainstream culture deigned to acknowledge the Beatles, it came through patronizing references in feature cartoons like Disney's *The Jungle Book*. In September 1965, a new character appeared on ABC-TV's prime-time cartoon series *The Flintstones*: Eppy Brainstone (who would have been recognized by young and old alike as a topical reference to the Beatles' manager); the same month also saw the premiere of *The Beatles*, an animated ABC Saturday-morning series, for which thirty-nine episodes—each based on a single song—would be produced through 1967. Mainstream TV had only begun to fully exploit the Beatles' popularity, co-opting it for bread-and-circus pabulum to mute its antiestablishment thrust.

That spring of 1965, President Lyndon Johnson sent the first American ground troops to Vietnam; previously, Americans had served there for four years in largely noncombat advisory roles, although pilots did fly defoliating missions. US bombing of Laos began in 1964 and then of North Vietnam in 1965 and Cambodia in 1969. American forces in Vietnam doubled from 250,000 in April 1966 to 500,000 that December. This escalation inspired the Students for a Democratic Society (SDS) to sponsor its first teach-in against the war on March 24, 1965, and huge Washington antiwar rallies in April and November that unexpectedly drew over twenty-five thousand people. This university-student organization, formed in 1962 with a call for more "participatory democracy" in its Port Huron Statement (reprinted in Hayden 2005), grew steadily from the same idealistic youths who had participated in civil rights leader Martin Luther King's marches and Freedom Rides of 1963. In addition to community organizing, the SDS made the antiwar effort a centerpiece of its activities. Many of these same students listened closely to the ideas blossoming on Beatles records and experienced a profound synergy with the band: a real-time coming-of-age saga that paralleled their own young adulthood and emerging political consciousness within a world of self-righteous, often sexist, racist, and homophobic adults. John Lennon had already made explicit his distaste for the Vietnam War privately, but not yet publicly, to reporters when Congress passed the Gulf of Tonkin Resolution in August 1964. The Beatles would flout their management's strict restrictions on antiwar speech in 1966, and Lennon in particular would exhibit ever stronger political stances for world peace in 1968 and beyond.

So a gap opened up between the Beatles in their duplicative 1965 schedule and a globe that seemed to turn on a new axis. A "youth culture" took root around shared antiwar values, an end to racial segregation, and more flexible sexual mores afforded by the popularity of the birth control pill (which hit the market in 1960). Even as early as 1965, this open argument of youths with their parents led to a "generation gap," where college students proclaimed "Don't trust anyone over thirty" to announce their solidarity. "Every American home has its Berlin wall," wrote media critic Marshall McLuhan (2001, 101). This generational conflict continued to ripple outward into issues such as the military draft, religion, marijuana, sexual politics, and ultimately feminism and environmental stewardship by the early 1970s. Rock music caught and reflected these antiestablishment values back to its listeners, creating an insubordinate subcultural counterweight to traditional mores and timeworn forms of entertainment.

Before fans could see the new Beatles film, *Help!*, or hear the rest of the soundtrack album, Buckingham Palace announced on June 11 that the Beatles would be given its highest cultural award, the MBE (Member of the British Empire) later in October. This meant they would tour to support their second film and soundtrack as honored subjects who had brought so much wealth into the British economy that the establishment felt obliged to acknowledge their position. If the 1950s had seen a postwar economic boom in America, Swinging London of the 1960s fed off the success of Beatles recordings.

The queen conferred the Beatles' MBE medals on October 28, and news reports flashed around the world that the group had accepted royalty's recognition, causing many infuriated previous recipients to renounce their awards now that long-haired pop stars had suddenly "cheapened" them. Rumors swirled for years that the Beatles had snuck off to smoke a joint in the palace bathroom, an event they would later deny in *Anthology*. But the royal event showed that (as with Lennon's "jewelry" remark for the November 1963 Queen Mother's audience) they straddled a line between rock's subversive subculture—universally acknowledged as the youth's vanguard—and the establishment's table, their invitation to dine coming in response to flooding British coffers.

Partly due to this MBE, Beatles scholars view 1965 as transitional in ways both incremental and dramatic. The material from this season made earlier work sound faintly nostalgic, as if created by a much younger group. The *Help!* film reworked *A Hard Day's Night's* nonchalance into buffoonery (and soon inspired ABC-TV's copycat sitcom, *The Monkees*, part of Fall 1966's prime-time lineup). Patterns set in 1964 progressed in growth to monumental proportions, as in an audience of 65,000 strong at Shea Stadium in New York on August 15, 1965, where crowd noise overwhelmed the most powerful amplifiers then available. The TV film made from this concert, where the Beatles seem drunk on the masses' ear-splitting pitch, barreling through "I'm Down" on waves of laughter, captures a peak Beatlemania moment. Although they would repeat a Shea appearance in 1966, by 1965 it was already clear to many that this level of idolization joined the Beatles to larger forces—the very idea of rock music as a rejuvenating and hegemonic channel of youth's values. A key to the Beatles' protean imagination lies in how they kept ascending new summits only to redefine them as springboards, not endpoints.

Where 1964's material seemed to both renovate and challenge existing forms, everything that came after pointed toward a new future; the band's 1965 content cried out for new formats, new contexts, and new technologies. This all remained tantalizingly out of reach, for the moment: nobody could predict what lay ahead, except for promise. Only in retrospect do future developments come into focus: the first seeds of heavy metal (spawned by the Kinks), raga rock, and even progressive rock took root in 1965 Beatles. New directions had been charted, and many musicians, managers, promoters, broadcasters, and journalists; studio producers and engineers; manufacturers of guitars, amps, and effects; cultural icons and commentators alike—all picked up the Beatles' musical hints and ran with them in the new age that followed.

If the underlying structure of the Beatles' 1965 calendar proceeded unchanged from the year before, great strides in compositional craft, unique instrumentations, and non-rock styles also deserve recognition. Lennon-McCartney lyrics gained new self-awareness: "Help!" particularly peels back its film's superficial James Bond parody to uncover new depths of personal insecurity; where the movie exaggerates the mop-top image, the soundtrack everywhere belies it.[1] Thus, a curious

---

1. That season's James Bond series (starring Sean Connery) followed 1964's *Goldfinger* with *Thunderball*. *Help!* was also a progenitor of taste in the *Batman* television series.

ironic distance opens between the wacky film spoof and its sometimes sardonic soundtrack. Some general points about the album will be preceded by a detailed look at how instrumental color combines with aspects of melody, harmony, rhythm, and form in the LP's lead single.

"Ticket to Ride"

Recorded February 15, 1965, for *Help!*

—the Beatles advance with a new command of simple yet highly contrasting electric guitar stylings that points directly to the creation of hard rock as surely as the song's details of rhythm and texture do in emphasizing an imposing formal structure. Discussion of pitch, especially chord choices, gets somewhat technical in appreciation of the new year's complexities.

From the opening moments of their first recording of the new year, "Ticket to Ride," electric guitars gain a new authority; Harrison's ringing twelve-string launches the song with a powerful line, but the track also features subtle timbral differences and rhythmic vitality from a newly intricate sort of ensemble, partly owing to advantages offered in studio procedures (moving the guitars to their own tape track, thus unlocking them from bass and drums; and overdubbing) unavailable in live performance. The shifts of coloring stem from three new guitars—matching Fender Stratocasters played by both John and George and an Epiphone Casino played by Paul—and a new pedal effect used by George. Ringo's drumming and tambourine playing combine for tension and release as transforming as that created in the retransitions of "From Me to You" and "I Want to Hold Your Hand," but in a quieter, more introspective way.

"Ticket" leads off with a bright melodic repeated riff from George's electric twelve-string. It's mostly a syncopated arpeggiation of the tonic triad, with one important exception: a dissonant ninth on an offbeat (B against the tonic root, A, articulated on the second half of beat 3) stubbornly pulls away from the first scale degree and leaps up to the chord's fifth, repeating the riff without a direct resolution of the non-triadic tone, to sneering effect. (The B neither returns immediately to stable root A nor passes to chordal third, C♯.) The ninth escapes the tonic triad, an appropriate emblem of the woman who jilts the singer, leaving him to lament his ex's newfound freedom. After a tom-tom flurry reminiscent of the "She Loves You" opening, John and Paul enter (0:03) with a growling Strat that doubles the bass on droning chord roots. Although the two repeat a long-unchanging pitch (tonic A supporting the I chord for two bars and then six more once John's vocal begins, finally moving to B for ii at 0:18 and to E for V, 0:21), John and Paul syncopate their attacks by following each strong downbeat with an accent on the second half of the second beat, and repeating this pattern through the entire verse.[2] Through the

---

2. There are two possible models for the syncopated drone: it's conceivable that when Lennon acquired the Stratocaster, he thought back to prior uses by others—principally Hank Marvin and Buddy Holly—whom he revered in his formative

six bars of tonic, no one plays a chord—just a drone that also colors the *Help!* outtake "If You've Got Troubles," pointing the way to unchanging drones throughout much of *Revolver*, culminating in the mystical bass and tamboura of "Tomorrow Never Knows." The full texture of the "Ticket" verse's ostinato—everything played in the recording of the basic track plus an overdubbed tambourine—is represented in Table 5.1, with x's marking the articulations on every half beat in the two guitars, bass, and drums (the twelve-string's escape tone, B, is marked "(esc)"):

TABLE 5.1. Components of the "Ticket to Ride" ostinato.

beat:	1	+	2	+	3	+	4	+
12-string	x		x	x		(esc)		x
Stratocaster	x			x				
bass	x			x				
rack tom								xx
snare			x			xx		
bass drum	x			x	x			
tambourine hit			x				x	

The Beatles' embrace of non-Western sounds normally gets traced to the late-1965 use of sitar, but Paul returned from a ten-day holiday in Tunisia on February 14 and, in recording "Ticket to Ride" the next day, asked Ringo to emulate an Arabian drum pattern he'd heard there.[3] This syncopated part is displayed in three strata, one line per drum, in the table's illustration of the ostinato; x's indicate hits on the various skins, with "xx" showing the flams that accent off beats through the second half of every bar.[4] (⊙ The flam is demonstrated in Video 3.1.) Note how the drums' composite rhythm is fully matched by George's Rickenbacker part—suggesting that if Ringo were following Paul's direction for rhythm, George must have created his signature line around the drumming. (Is this how the twelve-string/drums riff of "What You're Doing" had been put together a few months earlier?) Thus, the "Ticket" ostinato represents a subtle mix of blending and contrast, John and Paul paired against a united Ringo and George.

guitar-learning years. In the Shadows' big hit covered by the proto-Beatles, "Move It," Marvin plays exactly this open-string tonic drone in the "Ticket" rhythm. Another possible model is in the same guitar part featured in the major summer 1964 hit, the Beach Boys' "Don't Worry Baby" (which may also be heard as lending a melodic sequence to Lennon's much later "(Just Like) Starting Over").

3. In a February 2014 conversation with Walter Everett, London-scene expert Gordon Thompson pointed out that in his attendance at London's music clubs, McCartney could also have heard Davy Graham playing North African–influenced music—as in his "Maajun (A Taste of Tangier)"—in the second half of 1964.

4. In a March 2015 conversation with Walter Everett, North African music expert Richard Jankowsky said that Ringo's composite pattern is much like a slowed-down version of the multi-drum Tunisian folk rhythm called Bū Nawwāra.

The verse's refrain at 0:23 (repeating the song title) itself opens with a harmonic escape, a deceptive vi (following the previous ii–V) prolonged through two different chords that underline the word "ride": IV7 and ♭VIIM7. The first of these (at 0:25) sets up a bluesy cross-relation between the major scale's third scale degree, 3 (fifth of the vi chord), and the minor pentatonic's ♭3 (seventh of IV7), a favorite contrast of Lennon's as heard in "From Me to You" (1963), "Glass Onion" (1968), and "Cold Turkey" (1969). Tension peaks when vi returns to V at 0:32, at which point John sings a blue ♭7 against his own guitar's leading tone, 7, at the final "ride."[5] But before we get there, the song's newly invented chord, the ♭VIIM7 (strummed at 0:28), takes the ride to such an unexpected destination, the always-moving rhythm stops dead with a cymbal crash for John's "ri-hi-hide" vocal melisma on three pitches that are not part of the triad, scale degrees 6–5–3 over the ♭VII chord (spelled ♭7–2–4).[6] But just as he had added overdubbed color to the first verse's turnaround in "If I Fell," George superimposes another version of the ♭VIIM7 "Ticket" chord on his own Stratocaster, in a higher hand position whose voicing places the second scale degree on top, a recollection of the ostinato's non-resolving ninth, with a stunning, shimmering new pedal effect. The volume-tone control pedal (which George had first heard as used by Liverpool's Colin Manley in the Remo Four's mid-1963 B-side "On the Horizon"), removes a sound's attack and decay and creates a silvery tone like that of a bowed violin; it is also featured melodically throughout "Yes It Is" and "I Need You," both recorded along with "Ticket" on February 15–16. In this one chord, the confusing clashes of dissonant scale degrees over a chromatic root, the stop-time rhythmic interruption, and the otherworldly guitar timbre combine to show just how far the singer is thrown off his moorings by his loss.

An appreciation of "Ticket" is not complete without reference to two other important guitar effects, plus Ringo's own superimposition, all boosting the overall ensemble. John contributes one factor in the basic track, in the retransition from bridges to returning verses. Here (at 1:25–1:26), he chugs away with repeated downstrokes on the Strat's tense V chord, but without thirds, recreating the power chords with which he had built the retransition on V in "I Want to Hold Your Hand" sixteen months earlier. Ray Davies of the Kinks and Pete Townshend of the Who greatly amplify power chords in songs like "You Really Got Me" (1964) and "My Generation" (1965), respectively, but in "Ticket," Lennon's sonority resounds more subtly, covered by more attention-grabbing parts, just as in the retransition's climax in "Day Tripper," recorded eight months later.

5. This local peak associates the "girl" of 0:15 with the singer's painful loss at 0:31; at both points, John shouts the high blue ♭3 against a triad to which it does not belong. This contrasts strongly against the low fifth scale degree that John sings on "sad" at 0:09, a reminiscence of "I'm a Loser." Register as well as scale membership help differentiate the singer from his ex.

6. The same unusual chord, ♭VIIM7 over a bass scale degree 4, is heard at a stop-time moment just before the title refrain in Smokey Robinson and the Miracles' "Tears of a Clown" (1967).

At this point in the "Ticket" retransition, a highly charged overdub grabs our attention: Paul injects a note-bending minor-pentatonic blues lick from his new Epiphone Casino, a hot guitar often verging on feedback that he'd heard played in London's blues clubs. (This so impressed John and George that they order two matching Casinos; John's becomes his favorite electric for later work.) At this point, Ringo and George drop out while John's rock-hard open fifths contrast Paul's molten melody with impossible flash. Although Ringo does not play for most of this key passage, his crash cymbal lingers over John's and Paul's entrances, and the song's form returns at 1:25 with his alarming overdubbed tambourine rattle and face-slapping rapid-fire subdivisions into eight snare hits. (Enunciating structure, Ringo hits the tambourine on backbeats through the verse, and then shakes it loosely, four to the beat, in the bridge.) The climactic orgy of guitars and drums erupts as shown in Table 5.2.

TABLE 5.2. Components of the "Ticket to Ride" retransition.

1:23	1:24	1:25	1:26	1:27
RS cymbal crash!			RS tambourine rattle	. . . .
				RS snare roll!
				RS drums ostinato
	PM bluesy Casino lead	. . . .		. . . .
		JL Strat power chords	. . . .	JL drone w bass. GH 12-string riff.

With "Ticket," the Beatles played hard rock months before the Stones created "(I Can't Get No) Satisfaction." These intertwining elements forge a key step in the birth of rock out of rock 'n' roll.

CUE	SECTION	HARMONY	DETAIL
0:00	Introductory tattoo	I	GH 12-string gtr ostinato
0:07	Verse 1: antecedent	I–ii–V	
0:23	Verse 1: refrain	vi–IV7–vi–♭VIIM7–vi–V–I	
0:34	Tattoo	I	GH 12-string gtr ostinato
0:37	Verse 2		
1:05	Tattoo	I	GH 12-string gtr ostinato
1:08	Bridge	IV7–V–IV7–V	
1:22	Retransition		PM Casino / JL power chords
1:26	Verse 1		
1:53	Tattoo	I	GH 12-string gtr ostinato
1:57	Bridge		
2:11	Retransition		
2:15	Verse 2		
2:43	Tattoo into Coda	I	

HELP!

The Beatles add keyboards to their toolkit for early 1965 recordings: Paul plays an electric piano, the Hohner Pianet, for a blues progression in "The Night Before" and for an emulation of mariachi trumpets in "Tell Me What You See" (which also features more authentically Latin guiro and claves). Not to be outdone, John copies the mannerisms of Jerry Lee Lewis in sliding his elbow all over a Vox Continental organ in the raucous "I'm Down." Along with the Beatles' own fresh instrumental colors, outside session players made first appearances in these months: the Dylanesque "You've Got to Hide Your Love Away" would be capped off by two flutes in octaves for a bittersweet acoustic finish that counter Dylan's unruly harmonica, and "Yesterday" features a classical string quartet shadowing McCartney's gentle acoustic guitar. Previous rock 'n' roll tracks had been graced with strings, notably in Atlantic studios for the Drifters and Ben E. King ("Stand by Me," 1961), but George Martin's "Yesterday" quartet arrangement doubles the voice leading of the composer's guitar parts while adding pictorial ideas. Simply having McCartney solo with an acoustic guitar in front of a classical string quartet commanded attention and gave the number more European than "folkie" overtones. It also showed the Beatles' mutability, a willingness to bend their ensemble dynamics to suit the material, even if that meant spotlighting McCartney in a "solo" turn with a sharply unexpected style.

In parallel, the group's exploration of tonal variety reached new heights in "Yesterday," which opens with a thirdless chord and, before the listener can grasp tonic securely, moves in its second chord down a half-step for a rare minor triad built on the seventh scale degree (thus making scale degree #4 its fifth), to be turned around as ii of vi. Previously, as in "This Boy," "You Can't Do That," and "I Should Have Known Better," the Beatles had applied V/vi in tonicizing the submediant. In "Yesterday," McCartney extends this by one chord, moving ii/vi–V/vi–vi, thereby creating a highly sophisticated progression that seats the phrase deeply in a melancholy minor territory. Two film songs, "Another Girl" and "You're Going to Lose That Girl," modulate to the distant chromatic ♭III area for their bridges—rather than the more usual and comfortable IV of 1963 patterns—recalling a tonal structure not used since 1962 for the disquiet portrayed in "To Know Her Is to Love Her" and "Love of the Loved."

The Beatles' recording procedure adopted one important new twist. Although overdubs now featured prominently in most tracks, they were generally reserved for sweeteners: the basic-track performance would convey all fundamental instrumental parts, with the fourth track available for hand percussion and occasional guitar effects. In the new film's title song, everything we hear from lead guitar has been overdubbed. Born of a dilemma, this leads to new flexibility in recording such that Paul will come to overdub even his bass parts in 1966, allowing him to play keyboard on basic tracks. The dilemma: George could not keep a proper rhythm in the difficult stop-time riff played on his Gretsch Tennessean, especially while joining in singing "won't you please, please help me." Off-mike studio chat taped for the first forty seconds of take 4 reveals this discussion: George doesn't want to play the riff during the vocal performance; Paul suggests subdividing the beat, tapping quickly so George can properly place the notes, and John says he'll keep time by thumping the backbeat on his acoustic twelve-string as a guide (such thumping at 2:08 will carefully be muted out of mono, but not stereo, mixes). Ultimately, George records his Gretsch on its own in a second-generation overdub. For *Revolver*, more than one track would begin life similarly with just two Beatles at a time recording the basic track, then superimposing even elemental rhythm parts afterward.

The Beatles' burgeoning productivity knew no boundaries and was held to no constraints. Their identity became synonymous with expansive creativity. Still, tried-and-true traditions hold the day in most outward measures through mid-1965: heteronormative boy-girl topics govern song situations, and dialogue with musical conventions abounds. Formal structures maintain verse-chorus-bridge paradigms; styles continue to draw from generic situations. Case in point: "You're Going to Lose That Girl" draws from the advice-song tradition that made "She Loves You" possible, although with the twist that the singer now delivers a warning, not support. In the song's *Help!* performance, we can see Paul wagging his finger at 1:50 ("She's gonna change her mind"). Just as he borrows Little Richard's back-bending body language for "Long Tall Sally," here Paul refers to girl-group choreography. If you watch a televised performance by the Supremes of "Back in My Arms Again," for instance (as performed on *Hullabaloo* on May 11, 1965), you'll see a typical example—Mary Wilson wagging her index finger at Diana Ross as she sings, "How can Mary tell me what to do?" (It's a two-way street of style appropriation: before and after every chorus, Flo Ballard and Mary also punctuate this song with examples of a falsetto "woo" stolen from the early Beatles.)[7] These traditions tend to mask *Help!*'s advances, incremental as they are. Photo 5.2 shows the album cover.

PHOTO 5.2. The Beatles, photographed by Robert Freeman. *Help!* LP (released in UK August 6, 1965).

7. Jacqueline Warwick (2001, 165) discusses "You're Going to Lose That Girl" alongside the Motown girl-group tradition of advice songs, a topic developed further in Warwick 2007.

"The Night Before"

Recorded February 17, 1965, and "Another Girl" (February 16) for _Help!_

> —_a pair of film songs examine two sides of romantic trouble, their expression lying chiefly in matters of unusual chromatic chord relationships, one of which, the double-plagal succession, will become a Beatles staple._

Producing their second film put the Beatles in a scheduling vise that squeezed material from them sideways when most aesthetic impulses moved them forward. To keep things jumping, Lennon and McCartney, both together and separately, experimented with remote harmonic contrasts that previously might have seemed out of reach.

The suspicious narrator of "The Night Before" frets about a romantic triangle; he fears his new lover may be cheating on him. Electric piano colors the double-plagal I→VII–IV–V sequence in verses, before the bridge recaptures the harmony-softening formula of "From Me to You" and "I Want to Hold Your Hand" by banking off the minor dominant, v (A minor), at 0:56, which acts like ii of IV at 0:59, proceeding to V of IV and resolving into IV itself, where the singer revels in softer memories. (The double-plagal progression, where ♭VII is to IV as IV is to I, was a trope in early 1965, coming from the Four Tops' "Baby I Need Your Loving" into Martha and the Vandellas' "Nowhere to Run" and the Who's "I Can't Explain" while McCartney was writing it into many songs in _Help!_ and later work.) That ♭VII modification only becomes more important as rock's vernacular expands; Pete Townshend builds a cathedral to this progression in _Tommy_.) It uncoils back into the verse on the climactic word "cry" (moving through vi minor, II7, and a retransitional V7 back to tonic at 1:02–1:06), balancing fear of deceit against intense pleasure. "The Night Before" only flirts with poetry, however, and lacks the intensity of "If I Fell" or "I'll Be Back," which both treat the similar themes of balancing hope against doubt. But what's medium-tier on a Beatles album would be top-tier anywhere else. So McCartney's vocal assumes focus: it's a marvel of control and spontaneity, color and soul the way "Hey Jude" and "Oh! Darling" would be in coming years. When McCartney builds to the bridge's retransitional word "cry" at 1:06 and again at 2:02, he releases in one rising arpeggiation to the song's vocal apex all the coiled anticipation he'd invested in building up to it. You get the feeling he knows he deserves better material, and he's just waiting for the medium (the scripts, the fame, the touring) to catch up. It points in all the right directions without going very far.

"Another Girl" flips the narrative for romantic worry from the cheater, not the cheated. Here, McCartney's verses take root in a typical bluesy melody with a stop-time break at stanza's end for the boastful: "For I have got . . . _another girl_." (It could count as a riposte, or precursor, to triangles like "She Loves You," "Not a Second Time," or Lennon's "You're Going to Lose That Girl.") On the second break, the singer pivots the entire number onto a different harmonic track, shifting gears sideways (from I up to ♭III at 0:49 and 1:21). The bridge visits a brief hope of the pleasures this new romance surely brings and winds back down into the home key with a single ingenious step (through ♭III's purported major mediant resolving back to I more sensibly, through a reassuring V7 function at both 0:56 and 1:28. The harmonic reassurance underlines the sentiment, "She will always be my friend," not fickle as the singer is himself.) The narrator twists an emotional knife, telling one lover he's found another, but we already knew with "I'll Follow the Sun" that Paul was right at home with the subject of a disloyal protagonist. The harmonic plan mirrors the romantic duplicity.

Both songs glide on subtle, self-satirical attitudes, as if admitting: these are silly little numbers, but nothing's too silly for this film, a Bond satire. Bobbing heads to fill space might blunt the edges, but the harmonic patterns remain vivid—they can't rely on bluesy passages without inserting a couple of wayward bridges (that of "The Night Before" beginning with a IV tonicized just the way it was done in "From Me to You" and "I Want to Hold Your Hand"). These double harmonic plans will come into play in more sophisticated form in "Here, There and Everywhere," "Good Day Sunshine," "Doctor Robert," and "Penny Lane."

"The Night Before"

CUE	SECTION	HARMONY	DETAIL
0:00	Intro	I↠III–IV7–V7	
0:11	Verse 1: S, R	I↠VII–IV–V (repeated)	PM dbl-tracked lead
0:22	Verse 1: D, C	vi–ii°6–vi–ii°6–I–IV7–I	
0:32	Turnaround	♭III–IV	
0:34	Verse 2: SRDC		
0:56	Bridge	(ii–V7–I of) IV–vi–II7–V7	maracas
1:07	Verse 1: SRDC		
1:29	Turnaround		
1:30	Guitar solo	based on Verse: S-R	GH dbls gtr part in octaves
1:41	Verse 2: D, C		Vocals return
1:52	Bridge		
2:04	Verse 2: SRDC		
2:25	Tag ending	I↠III–I	Last line repeated

"Another Girl"

CUE	SECTION	HARMONY	DETAIL
0:00	Introductory motto	I7–IV7–I7–IV7	Chorus
0:06	Verse 1: phrase 1	I↠VII–I–IV7	4 bars
0:12	Verse 1: phrase 2	I↠VII–I–IV7–V7	expanded to 8 bars
0:22	Chorus (motto)	I7–IV7–I7–IV7	
0:28	Verse 2		
0:43	Chorus (motto)	I7–IV7–I7–IV7	
0:49	Bridge 1	(I–V7–I–V7–I of) ♭III–V7–I–V7	expansion of motto
1:00	Verse 3		

CUE	SECTION	HARMONY	DETAIL
1:16	Chorus (motto)		
1:21	Bridge 2		
1:33	Verse 3		
1:49	Chorus into Coda	I7–IV7–I7–IV7–I7	McCartney's guitar

"Yesterday"

Recorded June 14 and 17, 1965, for *Help!*

—perhaps the song of which Paul McCartney is proudest, "Yesterday" plumbs new emotional depths with an introspective text and an intimate melody a bit incongruous for a rock band. So McCartney and Martin call on a string quartet for the first time.

It came into the world through Paul McCartney's dream and early on bore the working title "Scrambled Eggs" as the mysteriously archetypal melody pursued the perfect lyric. In many spheres, it became the group's biggest song, ironically the one most identified with the Lennon-McCartney partnership, and remains a substantial piece of their catalog's publishing fortune, with new singers reframing the song annually in tribute.

But "Yesterday" occupies a curious position in the Beatles' catalog as a Tin Pan Alley standard from within the stylistic conqueror's camp. (Imagine Jerry Lee Lewis writing a song like Patti Page's 1953 hit "How Much Is That Doggie in the Window?") The Beatles' "Yesterday" has the unmistakable allure of a classic: a handsomely sorrowful melody gracing a universal heartbreak theme, desire tinged with regret framed with vocal yearning and a classy, formal set of strings.

So why do many rock critics consider this song a Beatles lemon? For starters, it's so closely identified with McCartney's solo performance, without any other band members supporting, that he likes to claim he wrote it all by himself. In 2001, McCartney told *Reader's Digest* of his foiled desire to reverse the "Lennon-McCartney" copyright credit:

But at the time of the *Anthology*, I was going through a bit of a tough period with Linda [who would die of cancer in 1998], and the song "Yesterday" was in the *Anthology*. Instead of Lennon/McCartney, someone proposed putting in the full names, so that all the songs would be by John Lennon and Paul McCartney. So with "Yesterday," with that particular one, I thought, "Wouldn't it be nice after all these years . . . if we just changed it and put "Yesterday" by Paul McCartney and John Lennon?

And I know John always said he had nothing to do with that song so I figured that would be okay. In fact, a pianist used to play it whenever he came into a certain restaurant: "Da, da, da" [hums the first few chords [*sic*] of "Yesterday"] and he'd go, "Oh no! It's not even mine." So, you know, I thought John would be okay with that.

But what happened is we got into a little sticky moment 'cause I rang Yoko and said, "Just on this one occasion could I have this as a favor? I'm not going through a great time in my life and I'd like it." And she first said, "Yeah," but then she rang back and said, "No." (Available online at http://www.macca-central.com/macca-archives/readersdigest/Paul_McCartney_interview.pdf)

However, in a 1967 interview for the *BBC Light Programme* about winning the 1966 Ivor Novello Award, McCartney claims Lennon came up with the title "Yesterday." A lot of Beatles scholarship leaves their individual memories in tatters, and history may never resolve this issue (Winn 2003, 103).

Producer George Martin suggested the track's setting by arranging a string quartet to accompany McCartney's acoustic guitar. By this point, during the *Help!* recording sessions, the band's ideas about instrumentation grew expansive; the nylon-stringed flamenco guitar (which signals formal taste) on "And I Love Her" swelled to embrace the doubled flute part on Lennon's "You've Got to Hide Your Love Away." But no material had ever suggested a non-Beatle ensemble, a completely non-electric group of outsiders, with McCartney as the sole group member on the recording. If a string quartet proved the right choice for the material, it also put a new premium on the authority of the composer: from this point on, the constraints on their own ensemble began to fall away, beginning with how any arrangement for the studio might be reproduced onstage. (For TV appearances of this song, McCartney simply performed it alone, with studio-orchestra principals adding their parts from the wings or the pit.)

Several McCartney songs point toward this "Yesterday" breakthrough, including "When I'm Sixty-Four" (which he started writing at age sixteen), "P.S. I Love You," "Things We Said Today," and "And I Love Her." All of these embrace a historical tradition of the dewy-eyed protagonist romancing his lover, all seem to recycle Tin Pan Alley models, and all position McCartney as a tidier, more genteel ballad singer than Elvis Presley, who could also descend into pure goop ("Love Me Tender," "Are You Lonesome Tonight?"). Combined with the exclusive McCartney spotlight, it brought new force to the internal tension within the band, between Lennon, a rocker who scorned sentimentality, and McCartney, the "all-around entertainer" who enjoyed parental diplomacy as much as he did returning his date home extra late.

The track's classical air gets simultaneously derided as pretentiously inappropriate for a rock band and lauded as opening up a limitless soundworld. One thing rock critics get right about "Yesterday" plays into wider misconceptions about the band's mission: if the Beatles stand as rock's greatest group, why is their best-known song a throwback to the prudish parental style they rebelled against? And if they count among the top rock performers, why does their staple omit three members completely? The counterargument involves the band's embrace of rock's larger role in music history: they celebrated all styles, even the gushing treacle rock meant to replace, as a way of diverting anything worthwhile into the new rock streams that came to dominate music's next chapters: prog rock, reggae, rap, techno, dance mixes, and digital mash-ups. Borrowing from previous styles needn't be heretical if it animates a larger idea. And the larger idea of the *Help!* album pushed all rock forward, from guitar sounds and drum patterns to how the role of vocal harmonies ("You're Going to Lose That Girl") and folk influences ("You've Got to Hide Your Love Away") could all find summary in a Lennon-led closer like "Dizzy Miss Lizzie." A number of old rock 'n' roll standby techniques have gone by the wayside: the guitar boogie, a core part of Lennon's rhythm guitar playing through 1963, does not appear in the four and a half years between "I Want to Hold Your Hand" and "Revolution," outside of the 1964–1965 cover recordings of "Long Tall Sally," "Kansas City," "Rock and Roll Music," and "Bad Boy." Even before they recorded *Rubber Soul*, rock grew big enough to cast huge shadows on previous styles, the Beatles proved, and folded in all of history to make that argument. Precisely by declaring a lack of boundaries, they allowed themselves to take what they wished, even from what had once been enemy territory.

The "Yesterday" recording session has descended into legend: on the afternoon of June 14, 1965, McCartney tracked six takes of "I've Just Seen a Face," overdubbing acoustic guitars and maracas, and then seven takes of the wildcat, irascible "I'm Down" with the full band. According to *Magic Circles* critic Devin McKinney, in "I'm Down," McCartney "nearly chokes to death trying to cough up Little Richard, who has somehow crawled in and taken over his body" (McKinney 2004, 399). After supper he came back for just two takes of "Yesterday" and sang like a eunuch.

CUE	SECTION	HARMONY	DETAIL
0:00	Introduction		Detuned acoustic guitar
0:05	Verse 1	I–(ii–V7 of) vi, IVM7–V7–I, vi7–II7–IV–I	McCartney lead, solo
0:22	Verse 2		strings enter
0:39	Bridge 1	(V7/4–3 of) vi–IV–ii7–V7–I	(repeat, with new melodic goal)
0:59	Verse 3		
1:17	Bridge 2		
1:37	Verse 4		high first-violin pedal
1:54	Coda	repeat final line	PM humming

THE BEATLES AS LIVE PERFORMERS

As their success continued, the Beatles used their increasing leverage to negotiate less touring, more vacation, and more time for reflection. Their schedule echoed 1964's: days passed with a series of concerts; the recording of a new single ("Ticket to Ride" / "Yes It Is") and film songs (for *Help!*) in February; that film's shooting and the completion of its companion LP in June; summer concert dates in Europe, the United Kingdom, the Far East, and North America; the recording of a year-end single ("We Can Work It Out" / "Day Tripper") and LP (*Rubber Soul*) for the Christmas market; and finishing the calendar with a series of London shows. There was, however, one profound change: a sharp reduction in music played before a live audience. With that came a diminishing degree of care taken with ensemble. Because they were inaudible in halls, the Beatles no longer worked at precision, especially with their vocals. John frequently sang incorrect words, even in television broadcasts where they could be clearly heard (watch him confuse his pronouns throughout "I Feel Fine" in the 1965 *Sullivan* show, for example). Their 1964 *Sullivan* debut held smart, crisp surprises; the 1965 farewell performance was sloppy to the point of disrespect for their art. Seen another way, despite the great care that went into their composing and recording and the behind-the-scenes difficulties of touring the world, this group consistently projected a fun-loving and self-effacing insouciance.

The number of performing days per year peaked at 305 in 1962, dropped to 248 in 1963, to 129 in 1964, to only 46 in 1965, and then to just 22 in 1966, the year of their final group concerts (excepting one last unannounced, impromptu mini-concert offered from the rooftop of their London offices in January 1969). More days of 1965 (twenty-six) would be spent in the recording studio than in the previous year (sixteen), as more leisure time (including two weeks at the beginning of June and a six-week break in September–October) opened up for composition, a trend that continued and expanded throughout 1966–1969. And the term "vacation" remained fluid: John, Paul, and now George discovered new creative worlds through writing, arranging, and recording over and above performing. Through all of these considerations, the Beatles began to redefine the nature of pop songs and rock recording, strongly announced by the year's second LP, *Rubber Soul* (see Photo 5.3).

PHOTO 5.3. The Beatles in Autumn 1965, photographed by Robert Freeman. *Rubber Soul* LP (released in US December 6, 1965). The cover differs only slightly from that of *Beatles for Sale*, but in the intervening year the Beatles learned how to use distortion as a tool.

"We Can Work It Out"

Recorded October 20 and 29, 1965, for double A-side with "Day Tripper"

—posing an unresolved pairing of McCartney's fundamental optimism in dealing with a frustrating interpersonal conflict, as against Lennon's exploration of its negative side.

The Beatles' middle period (1965–1967) sees the Lennon-McCartney collaboration detach into distinct parts before veering off in separate directions, and certain songs function like diagrams: "We Can Work It Out" poses as a romantic argument that doubles as a debate between two songwriters. Since the two voices happen to be McCartney's (verses) and Lennon's (bridges), and the song's structure neatly divides into major-mode verses and minor-mode bridges, it blinks like a neon sign for a partnership with a split personality. (It thus prefigures later bipolar collaborations like "A Day in the Life" and "I've Got a Feeling.")

The number starts on an unprepared downbeat: we join the argument already in progress, with McCartney posing as the neutral moderator. At first he suggests seeing things his way and vents his frustration that he has to keep on talking until he's spent; then he suggests seeing things his *partner's* way, in which case they risk everything—the relationship might be finished. The narrator's self-centered bias trickles from every line. But, just as with the similarly ironic "I'll Follow the Sun," the music rolls along with a friendly lilt: the harmonium resembles an accordion, a wheezy old-world symbol for authenticity and homegrown music making. And his tag line, "We can work it out," repeated for emphasis, has enough ardor to win you over; the question is, since he's aiming his words directly at his lover (*your* way), do *we* the listeners believe him? Where his logic falls short, his charm has sway. So we go along: the second verse starts with what she's saying (what *we're* saying) ("You can get it wrong and still you think that it's all right"), which doubles down on his lack of faith: you think you're right, but I know you're wrong. Think of what he's saying: straighten this thing out my way or we can say goodnight: my way or the highway, toots. And again with that repeated hook: "We can work it out"—yeah, if you see it the *singer's* way.

McCartney doesn't even try to straddle a line here: he insists he's right and his lover wrong, and there's no variation to this attitude in three verses. In verse 2 his only hedge is that time will tell if he's right or wrong. But the rejoinder to that is that his partner remains *definitely* wrong; if we go your way, we fall apart. This imparts a shadow on the imaginary relationship of the song and forecasts the Lennon-McCartney publishing feud that erupts in 1969.

The challenge to Lennon's bridges (at 0:37 and 1:22) goes unstated, and it strays completely from Paul's argument: this new vantage takes a bird's-eye view to turn philosophical. Life's too short for petty disputes, so why do even the most sincere romantic relationships wrestle with pint-sized squabbles? And Lennon's tag line, his musical punctuation, uses a clichéd oompah-pah waltz gesture to ridicule the petty nature of the conflict with large triplets like those that ended "I Want to Hold Your Hand" (1:31 and 1:44). But the dissonant suspensions that precede this cadence point up the triplets' rhythmic struggle.

Only after a couple of bar-form verses (organized asymmetrically as 3 + 3 + 2 bars) whirr past do you notice that the shape of this song has to do only with the articulation of the conflict, not a resolution: any anticipation/release quotient in the music deals with contrasting song sections, not settling a dispute. In fact, we hear two narrators singing past each other, as if they don't listen to one another at all: the dual storytellers (verse and bridge) barely seem aware of each other's presence in the same song. In the bridge, McCartney sings a descant to Lennon's lead, but it's not clear whether this expresses solidarity or a simple shadow. The only "reconciliation" occurs in musical terms, when Lennon's "oompah-pah" figure returns for the closing gesture after McCartney's final title line. But does this mean Lennon "wins" the argument? Or, alternatively, does it mean that the number coheres more in musical than literal terms, and the dispute is never truly worked out? This deliberate ambiguity signals a new layer of meaning in Beatles tracks: listeners are allowed to discern their own resolution or ongoing conflict in the track, and to imagine a settling of this dispute is to imagine something less compelling, less open-ended, and less stirring.

CUE	SECTION	HARMONY	DETAIL
0:00	Verse 1: *a*	I→VII–I	McCartney
0:00	Verse 1: *a'*	I→VII–I	McCartney
0:14	Verse 1: *b* (refrain)	IV–I–IV–V7	
0:18	Verse 2: *a–a'–b*	as above	
0:36	Bridge: phrase 1	(i→VI–V7 of)	Lennon lead over 4-3 susp.
0:46	(cadence to phrase 1)	vi	Triplet figure in minor
0:50	Bridge: phrase 2	(i→VI–V7 of)	Lennon lead
0:59	(cadence to phrase 2)	vi	Triplet figure in minor
1:03	Verse 3: *a–a'–b*		McCartney
1:21	Bridge 2		Lennon lead
1:47	Verse 3		McCartney
2:05	Coda	I–IV–I	Triplets in major

"Day Tripper"

Recorded October 16, 1965, for double A-side with "We Can Work It Out"

—a twelve-bar blues run amok amidst a highly confusing chord palette, answered by a retransitional enlightenment richly textured with a counterpoint of differently

motivated instrumental and vocal parts, altogether as celebratory in its own way as "She Loves You."

For many novices, the formal structure of a song is hardly worth pursuing, but this attitude is typically based on (1) an underappreciation of the topic's relatively abstract nature and (2) the simplistic manner in which it's often considered. But form is a highly expressive device for the Beatles. As if a study for future mazelike songs like "Lucy in the Sky with Diamonds," "Happiness Is a Warm Gun," and "You Never Give Me Your Money," John Lennon uses the experience of emerging from confusion—enlightenment—as inspiration for an unexpected twist on a standard form and a masterful manipulation of retransitional anxiety, resulting in an almost incidental classic rock song that helped define a genre—incidental in that the song was a last-minute idea developed when the Beatles needed a new single, largely created on the studio floor at EMI, an early indication of the direction rock composition was to take with the imminent explosion in the number of available recording studios and the concomitant relaxations in schedule and procedure. Genre-defining in its heavy doubling of bass and guitars in an ostinato of teasing chromatic and syncopated dissonances that would inspire such proto-metal textures as would be heard within four years in Cream's "Sunshine of Your Love," Blue Cheer's "Summertime Blues," and Led Zeppelin's "Good Times Bad Times." (▶ The doubled bass line is demonstrated in Video 1.7.)

The verse's first two phrases (labeled *a* and *a1* in the accompanying chart) promise a twelve-bar blues, especially given the iconic introductory tattoo's strong emphasis on lowered third and seventh scale degrees. It's only because of the stylistic ubiquity of the twelve-bar pattern that the listener understands immediately in bar 9 that things have taken a wrong turn and lead quickly into a seemingly hopeless quagmire. Salvation, however, arrives at the end of an instrumental break that requires three Beatle guitarists, each with his own voice, as if a first foray into the world of traded solos that would grace "The End."

The verse is a *bar form* composed of three phrases, the first two following the melodic and harmonic structure of bars 1–8 of a blues, repeating identical lyrics as *a–a1* in each of the three verses. (▶ Bar form and the twelve-bar blues structure are covered in Video 1.3.) (For a variation that brings to the surface the singer's nagging frustration and intensifies his renewed exasperation, the third verse uses heightened pitch, a common technique whereby a recurring melody is raised in its last appearance: the bluesier second time through "TRIED to PLEASE her.") But instead of moving to V for the expected harmonic high point in bar 9, the Beatles sit on four equivocating bars of a major II chord. In fact, it's a II7 chord, and we soon learn that the chord palette for "Day Tripper" consists of sevenths atop major triads built on all of the first six degrees of the major scale, a most confusing collection that pays little heed to any underlying diatonic set. The major II7 of bars 9–12 (0:32–0:38) moves to IV7, but this descends to III7 before the II7–IV7 motion might be considered in light of its prior appearances in "She Loves You" or "Eight Days a Week." IV7–III7 makes sense only when the next chord, VI7, arrives, making these three sonorities work together (as ♭VI7/VI–V7/VI–I7/VI) in an unusual tonicization of the major VI area (putting IV7 into the role of what is called the German augmented sixth, a highly charged chromatic chord that had been very unusual in rock and pop music, although Lennon had previously used ♭VI7–V7 to end the bridge of "I Call Your Name"). All of this, the refrain of bars 9–16, portrays ambiguous digressions in phrase rhythm and harmony. The bar of tonicized VI7 (0:42) sidesteps to V7 (0:44) as a transposed pun on the once-withheld V7–IV7 (of the abandoned prototypical blues structure's bars 9–10). This yields a retransitional half cadence, just as the singer emerges from darkness into light. The full excursion from bar 9 lasts eight bars, the length of the first two lines put together; "It took me soooooo long to find out." Gratification had been delayed far too long; it is now understood that no such release will occur with the participation of the song's teasing object, and melismas in chromatically distant tonal centers work as ciphers for the singer's evolving frustration.

Resolution arrives only in the climactic culmination of the break's orgiastic retransition. Sitting on a dominant chord that lingers beyond the half cadence that ends verse 2, the tattoo reappears in a tense new light, transposed for the first time from E to B, a fifth higher than at the opening. All guitars have their individual roles here, most prominently Harrison on the ostinato and McCartney simply repeating the fifth-scale-degree root as a dominant pedal, at first once per beat but then faster from 1:31 onward. As a post-"Ticket to Ride" overdub, Paul picks up his Epiphone Casino to protest the oppressive environment in a wanton, bluesy solo at 1:31–1:42, beginning just as the bass revs up. For his part, Lennon begins to chug away on a rakish power chord that grows in dynamic intensity through the peak of this retransitional passage, again a "Ticket to Ride" hangover.

While tension is prolonged in the bass, it is intensified by a guitar overdub from George: a rest on every downbeat is followed by a sustained second-beat articulation of a different pitch in each bar throughout all twelve bars of the passage, rising stepwise over that twelfth from scale-degree 5 up past the octave mark and soaring another fifth to scale-degree 2. This backbeat line—climbing out of murky depths to find the unmistakable sunlight of a tense high register—is colored by Harrison's first use in months of the volume-tone control pedal, forcing a late realization of every note in the scale, each tone fading into existence.

And late realization—an understanding that fades in from obscurity to clarity—is what this passage, and the song as a whole, is all about. The final dawning of the recognition of past deceptions is expressed vocally, with the "ahhh!" of parallel triads sung by Paul, George, and John ascending the scale to V, exploding in a gradual, measured acceleration of articulations: The first "ah!" connects three full-bar chords (1:31–1:35); after a breath, the second "ah!" sustains for two bars (1:36–1:39), and then a third "AH!," the "Eureka!" moment, erupts on a single bar of V (1:40–1:41). (This entire break resembles the rave-ups from "Twist and Shout," tempered for the middle of a track.) The deception is finally uncovered. Everything once pent up begins to spill over at the return of the tonic ostinato at 1:42, but we are not presented with a full and immediate release; the resolution of tension washes over a stop-time tambourine shake before a spasmodic fill (1:44) returns the drums, rhythm guitar, and band as a whole to its senses at 1:45 so Paul may direct a newly exasperated third verse. The subject only took the singer half the way there, but he discovered his destination himself in the understanding that he had been just a plaything all along. Frustration persists beyond resignation in the lowered seventh scale degree that endures through the fadeout coda. "Day tripper, yeah."

CUE	SECTION	HARMONY	DETAIL
0:00	Introductory tattoo	I7	Bass / guitar ostinato
0:18	Verse 1: a	I7	"Got a good reason"
0:25	Verse 1: a'	IV7–I7	
0:32	Verse 1: b (Refrain)	II7–IV7–III7–VI7–V7	
0:46	Tattoo		
0:52	Verse 2		"She's a big teaser"
1:20	Break	V7	
1:31	Retransition	V7	
1:42	Tattoo	I7	
1:48	Verse 3		"Tried to please her"
2:17	Tattoo and Coda		

RUBBER SOUL

Rubber Soul offers a new paradox: largely because of John Lennon's interests, the album combines the personal with the universal. Challenged to write about his childhood, Lennon drafted "In My Life" as a series of Liverpool remembrances:

> Penny Lane is one I'm missing
> Up Church Rd to the Clock Tower
> In the Circle of the Abbey
> I have seen some happy hours.
>
> And the 5 Bus into town
> Past the tramsheds with no trams
> Past the Dutch and St Columbus
> To the Dockers Umbrella that they pulled down.[8]

8. The Picton Clock Tower stands in a traffic circle nearby the (long since defunct) Abbey Cinema along Church Road in Wavertree, within a few blocks of George Harrison's birthplace, John Lennon's first home, and the Penny Lane round-about. The Dockers' Umbrella, an overhead railway along the River Mersey that served workers both as transportation

Dissatisfied with the specificity of such references (although Paul will retain a liking for the bouquet thrown to Penny Lane and make use of it once John writes of his neighborhood orphanage, Strawberry Field), John's finished song welcomes a larger audience, ultimately reminiscing only about "places I'll remember." Lennon, again, contemplates his own particular inadequacies but offers an outsider's optimistic perspective when his faults are ascribed to an Everyman, a "Nowhere Man." The cast-a-wide-net generality of "The Word" features a particularly bold statement of social consciousness, strongly marking the Beatles as singular, not just a talented rock band.

Even while sidestepping protest songs or race-riot references, the Beatles seemed uncannily sensitive to the world's apprehensions: "Norwegian Wood (This Bird Has Flown)" told of an atmospheric rendezvous outside marriage, a taboo matter at the time, never mind one framed within a "pop" narrative. It contained a vague reference to smoking marijuana, and the background vocals to "Girl" alternated between suggestive inhalations (0:23–0:25 and 0:53–0:55) and a deliberately provocative "tit-tit-tit-tit" (1:00). "The Word" openly proclaimed a youth-movement bumper sticker as if cribbed from a campus SDS meeting, built around the antiwar faction's most cherished value—love—and keyed the psychedelic wave almost two years in advance. In a variety of cues and code references, the Beatles confirmed everybody's hunches about the emerging youth movement while stretching their imaginations and challenging their own thinking. It took particular cunning to pull off messages this subversive while still pop stars, but the Beatles had enough guile and intrigue to keep attracting new listeners. The year 1965 would have gone down as an apogee in rock culture if it weren't immediately upstaged by 1966.

With *Rubber Soul* and its attendant single, "We Can Work It Out" / "Day Tripper," the Beatles turn up the intensity on the level of the experimentation that grew throughout *Help!* Harmony turns into a Rubik's cube: the aggressive dissonances in "Drive My Car" (verse-ending vocal C, F and G over A7) and "We Can Work It Out" pronounced layered contradictions; new relationships between the bass and upper lines in "Wait" and "Michelle" take advantage of the balance between upper and lower registers for increasingly innovative and nuanced textures, particularly involving dissonance treatment. Through the influence of Motown's bassist James Jamerson and Stax's own Donald "Duck" Dunn (compare his bass line on Otis Redding's "Respect" and that of "Drive My Car"), McCartney's new Rickenbacker bass awakens to a new rhythmic independence from the drums (see especially "Michelle" and "The Word"), which later commands attention in "Rain" (1966) and ripples outward through its fully self-governing melody in "Something" (1969). This lends far greater depth to the Beatles' sound, befitting the expansion of tone and topics in their lyrics. Only in the earlier-recorded "Wait" and "Girl" does the bass guitar hide in the wallpaper.

An explosion of overdubbed guitars continues from *Help!*, particularly in doubling one or more parts with the bass (as in the "Drive My Car" and "Day Tripper" ostinatos, pointing from soul to hard rock), once (in "Think for Yourself") with a high level of distortion in his distinctive countermelody. New effects multiply, from the lascivious bottleneck slide in "Drive My Car" to the ultra-high harmonic that ends the "Nowhere Man" solo, ironically juxtaposing a flash of enlightenment against the song's complaint of ignorance. The jangle of the electric twelve-string took on a

---

from dock to dock and as shelter from the rain, closed in 1956; the city's tram service was discontinued in 1957 (Belchem 2006, 48–49, 401). The "Dutch and St Columbus" remain obscure, although Hunter Davies (2014, 132) respells this as St. Columba's Church (lying in Hunt's Cross, miles south of all Wavertree locations). A later verse refers to Calderstones Park, which lay just across Menlove Avenue from Mendips, John's home with his Aunt Mimi to 1963. A similar reference to Liverpool's docks, the "Cast Iron Shore," is memorialized in "Glass Onion" (1968).

harder, post–1964 Byrds edge in George Harrison's "If I Needed Someone," partly due to the capo that therein shortens strings to two-thirds of their open length; this game of leapfrog that pushed the Byrds to greater distortion of their own the next year in "Eight Miles High" matched in its intensity other examples already noted with the Supremes, the Beach Boys, Bob Dylan, and Booker T. and the M.G.'s (which group featured bassist Dunn). More conservative is the strong original rockabilly that opens up on George's Gretsch in "What Goes On," Ringo's solo vocal number on the LP.

Then there's George Martin's "wind-up piano": He recorded the solo to "In My Life" at half speed, in a low register, so that when replayed at proper speed, the tape sounded an octave higher with a clipped articulation that gave it the desired (yet cunningly synthetic) tonal quality of a harpsichord.[9] The rhythmic slipknot that opens "Drive My Car" and the transition points in "The Word" showcase a bedrock confidence in Ringo Starr's drumming, and the metric cross-accents of triplet quarters vividly express the end-of-bridge struggle (just after the resolution of tense 4–3 suspensions) of "We Can Work It Out." A new sort of vocal counterpoint introduced in "You Won't See Me" portends the use of voice parts representing different and even conflicting agencies in "Eleanor Rigby," "She's Leaving Home," "Getting Better," and "Happiness Is a Warm Gun," advancing far beyond the prior Motown-based call-and-response conventions in "You're Going to Lose That Girl" and "Help!" As we've seen, even formal structure becomes expressive when the twelve-bar promise of "Day Tripper" expands to unforeseen length with frustrating harmonic excursions that suggest the prolonged manner of unraveling sexual deception. By reaching back and expanding their own resources exponentially, they did not need to call on outside session musicians as was done for "You've Got to Hide Your Love Away" or "Yesterday."

More and more, McCartney's inspiration for his bass sound came from Motown and Stax. The Beatles dug deeper into R&B as something beyond a style to be imitated or obliquely referred to (as the Rolling Stones, the Animals, and the Yardbirds did) but an intricately woven part of their own language. After the example of the Stones, who recorded at Chess Studios in Chicago and RCA in Hollywood, the Beatles hoped to follow *Rubber Soul* by recording their next album in Detroit (at Motown studios, with songs reportedly commissioned from the stable's most successful composers, Eddie and Brian Holland and Lamont Dozier) or Memphis (at Stax). Although the location ultimately did not move away from London's familiar EMI den, the work of 1965–1966 churned in strong R&B grooves. As suggested by clashing organ chords in "The Word," the fit was rough but rich.

By the end of the year, the Beatles eclipsed any possible MBE-aroused suspicion of the group's integrity with the first of three mid-period albums that cemented their reputation as artists, never sell-outs. *Rubber Soul* marked a new way of experiencing pop music; like a string of short stories from a major literary figure, the song sequence itself had an inexorable sway, the way Lennon's left-behind misanthrope in "Norwegian Wood" gave way to McCartney's romantic ironist in "You Won't See Me." From this point forward, all their LPs exceed the sum of their parts. No longer arbitrary gatherings of independent songs, albums—no matter how

9. Beatles engineer Norman Smith would borrow the "wind-up piano" for a passage in Pink Floyd's "See Emily Play," and in tracks by the Pretty Things, which he produced in 1967 and 1968.

varied their content—become whole units, with imagined interconnections that define overall coherence, a collective aesthetic.

In later years, *Rubber Soul* would often be cited as the earliest of fans' "favorite" Beatles albums, whereas previous product would often be referred to as one or another favorite Beatle song—an example of how the band had grown out of the adolescent marketing of 45 rpm singles and into the new young-adult format of more thoughtfully integrated 33 1/3 albums. Even though British and American versions of *Rubber Soul* offered different track listings, as did all predecessors, neither lineup contained a song that was also made commercial as a single (and thus marked for individual recognition)—a stunning change for the American marketplace, but one that would be repeated with *Sgt. Pepper's Lonely Hearts Club Band* (1967) and *The Beatles* (1968).

As rock came of age and teen spending habits pushed more and more pop and rock albums up the charts (crowding out the adult-oriented film soundtracks, Broadway cast recordings, lounge singers, folkies, and comedy acts), content would be created and perceived differently: as its poetry demanded contemplation, rock music became a more thoughtful enterprise that no longer entailed changing records every two minutes both to maintain variety and allow for frequent breaks on the dance floor. Graduating from music's physical temptations, young listeners more frequently sat back and considered music by the hour, the way previous generations read fiction, followed radio serials, or watched movies. Perhaps it was the warped cover photo, the vaguely exotic sitar alongside a puzzling lyric in "Norwegian Wood," or the openly spiritual glow surrounding "The Word"; *Rubber Soul* introduced to pop music a new mystique, yet posed somewhat more approachable quandaries than Dylan did. The idea of the coherent rock album led in two years' time to the idea of a concept album—a series of songs bound in one LP with an overarching theme, much like the nineteenth-century song cycles of Schubert, Schumann, or Brahms.

These become important considerations, especially since the turn of the twenty-first century, when virtually any piece of music from any point in history—and from many of the world's cultures—lies mere clicks away on the internet, and when few sit down anymore to listen to a forty-minute work of music without interruption or distraction. Through the years of biggest album sales in the 1970s and '80s, before the eras of rock videos, mixtapes, downloads, and streaming (before the dawn of cable TV, home video, and social media), listeners settled in for hours of close listening, often through headphones, playing one album after another in their entirety. For millions, this started with *Rubber Soul*.

"You Won't See Me"

Recorded November 11, 1965, for *Rubber Soul*

> —*Paul's persona seems to grow in strength of spirit as the ensemble's backing vocal parts become ever more robust and resolute with each new verse.*

In yet another personal-pronoun weave, "You Won't See Me" yanks the listener in with an unprepared plagal cadence (IV–I), turning a corner into the song in a gesture that goes unrepeated: those sharp opening chords open a trap door that lands you on an elaborately smooth conveyor belt. Once McCartney's lead vocal enters and his short-burst phrases get swallowed up by the background velour, there's just enough energy and detail pushing him along that the singer becomes less the focus than just another thread in a finely braided tapestry of sound. The ensemble pulls harmonic taffy out of the simple sequence: two short, detached phrases ("When I call . . . you up . . .") set up a long held note ("your liiiiiiine's engaged" at 0:08), which gets repeated, and shorter phrases bring the harmony back home at the end of each verse.

The anticipation here stems from a slow layering of vocal harmonies, added in each successive verse, like a kaleidoscope that adds colors with each rotation. The effect is hypnotic, even levitating, especially when you keep tuning in to hear more detail and the mostly common elements float by in elaborate symmetry. (As critic Robert Christgau declared, the secret to good rock—or any strong style—is "repetition without tedium.") The only vocal variation comes at the retransitional ends of bridges when the backing singers dissolve from "oohs" into "Oh I wouldn't, no I wouldn't" (at 1:30 and 2:24), the only rejoinders offered to the lead singer's woe.

Finally, a calming irony settles down in the last two verses: the singer keeps appealing for mercy while the frame keeps adding blankets of calm and reassurance; it's as if the entire band summons all its empathic affability to prevent the singer from stressing out. By the final repetitions into the fadeout, the singer has absorbed the affection around him; he chirps happily as the undulating warmth gets enveloped by the silence.

As a McCartney vehicle, the song resembles the words versus music irony of "Can't Buy Me Love," its carousel repetition effect spinning on delight even as it waves goodbye. Each successive verse comes back on itself, finding more pleasure in its stacked vocals, like a dreamy wedding cake that ascends toward a mannequin couple. "Filled with tears," he keeps singing, sounding more and more like he's won the prize with each revolution.

CUE	SECTION	HARMONY	DETAIL
0:00	Intro	IV–I	Disorienting harmony
0:03	Verse 1: S, R	I–II7–IV–I	(Repeated)
0:20	Verse 1: D	I7–IV–iv–I	
0:28	Verse 1: C	I–II7	Background vocals enter
0:33	Verse 1: refrain	IV–I–IV–I	Extended C-gesture
0:40	Verse 2		Descant line enters
1:09	Refrain		
1:17	Bridge 1	ii–iv–iv°–I	
1:25	Retransition	II–V7	
1:34	Verse 3		3rd vocal part added
2:03	Refrain		
2:11	Bridge 2 and Retransition		
2:28	Verse 3		4th vocal part added
3:06	Outro	(based on verse)	Vamp on verse changes

"Michelle"

Recorded November 3, 1965, for *Rubber Soul*

> *—with this cabaret number, Paul McCartney once again leads the Beatles into new non-rock styles. Harmonically sophisticated, especially with its chromatic blur of constantly coexisting major and minor modes and a bass line that exemplifies in a subtle way the composer's bold invention heard throughout the album, "Michelle" also employs the contrast of high and low vocal registers to portray vivid emotional contrasts.*

If "DayTripper" brandishes guitars in debauchery, "Michelle" coaxes them with seductive delicacy. Here, passion is thinly disguised by a subdued, largely acoustic instrumentation at a moderate tempo, with tamed dynamic extremes. Many factors contribute: chromatic tension, a rosy glow put on the contrasting major mode, retransitional lines of long-repeated pitches that give Paul's vocal the same trance-like intensity ("say the only words I know that you'll . . .") that John will later achieve in "Julia," and an upper-register surge ("I need to, I need to, I neeeeed to") that lays bare the singer's underlying desire, leading into domesticated maturity and a stark humility, and away from the indulgent eruptions of 1963. The surge acquires added emphasis from Paul's brave mordents on "need" at 1:07 and "want" at 1:40. One very nice touch with which the suitor rests his case is the final beautification of the retransitional line—already heard three times with lyrics on a repeated pitch as well as in the instrumental intro—that recasts the final phrase, "and I will say the only words I know . . .," with freshly moving, emotionally revealing scale degrees in a lower register that find fulfilment in a complete descent to 1 and an authentic cadence on the major tonic, whereas all previous performances end questioningly with half cadences, scale degree 2 above V. The close is all the more fulfilling because Paul's vocal approaches the final tonic resolution from an alluring leading tone, 7, a tone that had been completely absent from the intro's culminating thirdless V chord, and which tone appears in the lead vocal for the first time only in the song's penultimate vocal downbeat

Is "Michelle" in F major or in F minor? Yes. Both, not simply in the usual sense whereby modes are mixed, but in a more profound way, with both FM and Fm claiming equal prominence and centricity. Both together characterize the subtle chemistry that paints hope in melancholy. Major-mode songs would not contain the abundance of lowered third, sixth, and seventh scale degrees that form the majority in "Michelle," and while minor-mode songs often end on a major tonic chord for a "Picardy third" light at the end of the tunnel, none begins with one, as these verses do. Although the bridge opens in a needful F minor, it turns bright with a soothingly tonicized ♭VI ("I think you know by now"), which scale degree had previously lain at the depths of falling hopelessness to end the chromatic descent, 1–7–♭7–6–♭6–5 (with this ♭6 sustained for a full bar, twice the duration of previous tones) in introductory and retransitional pleas.

Paul McCartney's late-1965 concentration on interesting bass lines brings new meaning to the very first sound in "Michelle." He consciously explores all of the implications his bass line has for supporting upper parts when he tells one columnist:

If you're in C, and you put [the bass] on G—something that's not the root note—it creates a little tension. It's great. It just [*takes a long, expectant, gasping breath*] holds the track, and so by the time you go to C, it's like, "Oh thank God he went to C!" And you can create tension with it. (Mulhern 1990, 20)

In playing a long-sustaining C in the bass while the guitar chord above claims F as its root, McCartney brings a pronounced yet subtle tension to the song's intro, which concludes with that C in the bass but the guitar falling into line with its sunken, thirdless C chord (0:06–0:08). It's a related sort of bass-derived dissonance underlying the growing number of 4–3 suspensions that bring stress and tension to many 1965 songs, at first to portray anticipation in "Wait" and later to bring out the strife in the verse's cadence and the bridge of "We Can Work It Out."

The all-encompassing outer voices—bass and lead vocal—create a new personality for the (025) blues trichord. The bridge opening cancels out the bass's recent upward-walking leading tone, 7 (0:32), with a protesting lowered 7 that boldly insists "I love you, I love you, I love you" in both the bass (F–C–E♭–F–C–E♭) and in the heightened, suddenly solo vocal (C–F–E♭–C–F–E♭–C, all a half-step below the "Ticket" outburst) simultaneously. But the second bass E♭ resolves not as lowered 7 to F but as fifth of a disarming A♭7 chord (0:36) that tonicizes ♭VI, D♭, as the gently calming "oohs" return in all-embracing thirds-plus-octaves backing vocals. It's as if the major triad on D♭ recasts the portentous ♭6 of the chromatic introductory descent as pure, open, and non-threatening: "That's all I want to say." Tension returns as D♭ drops directly to C (at 0:41), placing us firmly back in the minor mode when the singer realizes he still does not have the words he needs.

Chromatic strain is everywhere, even if mostly kept in abeyance. "Michelle" revels in the fully diminished seventh chord, a multiply valent sonority expressed in three successive neck positions that "go together well" at 0:14–0:16 as in no other Beatle song. The complexity of the object's beauty, "ma belle," is captured in a cabaret atmosphere in the "Gretty" chord, the jazzy ♯9/♭7 chord at 0:11–0:12, which the young Beatles had learned from Jim Gretty, a Liverpool guitarist. The Gretty chord combines both the D natural—scale degree 6—of the major mode and D♭, the root of the song's core chromatic issue, ♭VI. But it's all grace under pressure, most chords only lightly touched on, with the capo on the fifth fret to pique their brilliance. The solo electric guitar heard in the break (1:26–1:39) and coda (2:20+) is overdriven for a full sustain yet muted by bridge-pickup coloring and strong filtering of treble by the tone knob: it is gloomy amid the acoustic guitars' attempts to maintain a major-mode countenance. "Michelle" is perhaps the Beatles' most complex love song before "Something," and certainly the one most deeply enveloped in a smoky conundrum.

CUE	SECTION	HARMONY	DETAIL
0:00	Introduction	i/5–chrom desc–iv/1–V5	based on retransition
0:08	Verse 1	I–IV♯9–v6/5–vii°6/5/V–V–II♭9–V	
0:20	Verse 2		repeated, *en français*
0:33	Bridge 1	i–V7/♭VI–♭VI–V7–i	
0:45	Retransition 1a		
0:53	Verse 2		
1:05	Bridge 2		
1:17	Retransition 1b		
1:26	Break		based on verse
1:37	Bridge 3		
1:50	Retransition 1c		
1:58	Verse 2		
2:10	Retransition 2		
2:19	Coda		based on verse, fades out

POINTS FOR DISCUSSION

1. How did the Beatles both repeat themselves and break new ground in 1965?
2. Name some ways in which instrumentation, harmony, melody, rhythm, form, engineering, and poetic topics advanced in the Beatles' music in 1965.
3. Describe how the changing character of Paul McCartney's bass lines in this period adds depth to the Beatles' musical textures.
4. In what ways do keyboard instruments play a larger role in the Beatles' music of 1965?
5. Describe how the Beatles begin to tweak the idea of backing singers as more than just call-and-response players in a gospel formula.
6. What aspects of 1965 world politics contradict the generalization that the Sixties were all about peace and love? What were America's cultural tensions in 1965?
7. Provide some clues from *Rubber Soul* that the Beatles were attuned to the changing world around them.
8. How does the music of Motown and Stax and other R&B sources play more of a role in the Beatles' 1965 sound?
9. Discuss some of the Beatles' varied uses of the ♭VII chord on the *Help!* album.
10. Where can you hear the volume-tone control pedal? Distorted guitar signals? Describe the sounds.
11. How do the string parts in "Yesterday" relate to McCartney's guitar part? How are they similar, and how are they different? How are the seven bars of the verse of "Yesterday" divided into smaller phrases? Is there more than one possible way to consider organizing them?
12. Choose one Beatle and discuss the nature of his performing role (as singer and/or instrumentalist) and how it changed from 1962 to 1965 by referring to his participation in at least four recordings.

13.   Choose five songs, at least one from each year (1962–1965), and discuss how the Beatles' sense of ensemble changed, by referring to the interaction of specific instrumental and vocal techniques.

FURTHER READING

Belchem, John, ed. *Liverpool 800: Culture, Character and History*. Liverpool: Liverpool University Press, 2006.

Davies, Hunter. *The Beatles Lyrics*. New York: Little, Brown, 2014.

Hayden, Tom. *The Port Huron Statement: The Visionary Call of the 1960s Revolution*. New York: Perseus, 2005.

McLuhan, Marshall. *Understanding Media: The Extensions of Man*. New York: Routledge, 2001.

Mulhern, Tom. Interview with Paul McCartney. *Guitar Player*, July 1990.

Sale, Kirkpatrick. *SDS*. New York: Vintage, 1973.

Warwick, Jacqueline. "You're Going to Lose That Girl: The Beatles and the Girl Groups." *Beatlestudies* 3 (2001): 161–167.

Warwick, Jacqueline. *Girl Groups, Girl Culture: Popular Music and Identity in the 1960s*. New York: Routledge, 2007.

Wyatt, David, 2014. *When America Turned: Reckoning with 1968*. Amherst: University of Massachusetts.

CHAPTER 6

FROM THE STAGE TO THE STUDIO (1966)

After climbing to the top of the entertainment world, the Beatles saw only a dull plateau. They may have felt frustration over glimpses of advancement that could not easily be realized due to limits beyond their control. A script for a third film foundered on disagreements. Security concerns and signs of exploitation nixed plans to record in America, or even to tape songs written by Motown staff composers or produced by Stax staff (besides, the travel, storage of growing amounts of gear, and unfamiliar environments of such an enterprise would have caused unnecessary hassle). In 1966, the increasingly independent Beatles went in separate directions, but the group mission allowed for each to learn from the other so that when they did gather, the whole always exceeded the sum of its parts. The band concertized but lost interest in rehearsing, since reproducing studio effects held no interest for screaming fans. The disastrous—for them, not for their fans—world tour in the summer of 1966 brought their all-consuming public personas hard up against their studio creativity.

The year 1966 marked a new distance between the Beatles and fans who couldn't understand the strange squawks of "Tomorrow Never Knows" or why John Lennon casually remarked how they were "more popular than Jesus," or how they disappeared without a word, with no BBC Radio performances, with only a single television-studio appearance in 1966 in the United Kingdom and none elsewhere, releasing no new music after August. The wonders of 1967 would quiet most of the growing doubts from naysayers, but the Beatles' status as press darlings met a backlash throughout 1966.

PHOTO 6.1. The Beatles on May 19, 1966, performing for the "Rain" video in EMI's Studio One. "Strawberry Fields Forever" / "Penny Lane" 45 (as released in Japan March 15, 1967).

They began routinely enough, with *Revolver* recording sessions occupying the months between March and May of 1966; you can see the group as they appeared midway through these sessions in Photos 6.01 and 6.02. The first and most adventurous session produced "Tomorrow Never Knows," which became the album's wormhole finale. And as on *Rubber Soul*, instrumentation now stretched to include sitars, string ensembles, brass, and backward tape loops. While these sessions took place later and later in the evenings, Beatlemania continued on the outside as fans anticipated new recordings. During the summer months they toured Germany, Tokyo, the Philippines, and America. And then, because they had argued successfully to skip a third film, they spent the autumn months apart, pursuing various solo projects. They regrouped in November for more sessions with fresh material that would extend their experimentalism even further.

1966 Original Releases (British):
Single: "Paperback Writer" / "Rain" (rel. June 10)
LP: *Revolver* (rel. Aug. 5)

Side 1:
"Taxman"
"Eleanor Rigby"
"I'm Only Sleeping"

Side 2:
"Good Day Sunshine"
"And Your Bird Can Sing"
"For No One"

PHOTO 6.2. The Beatles on May 19, 1966, in EMI's Studio One. Photographed by Robert Whittaker for the reverse ride of the *Revolver* LP (released in UK August 5, 1966).

"Love You To"   "Doctor Robert"
"Here, There and Everywhere"   "I Want to Tell You"
"Yellow Submarine"   "Got to Get You into My Life"
"She Said She Said"   "Tomorrow Never Knows"

THE FINAL TOURS

During the final 1966 tours, four Beatlemania incidents spiraled out of control, leading to the greatest crisis of group unity they'd experienced since skulking away from Hamburg in December 1960. Their *Revolver* sessions convinced them they were most at home creating in and for the studio; the tour to support the album—which exploded custom by omitting any album tracks from their set lists—confirmed their inclinations. They were truly no longer a performing group: once, their stage roles (Paul on bass, Ringo on drums, George on lead guitar and John on rhythm guitar) defined their musical contributions. In *Revolver*, Paul at times plays piano or clavichord in basic tracks accompanied only by Ringo, composing and recording his bass line at some later point. Ringo would overdub cymbals, as with the subtle roll that opens "Good Day Sunshine," fading in as naturally as "Eight Days a Week" did artificially. In "Taxman," Paul continues to explore lead guitar while George introduces a band of Indian musicians to accompany "Love You To" (the nonsyntactical title being George's play on "Love Me Do"?) The overdubs in *Revolver* constituted key elements of formal and harmonic structure as well as texture. The new spring 1966 studio applications such as backward tape ("Rain," "I'm Only Sleeping"), rotating Leslie speaker and artificial double tracking (both applied to John's voice in "Tomorrow Never Knows"), and the numerous effects created for the hit single "Yellow Submarine" could not be reproduced onstage, nor could the subtler touches such as strong electronic limiting, which gave cymbal attacks an unnatural whoosh. On a larger scale than with the situation posed by possibly recording in Detroit or Memphis, the Beatles had to ask: Why bother?

On their route from London to Tokyo in late June, a huge storm forced a nine-hour layover in Alaska. They arrived for their only Japanese appearances ever, greeted by death threats and protesters. Crowds objected to the Beatles' three-night stint at the Nippon Budokan Temple (a judo arena) because of its traditional spiritual associations. The armed-guard security in Japan exceeded that in all previous tours. While the concerts came off successfully, the Beatles' experience of Japan was so tightly controlled that they felt straitjacketed by their own entourage.

Then they few to Manila for a concert at the Rizal Memorial Football Stadium, where over twenty-four thousand fans heard afternoon and evening sets on July 4. The following morning, they were surprised to see themselves on TV, where a weeping Imelda Marcos, wife of President Ferdinand Marcos, decried the band ignoring her invitation to Malacañang Palace. A miscommunication quickly became an international diplomatic incident. Insulting the Philippines leader was seen as a political affront: the Beatles and their crew struggled to the airport through a dangerous withdrawal of police security, where a frightened Brian Epstein had to turn over all concert receipts as extortion before they could take off.

In America, an unrelated scandal loomed: in-house photographer Robert Whitaker shot the cover to Capitol's *Yesterday and Today* as a sick joke: the four Beatles posed on March 25 in white smocks draped with dismembered dolls and slabs of meat (as shown in Photo 6.3). Capitol Records had never released an American album comparable to the content of their British counterparts; *Yesterday and Today*, released June 15, was compiled from both sides of three recent American singles, two leftovers from *Rubber Soul*, and three advance tracks from *Revolver* sessions. Because the American label had routinely released Beatles albums with fewer tracks and rearranged song sequences, the Beatles' cover photo was seen as a multilayered protest, against the gap between their album layouts and Capitol's, but also between their public mop-top image and desire to graduate from the teen market. Their music had grown and taken on serious issues; why couldn't their public persona follow suit? John Lennon offered up a plumb quote, saying he thought the butcher cover appropriate for a country intent on butchering innocent people in the growing Vietnam conflict. Even if the photo session had originally been a random, eccentric idea on Whitaker's part (as claimed by the principals), the record cover has assumed all sorts of received meanings.

In retrospect, it's a wonder Capitol printed up any copies of this cover. It was immediately howled down by both DJs and retailers, and Capitol had to hastily recall it and issue a replacement. For a long time, fans steamed and peeled away innocuous replacement cover slicks to find the original "Butcher" cover underneath; the original record jacket remains a valuable collectors' item. The album went on to be a bestseller, but the controversy lingered.

PHOTO 6.3. The Beatles on March 25, 1966, as photographed by Robert Whittaker for the original "Butcher" cover of the *Yesterday and Today* LP (released in US June 20, 1966, but immediately withdrawn and replaced with new cover).

The fourth fracas erupted over a Lennon quote from a March 1966 interview by his close confidant Maureen Cleave for the *London Evening Standard*, saying, "Christianity will go. It will vanish and shrink. I needn't argue with that; I'm right and I'll be proved right. We're more popular than Jesus now; I don't know which will go first—rock and roll or Christianity." Although his tone came off as typically arrogant, he was trying to thoughtfully answer a question regarding his reading habits and join the ongoing conversation on Britain's decades of declining church attendance. On the eve of the US tour, the American teen magazine *Datebook* reprinted John's comment as a cutaway boast on its cover. This created an uproar, especially throughout the Bible Belt South. To dispel the backlash, Brian Epstein arranged for Lennon to open the US leg of the tour in Chicago with what amounted to a confused and humiliating apology for statements taken as blasphemous comparing the Beatles to Christ. "I'm not anti-God, anti-Christ, or anti-religion. I was not saying we are greater or better. . . . I'm sorry I said it, really."

The press conference remains among the few clips where Lennon appears anxious and rattled in public, afraid for both his own safety and that of his fellow Beatles. Death threats streamed in, and crowds became perilous, surrounding airport and hotel arrivals. Where Beatlemania had once seemed exotic and fun, now it turned menacing. Radio stations in Birmingham, Alabama, banned airplay and organized record burnings. Hooded Ku Klux Klan members openly demonstrated against the Beatles' performances. Lennon expressed horror at these exaggerated reactions and how he had "created another little piece of hate in the world." In the Memphis performance, when a firecracker went off in the stands, the Beatles instinctively looked toward John to see if he had been shot. Otherwise, teen crowds seemed oblivious, ecstatic to share even a large disorderly space with their heroes. Lennon's eventual murderer, fourteen years later, acted precisely on delusions based on the "more popular than Jesus" observation.

All of these protests conveniently ignored the lengthy interview the Beatles had given to *Playboy* in its February 1965 issue, where they debated the difference between atheism and agnosticism, declaring they didn't believe in God. George Harrison joked that Lennon served as the group's "official religious spokesman" (Frontani 2007, 100). At the time, such open disregard for "standard" religious beliefs remained highly controversial. The conformist overhang of the Cold War had very little wiggle room for such outspoken secular pronouncements.

The world itself had changed drastically in the previous twelve months. Indira Ghandi assumed the prime ministership of India in January 1966, celebrating a heroic nonviolent struggle against Britain's empire rule. In the United States, President Johnson had committed 250,000 troops to the effort in Vietnam, arousing antiwar passions even further among college students and leftists. In the San Francisco Bay area, "acid tests" with the Grateful Dead—light shows with rock music where listeners shared LSD and amphetamines openly—finally led to criminalization of these hallucinogens, even as their use continued to spread. And the early stirrings of a violent Black Panther chapter began in Oakland, California. After years of strife and terrorist tactics by white police, many ideals had been shattered, and Martin Luther King had trouble keeping his nonviolent coalition together.

Beatlemania's increasing chaos punctuated a dismal scene overall: the band's underrehearsed approach to challenging music rendered undersold stadium performances dissatisfying. As the Beatles left San Francisco on the tour's final night, August 29, George said, "That's it. I'm not a Beatle anymore." Instead of regrouping in London to record an album for the Christmas market as they had done every year after 1962, the four members dispersed to the world's four corners for three months apart.

REVOLVER

Revolver, the only album the band released in 1966 (one week before that fateful American tour), signaled a leap as great as the one between *Help!* and *Rubber Soul*—perhaps greater. Its cover, drawn by Hamburg friend Klaus Voormann, is shown as Photo 6.4. Anyone setting the needle down at the opening song realized these tracks made dancing secondary—the jerky strut of "Taxman" and lopsided meters in "She Said She Said" charmed with unfamiliar patterns. The new album posed serious riddles that challenged every known pop convention: unprecedented uses of backward tape, sped-up and slowed-down playback, tape loops, vocals and guitar lines duplicated slightly out of phase with one another—the voices seeming strangely human and mechanical at once— voltages distorted by spinning Leslie speakers, and even a keyboard instrument, the Mellotron, made entirely of prerecorded sounds, made early and pronounced appearances here. Outright

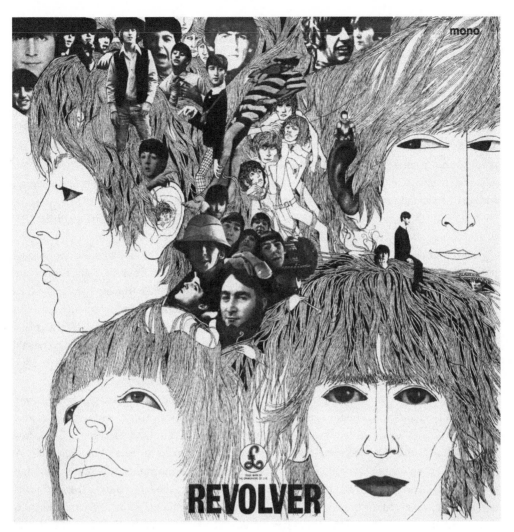

PHOTO 6.4. Hamburg friend and future Plastic Ono Band bassist Klaus Voormann's illustration and collage for the Beatles' *Revolver* LP (released in UK August 5, 1966).

North Indian instrumentation and compositional structures, in George Harrison's "Love You To," took their turn. In "Good Day Sunshine" and "Doctor Robert," dueling tonal centers shifted in ways that made taken-for-granted certainties now fragile. Deadly serious moods slithered amongst the silly ("Yellow Submarine"): non-rhyming lyrics for one song taken directly from a book on Tibetan wisdom proclaimed "It is not dying," those of another portrayed two lonely souls who meet only at a grave, and a third declared: "I know what it's like to be dead."[1] This music addressed all areas of the mind and body. Its mood, method, and frame all flaunted the layered qualities of poetry and implicitly reflected recreational drug use.

1. As in Elizabethan blank verse, most of the non-rhyming lyrics for "Tomorrow Never Knows" are set in iambic pentameter: "Turn off your mind, relax and float downstream," "Lay down all thoughts, surrender to the void," "that you may see the meaning of within," etc.

The Beatles used their hard-earned downtime for exploring. The world at their feet, they turned inward, partly out of an interest in spiritual matters that would culminate in an early 1968 retreat to Rishikesh, India, to practice transcendental meditation, and partly through the mystical insights gained through psychedelic drugs, LSD being their favorite. The LSD molecule, produced and studied as part of psychiatric and psychological research in the 1950s and '60s, overstimulates cortical neurotransmitter receptors and processing in the amygdala, intensifying sensory and limbic effects, causing visual distortions such as rippling, vibrant, and trailing colorizations and similar auditory distortions; strong mood changes; altered perception of time, memory, awareness, and proportion; extreme disorientation; and loss of identity. Normal and weird seem inverted, and sustained nightmarish perceptions can lead to "bad trips," but subjects often report feeling united with their surroundings, at one with the world.

Still legal in the United Kingdom until late 1966, LSD burst into public consciousness with the 1964 publication by Harvard researchers Timothy Leary and Richard Alpert, *The Psychedelic Experience: A Manual Based on the Tibetan Book of the Dead*, a spiritual guide to the death of the ego through psychedelics, akin to ancient funerary texts guiding the soul's liberation from the body. Lennon and Harrison were given LSD in March 1965, and Starr joined these two in their tripping a second time at a Los Angeles party on August 24. There, actor Peter Fonda told Lennon of his having experienced death; this discussion led Lennon to write "She Said She Said." McCartney would explore LSD a year later, with enthusiasm. In June 1967, *Life* magazine reprinted a British interview with Paul in which he said, "After I took it [LSD], it opened my eyes. We only use one-tenth of our brain. Just think what we could accomplish if we could only tap that hidden part. It would mean a whole new world."

The Beatles, especially Lennon, took LSD frequently, and their expanded imaginations showed most vividly in the drones, imitative guitars and vocal parts, and the many types of aural distortions in *Revolver*. Lyrics unrelated to normal waking consciousness ("I'm Only Sleeping," "Tomorrow Never Knows," and "She Said She Said") made a clean break from everything previous. As partygoers, group members moved from "Swinging London" to the avant-garde underground; in October 1966, Barry Miles sought McCartney's help in founding the *International Times*, a journal of the artistic vanguard. At the Indica Gallery, Miles introduced Lennon to New York artist, musician, and provocateur Yoko Ono at her first London show on November 9. All that being said, "Tomorrow Never Knows" also depends on an extremely conservative structure: the lack of rhyme and use of the iambic pentameter of Shakespeare's, Milton's, and Wordsworth's blank verse, somehow resurrected from Lennon's Quarry Men schooldays.

"Here, There and Everywhere"

Recorded June 16 and 17, 1966, for *Revolver*

—*being a brief yet technically involved recognition of McCartney's inseparable melodic and harmonic intuitions.*

One of the biggest surprises of the Beatles' *Ed Sullivan* appearance in 1964 lay in their range of song choices, even though at the time, their hair upstaged their sources. "Till

There Was You" (from *The Music Man*, which beat out *West Side Story* for Best Musical at the 1958 Tony Awards) was a sop to the establishment, a song that would have sunk the Rolling Stones, one that mothers everywhere approved of. Surrounded by "All My Loving" and "I Want to Hold Your Hand," it had a touch of Trojan Horse: McCartney usurping the enemy's material inside a rebellious rock 'n' roll frame, charming the establishment while seducing its daughters. (Its part in the set list continues a line of similarly sentimental breaks—such as those provided earlier by "The Honeymoon Song (Bound by Love)," "Falling in Love Again," and "A Taste of Honey"—that connect the Beatles, or at least Paul McCartney, to their variety-show music hall roots; it was also encouraged by Elvis's softer repertoire.)

But the Meredith Willson number also signals a respect for the Tin Pan Alley tradition that carried into the many songs by Gerry Goffin and Carole King covered by the Beatles in the early days. In most rock recordings, there's no time for a preamble or a précis, a brief introductory passage that introduces the material to build suspense for the main melody. "Here, There and Everywhere" has a classical build, both a formal synopsis and then a spinning out of all its implications through verses and bridges that would have impressed Richard Rodgers. (The tempo-free intro recalls the slow beginning to Goffin-King's "Take Good Care of My Baby," which George Harrison had sung in the Decca audition, as well as Lennon's "Bad to Me" and "Do You Want to Know a Secret.")

Accompanied by just vocals and soft electric guitar, the track opens with McCartney taking a wildly unnatural leap on the second phrase (at 0:04), his voice arpeggiating up in octaves while the chord shifts from diatonic iii to a chromatic ♭III, only to settle back into the home key for the opening verse (0:10).[2] The downbeat chords this preamble visits (I and ♭III) map the key structure to the entire song; the verses are in I, the bridges begin on ♭III.[3] The binary tonal-area format for romantic songs now assumes a formal, almost regal, prevalence in McCartney numbers. As delineated in the opening bars, he tips his hat to himself, congratulates his own method as he unfurls one of his more seductive melodies. After first planting a key word on the first scale degree ("here" and "there"), the "making each day" (3–5–9–8–4–6–5) line resembles the upward curve in "Yesterday" ("Love was such an easy game to play" (3–♯4–♯5–6–7–8–7–6–6)); "everywhere" stretches into the bridge in the contrast provided by the parallel minor, moving from G major to G minor through the world-expanding ♭III. The bridge begins with a fluorescent ♭III, but settles right away into a forlorn G minor that portrays the "care" that will never concern him (verse phrases at 0:22–0:27 and 0:45–0:51, echoed at "never care" at 1:02 and 1:37), glimpses a brief balalaika-like passage (recalling the suggestion of a mandolin in "Girl"), before winding gently down in the major home key for verses. The overall texture

2. The introductory progression, I–iii–♭III–ii–V7, moves through a similar passing motion to that learned in "Till There Was You" (iii7–♭iii7–ii7), which turned up in both "Do You Want to Know a Secret" and "If I Fell," and later a riff in "Yer Blues."
3. McCartney learned this relationship from "To Know Her Is to Love Her" and first applied it to "Love of the Loved"; it would appear once again in "Two of Us."

resembles a lush orchestra, only it's done through plush vocal harmonies (singing triads), as if instruments would be too crass for such delicate sentiments.

CUE	SECTION	HARMONY	DETAIL
0:00	Précis	I–iii→III (!)–ii–V7	
0:09	Verse 1: S-R	I–ii–iii–IV	melody altered in repeat
0:20	Verse 1: D	(ii–V7–ii–V7 of)	
0:26	Verse 1: C	vi–ii–ii7–V7	
0:33	Verse 2	[= Verse 1]–(V7 of)	
0:56	Bridge 1	♭III–i–iv–V7–i	
1:02		iv–V7	balalaika
1:07	Verse 3		
1:30	Bridge 2		
1:42	Verse 3		
2:06	Coda	I–ii–iii–IV–I	

"And Your Bird Can Sing"

Recorded April 26, 1966, for *Revolver*

—close attention to chord functions and melodic stasis, as harmonic ambiguity leads to clarity, illustrates how John Lennon leads his fans away from worldly distractions with a spiritual call.

Bob Dylan's blues-leaning version of the old folk number "Corrina, Corrina" includes a line borrowed from Robert Johnson, "I got a bird that whistles, I got a bird that sings; but I ain't got Corinna—life don't mean a thing" (*The Freewheelin' Bob Dylan*, 1963). In "And Your Bird Can Sing," John Lennon tropes this idea for a subtle antimaterialist statement a full year before the message would become more overt in songs like "Baby, You're a Rich Man" and "Within You Without You." Lennon's theme is larger in "Bird"—not only does the singer devalue material possessions, but he calls the listener to awaken as if from slumber and seek clear, important goals by ignoring the distractions of superficial everyday business. Lennon might also be heard to offer himself as a spiritual as well as cultural Messiah figure, a self-characterization that would be suspect for other reasons in mid-1966. "You don't get ME," he taunts with a sudden multiply-voiced ego in the I triad (0:17–0:20); "Look in my direction," he hints, guiding the way with the reassuringly goal-directed dominant preparation chord (ii) and then the song's only expression of V harmony reserved for the retransitional promise, "I'll be 'round." (Perhaps "Ain't She Sweet," recorded in 1961 and used as a warm up at least in 1969, was also on Lennon's mind: therein, he ended a bridge phrase with "in her direction" on the same pitches, B, C♯ and E, which which he ends the "my direction" phrase in "Bird.")

Clarity wins out over ambiguity, direct simplicity over confusing complexity. The song's stable diatonic basis through verses contrasts against an uncertain bridge section, where the iii chord (a deeply involved ii of ii) expands with the sort of descending chromatic line heard in "Michelle" that would later become a Lennon staple ("Lucy in the Sky with Diamonds," "Dear Prudence") and would eventually be adopted by Harrison ("While My Guitar Gently Weeps," "Something"). (The chromatic progression comes most directly from the bridge of "It Won't Be Long" (at "Since you left me"), its descending bass line, G♯–F𝄪–F♯–E, taken from the high backing vocal of the 1963 track to support the lead vocal, which ornaments B with its upper neighbor C♯ in each case.) John's guitar carries a simple and direct droning tonic chord through verses, strummed in a generous rhythm, once on every pulse. This steady, stable foil stands against George's and Paul's self-consciously intricate guitar-and-bass trio tattoos, prized but taxing (under the weight of worldly possessions), surrounding John's verses, busily dividing beats with parallel thirds, horn fifths, and then parallel sixths. Additionally, Lennon uses his vocal accents to clarify the notion of rhythmic contrast: every syllable articulates its own beat in verses, but syncopations push each syllable onto an offbeat in bridges, wherein the "bird is broken" (presaging an image of racially divisive struggle in McCartney's "Blackbird"). For his part, Ringo's open jangles in verses turn to tense hi-hat chokings in bridges and illuminating cymbal crashes whenever V finds I.

John's vocal part in bridges shows constancy in the face of change in pitch as well as rhythm. Whereas his line builds largely on an unchanging fifth scale degree (with some ornamentation, as with the upper neighbor to 5 so common in his melodic writing in 1962–1964: note in "Please Please Me" the attention to 5–6–5 at "said these words," and in "A Hard Day's Night," note the high degree of Chuck Berry–like repetition on 5, ornamented by a bluesy 7 above, as in "work-*ing*"), John's vocally stressed B is harmonized in numerous ways that begin in obscurity but come into focus as the harmony becomes more clearly defined: to open the bridge, B functions as the chordal third of ii/ii; it then becomes the seventh of V7/ii, the fifth of IV/V, the suspended and anticipatory eleventh of ii, and then the powerfully clarified root of the retransitional V. (This is a similar process of discovery in the reharmonized ending of "She Loves You" and the introductory motto of "Help!," presented here with masterly understatement.) The singer sounds at one with all phases of the universe, but this only approaches clarity with the words "I'll be 'round." The listener's awakening emerges in a similar, gradually unfolding sense out of the hazy introduction to "If I Fell" and corresponds to the reassurance John gave himself in the retransitional line "The world is at your command" in "Nowhere Man."

In verse 2, John describes the bird as "green," the color he once used to paint others' jealousies over the singer's possession of a woman (in "You Can't Do That"). The disparagement here of vivid color (greenness is too much of this world and does not lead the true seeker to aspire to invisible bliss) might be interpreted as an early reaction against psychedelia—a position the composer would soon reverse: "Listen to the color of your dreams," he advises in "Tomorrow Never Knows." Lennon specialized in such absolute, all-then-nothing about-faces, as with his later embrace then spurning of the Maharishi and his rejection then promotion of political protest (stunningly changing his mind in a single phrase of "Revolution:" "you can count me out—in"). After he was initially upset by the LSD once dropped surreptitiously into his coffee, the chemical would for a time become mother's milk once John discovered its cosmic potential, an elixir of escape from the real world's traps and doldrums.

Throughout, distraction gets drawn by busy guitars, unfathomable chords, pushy rhythmic accents, and material colors. One near-final complication of inharmonious pitches reiterates this: in verse 3, the line "every sound there is" acquires a new pair of descant vocals noisy in their dissonance against the ruling texture, leading at 1:19 to a V chord sung incongruously over the governing I. Once again, a tangle of trees diverts attention from the forest of larger goals; one must not attend the flashy confusion of "every sound" when a harmonious "om" underlies everything. See beyond the seven wonders, hear beyond the tantalizing birdsong, for a revelation of communal truths in one single, constant vibration.

"And Your Bird Can Sing" remains an under-celebrated *Revolver* song, partly because its message employs veiled language in post-Dylan metaphors of impressionistic poetry and music. Like the best of Lennon, appreciation of its value requires thoughtful interpretation of its symbols. Ultimately, he sings, one may have everything one wants, but without investing at more spiritual levels, love will be out of reach, and life will have no meaning. In the song's final display of worldly confusion, an inconclusive IV chord overrides an insistent 1 in the bass that seems to ask, "What do *you* think?" Quite a profound statement made complete in two minutes.

CUE	SECTION	HARMONY	DETAIL
0:00	Introductory tattoo	I	trio: GH/PM guitar duet, PM bass
0:07	Verse 1	I–ii–IV–I	JL strums
0:20	Link	I	Tattoo reference
0:22	Verse 2		
0:36	Bridge 1 >	exp iii–V/ii	JL syncopated vocal, GH/PM gtrs/bs trio
0:43	Retransition	I–ii–V	
0:50	Break 1	(from verse)	Tattoo trio
1:05	Bridge 2 >		
1:12	Retransition		
1:19	Verse 3		noisy PM/GH descants
1:34	Break 2		Tattoo trio
1:48	Coda	I–IV/1 (!)	Tattoo trio

"Doctor Robert"

Recorded April 19, 1966, for *Revolver*

—a close look at harmonic relations elucidates the modulations of key that depict the good (?) doctor's druggy injections of energy.

Paul McCartney typically gets credit for his Tin Pan Alley pretensions and pleated chords (the dual home keys in "Here, There and Everywhere" and "Penny Lane," the French pillow talk and diminished sevenths in "Michelle"), but Lennon proves equally deft at playing games with key relationships. Several of Lennon's numbers ("Day Tripper," "Lucy in the Sky with Diamonds," "Dig a Pony") deploy harmonic frames like conundrums, where home keys always surprise the ear, and bridges take root in faraway places.

The "Dr. Robert" story is legend: during their stay-overs in Manhattan, the Beatles caught wind of a mythical doctor who wrote prescriptions for the stars: as played out in episode 608 ("The Crash") of AMC's *Mad Men* series in 2013, the Dr. Feelgood physician made house calls and gave respectable professionals shots of vitamins mixed with amphetamines so they could work through the night and make their impossible deadlines, all as "legit" prescriptions. (The suits called these shots "energy serum," or "miracle tissue regenerator.") In an era when youth culture defined itself by choosing alternatives to alcohol (chiefly marijuana, but increasingly stronger psychedelics such as LSD and barbiturate pills), the fast-life establishment turned to wayward medics for juice. Elvis Presley, for example, notoriously relied on prescription medications as a "respectable" alternative to hallucinogens. According to Jean Stein and George Plimpton's oral history of the Warhol scene centered on model Edie Sedgwick (*Edie*), this doctor, Charles Roberts, played a well-known role "servicing" the downtown bohemian art scene. *Mad Men*'s creator, Matt Weiner, cites Max Jacobson, who treated John F. Kennedy. There had to have been others.

The song has a cleverly shifting subtext: while it laughs at its subject, the harmonic footing of the song swaps out carpets beneath characters for a maze of colors: each time the verse returns, you never know where it will land. The track opens almost too casually, vamping to kill time, pivoting between I7 and a syncopated IV. But after the first phrase, the narrator steps through a mirror (as the tonal level drops from A to F♯, VI7, at 0:16), mimicking the effect of drugs hitting the bloodstream. Approached by a lurch, VI7 is neighbored by an E7 chord at 0:25 that is not understood as the original key's dominant, but IV of its replacement tonal center, when VI7 is revealed as V7 of II, only when it resolves there for the B-major bridge. Meanwhile, to start the second verse, the band has to step back *down* to I (A), which sounds as if everything starts up again in a new key. But it's not a new key; it's just the way the gears have shifted to wind up once on II (B major), to make the I (A major) sound like a deceptive or false return. A year hence, similar modulatory jolts will make a tonal three-ring circus out of "Being for the Benefit of Mr. Kite."

Lennon's paean to the sleazy doctor paints a guiltless antihero haloed by a homophonic boys choir for the bridge ("Well, well, well, you're feeling fine" at 0:58 and 1:40). The choirboy routine stays in B, which gives the harmonic layout some resolve: the narration passes through I and VI major; the bridge plants itself in II as the drugs deliver the user to a different consciousness. The rush of the verse answered with sublime sarcasm of mop-top cherubs, giving their blessing in chorale finery backed by church organ. (How did the Don Drapers of the world feel hearing this track when their young trophy wives cued it up for them? Flattered? Honored? Betrayed?)

For the final touch, the Beatles toy with an ironic "finished" ending as the sound disappears. Other tracks deploy every variety of fadeout possible, from the simplest dimming ("Not a Second Time," "I Should Have Known Better") to the most creative trick endings ("Strawberry Fields Forever," "Get Back"). Even into their late period, they keep tweaking how outros can work: surging into the silence (the "Hey Jude" fadeout stretches toward infinity), marching into increasing mania ("All You Need Is Love," "I Am the Walrus"), or landing on an unresolved cadence on IV ("And Your Bird Can Sing"). "Doctor Robert" uses one of the strangest devices for an ending: the fade to proper cadence. You can hear them land on its final chord for a very satisfying resolution at 2:09–2:10. This plays into their awareness of silence, how every track emerges from and returns to quiet, and how best to insert pauses to create tension or subliminal punchlines (from the stop-time silences and fermata-marked caesuras in "There's a Place" and "She Loves You" to the later stop-time breaks in "I'm So Tired," "Don't Let Me Down," and "Dig a Pony"). It's almost as if the song's rush shuts the band down, and its last thought before it loses consciousness becomes a proper finale.

CUE	SECTION	HARMONY	DETAIL
0:00	Intro	I7–IV	
0:06	Verse 1: phrase 1	I7–IV	JL lead vocal
0:17	Verse 1: phrase 2	VI7–(IV7–V7 of) II7	
0:32	Verse 2		Duet
0:55	Guitar interlude		
0:58	Bridge 1	(I–IV/1–I) of II–V/2–I7	Chorale, ironic
1:10	Verse 2	I7–IV	Duet, guitar
1:40	Bridge 2		
1:51	Verse 3		
2:09	Outro	I7–VI7–II	Proper cadence on II

"Paperback Writer"

Recorded April 13 and 14, 1966, for A-side

—focusing solely on the vocal counterpoint that lifts the wittily busy poetry of this post-"All My Loving" McCartney dispatch.

Luxuriant vocal harmonies have swelled in Beatles tracks since the intricate cross-court volleys between lead and backups in "It Won't Be Long," the girl-group arguments between singer and backups in "Devil in Her Heart," the Greek chorus effect in "You're Going to Lose That Girl," and the smooth-rolling irony of "You Won't See Me." Even more innovation came with "Nowhere Man," and witty calls and responses lay ahead in "Getting Better," on up through *Abbey Road*'s "Because," a late vocal flourish. Along the way, new layers of self-consciousness emerge as arrangements comment on one another: the "Paperback Writer" intro pattern reverses itself in the "Good Day Sunshine" fadeout. Because of their skill in so many other areas, the Beatles' intricate line writing and robust vocal-ensemble work often get overshadowed by rivals like the Beach Boys and the Byrds.

Opening a pop single with the a cappella waterfall (a "motto") that propels "Paperback Writer" instantly dates a lot of these earlier chorales. Although they attempted this number onstage during the 1966 tour (and lip-synched it on their *Top of the Pops* appearance), the results fell way short of what they achieved on tape. The opening phrases climb stepwise to sustained notes which rest atop lower voices peeling downward, falling in a sequence of two echoes: the opening phrase (at 0:00), the first echo ("writer" 0:03), and the second echo (0:05), all bathed in reverb and left hanging in anticipation.

The vocal motto melts right into the guitar lead, a riveting riff playing off an arpeggio idea that could have anchored the track if it hadn't followed such a tour-de-force vocal display. In fact, this recurring vocal motto operates the way a guitar tattoo would—it's the sound you keep anticipating, the expectation that seeks new release on each return. The three-part chorale motto has three distinct unaccompanied appearances: at the top, at 0:49, and again at 1:38.

On verse three, at 1:01, the background vocals join in behind with "Frère Jacques," and sequence the silliness up a third at 1:20. Because it's in the background and doesn't draw attention to itself, many people listened to this track for years before they started noticing this sly inside joke. In a magnificently uncorrected mistake, on the second tier of this backup line the lower part (Harrison's?—the purer timbre of the falsetto makes it difficult to be certain) joins only after the first note, at 1:21, running fast to catch up.

The repeated stop-time vocal breaks follow an enticing pattern: first vocals alone, then guitar with drums, and finally bass, which enters as if delayed, an instant before the verses. Each time the chorale motto dissolves through the guitar break, McCartney's bass entrances acquire increasing suspense: at first (0:11) he's panting just behind the others; at the second break (1:01) he surfs and glides; on the third go-round (1:49) he dips and swerves with thrilling delay, yanking back on the others, his bass wagging the band.

The repetitions into the fadeout (1:50) mix all these elements together, the vocal chorale motto, the preening guitar tattoo, the bass angling from beneath, for three repetitions of the tag phrase. On the third repetition, the upper background vocal (Lennon's?) takes a little jump (2:10–2:11), signaling the fadeout. This one little gesture, the tiniest detail right near the end of the track, punctuates their four-bar phrases; coming at any other point, it would sound out of place.

CUE	SECTION	HARMONY	DETAIL
0:00	Motto	IV–I7	Chorale with echoes
0:05	Tattoo	I7sus4	Guitar lead
0:12	Verse 1	I7–IV–I7	McCartney lead vocal
0:30	Verse 2		
0:48	Motto		
0:54	Tattoo		
1:00	Verse 3		"Frère Jacques"
1:18	Verse 4		
1:36	Motto		
1:42	Tattoo		guitar
1:49	Outro	I	Call, response; repeat into fadeout

"STRAWBERRY FIELDS FOREVER" / "PENNY LANE"

Paul McCartney spent the fall of 1966 on safari in Kenya and writing the soundtrack for *The Family Way*—the first music to be credited to a solo Beatle.[4] Lennon also had a film role, acting in *How I Won the War*, shot in Germany and Spain that September through November. Harrison studied sitar under Ravi Shankar in Bombay and toured the Indian subcontinent. Ringo Starr caught up with family at home in Surrey. Lennon in particular seemed at odds with himself; the group he'd led for nine years was disintegrating with no goals in sight. Because John used his art as an emotional release—as he acknowledged doing in "I'm a Loser" and "Help!"—the deeper identity crisis that overtook him in the fall of 1966 might have brought him to a similarly productive catharsis. He picked up a nylon-string classical guitar in Almería, Spain, churned over his nagging childhood emotional trials, and began composing "Strawberry Fields Forever." As the composer said himself, " 'Strawberry Fields' was psychoanalysis set to music, really." Such an inspiration for his anguished work would be an early parallel of the Beatles' final dissolution in 1970 leading to primal screams for help on the *Plastic Ono Band* album.

---

4. Much of the following discussion of "Strawberry Fields Forever" and "Penny Lane" is taken from Everett 2014.

When Paul heard "Strawberry Fields," he decided to write his own song memorializing childhood memories, all situated in the popular bus roundabout known as Penny Lane. The Beatles devoted several weeks at the end of 1966 to recording "Strawberry Fields Forever" and followed this by taping "Penny Lane" and a very early McCartney composition, "When I'm Sixty-Four," recently completed in honor of Paul's dad's sixty-fourth birthday. All of these tracks were initially intended for some future album, but EMI and Capitol insisted they put out a single to break up the lull between releases. They chose two tracks and designated each as A-sides (both directed for radio play), "Penny Lane" / "Strawberry Fields Forever." Because both songs circled childhood with contrary tones, critic Greil Marcus later dubbed this "the first concept single."

When "Strawberry Fields" was released with "Penny Lane" in February 1967, listeners swung helplessly at musical curveballs. The Beatles' once-unified fan base was slow to accept radical facial hair and unconventional clothing; the inscrutable baroque surfaces of these songs harbored peculiar interior fantasies; and the films promoting the two sides of the new single (full of backward motion, color negatives, odd costumes, surreal behavior, and non sequiturs of every order) screamed bizarre by any measure. (Decades later, of course, music videos could take any form a director might imagine, but in the mid- and late 1960s, the Beatles created the pairing of abstract visual imagery to song that, for the first time, did not represent a stage performance.) If *Revolver* posed riddles, the new single wove deliberately vexing, out-of-reach mystical koans, not least the gaping tonal shift between the ironic cheer of Paul's "Penny Lane" and the sour sonic hallucination of John's "Strawberry Fields Forever." They could have come from two completely different bands. Other puzzles surrounded whatever meanings might lie behind both the four snapshots of toddlers (the band members themselves) on the reverse side of the record's sleeve and the perplexing monochrome aerial photo of Liverpool's suburban Penny Lane district used in print ads. (An outtake from the same photo session that produced the "Strawberry Fields Forever" / "Penny Lane" sleeve would be used later in the year on the American release of "Hello Goodbye," shown as Photo 6.5.) The public scarcely perceived that the Beatles were attempting new poetic expressions of a return to innocence.

We don't know what led Paul to create a companion piece to John's new offering, but with the "Strawberry Fields Forever" / "Penny Lane" single, recorded from November 1966 into the following January, we hear two complementary Liverpool odes. McCartney's Edenic "Penny Lane" has a chipper stride, graced with direct, representational lyrics tracing quaint and quixotic characters who inhabit a clearly drawn picture; the barber, the banker, the fireman, the nurse—habitués of the retail neighborhood in the Penny Lane bus roundabout—all ring familiar. Yet in part because of the way the narrator keeps labeling everything "very strange," we also engage in a scene full of types, mannequins as stand-ins for lived experience, or the starry-eyed way a child might glamorize the life of a fireman or barber. McCartney's choice of a piccolo trumpet for the solo (at 1:10) dramatizes this skewed vantage of an "ordinary" street scene. As the high-pitched sound of a "toy" trumpet, evoking an age-old eighteenth-century style, it doubly accents a fading innocence, as the nurse begins to feel that "she's in a play," fulfilling the cast's expectations of her, when "she is anyway." McCartney had heard this specialized trumpet during a broadcast of Bach's Brandenburg Concerto no. 2 on the BBC and had George Martin notate his hummed melody for the solo.

Lennon's "Strawberry Fields Forever," on the other hand, swims in indecipherable, impressionistic imagery vaguely evoking misunderstanding, abandonment, and indifference, all somehow

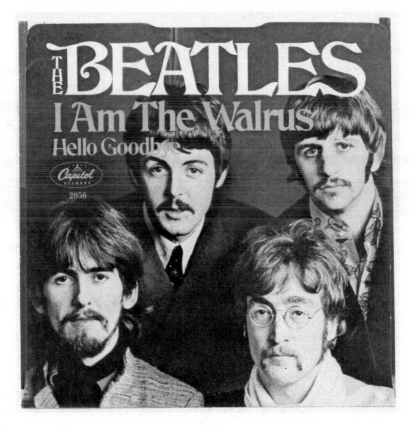

PHOTO 6.5. The Beatles in January–February 1967 as photographed by Henry Grossman. "Hello Goodbye" / "I Am the Walrus" 45 (released in US November 27, 1967).

tied to a treasured hallow of trees and fields—a child's idyll. Paul's hometown side might be heard as a delightful adaptation of John's year-old draft for "In My Life," which originally reminisced about a number of Liverpool landmarks. Although specific references in the draft did not appear in either "In My Life" or "Penny Lane," they nevertheless suggested a trip half consummated in John's Spanish melancholia, dreaming of his youth, contemplating where he came from and how long he had perceived himself as fundamentally different from his peers.

Strawberry Field was a Salvation Army home around the corner from Aunt Mimi's Mendips. Abandoned by both parents when very young, John identified with the institution's orphaned children as he attended their annual summer fundraising fair or played in their gardens just a leap over the wall. (The orphanage itself is now long gone, but Yoko's Strawberry Fields memorial to John lies directly across New York's Central Park West from their home for his final seven years, the Dakota building on Seventy-Second Street, whose tall carved-stone gables and arched window surrounds echo the now-lost Liverpool edifice.)

Lennon uses an indirect mode to recall his childhood and consider a lifelong otherness to root his fantasy at artistically profound depths. "Nothing is real and nothing to get hung about"; "It's getting hard to be someone"; "It doesn't matter much to me"; "That is, you can't, you know, tune in but it's all right": these and other lines express a fluid identity, an insecurity in one's surroundings, an inability of others to understand him, and a detachment from the everyday in a loose, anti-poetic, conversational style. The lyric speaks directly, without artifice, but resists clarity in fated clouds of obscurity. The song's complexity and indirectness might be defense mechanisms that filter lifelong negative memories.

Like its lyrics, the song's musical factors convey a vague and wondrous sense of disassociation. McCartney's Mellotron introduction articulates flute samples made alien by trimming away their sonic attacks and decays. Lennon's ambivalent chord choices portray a tonal elusiveness through unprepared pitch alterations and forward-reverse motion in relation to a stable harmonic center. Most pop songs seek and find their tonal home through anticipation and achievement; this one avoids any such center of gravity. Chord connections, such as the unnaturally minor v chord followed by the unnaturally major VI chord, resist clarity in the same obscure posture painted in the song's lyrics. The same v—VI chord connection will appear in 1968's "Julia" (first heard at "Julia, ocean child"), at a place where Lennon again filters lifelong memories, joining Oedipal images of his dead mother to those of Yoko Ono, his new lover.

An abrupt jump from guitars and keyboards to cellos and trumpets thwarts any attempt at secure grounding. This transition, which occurs at 1:00 in, famously unites two distinctly different takes of the track: one with guitar band, the other arranged for strings and horns. Lennon had waffled on which version he liked more until he instructed producer George Martin to simply combine the two after the first verse. "I said it was impossible," Martin replied, knowing that the two takes occupied completely different key areas. "You can fix it then," Lennon quipped (Martin 1979, 204). Martin's backroom solution neatly joins these two separate sessions by slowing the first down and speeding the other up just enough to match pitches—only in the "Strawberry Fields Forever" world, each resulting section sounds oddly off-kilter, as if spied through a thick lens, intensifying the overall sense of identity anxiety. Along with the timbre-distorting tape speeds and intermittent backward percussion, the sounds transport the singer and listener deep into the past, to a time preceding exile—or fame. Coming from the most famous pop star in the world, "Strawberry Fields Forever" plumbs irony in how beloved it became, the huge emotional nerve it struck in its boomer audience.

Listeners greeted "Strawberry Fields Forever" with waves of misunderstanding and awe, the composer's psyche heard center stage but buried under cryptic armor—a habit revisited in "I Am the Walrus," "Glass Onion," and "Come Together." In more recent decades, the song has emerged as a keystone of the Beatles' artistry and their commitment to human understanding and peaceful transcendence. As fans waited an unprecedented eleven months between Beatle albums, their only clues to what lay ahead seemed both baffling and poetic beyond all previous excursions.

POINTS FOR DISCUSSION

1. Name three ways experimentalism in the Beatles' music increases during the period encompassing 1965 and 1966.
2. Of the controversies that bedeviled the final 1966 Beatles tour, what aspects of Beatlemania seem to have led to trouble? When and how does over-ardent affection turn into zealotry and unpredictable mob chaos?

3. Name some examples of how the Beatles already began to see themselves as studio-centric musicians in 1966.

4. Examine the Lennon-McCartney songwriting partnership as it reaches "Penny Lane" / "Strawberry Fields Forever." How have they grown apart as songwriters? Can you think of other examples where a band contains two such distinct voices? Support your argument by comparing these songs with others.

5. Name some standout production touches across 1966 recordings: Which of these seem most experimental, or most judicious? Do any steal attention from the song's expression, or do they all suit their material? Why or why not?

6. Which *Revolver* songs have no guitars? Do other instruments fulfill their functions?

FURTHER READING

Frontani, Michael R. *The Beatles: Image and the Media.* Jackson: University Press of Mississippi, 2007.

Guralnick, Peter. *Sweet Soul Music: Rhythm and Blues and the Southern Dream of Freedom.* New York: Harper & Row, 1986.

Leary, Timothy, Ralph Metzner, and Richard Alpert. *The Psychedelic Experience: A Manual Based on the Tibetan Book of the Dead.* 1964. Reprint, New York: Citadel, 1995.

Martin, George. *All You Need Is Ears.* With Jeremy Hornsby. New York: St. Martin's, 1979.

O'Brien, Geoffrey. *Dream Time: Chapters From the Sixties.* New York: Counterpoint, 1988.

Stein, Jean, and George Plimpton. *Edie: An American Biography.* New York: Alfred A. Knopf, 1982.

CELEBRITY PSYCHEDELIA (1967)

The winter and spring sessions of early 1967 brought the Beatles to new artistic heights, transcending everything they had been working toward with *Rubber Soul* and *Revolver*. *Sgt. Pepper's Lonely Hearts Club Band* was the biggest game changer in rock history; it's a sprawling masterpiece that combines familiarity with surprise, innovation with technique, and imagination with technology. Alongside its prefatory single ("Penny Lane" / "Strawberry Fields Forever"), it signifies an artistic and commercial high point in their career, a ringing fulfillment of their promise, and of pop style's staying power.

However, the historical circumstances that brought *Pepper* to life contrast radically with its flamboyant reputation. As the Beatles worked on this recording, they watched their peers Mick Jagger and Keith Richards of the Rolling Stones jailed for drug use, the Vietnam War escalate dramatically, urban race riots continue, and the anxiety between generations only intensify.

1967 British Releases:

Single: "Strawberry Fields Forever" / "Penny Lane" (rel. Feb. 17)

LP: *Sgt. Pepper's Lonely Hearts Club Band* (rel. June 1)

Side 1:	Side 2:
"Sgt. Pepper's Lonely Hearts Club Band"	"Within You Without You"
"With a Little Help from My Friends"	"When I'm Sixty-Four"
"Lucy in the Sky with Diamonds"	"Lovely Rita"

<table>
<tr><td>"Getting Better"</td><td>"Good Morning Good Morning"</td></tr>
<tr><td>"Fixing a Hole"</td><td>"Sgt. Pepper's Lonely Hearts Club Band (Reprise)"</td></tr>
<tr><td>"She's Leaving Home"</td><td>"A Day in the Life"</td></tr>
<tr><td>"Being for the Benefit of Mr. Kite"</td><td></td></tr>
</table>

Single: "All You Need Is Love" / "Baby You're a Rich Man" (rel. July 7)
Single: "Hello Goodbye" / "I Am the Walrus" (rel. Nov. 24)
EP: *Magical Mystery Tour* (rel. Dec. 8)

<table>
<tr><td>Side 1:</td><td>Side 2:</td></tr>
<tr><td>"Magical Mystery Tour"</td><td>"I Am the Walrus"</td></tr>
<tr><td>"Your Mother Should Know"</td><td></td></tr>
<tr><td>Side 3:</td><td>Side 4:</td></tr>
<tr><td>"The Fool on the Hill"</td><td>"Blue Jay Way"</td></tr>
<tr><td>"Flying"</td><td></td></tr>
</table>

THE SUMMER OF LOVE

The year 1967 resists oversimplification as a psychedelic idyll. After taking their longest vacation from public life since 1963 in the autumn of 1966, the Beatles returned to the studio in December 1966 for work on a major new project. While this recording became their most famous title, *Sgt. Pepper's Lonely Hearts Club Band*, the racial, class, and generational conflicts surrounding them tilted toward extremes. Now that a sexual revolution, drug lifestyles, and rock's universal popularity transfixed the young, the world's inequities and military conflicts barreled ahead without notice. To many in the older generation, it seemed as if young people hoped to construct a delirious bubble in which they might escape the world's troubles. But to the rock artists and audience, the utopian impulses to transform the world through sound, color, and protest had an urgent sincerity even as innocence began to fade. The Beatles had striking and original comments on this situation, even though they were filtered through fictional mirrors.

The summer pop audience greeted *Pepper* like a prophecy, perhaps because of a buildup of anticipation, and perhaps because current events made it feel so needed, so necessary. Its June release kicked off the "summer of love," even though day-to-day life on the streets was far from tranquil. A right-wing coup took power in Greece in April and led to a military junta ruling until 1974. The same week *Pepper* appeared, Israel launched pre-emptive strikes against Egypt (the Six Day War) after Egyptian forces gathered on the Sinai Peninsula, adjoining the trade-sensitive Suez Canal. Before the peace agreement was signed on June 11, Israel had launched air strikes on both Jordan and Syria and began to occupy the Gaza strip. A highly efficient and fierce Israeli army suffered something under one thousand casualties against twenty-thousand-plus Arab deaths. A civil war also broke out in Nigeria that July, which led to famine and over a million deaths through 1970.

In America, President Johnson's mandatory conscription began siphoning young men for combat service in Vietnam, building troops levels up to 475,000. The year 1967 would be its bloodiest chapter yet, with over sixteen thousand American casualties. In May, seventy thousand protesters marched against the war; the following October, "Yippie" protestors Abbie Hoffman and Jerry Rubin promised to "levitate" the Pentagon with good vibes, leading demonstrators from the Lincoln Memorial.

(Norman Mailer wrote a hallucinatory account of this event for his Pulitzer Prize–winning *Armies of the Night* in 1968.) As if admitting failure, Secretary of Defense Robert McNamara resigned that fall, and Senator Eugene McCarthy (Democrat of Wisconsin) announced his presidential candidacy on a peace platform, challenging his own party's president. This exacerbated the arguments between young and old. The draftees, eighteen-to-twenty-one-year-olds forced to enlist even before they could vote, complained about hypocrisy and civilian casualties as their parents clung to the idea of "American exceptionalism." The World War II generation, steeped in heroic accomplishments, couldn't conceive that its government was systematically lying about its military mission and progress. In symbolic terms, many saw this as a father-son betrayal: the government conscripting teenage boys to fight an immoral war shielded by military fraud.

If hippies stood for the naive side of the counterculture, disappointments surrounding troop buildups pressured groups like the Students for a Democratic Society (SDS) and Stokely Carmichael's Black Power movement to swerve even further to the left. Beginning with its Port Huron Statement in 1962, the SDS had grown from regional chapters at the Universities of Michigan, Columbia, and Yale to a booming national movement of over half a million students. As the Vietnam War heated up, SDS protests led to sit-ins, teach-ins, and peaceful marches involving tens of thousands by 1967. Ultimately, tactical conflicts within the group led to the founding of the Weather Underground, which practiced "controlled" bombings of government property. This radical splinter sect named itself after a line from Bob Dylan's "Subterranean Homesick Blues": "You don't need a weatherman to know which way the wind blows." Heavyweight prize fighter Muhammad Ali (formerly Cassius Clay) refused to be drafted when his number came up in April 1967 as a conscientious objector, which led to the New York State Athletic Commission stripping him of the championship title he had seized in 1964. "I ain't got no quarrel with them Viet Cong," the quotable boxer declared in reference to the communist South Vietnamese united in resistance to American forces. "No Viet Cong ever called me Nigger." The bigger-than-life Ali crystallized the young person's refusal to accept racist hatred, murderous war, and religious intolerance. In 1971, the Supreme Court overturned his felony conviction, but only after he'd lost four peak years for refusing to serve. Ali's exoneration hinged on deprivation of due process in conflicting earlier decisions that had characterized his Islamist beliefs as insincere.

Urban riots continued in New Jersey and Michigan. Newark saw five days of looting and anger over police brutality that brought out the National Guard and left twenty-six dead that July. The disproportionate number of underclass and black troops in Vietnam only aggravated racial divisions. Wealthier and well-connected middle-class college students could often get education deferrals, whereas lower-class teenagers had fewer options. This continued prejudice against African Americans splintered the civil rights movement: Martin Luther King gave his first explicitly antiwar speech on April 4, called "Beyond Vietnam: A Time to Break Silence," as one of his voting rights activists, Stokely Carmichael, argued for great resistance to military imperialism, armed if necessary. The gap between young and old took on charged symbolic status as men grew their hair to their shoulders. Shouts of "Get a job" and "Cut your hair" from hardhat construction workers met with "Make love not war" and "Let your freak flag fly" from longhairs. Paul McCartney's *Pepper* song, "She's Leaving Home," conveys an elegant and largely sympathetic portrayal of the difficulty of one generation failing to communicate with the other ("What did we do that was wrong?"); the nonet of harp and strings places this song across an instrumentational divide from the remainder of the album. Steps toward equal opportunity for blacks proceeded with the confirmation of Thurgood Marshall as the first African American Supreme Court justice in August 1967.

In addition to rock's major themes of race, class, and generational tensions, religion began to play a bigger role. The Beatles took Harrison's Eastern mysticism seriously, and—following the lead of George's wife, Pattie Boyd Harrison—began to investigate Transcendental Meditation. In August 1967, while attending a weekend workshop in Wales led by their future guru, Maharishi Mahesh Yogi, the Beatles learned of the death of manager Brian Epstein from a barbiturate overdose. Although Brian's management duties shifted, with the end of the Beatles' touring, to booking other acts for his Saville Theatre in London, the Beatles' business anchor fell away, forcing them to reconceive their empire. The death was particularly tragic because as a gay man, Epstein had always been subject not only to bullying ridicule but also to prosecution under criminal anti-sodomy laws that were rescinded only a month before his death. The Maharishi became a father figure, and an Indian meditation retreat was planned for the fall. The group formed a new company, Apple, as a tax strategy and opened a clothing boutique in London that lost money hand over fist with criminally negligent mismanagement.

As their ambitions ballooned, so did their cultural relevance. The Beatles took a serious stand on world peace even though Britain never sent troops to Vietnam; when asked to represent the United Kingdom as one of nineteen countries participating in the first-ever live global satellite television broadcast, *Our World* of June 25, 1967, they performed their new anthem, "All You Need Is Love," which opened to mocking strains of France's "La Marseillaise," the national anthem the Allies once sang to drown out the Nazis' "Die Wacht am Rhein" in *Casablanca*. In musical terms, quoting "La Marseillaise" threw down a glove: Lennon wrote his own rock mission statement, an anthem to update the previous generation's antifascism.

Hippies, flower children, comprised the tender side of a counterculture centered in the Haight-Ashbury district of San Francisco, home to the Grateful Dead, the Jefferson Airplane, the Steve Miller Band, and other purveyors of "acid rock," which played out in Britain with Cream. The three-day Monterey Pop Festival in June 1967, a small-scale precursor of the Woodstock Music and Art Fair of 1969, featured some of these bands, as well as Janis Joplin, the Who, and the American "debut" of Jimi Hendrix (see Photos 7.01 and 7.02). Paul McCartney had personally recommended the Jimi Hendrix Experience to the organizers. Frank Zappa's arch social critique made fun of the hippies as well as the establishment they countered; the opening track of his 1968 release *We're Only in It for the Money* (with an inverted parody of *Pepper's* cover) skewered the runaways who dropped out of society to take drugs in San Francisco. George Harrison famously visited the Haight in August 1967 but became so turned off by flower-power naifs he renounced hallucinogens and recalibrated his spiritual search.

By this time, governments and the press had vilified LSD and recreational drugs, making their ingestion the perfect rebellious acts against "straight" culture. Many rock stars glorified their use, leading to law-enforcement crackdowns, particularly those led by London's zealous Sgt. Pilcher, who busted Mick Jagger, Keith Richard, and Brian Jones of the Stones in February and May 1967, John Lennon in November 1968, and George Harrison in March 1969. Throughout the spring of 1967, as *Pepper* sessions progressed, the Rolling Stones served time in jail for drugs Pilcher had planted on them and became early icons for the decriminalization of marijuana. For defrauding these high-profile defendants, Pilcher ultimately saw prison himself for four years on a perjury charge. (The charge against Lennon became particularly troublesome as a pretext for deportation attempts made while he was living in the United States in the early 1970s, subject to abuses of power in the Nixon White House, which feared that John would be formidable in galvanizing the

PHOTO 7.1. The Jimi Hendrix Experience, reverse of *Are You Experienced?* LP (originally released May 12, 1967; as reissued in US for CD in 2011). Hendrix is at center.

youth vote against Nixon in his 1972 bid for re-election.) The Beatles were always considered role models for the young, and the more outspoken they became, the harder those in power worked to tamp down their antiestablishment mystique. Although there was no draft in Britain, this became a hard line in how the state treated countercultural heroes. If the rock 'n' roll worldview involved drugs, busting rock stars became a key propaganda tactic in the early culture wars.

At the end of his short life, John Lennon turned philosophical about the Beatles' influence; in an interview held just a few weeks before he died in December 1980, he said,

> Whatever wind was blowing at the time moved the Beatles too. I'm not saying we weren't flags on top of the ship. But the whole boat was moving. Maybe the Beatles were in the crow's nest shouting "Land ho!" or something like that, but we were all in the same damn boat. (Sheff 1981, 205)

PHOTO 7.2. Psychedelic poster advertising Big Brother and the Holding Company, fronted by Janis Joplin, and Jack the Ripper at the Ark in Sausalito, California, October 6, 1967.

SGT. PEPPER'S LONELY HEARTS CLUB BAND

During the unprecedented ten-month gap between the release of *Revolver* in August 1966 and *Pepper* in June 1967, rumors swirled: the Beatles had run out of steam, they were working on a turkey, they were finished. The abstract promotional TV films for "Penny Lane" and "Strawberry Fields Forever" fed such talk. But the moment *Pepper* appeared, all negativity vanished. The music lit up the airwaves in a starburst of melody; radio stations competed with one another to see who could broadcast the album in its entirety the most times in a row; and the overwhelming audience response made their entire early career seem like a mere overture to this moment. When Jimi

Hendrix opened his June 4 show at Brian Epstein's Saville Theatre with the album's theme song, his audience knew every word, and the gesture was less a stunt than an oracle. "I put that down as one of the great honors of my career," McCartney said (McDermott 2009, 52).

Pepper's triumph was far from assured. Fans found the promotional films for "Penny Lane" and "Strawberry Fields Forever," broadcast on *American Bandstand* in February 1967, incomprehensible. Only those with considerably more musical experience, especially with a background in early twentieth-century classical works, understood the songs' originality and brilliance. These were highly expressive artworks, even if "Penny Lane" displayed a fanciful common touch, its layered meanings revealed only through repeated listenings. Poetry and musical craft reached an all-time peak, capping and expanding on a sequence of 1966 rock masterpieces like Bob Dylan's *Blonde on Blonde*, the Rolling Stones' *Between the Buttons* (see Photo 7.3), and the Beach Boys' *Pet Sounds*.

Sgt. Pepper's Lonely Hearts Club Band altered the pop world dramatically. The album's highly imaginative explorations of altered states, with Day-Glo colors in shifting forms, earned the term "psychedelic." These aural keepsakes resembled the light shows at Ken Kesey's acid tests, cosmic dance parties held with the Grateful Dead in San Francisco in the last months of 1965, while LSD was still legal. In London, psychedelic light shows drew hipsters into clubs like the UFO, where Pink Floyd improvised to trippy films, culminating in the "14 Hour Technicolor Dream" in April 1967. The Beatles even recorded an unpublished but legendary fourteen-minute tape piece,

PHOTO 7.3. The Rolling Stones, *Between the Buttons* LP (released in UK January 20, 1967).

"Carnival of Light," for "The Million-Volt Light and Sound Rave" hosted by a London theater in late January 1967. Despite frequent teases from McCartney, "Carnival" remains the holy grail of unreleased Beatles tracks.

Originally, McCartney brainstormed the larger *Pepper* concept as a way of refurbishing the image of the Beatles from teenybopper heartthrobs into a socially conscious young adult act. He pitched it to his bandmates as a way of changing from entertainers to artists:

> We were fed up with being the Beatles. . . . I thought, "Let's not be ourselves. Let's develop alter-egos so we're not having to project an image which we know." . . . What would really be interesting would be to actually take on the personas of this different band. . . . Then when John came up to the microphone or I did it, it wouldn't be John or Paul singing it, it would be the members of this band. It would be a freeing element. I thought we can run this philosophy through the whole album. . . . It won't be the Beatles, it'll be this other band, so we'll be able to lose our identities in this. (Martin 1992)

The Beatles realized this conceit by discarding their individual and collective egos in favor of a unified collaboration driven by a fictitious group. More than any singular visual, poetic, or aural feature, this reborn group identity maps the lasting impact of LSD on the Beatles' art. The album's concept took shape as an illusory performance by an unreal band, pictured on the cover as if exploding the Jefferson Airplane's *Surrealistic Pillow* pose, showing band members holding orchestral instruments they didn't really play.

McCartney sketched out the design, and Robert Fraser (an art dealer and mutual friend with Barry Miles) hired Peter Blake and Jann Haworth to supervise Michael Cooper's camera with a collection of life-size photographs, props, and wax figures (including the Beatles' own mop-top likenesses from Madame Tussauds). The photo session assembled an elaborately staged picture to recreate earlier motifs like Raphael's *School of Athens* (1509–1511), which positioned Greek intellectuals in a tableau, or the surrealist Max Ernst's *Au rendez-vous des amis* ("At a rendezvous of friends," 1922), where he posed his colleagues as both peers and mystics of surrealism. The notorious *Pepper* cover (Photo 7.4) has entered pop history as an example of Blake's postmodern "pop art," which already included a prominent canvas titled *The 1962 Beatles* (1963–1968). The *Pepper* image built off his earlier work where Blake lionized American pop culture icons, in paintings like *Self-Portrait with Badges* (1961) and *Got a Girl* (1961–1962), but he has long expressed bitterness that he was paid a flat fee of £200. In the Beatles catalog, this image carried through on collages from the *Beatles for Sale* inner gatefold, the family assortment adorning the "Strawberry Fields Forever" 45 rpm sleeve, and Klaus Voorman's *Revolver* patchwork.

This celebrity montage outlines a major *Pepper* theme: the triumph of twentieth-century pop culture, a postmodern lust for notoriety, and the new claims for pop art's legitimacy. At the time, most of the figures leading the style were recognizable but were not considered respectable "artists"; largely through *Pepper* and the Beatles' catalog, pop culture has since entered academia as a respectable course of study. In the Beatles' case, their career signified the triumph of commercial success combined with poetic gravity, and as they stand self-consciously in front of a host of popular figures from the century leading up to the time of their exalted status, they signal a knowingness about fame's brevity, how most celebrities seem oddly nostalgic and two-dimensional in

PHOTO 7.4. The Beatles as photographed on March 30, 1967, by Michael Cooper for the *Sgt. Pepper's Lonely Hearts Club Band* LP (released in UK June 1, 1967).

modern technology's rearview mirrors, and how being the most famous of the famous can obscure your best work. The sustained popularity of this image creates its own paradox.

Because they had given up two of the three songs they had already produced toward their next album, the Beatles built *Pepper* around the remaining number ("When I'm Sixty-Four"), and the next track they produced ("A Day in the Life"). Or, to be more precise, they conceived a frame that included the former and positioned the latter *outside* the album proper, delivered by a deflated narrator who presented *Pepper*'s fictions with a final sense of resignation. (A favorite parlor game involves considering how *Pepper* might have been inflected if it had included "Penny Lane" and/or "Strawberry Fields Forever.") While recorded early, "A Day in the life," the band's most ambitious songwriting collaboration and orchestral production, served as the album's coda, a morning-after hangover from the revelry of the night before. This shadows the rest of *Pepper*'s mood, and gives the lie to any two-dimensional readings. If *Pepper*'s fantasies and technicolor costumes create a utopian hope, "A Day in the Life" finishes the record off with a cold splash of dismal reality.

That the Beatles created *Pepper* under these reclusive conditions made their commitment to the project and its ambitious concept all the more remarkable. The opening sound of the album, of an orchestra warming up and a crowd murmuring excitedly before a live concert, hints at the conundrums most contemporaneous listeners appreciated: for their first all-studio effort, the Beatles pretended to be a Victorian brass band, "guaranteed to raise a smile." Even in these early moments, the Beatles knew they had crafted a series of songs they never intended to perform live, and beyond this, these tracks referred to the wild live setting as counterpoint to the immaculate production of a controlled environment. Engineer Geoff Emerick won a Grammy Award in the non-classical category for his work on this production, the first such technical recognition for a rock album.

The LP opened and closed with a theme song, marked by an anticipation-filled and appreciative audience, with "A Day in the Life" rising from the experience more like an after-concert apparition than an encore. With this concluding song from *Pepper*, its interior "Lucy in the Sky with Diamonds" and other key Beatle releases of 1967—"Strawberry Fields Forever" and "I Am the Walrus" from *Magical Mystery Tour*—John Lennon wrote his group's defining masterpieces, but Paul McCartney shaped the large-scale framework (album-cover concept and the "live" show conceit). Just as he counted off the Beatles for their first LP, he conceived the concepts for both large 1967 projects: the clock-face "script" Paul had sketched to determine the structure of *Magical Mystery Tour* can easily be found online.

The *Pepper* "show" begins with colorful, entertaining sing-alongs ("With a Little Help from My Friends") and moves through innocence and fun ("Getting Better" and "Lovely Rita") to greater and greater complexity (the major-minor instabilities of "Fixing A Hole," the elaborate tape manipulations for the whirligig effects in "Being for the Benefit of Mr. Kite"). "She's Leaving Home" describes the unsatisfying home life of a runaway from her parents' point of view; it remains one of the very few explicitly topical songs in the Beatles' entire catalog. At the end of side 1, "Being for the Benefit of Mr. Kite" details an 1840s handbill from a traveling circus that Lennon analogizes with rock 'n' roll (penning many phrases straight from the vintage poster), with shifting tonal centers (C minor, D minor, and E minor) for a three-ring circus. At the opening of side 2, an Indian interlude (with sitar, tabla, svaramandal, dilruba, and tamboura) interrupts the show for Harrison's "Within You Without You," which (even with George Martin's overdubbed string arrangement) casts a chimeric glow, especially next to the corny nostalgia of "When I'm Sixty-Four." "Good Morning Good Morning" is less a song than a manic episode (seared by a gleaming McCartney guitar solo), a breathless Corn Flakes ad that swallows up the narrator's daily routine.

People quickly pointed to "Lucy in the Sky with Diamonds" as an acronym for LSD, although Lennon maintained he was simply attaching childlike, Lewis Carroll imagery to the name of a painting by his three-year-old son, Julian. Carroll's way of thinking links Lennon's 1966 appropriation of Leary in "Tomorrow Never Knows" and 1967's "A Day in the Life," a song with two topics suggested by newspaper stories. (George would thereafter be the one to rely most often on found lyrics, as in "The Inner Light" and "Savoy Truffle," while a Beatle, and—from among his solo works—"The Ballad of Sir Frankie Crisp (Let It Roll)," its images drawn from a map of his Henley-on-Thames grounds.)

Despite its considerable charms and these heavy borrowings, *Pepper*'s colorful veneer masks a painstaking technical project. It required 324 hours of studio time for arranging, recording, mixing, and preparing masters. (Recall that the fourteen songs of *Please Please Me* were fully done, recorded, edited, and mixed, in twenty-eight total hours' work just four years earlier.) *Pepper's* tonal shifts alternated the cheery with the avant-garde, the reassuring with the confessional, with little or no silence between songs—a seamless parade of situations held together less by common theme than by the colorful arrangements and harmonies. Aside from the degree of composition and arranging now done in the studio at all hours of the night and early morning, the Beatles devoted far more time to figuring out how to commit ideas to tape, often by inventing new gadgets (such as the use of a control voltage to gang together multiple tape machines for the orchestra in "A Day in the Life") and multiple generations of four-track tape. The results sound delightfully artificial, skirting attempts to sound "live" as they strove to seem as unreal as possible, with heavy reverb applied to some parts and not others, as well as expressive panning from one speaker to the other and back (especially in the "A Day in the Life" lead vocal), effects that would never occur in real performance space. This, as much as any aspect of the otherworldly lyrics or the psychedelic music's form, colors, or rhythmic structure, laid the groundwork for the progressive rock of the Zombies, the Moody Blues, Pink Floyd, Jimi Hendrix, Cream, and Yes. Add conceptual artist Yoko Ono, who had worked with John Cage and the performance-artist collective Fluxus before intensifying a relationship with John Lennon in late 1967, and you have the pinnacle of experimental pop when a broadcast of Shakespeare's *King Lear* seeps into the dire, masterfully creepy "I Am the Walrus."

As links between tracks vanish, thematic connections stray until the reprise, when the show returns and the album draws to a close. Only upon its self-conscious ending does the entirety of *Pepper* come into view as a series of entertainments, distractions, and situations encased in a show with an opener reprised at the end for a proper finish. The fictional *Pepper* band re-emerges to the sound of Ringo Starr's propulsive backbeat (after the closing sounds of "Good Morning" morph into the cries of farm animals) and frames all the proceedings as harmless diversion. All winds to a close with false modesty and showbiz flattery (even a corny truck driver's modulation from F major to G major at 0:42) as the disc just about runs out of grooves. *Pepper* artfully exploits its own medium's contours: the pop album as two-sided vinyl, complete with an unprecedented lyric sheet on the back cover. The celebrity culture that had swirled around the band for four years now became one of Lennon and McCartney's great subjects.

"Lucy in the Sky with Diamonds"

Recorded March 1 and 2, 1967, for *Sgt. Pepper's Lonely Hearts Club Band*

—investigating what is perhaps the Beatles' creative peak in the blending and contrasting of psychedelic colors, this essay details the track's careful construction of experimental instrumental timbres and control-room tape manipulation. The song's formal structure has the listener meander down the rabbit hole from enigmatic verse through tonally unexpected pre-chorus to heartily announced chorus, as the singer searches for—and ultimately finds—Lucy!

"Lucy in the Sky with Diamonds": a song whose title was the product of the imagination of a three-year-old Julian Lennon (who used the phrase to describe a picture he had drawn) and whose fantastic imagery was inspired by the Beatle father's fond memories of Lewis Carroll's *Alice* books. The coincidence that the initialism of Julian's phrase, LSD, matches the common name of John's then-favorite form of chemical mind expansion is happily cosmic, and the recording combines one of Lennon's most perfect blendings of evocative lyrics, ingeniously appropriate formal structure, tonal intrigue, and vibrant color palette.

The Beatles' many song manuscripts (such as those collected in Davies 2014 and Harrison 1980), from first drafts to fair copy, contain nothing but lyrics (and occasionally a reference to "Intro," "Middle 8," or "Chorus"), with only rare exceptions: John has written out the complex chords to the intro to "If I Fell"; Paul keeps track of some unusual tonal shifts in both "Good Day Sunshine" and "Penny Lane"; an enigmatic jotting, "D–C–E–C–E–A" appears for the "Something" solo; and a number of interesting notes are preserved in three "Lucy" documents. The first (Davies 2014, 201) indicates "break/drums etc." before the chorus lyrics and "D to A" after them. The "drums" and chord ideas were worth preserving: it was key that Ringo (alone) mark the radical changes of both tempo and meter that lead into the chorus with his stop-time four-on-the-floor doubling of bass drum and toms, and that the D major–A major progression mark the "ahhh" plagal retransition from choruses to verses. A second copy of the full lyrics (Davies 2014, 202) is likely the sheet from which John sang in rehearsal and recording; it includes several notes on instrumentation written afterward:

"ORGAN" at the top (this is the harpsichord-like solo Lowrey organ with which
    Paul introduces the track, as a reworked performance of his Mellotron intro to
    "Strawberry Fields Forever")
"drums" after the word "skies," which is where Ringo's cymbals enter
"ORGAN, TAMBURA" just before the second phrase of the first verse ("Somebody
    calls you"), where the tamboura fades in
"Guitar, dropping bass" for the pre-chorus ("Cellophane flowers"), which is marked by
    the entries of two guitars played by George and a change in Paul's bass part from a
    stepwise descent to a simple alternation of roots and fifths (and this may suggest
    a late entry of the bass during rehearsals, before Paul ultimately composed the
    eventual bass line); and
"Piano" before the titular chorus, where the Vox Continental enters (studio
    documentation often refers to this Vox electronic organ as an "(electric) piano," to
    the confusion of many scholars).

In the third, most interesting document (Davies 2014, 242), Paul has written cues from the lyrics, along with his own notes on arrangement, which would make it seem as though Lennon and McCartney both kept track of the same instrumentation decisions made as rehearsal progressed:

"organ" for the first verse

"Drums, cymbal, out, tambura + organ left hand" before "kaleidoscope eyes" and
   "drums again, cymbal" after (the hi-hat enters after the first and second phrases
   but is out while they are sung)

"guitar enter drums (middle) Bass" (suggesting that Paul considered the pre-chorus
   to be a "middle 8")

"F (D min)" (an almost unique notation of chord changes for the complex modulation
   from A major to B♭)

"No gap" before the chorus lyric and "Piano, drums / guitar, fast comp jigger jigger.
   Organ on D to A" (an indication of fill to appear before the chorus; "piano" and
   "organ" roles would both be played on the Vox Continental in the recording; the
   "jigger jigger" seems to be the only notated suggestion of rhythm in a Beatles
   manuscript).

This sheet also includes John's citation of the book *Brotherhood of Light*, a
compendium of tarot cards, and Paul's suggestion for the running order of *Pepper* tracks
with John's filling-in of his abbreviations; the reverse side of the sheet includes John's
late-March notation of lyrics for "Fool on the Hill." The lengthy rehearsal at which all of
these instrumentation decisions were made, on February 28, 1967, was documented with
250 photographs taken by Henry Grossman for *Life* magazine and collected in the 2008
book *Kaleidoscope Eyes*.

We label the song sections thus:

Introduction: A triple-meter arpeggiation of the fifth in the tonic A-major triad, over a
   chromatically descending bass, played solo by Paul on the Lowrey Heritage Deluxe
   organ. In its way, this is a descendent of the "And Your Bird Can Sing" bridge and
   a progenitor of sections of "I Am the Walrus," "Dear Prudence," "While My Guitar
   Gently Weeps," "Something," and "I Want You (She's So Heavy)."

Verses: Led by John's singing "Picture yourself" or "Follow her down," initially on
   an unchanging pitch in a choppy rhythm, but following a suggestion from Paul to
   sing it more flowingly, John passes down and up from that pitch with smoother
   phrasing. Two similar phrases, of nine and then ten bars, with different endings
   (the second one dwelling on newly minor triads). The verse leads smoothly to the
   pre-chorus over a stepwise-descending bass line that modulates from A major to a
   tonally distant B♭ major.

Pre-choruses: "Cellophane flowers," retaining more of the monotonous melody, with
   occasional neighbors, all over a new tonal center, B♭. Appears only following the
   first and second verses (the third verse moves, instead, directly to the final chorus
   without intervention of a pre-chorus), with a strong half cadence of the next key, G
   major, on "gone" an unprepared drum transition, suggesting the sudden vanishing
   of a triple-meter apparition, replaced by the quadruple-meter celebration.

Pre-choruses are slightly faster than the verses; choruses have a slower pulse, but their beat divisions and subdivisions are faster than preceding sections.

Choruses: Repeating the song's title, in G major but concluding with a plagal cadence in A major, as noted above. The chorus melody and the descant Paul adds above it descend while the bass line climbs the scale, the contrary motion reminiscent of "All My Loving." The final chorus moves directly into the

Coda, with the plagal cadences in A followed directly by repetitions of the G-major chorus.

A detailed focus on the song's atmospheric performing forces, showing the group's greatest attention to date to tone-color details—and therefore the peak of the psychedelic tonal palette, will be organized by chronology of their recording for the final master. In working up a reconstruction of the recording process for "Lucy," all available performances and mixes have been carefully examined, as have the best prior attempts at reconstruction.[1] The basic track, recorded in take 7 on March 1, was comprised of:

Lowrey organ, played by Paul. Babiuk (2015, 395) gives the registration as harpsichord, vibraharp, music box, and guitar stops, and this is borne out by our own experimentation. (All registrations shown in Grossman's photos from the night before show other settings, when compared to the Lowrey owner's manual, also marked by full brilliance, vibrato, and long sustain.) This exotic-sounding part (left-hand descent, right hand marking the A-major arpeggiation) is played only in the intro and verses and given heavy reverb; in most mixes, the Lowrey fades up in entering second and third verses, partly to mute out some infelicitous notes from Paul.

Ringo's drums, played differently in each section. Silent until the end of the first verse's first phrase (downbeat bass-drum hits are muted out through the verse), Ringo announces himself with an incongruous shuffle on the closed hi-hat (0:15–0:19) that disappears with the vocal re-entry; this second phrase is marked only by one hit on the open hi-hat. The verse ends with bass-drum downbeats and the open hi-hat struck on each beat (0:26–0:32). In pre-choruses (0:32–0:47), Ringo strikes a ringing ride cymbal on each beat with the tip of the stick (with occasional shuffle) over the continuing bass-drum downbeats: the continuous rhythmic pattern covers the seam between verse and pre-chorus, but the cymbal color changes between sections. Four stop-time hits, one per beat, on bass drum and slack-tuned floor tom

1. Recordings include an "early rehearsal take" (take 1?) of the basic track (heard on George Martin's 1992 television special *The Making of Sgt. Pepper*), mono and stereo mixes released in 1967, the scuttled November 1967 mono mix (RM 20) given a new first verse sung by the actor who portrays "Jeremy" for the *Yellow Submarine* soundtrack. The 1987 stereo mix (essentially the same as that for 1967), the "outfake" based on take 6 for the second volume of the *Anthology* CDs (1996), true digital remixes made for the *Yellow Submarine Songtrack* (1999, highly recommended), *Love* (2006, given unfortunate extra strings and guitars), and Rock Band (2009) projects, plus out-of-phase remixes of all stereo tracks and the individual Rock Band MOGG stems. Prior scholarly attempts at reconstruction are found in Lewisohn 1988, Everett 1999, Winn 2003 and 2005, and Kehew and Ryan 2006.

together, set up the tempo for choruses. Here and through the coda, Ringo moves to the shoulder of the stick on the constant ride cymbal over a backbeat on snare and bass drum (with frequent division of the bass drum beats).

Gibson acoustic-electric J-160, played by George, and *Steinway piano*, played by George Martin. The guitar is present for pre-choruses and choruses only (strumming chords on each beat), and the piano is played only for a single loud, long-sustaining D-minor chord at the end of each verse (first at 0:29), as if a foreshadowing of the final "A Day in the Life" chord. Both piano and guitar are heavily processed, with both strong ADT and unnatural equalization (possibly through the RS 56 Curve Bender unit that George is pictured adjusting in the control room on February 28). The ADT creates what became known as a "flanging" effect, as multiple identical signals move in and out of phase with each other. Although the piano is played loudly, both piano and Gibson are low in all mixes.

Vox Continental II organ, probably played by John. Unconnected right-hand block-chord triads played on offbeats through the first and second choruses, but on strong beats through third verse and coda, and out during verses and pre-choruses. (This is not likely Paul, even though he agrees with Martin, in Martin 1992, that it was "probably" him on this part). John may also be shaking a maraca in his left hand through pre-choruses and choruses; sound sources suggest this but are not conclusive in corroborating written documentation.

Tamboura, played by George. Replacing John's guide vocal, which can be heard on the *Anthology* and also bleeding onto the drum track, the tamboura fades into the second phrase of the first verse and sustains through all other full verses.

These instruments filled all four tracks of the first generation of tape and were reduced to a single track for overdubs made the next day:

Vocals by John and Paul: John sang verses and pre-choruses alone; Paul added a descant line to choruses (moving from unison to descant at different points in the first and second choruses). Colors are radically altered by both ADT and varispeed for very unreal "down the rabbit hole" sonorities. John's initial vocal is taped slowly to sound sped up (higher and faster) on replay at conventional speed. For the pre-chorus, John tapes a second vocal track, to sound even faster. These two tracks actually overlap at the unison for the entirety of all lines referring to the "girl with kaleidoscope eyes" and "that grow so incredibly high" for a highly unusual blend in transitioning between vocal speeds from verses to pre-choruses. With "eyes," the echo is brought up strongly for pre-chorus vocals, but choruses contain no echo beyond light reverb. Either John or Paul cannot resist backbeat handclaps in the coda's final chorus run-through.

Paul's Rickenbacker bass: This is probably recorded both by microphone at the amplifier and direct-injected into the board, both signals mixed on tape in varying ratios through the song. Verses seem fully direct-injected, but pre-choruses feature leakage from the room (plus a touch of tape echo and what seems to be a slowly rotating Leslie drum); choruses add more reverb to the Leslie artifact. Paul articulates downbeats only through verses, doubling his left-hand Lowrey descent, but anticipates the even three-notes-per-bar rhythm of pre-choruses already on the minor chords as Ringo opens his hi-hat. Arpeggiation in the pre-choruses gives way to scalar ascents in choruses, creating the contrary motion noted above. The line becomes freer in the coda, incorporating syncopated rhythms at 3:01–3:03 and with lowered seventh scale degrees added at 3:15–3:22. The bass is given prominence in all mixes.

George's two electric guitars: George adds two distinctive electric-guitar colorings. In pre-choruses, he doubles John's vocal with pronounced slides like those heard on the dilrubas or sarangis played elsewhere on 1967 Beatle tracks, such as "Within You Without You" and "Blue Jay Way." In choruses, we hear his Leslie-laden guitar double the bass line. The Leslied guitar may have been punched into the same track that the slide guitar had occupied first. Aside from the J-160, the only guitars pictured in Grossman 2008 are John and George's Casinos and John's Stratocaster. This does not mean that others were not available during the overdub session two days later (they were stored in EMI closets; it's also noted that the Leslie cabinet is not seen on the floor in any February 28 photos), but the slide part is consistent with the Casino's sound, and the Leslied part has a Strat's growl.

In the year when guitarists Jimi Hendrix and Eric Clapton demonstrated that rock music had room for instrumental virtuosity, the Beatles showed no interest in flashy displays of dexterity. But no one could conjure such variety within these constraints. While the contrast of so many performance techniques and electronic timbres makes for a highly varied mix of unusual tone colors, the way they relate to each other is more interesting still. All basic-track instruments are mixed to one tape track with heavy ADT that camouflages the acoustic guitar and piano. We've already noticed the overlaps in differently sped-up vocals. The first entry of electronically altered cymbals is almost lost in the Lowrey, and the tamboura, cymbals, and Lowrey together blend in ways that may be recognized as having been attempted in some *Revolver* mixes but that seem much more thoroughgoing here. The doublings of vocal and then bass lines with differently hued electric guitars shift colors just like Lucy's kaleidoscopes and Alice's experiences. The extreme phasing given to the slightly slower/lower mono mixes provides a constant envelope across the ever-changing thickness of their textures. "Lucy in the Sky with Diamonds" is a wonder-filled impressionistic journey from one unreal place to another, its unusual contrasting timbres coalescing around unexpected tonal twists in a labyrinthine formal structure that portrays a wryly crooked step through a mirror's reflection to take the listener from the Red King's dream to a mad tea party.

CUE	SECTION	HARMONY	DETAIL
0:00	Intro	A: I over descending bass	PM on Lowrey organ
0:05	Verse1: phrase 1	I over descending bass→VI	JL vocal
0:18	Verse 1: phrase 2	I over descending bass–vi–iv	GH tamboura enters
0:32	Pre-chorus: phrase 1	B♭: I–II9/7–V add6–I	JL higher vocal, GH slide guitar
0:42	Pre-chorus: phrase 2	G: IV9/7–I–V	Leads to transitional HC
0:50	Chorus	G: I–IV–V rptd; A: IV	PM/JL vocal duet with plagal retrans.
1:07	Verse 2	A: I . . . vi–iv	
1:32	Pre-chorus	B♭: I to G: V	
1:50	Chorus	G: I to A: IV	
2:08	Verse 3	A: I–vi–iv	
2:32	Chorus and coda	G: I–IV–V rptd; A: IV–I	

"A Day in the Life"

Recorded January 19 and 20, and February 3, 10, and 22, 1967, for *Sgt. Pepper's Lonely Hearts Club Band*

—Lennon and McCartney complement each other as they goad themselves into new depths of angst amidst a banality shattered by a new use of symphony orchestra that catches the ear of classical composers, just as the day's leading poets find respect for these self-taught one-time mop tops.

For the finale, the reprise to the *Pepper* theme song segues directly into Lennon's forbidding acoustic guitar introduction for "A Day in the Life." After waving goodbye to the fictional audience, the curtain descends on the album's illusory world, and a new narrator greets us from a private, hyperrealistic realm: alone with ominous piano, bass, and despondent maracas, Lennon recounts his daily ritual of reading the newspaper, whose stories provoke anguished, existential sighs: "oh boy." The first two verses relate a fatal car crash, with the detail hovering around the unrecognizability of the victim: "Nobody was really sure if he was from the House of Lords."[2] The British think of their House of Lords as one antique remnant of the British Empire: if you're loaded and born into a family with a title, you serve in that uppermost chamber as a matter of birth, not aptitude; in power circles, it's the ultimate "men's club." In the House of Lords, you can be "famous" without quite being familiar, renowned yet anonymous.

2. The real-life crash victim is widely believed to have been the twenty-one-year-old scenester Tara Browne, heir to the Guinness ale fortune. The *Daily Mirror* headline from Dec. 16, 1966, reads *"Guinness Heir Saved Girl's Life in Crash"* (Harry 2001, 135–136).

In the third verse, Lennon reads about a movie he's seen (it's actually *How I Won the War*, in which Lennon stars), in which the English army has just won the war, and the violence makes a crowd of people turn their heads away. Pop audiences don't want to know how wars are won any more than how sausages are made. But Lennon's narrator can't turn away from the gore; he simply has to look, "having read the book"; he feels a moral responsibility to the material. At the end of this verse, he ascends into guileless falsetto for the song's lingering rejoinder, "I'd love to turn you on." At the time, this was an explicit drug reference, a pickup line people might use at parties to share premium weed or acid. But in the context of the song, the line works poetically on different levels: it's the narrator wishing for a more enlightened world, one where violence and carnage doesn't intrude, where the poetry of everyday life can elevate monotonous routine and innocence answers evil.

The second time he lands on this line, a huge orchestra swoops into the mix for a transition that mixes escalating fear with a fearsome resolve: in an avant-garde move, musicians were told to play whatever notes they wished in a generally rising motion and land together on a target, and once they hit their peak, the noise suddenly drops away and an alarm clock goes off (left, at 2:18). A new character enters (in the voice of Paul McCartney), and the listener wonders whether the preceding section has been a dream, or nightmare, that this new singer awakens from. McCartney's character has a completely different outlook than Lennon's: he wakes up late, falls out of bed, dashes to catch his bus, and lights up a smoke (marijuana?) as he heads off to work. McCartney's busybody replaces Lennon's oversensitive narrator—he's a bureaucrat, say, who doesn't pay any mind to the world around him, let alone read the paper. He remains sublimely checked out of reality, until a drag on his smoke sends him off into a dream, and the orchestra re-enters with Lennon singing "Aaaaah." After a brass flourish, we land back in Lennon's world for the final verse. Does McCartney parachute down into Lennon's song, or does Lennon's narrative simply let McCartney's sideshow in from some trap door? This song-within-a-song structure remains striking for how elegantly it suits the larger idea: that simple engagement with the contemporary world involves suffering, and staying "sane" relies on tuning everything out.

This last verse turns the most commonplace detail into the song's most disturbing image: someone like a Kafkaesque clerk has counted how many potholes speckle the streets of Blackburn, Lancashire, and as a deliberate anticlimax to Lennon's and McCartney's triptych, it emphasizes how wayward and meaningless modern bureaucracy has become, and how many empty souls populate the world (echoing the obliviousness of "Nowhere Man," and "all the lonely people" from "Eleanor Rigby"). By the last time John sings "I'd love to turn you on," the track has built up a scaffolding of philosophical dread, and as the orchestra re-enters for its final horrific ascent, the soundscape turns frantic, brutal, unyielding. By the time they reach their top pitches, a rush of anxiety and paranoia has built up that can't be assuaged. After a moment's suspenseful pause (at 4:20), a gigantic E-major chord played on multiple keyboards (4:21) brings the track to a crushing close, like a huge, heavy door slamming shut on some cultural dystopia. Engineer Geoff Emerick artificially extended the piano's decay across forty seconds of unbearable tension, even more unsettling than either orchestral climax in that it nullifies all possibility of resolution, or escape. Both those orchestral peaks cry out for release, and this declamatory yet hollow chord reverberates just long enough to deny it.[3]

As a finale, "A Day in the Life" casts a gigantic shadow over the album it closes. It's impossible to listen all the way through without the illusory promise of its opening moments dropping away for its dreadful, inelegant close. This single track lifts *Pepper* out of the pop context and gives it a weight and self-consciousness it wouldn't otherwise have: fame and fortune and pop fantasy all have their pleasures, the Beatles seem to be saying, but after the show's over we all return to modern life, which is brutal, full of random savagery, answered by neglect and worse: mundane tasks—the counting of potholes. When Bob Dylan eulogizes Lennon in "Roll On John" (which ends *Tempest*, 2012), it's "A Day in the Life" that provides the first quoted Beatle lines. When *Pepper* gets referred to as a masterpiece, "A Day in the Life" is the main reason why: it elevates everything it follows, and works as a diagram of Lennon's and McCartney's opposing concerns like a negative image of "We Can Work It Out." The subtext to that song was "No we can't, really." This song recontextualizes that theme in artistic terms (two songwriters, stitching different worldviews together) and goads the listener to listen beyond the color, texture, and promise of hallucination to the other side of fantasy, the daily prompts for escape. Folded into the structure of this dual narrative lies the suggestion that Lennon dreams McCartney and McCartney dreams Lennon, an astral metaphor for the songwriting partnership as it begins to crack open. It also echoes the cover's visual collage with an audio montage. Reality intrudes on fantasy, and while *Pepper* stands as a psychedelic carousel, its greatness stems from how Lennon and McCartney use their own sparring partnership to stitch a masterpiece about the limits of entertainment. From this point on, their utopian promise for a world rejuvenated by music becomes inexorably shaded by a dark undertow.

CUE	SECTION	HARMONY	DETAIL
0:00	Intro	G: I–iii6/4–vi–4/2–IV	
0:12	Verse1: *a'*	I–iii6/4–vi–4/2–IV–4/2–ii9	JL vocal (4 bars of 4/4)
0:25	Verse 1: *a"*	I–iii6/4–vi–4/2–IV–♭VII–vi–4/2–IV	with extension (6 bars)

3. Walter Everett is grateful to Megan McDevitt for noting in a March 2015 conversation that this ending of a G-major song with an E-major triad is a full-blown explosion of the final added-sixth chord (an E added to G major) of "She Loves You."

CUE	SECTION	HARMONY	DETAIL
0:44	Verse 2: *a'*		(4 bars)
0:56	Verse 2: *a"*		w/o extension, but expanded (5 bars)
1:11	Verse 3: *a'*		(4 bars)
1:23	Verse 3: *a"*		(5-bar version, given tag)
1:39	Transition tag	IV >>>> E: I	(14 bars, with orchestral rise)
2:20	Bridge	E: I→VII–I–V9–I–V9	PM vocal (10 bars of 4/8) (repeated)
2:48	Retransition	E:♭VI→III→VII–IV–I	(5 bars of 4/4) (repeated)
3:17	Verse 4	(same as Verse 3)	
3:46	Transition tag	IV >>>> E: I	(13 bars, w/ orch. rise to final chord)

MAGICAL MYSTERY TOUR

After Epstein's death, the group delayed a fall trip to India and decided instead to keep working, stay busy, and deal with its grief by concentrating on music. Unfortunately, this came with a parallel contract to shoot a one-hour TV film. In the spirit of Ken Kesey's Merry Pranksters, who had sojourned across America in a psychedelic bus named *Further* in 1964, the Beatles followed McCartney's concept: hire a bunch of eccentric actors and extras, climb on board a tour bus with no fixed destination, and improvise dialogue. Having repeatedly charmed the world's press, they reasoned they were good enough at extemporizing to carry the patter between musical numbers and had earned the self-governing status to create and produce their own film instead of relying on established hands for a prefabricated rerun of *Help!*

They had been recording steadily ever since wrapping *Pepper* and knew more tracks would come of their own volition, so they forged ahead. The history of film is rife with egotists who think they can outsmart the medium; Ingrid Bergman left her husband to join Roberto Rossellini in 1949 to make the experimental "neo-realist" movie *Stromboli* without a script, inspired by reality. But a weak script tends to work better than no script at all: improvising entire scenes based on whimsy undervalues the frames that most good improvisation clings to, and even when laced with Beatle tracks, a mass-movie audience expects characters, plot, and conflict. Unfortunately, again, these Beatle tracks came hard upon the spring's masterpiece and suffered from the comparison: if *Magical Mystery Tour* had been *Pepper* with a contrived plot outline, at least it could have leaned on better music. For the soundtrack, numbers like "Your Mother Should Know" seemed like a dim reprise of "When I'm Sixty-Four," and "Blue Jay Way" was an exotic indulgence that made "Within You Without You" seem downright terse. Only "I Am the Walrus" (a still from which scene appears as Photo 7.5) holds up as a bold piece of experimental stream of consciousness, a Lennon salute to Lewis Carroll complete with talking animals and wayward symbols.

PHOTO 7.5. The Beatles miming to "I Am the Walrus" on an airfield in West Malling, Kent, in mid-September 1967 for gatefold for inner booklet of *Magical Mystery Tour* EP (released in UK December 8, 1967).

In postproduction, the film project unspooled still further, with McCartney and Lennon competing as film editors and McCartney running off to France for the only professionally shot camerawork in the piece, for "A Fool on the Hill," which made the result both ponderous and discontinuous.

The resulting homemade bomb, *Magical Mystery Tour*, was shown on BBC-TV on Boxing Day, December 26, but unfortunately in black and white, draining the project of its mind-altering color and heightening the contrast between its flowery goals and amateurish realization. (It's impossible to imagine their first self-directed color film airing in black and white on Epstein's watch.) *Pepper* had restored the Beatles' credibility after the backlash of 1966, but by the end of 1967, *Magical Mystery Tour* collected new critical drubbings. The year ended with a level of discomfort not felt since they had quit performing. The musical soundtrack appeared in Britain in a unique format: across two 45 rpm EPs in a colorful package with booklet (see Photo 7.6); in America, Capitol combined the movie material on side 1 of an LP with the year's A- and B-sides (including "Penny Lane" and "Strawberry Fields Forever") on side 2. Monumental greatness still lay ahead, but at the beginning of 1968, the Beatles strongly felt they deserved a break from fame and recording. So they finally headed off to India.

PHOTO 7.6. The Beatles in mid-September 1967, *Magical Mystery Tour* EP (released in UK December 8, 1967).

"The Fool on the Hill"

Recorded September 26–27 and October 20, 1967, for *Magical Mystery Tour*

—*as if in reaction to the complex mystery of "A Day in the Life," Paul offers a musically simplistic portrait of an unaffected soul.*

Most hear the second half of 1967 as the only dip in an otherwise brilliantly consistent aesthetic drive and forgive *Magical Mystery Tour*'s indulgences in light of *Pepper*'s brilliance. *Magical Mystery Tour* has its strengths: in its sheer effrontery and strangeness, "I Am the Walrus" continues to baffle in interesting ways (even if the production sounds comparatively flat). Ringo's crisp drumming elevates the title track, and singles like "Hello Goodbye" bubbled onto radio even when the material's reach exceeded its grasp. When tacked onto an inferior piece of material, the fake Maori ending to "Hello Goodbye" came off as a gimmick.

"The Fool on the Hill" has entered the catalog as one of McCartney's minor character portraits, alongside "Eleanor Rigby," "Penny Lane," "Lady Madonna," "Maxwell's Silver Hammer," and "Rocky Raccoon." Except for the first, these types stride about in typically airy, benevolent settings that range from tragic to ironically sunny to darkly cartoonish, and they allow McCartney to wear different genre hats while stretching his elastic vocal delivery.

"The Fool on the Hill" remains the least of these: the lyric goes unfinished; the major-minor design of verses against their refrains and the instrumentation and production all reveal a weakness for that tired cliché, the wise simpleton who belies depth, range, or substance. We're supposed to feel sorry for this figure because his gaze captures the magic of the planets in motion, but McCartney's really just trying to gin up sympathy for his everyman pose: he gets more out of the similar major-minor tension in "I'll Be Back," "We Can Work It Out," and "Fixing a Hole," and far more intricate double meanings from the nurse selling poppies in "Penny Lane."

The character itself had grown tired before McCartney got to it. The Tin Pan Alley precedent, "Nature Boy" (Nat King Cole's 1948 hit written by the idiosyncratic composer, eden ahbez), posits a self-taught eccentric who reveals enlightenment in the concluding couplet: "The greatest thing you'll ever learn / Is just to love and be loved in return." Thirty years later this character reemerged as *Forrest Gump* (1994), hovering over post-1950 pop culture like a mental puppy who spouts fathomless insight via his mother's mantra: "My Momma always said life was like a box of chocolates. You never know what you're going to get."[4] Gump (Tom Hanks) winds up rich at the end of his movie; First Lieutenant Dan Taylor (Gary Sinese), his paraplegic Vietnam vet buddy, grows a heart of gold to replace his legs. (Bubba, the African American vet, dies in battle.)

Gump has it all over McCartney's fool. Instead of developing the idea or lending this figure any detailed colors, McCartney simply goes into repetition, as if flutes, his own plastic recorder, and the circular progression can bring this tired trope to life. The second bridge betrays a partial lyric ("They don't like him") to rely on arid repeats, tedious at first, and finally vapid.

CUE	SECTION	HARMONY	DETAIL
0:00	Intro		piano and flutes
0:03	Verse 1a	I add6–ii7/1–I add6–ii7/1	PM double-tracked vocal
0:17	Verse 1b	ii7–V7–I add6–vi7–ii7–V7	offset doo-wop
0:27	Chorus 1	i5–↓6–5–↓6–↓VII7–i7	
0:40	Transition	I6	
0:44	Verse 2		add acoustic 12-string
1:07	Chorus 2		
1:23	Break		PM recorder, harmonicas & flute

4. Peter Sellers plays another sagacious idiot, Chauncey Gardiner, in *Being There* (1979).

CUE	SECTION	HARMONY	DETAIL
1:37	Verse 3b		PM vocal re-enters
1:47	Chorus 3		
2:03	Verse 4		PM ad-lib
2:16	Verse 4b		Lyrics re-enter; heightened pitch
2:26	Chorus 4		
2:41	Transition		Birdlike sound effects
2:43	Outro		fadeout

"I Am the Walrus"

Recorded September 5, 6, 27, and 29, 1967, for *Magical Mystery Tour*

—an uproarious discord in all its poetic and musical aspects, "Walrus" is meant to frustrate the analyst. Its flexible phrase rhythms and studiously ungrammatical chord connections make for an ever-developing formal structure that evidence the craze of its composer's reasoning.

By design, "I Am the Walrus" is John Lennon's most irregular Beatle song in every manner possible. Hearing that his lyrics were under study at Quarry Bank High School—led by the literature masters who had once branded him as "bound to fail"—Lennon resolved to weld poetic and musical nonsense into a form so inscrutable only a fool could pretend understanding. Peopled by characters such as "Semolina Pilchard" and "Edgar Allan Poe," the song's dark tales move between the cockeyed utterances of Stanley Unwin and Bob Dylan in invoking Lewis Carroll's Walrus and Humpty Dumpty—"the Eggman." If John had heard William Burroughs—the beat novelist and companion of Barry Miles, Robert Fraser, and Richard Hamilton (all with Beatle connections)—when he publicly read in London, in 1967, his 1963 poem "The Addict," he might well have noted Burroughs' self-identifying line "I Am the Wall." If so, the "wall" might have reminded John of Humpty Dumpty, Carroll's creator of the portmanteau, the literary device that would convert "I Am the Wall" to Lennon's own title. As nonsensical as the lyrics are, twisted music parodies the performing forces, formal structures, phrase rhythm (compare the unbalanced phrase extensions here with those of "A Day in the Life"), and pitch relations of the typical pop song in a snide acid trip of lost ego. Lennon's identity crisis ("I am he as you are he as you are me") is inspired by *Alice's Adventures in Wonderland* and set in a dire, paranoia-induced police siren of fifth scale degrees repeatedly alternating with their chromatic leading tones, first stated by the heavily distorted and compressed lead vocal but later echoed by cellos that undermine the song's core at 1:23.

The form of "Walrus" may be the most complex construction ever to shape a pop song under five minutes. As indicated in the accompanying chart, phrase lengths and patterns seem almost arbitrary. An introductory tattoo lasts seven bars (it is actually a trimmed 7.5 bars in original performance) but is cut to three for a transition that appears midway through (at 2:03). The verses are in bar form, a–a'–b, but each phrase expresses a different harmonic progression (only the first containing a repeat), and the last, a refrain, is half the expected length. The second verse is expanded in two places: first, in getting to the song's core with Lennon's sustained, dissonant, repeated, and finally falsetto "crying," an inserted retransitional phrase as alarming in its own weird way as the arresting stop-time "cry-hi-hi-hi" eruption was in "This Boy." Prior to the tattoo's return, at 2:01, the "Eggman" refrain takes an extra bar of V embellishment with a rude, foul mix of a disjointed operatic yodel, a radio's harsh frequency modulation, and group glissandi from a dissonant interval in cellos. The opening tattoo is given a set of lyrics in the bridge, which turns to the currish ♭VI–II tritone from the end of the verse's second phrase and comes out through the refrain, now extended with a plagal softening, V–IV. ("Thank You Girl" was the Beatles' only other song to lead from the bridge into a refrain.)

Opening with a solo electric piano (John's answer to Paul's exotic keyboard intros to "Strawberry Fields Forever" and "Lucy in the Sky with Diamonds"), "Walrus" quickly gives itself up to a wild use of strings, horns, bass clarinet, and chorus for which the brilliant George Martin must be given credit. Of greatest interest is the choir, actually the Mike Sammes Singers, an expert jazzy a cappella–style group with the facility of the Swingle Singers, often hired as backing vocalists for pop-hit arrangements recorded in London. Later on, they would provide the soothing phrases behind Ringo's singing in "Good Night" and Paul's in "The Long and Winding Road," but that is not their role in the vile cacophony of "Walrus." The glissandi on an atonal pitch collection may have been a signature of theirs; elsewhere, it's featured for several seconds in their challenging rendition of Jerome Kern's "Pick Yourself Up" (at 2:18 for "fall" in their televised performance of ca. 1958). The Sammes Singers practice the same mess of glissandi several times in "Walrus," always on hand to suggest the ignoble "fall" of Humpty Dumpty (first at 0:57) and in the song's "crying" retransitional core at 1:30–1:33. This is infectious, as the Eggman glissandi are doubled by the celli, which are then divided at 2:01 for a most schizoid stop-time plunge but reintegrated for a rising transition to the bridge at 2:09 (a repeat of the end of the intro). Glissandi are also characteristic of the tuning of the radio dial at 2:01 and thereafter (in an avant-garde mixing in of a broadcast of a death scene from Shakespeare's *King Lear*), and the horn solo at 3:55–4:04. Along with the plastic recorder of "Fool," it's the string glissandi that are quoted as the "Walrus" totem in "Glass Onion." Beyond the glissandi, and their sung-shouted joker's "ho ho ho hee hee hee ha ha ha," the Sammes Singers are best known for Lennon's mix in the coda of men chanting "Oompah, oompah, stick it up your jumper" (at 3:30) and women with "Everybody's got one! everybody's got one!" The first-named chant is an old British catchphrase captured in the 1935 British novelty record "Umpa, Umpa, Stick It up Your Jumper," by the Two Leslies.

But it is with the song's harmony that Lennon is his most cynical. As if the son of "Day Tripper," "Walrus" is comprised of all-major triads built on every white key of Lennon's electric piano, confounding the home scale with mode mixture from realms outside of functional tonality. To confuse matters more, A is the tonal center of an Aeolian collection (A–B–C–D–E–F–G–A, identical to the natural minor scale), rather than the C major that would seemingly be the home base of so much major-triad sonority. At times, the bass line moves somewhat sensibly (as in the initial lament bass moving to an introductory V), but other changes are governed by the tritone (as when moving directly from F major [♭VI] to B major [II]). Beatle references include the bass-line descent of A–G–F♯–F–E of "Lucy" suggested in phrase *a'* and the ♭VI–♭VII–I Aeolian cadence of "With a Little Help from My Friends" that makes up the "Eggman" refrain. In the coda, the metrically free orchestral ascent from "A Day in the Life" is mocked by a measured, plodding rising *Dorian* line in violins against a descending *Aeolian* line in cellos and basses, producing a string of root-position chords in contrary motion that gets progressively more dissonant: A major bounded by an octave; G major bounded by a tenth; F major bounded by a fifth; E major bounded by a seventh; D major bounded by a ninth; C major bounded by a tritone; and B major bounded by a minor sixth; repeating in ever-rising over ever-falling lines. George Martin said it best when he described "Walrus" as an exercise in "organized chaos" (Lewisohn 1988, 122).

CUE	SECTION	HARMONY	DETAIL
0:00	Introductory tattoo	II–I→VII→VI–V8–7–IV8–7	7 bars led by JL's distorted Pianet
0:22	Verse 1: *a*	I–4/2–III–IV–I repeated	6 bars ("I am he")
0:39	Verse 1: *a'*	I–4/2–IV6→VI→VII–I–4/2; ♭VI–II	6 bars ("Sitting on a cornflake")
0:56	Verse 1: *b* (Refrain)	♭III–IV–V	3 bars ("Eggman")
1:04	Verse 2: *a*		6 bars ("Mister City")
1:22	Verse 2: core	IV4–I–V–IV	5 bars; plagal "crying" retransition
1:36	Verse 2: *a'*		6 bars ("Yellow matter custard")
1:52	Verse 2: *b'* (Refrain)	♭III–IV–V	expanded to 4 bars
2:03	Tattoo	II–I→VII→VI–V	abbreviated to 3 bars
2:12	Bridge	II–I→VII→VI–V→VI–II	5 bars ("Sitting in an English garden")
2:25	Refrain: *b"*	♭III–IV–V–IV	expanded to 4 bars
2:36	Verse 3: *a*		6 bars ("Expert texpert")
2:53	Verse 3: *a'*		6 bars ("Semolina Pilchard")
3:09	Verse 3: *b³* (Refrain)	♭III–IV–V–IV→III–II	expanded to 6 bars
3:25	Coda	I→VII→VI–V7–IV9–♭III♯4–II♭6	7 bars repeated 4 times through fadeout

POINTS FOR DISCUSSION

1. Describe what makes rock music sound "psychedelic" to you.
2. Give examples of how Lennon's and McCartney's songwriting themes separate and converge on *Pepper*.
3. Compare how *Pepper*'s tracks enlarge ideas first set forth on *Rubber Soul* and *Revolver*.
4. Detail the ways in which *Pepper* represents a break from the Beatles' earlier career: musically, visually, and symbolically.
5. Offer and support some arguments against *Pepper* as a rock masterpiece. Does any of it deal explicitly with race, class, generational conflict, or gender?
6. How did the Beatles' career advance and suffer in their first full year away from live performance?
7. In what ways does John Lennon explore the nature of self and personal identity in Beatle songs released in 1967?
8. Choose a song from *Pepper* and discuss its instrumentation and vocal roles and how these forces complement each other. Suggest how the song might have been recorded. (You may wish to consult Lewisohn 1988, Everett 1999, and Winn 2003.)
9. What aspects of "I Am the Walrus" might have led George Martin to refer to the track as "organized chaos"?
10. Can you find any songs released in 1967 that the Beatles could have played in live performance had they desired to?
11. Discuss the metric organization in the verses of "All You Need Is Love" or "Good Morning Good Morning."

FURTHER READING

Babiuk, Andy. *Beatles Gear: All the Fab Four's Instruments, From Stage to Studio*, rev. ed. San Francisco: Backbeat, 2015.

Davies, Hunter, ed. *The John Lennon Letters*. New York: Little, Brown, 2012.

Emerick, Geoff, and Howard Massey. *Here, There and Everywhere: My Life Recording the Music of the Beatles*. New York: Gotham, 2007.

Grossman, Henry. *Kaleidoscope Eyes*. Houston: Curvebender, 2008.

Harris, David. *Dreams Die Hard: Three Men's Journey Through the '60s*. New York: St. Martin's, 1982.

Harrison, George, 1980. *I Me Mine*. New York: Simon & Schuster.

Harry, Billy. *The John Lennon Encyclopedia*. London: Virgin, 2001.

Mailer, Norman. *The Armies of the Night: The History as Novel, the Novel as History*. New York: New American Library, 1968.

Martin, George. *All You Need Is Ears*. With Jeremy Hornsby. New York: St. Martin's, 1979.

Martin, George, exec. prod. "The Making of Sgt. Pepper." Aired June 14, 1992, on ITV and September 27, 1992, on the Disney Channel.

Martin, George, and William Pearson. *The Summer of Love: The Making of Sgt. Pepper*. London: Macmillan, 1994.

Sheff, David. "Interview: John Lennon and Yoko Ono" *Playboy*, January 1981.

Taylor, Derek. *It Was Twenty Years Ago Today*. New York: Simon & Schuster, 1988.

CHAPTER 8

LISTENING THROUGH A GLASS ONION (1968)

THE SUMMER OF LOVE, INVERTED

The year 1968 was one of the most tumultuous of the twentieth century. The spring and summer of 1968 erupted with startling violence, complicating the fierce tensions between races, social classes, generations, genders, and ideologies the world over. In America, the chaos intensified beyond the civil rights movement's worst nightmares with two savage assassinations—those of the Rev. Dr. Martin Luther King, Jr., and New York senator Robert F. Kennedy—dashing everybody's best hopes. To many, it seemed as if mayhem had been set loose between the young and old, between the ruling establishment and its subjects, and the fallout felt both unknowable and unpredictable. The Beatles' and the hippies' soft pleas for love and peace, no matter how well meant and no matter how powerful the music that carried the message, seemed like cries in the wilderness.

Protests against the Vietnam War moved from radical to mainstream culture in the first months of 1968. In January, beloved pediatrician Benjamin Spock was indicted for encouraging resistance against the military draft. On many college campuses, antiwar sentiment surged as the official state narrative turned transparently fraudulent. The North Vietnamese launched the surprise Tet Offensive on January 31, an assault that saw Communists hold Saigon's American embassy for six hours. Vietcong guerrillas managed to hold the South Vietnamese city of Hué for weeks. The *New York Times* ran a front-page photo of Saigon's police chief, General Nguyen Ngoc Loan, executing a Vietcong officer on the streets of his city. Despite the shooting victim's enemy status, the brutality of the photograph proved as chilling as the 1963 image of the Buddhist monk Thích Quảng Đức's self-immolation. The Tet surprise attack prompted the bloodiest stretch of the war and persuaded most observers—except the military brass—that the American strategy was failing. Boorish even in the face of flagrant counterevidence, the US Army's commanding general, William Westmoreland, boasted that the assault brought the North Vietnamese a "massive military defeat," then requested an additional 206,000 American troops to answer the threat. By this point, Johnson demurred and sent only 22,000 draftees. The war's supporters and detractors alike were stunned in March by the My Lai massacre—in which renegade American forces murdered helpless Vietnamese citizens in their homes, the resulting carnage appropriated in a Yoko Ono record sleeve (Photo 8.1). This made clear just how irrational and horrific such a course was, which only expanded with the secret US bombing of Laos and Cambodia. At the end of February, CBS news anchor Walter Cronkite made a famous prime-time reckoning, predicting stalemate. "If I've lost Cronkite," a stunned Johnson commented, "I've lost the war" (DeGroot 2008, 283–285).

PHOTO 8.1. Victims of the My Lai massacre in 1968, as reproduced on the sleeve for Yoko Ono and the Plastic Ono Band's "Now or Never" / "Move On Fast" 45 (released in US, November 13, 1972). The sleeve makes the Beatles' "Butcher" cover seem prescient.

All this occurred in the context of the American presidential primary campaigns. Upstart Minnesota Democratic senator Eugene McCarthy challenged his party's incumbent with a surprisingly successful antiwar platform. Even though McCarthy came in fourth in New Hampshire's March 12 primary, pundits proclaimed the blow devastating for Johnson's re-election prospects. That same week, on the sixteenth, Bobby Kennedy, the Democrats' most vocal antiwar figure, who inherited his slain brother's mythic presidential pedigree, declared his candidacy. By month's end, a battered President Johnson announced he would neither seek nor accept his party's nomination, throwing the race into turmoil. For all his advances in civil rights and the fight against poverty, Johnson's legacy would forever be stained by his support of the Vietnam War.

Within a week of his announcement, even this stunning news—a sitting president stepping down, admitting defeat in a war he couldn't convince himself was worth winning—got plowed under by more chaos. Martin Luther King, Jr.,'s 1967 address "Beyond Vietnam" had the paradoxical effect of weakening his civil rights credibility, giving narrow-minded and bigoted opponents pretense to paint him as unpatriotic and worse. Publicity once given to his nonviolent movement was quickly co-opted by threatening splinter groups such as Oakland's Black Panthers, which espoused Black Power. King had been a marked man even before his anti-Vietnam stance, but increasingly, his bold coalition of liberal establishment and mass activists seemed to be fracturing, and his speeches took on existential notes. In Memphis to support an anti-poverty campaign pegged to sanitation workers' pay, King was murdered on a motel balcony by a racist's long-range rifle on April 4.

Following increasing numbers of riots over the previous two summers, King's death only emboldened the frustrations of blacks and others who supported their cause, and crystallized the sense that white supremacy exercised only brute power against the most basic reforms. King's killing kicked off riots in over a hundred cities, leaving dozens killed and thousands wounded. The biggest flare-ups came in Washington, DC, Baltimore, Louisville, Kansas City, and Chicago. President Johnson sent federal troops into the national capital's neighborhoods to quiet looting, vandalism, and arson. After a night of unrest in Roxbury, Boston's newly elected Mayor, Kevin White, scrambled to stave off more unrest; aides convinced him that the live, public TV broadcast of a scheduled concert by James Brown, the African American "Godfather of Soul," might quell the violence. But before he could move forward with the plan—which would come off as a success—they had to inform White just exactly who Brown was.

The night Dr. King was killed, Senator Kennedy was met on a campaign stop in Indianapolis by a crowd he had to inform of the murder. In efforts to soothe his audience, he spoke openly for the first time of the death of his brother, President John F. Kennedy, four and a half years before. His moving impromptu words included a quotation from the ancient Greek tragedian Aeschylus that he had rehearsed many times in the depths of his own grief:

> Even in our sleep, the pain which cannot forget
> Falls drop by drop upon the heart
> Until, in our own despair, against our will,
> Comes wisdom through the awful grace of God.

Kennedy's exhortations toward love and forbearance were largely credited with stemming violence in Indianapolis. But just two months later, after scoring a major antiwar victory in the

California primary election on June 5, Kennedy himself fell to an assassin's bullets in the kitchen of Los Angeles's Ambassador Hotel. The convicted gunman, Palestinian Sirhan Sirhan, opposed Kennedy's support of Israel during 1967's Six Day War. Two assassinations in as many months made any progress with racial, class, religious and generational divisions—vexing for so long—now seem forever out of reach.

All these forces met at the Democratic Party convention in Chicago near the end of August, where a prideful Mayor Richard Daley, paranoid about how his fair city might be perceived, armed his police with bats and tear gas. The dispirited antiwar movement gathered a mere five thousand to peacefully protest the Democrats' drift toward the center. Officers dutifully arrested and clubbed disorganized youths outside the hall. TV cameras beamed the brutal scene nationwide as picketers chanted, "The whole world is watching!" Eventually, the Democratic race fell to the sitting vice president, Hubert Humphrey, who tried in vain to unite the party by defending Johnson's Vietnam policy. The Republican nominee, Richard Nixon, portrayed the Democrats as having been destabilized by wayward, disrespectful youth. Behind the scenes, Nixon went on to sabotage the Paris peace talks, giving him a razor-thin electoral victory that November.[1] "Chicago" became an enduring metaphor for how constitutionally protected dissent continued to meet a repressive police state.

European youth watched America's antiwar unrest and erupted in their own defiance. In Paris, where living standards trailed most of the West, university students mounted springtime protests against collegiate living conditions and antiquated social codes. Activists there invoked the ideals of the Chinese Cultural Revolution, led by Chairman Mao, and South American Marxist guerrilla Che Guevara, as inflated solutions to Western inequities. These French protests embraced hints of anarchy, and they stressed lifestyle, entertainment, and stagecraft, self-consciously constructing barricades as symbolic references to earlier revolutions, those of 1789, 1848, and 1871. Some sloganeering carried faint rock 'n' roll echoes, as if Dylan had scripted the catchphrases: "I have something to say but I'm not sure what," read one piece of graffiti (DeGroot 2008, 352). Eleven thousand Parisian workers soon joined the students, and by May the country came to a two-week standstill as an unlikely million people marched on the Champs-Élysées demanding political change. In one of those eerie moments where the Beatles suddenly seemed prophetic, it was as if the snatch of "La Marseillaise" at the top of "All You Need Is Love" had suggested what lay ahead. Ironically, June's election returned the conservative General Charles DeGaulle to the presidency, with an even stronger margin than in his original victory.

Soon after, the protesting of universities' dormitory living standards in Czechoslovakia flared when police brutality sparked widespread street marches, and soon anti-Soviet activists tested the Soviet Union's grip on its Eastern European satellites. Aiming for a thaw in the Cold War, a "Prague Spring" held promise for young Czechs who yearned for Western freedoms and open markets. But 4,600 Soviet tanks rolled into Czechoslovakia on August 11, echoing the brutal end to the Hungarian revolt of 1956 and smothering any hope of reform within the Soviet sphere. A hemisphere away, in October, government forces in Mexico City killed scores, or even hundreds, of protesting students and other political opponents.

1. For an illuminating account of Nixon's deception, see Wyatt 2014, 259–266.

Although Britain had no troops in Vietnam, antiwar demonstrations protested its support for the war on March 17 as hundreds marched on London's embassy—surrounded Grosvenor Square, a scene depicted in two Rolling Stones numbers: "Street Fighting Man," which droned through a crunching, violent beat to an ambivalent lyric on their 1968 blues breakthrough LP, *Beggar's Banquet*, and "You Can't Always Get What You Want," in which frontman Mick Jagger sings "I went down to the demonstration / To get my share of abuse," a highlight on 1969's *Let It Bleed*. But right within the United Kingdom, police storm-trooper brutality against marchers in Londonderry, Northern Ireland, in October 1968 marked the beginning of "the Troubles," a thirty-year period of fighting between Catholics and Protestants that led to 3,200 deaths and fifty thousand casualties, with the involvement of British troops beginning in August 1969. For many observers in the shrinking global village heralded by worldwide media, young demonstrators' expanding messages of equal treatment of minorities, women, and other victims of bias; world peace; and ecological awareness got drowned out by their lifestyle choices—long hair, flagrant sexuality, loud music, and overblown rhetoric. The middle-class drug culture measured the distance between the cocktail set and its "counterculture" offspring; ever longer and more unkempt hair became a potent symbol of rebellion against the war machine's entrenched powers. Merely challenging one's elders became a larger affront than anything else; to the establishment, it seemed like youth protests pursued less an antiwar agenda than a degenerate all-out rejection of the American Dream. Bobby Kennedy's Aeschylus quotation might well have been applied to any of a number of cultural realms in 1968; some of its suggestion of resulting wisdom, both awful and consoling, would be realized in the Beatles' work of the same year.

1968 British releases:
Single: "Lady Madonna" / "The Inner Light" (rel. Mar. 15)
Single: "Hey Jude" / "Revolution" (rel. Aug. 30)
LP: *The Beatles* (rel. Nov. 22)

Side 1:
"Back in the USSR"
"Dear Prudence"
"Glass Onion"
"Ob-La-Di, Ob-La-Da"
"Wild Honey Pie"
"The Continuing Story of Bungalow Bill"
"While My Guitar Gently Weeps"
"Happiness Is a Warm Gun"

Side 2:
"Martha My Dear"
"I'm So Tired"
"Blackbird"
"Piggies"
"Rocky Raccoon"
"Don't Pass Me By"
"Why Don't We Do It in the Road?"
"I Will"
"Julia"

Side 3:
"Birthday"
"Yer Blues"
"Mother Nature's Son"
"Everybody's Got Something to Hide Except Me and My Monkey"
"Sexy Sadie"
"Helter Skelter"
"Long, Long, Long"

Side 4:
"Revolution 1"
"Honey Pie"
"Savoy Truffle"
"Cry Baby Cry"

"Revolution 9
"Good Night"

EARLY 1968 RECORDING PROJECTS
AND RISHIKESH

After the triumph of *Sgt. Pepper's Lonely Hearts Club Band* and the calamity of *Magical Mystery Tour*, the Beatles took their longest career sabbatical as cultural tensions blew out political gaskets. While an extended Indian meditation retreat with the Maharishi Mahesh Yogi took up most of the opening quarter of 1968, *Pepper* lingered in the cultural mind as both a totem and a turning point. It overshadowed the *Magical Mystery Tour* charade as it reframed rock history. Each repeated listening brought new detail, new authority to *Pepper's* grooves, and it kept trumping *Magical Mystery Tour* in both charm and design. As the third of the celebrated middle-period albums begun with *Rubber Soul* and *Revolver*, *Pepper* made their previous work sound as if pointed toward something larger, more poetic and sweeping than rock had seemed capable of. "A Day in the Life" especially put a new frame on the familiar pattern of track sequences ending with Lennon leads, begun with the first two albums, with "Twist and Shout" and "Money," on through *Revolver's* "Tomorrow Never Knows," and showed the Lennon-McCartney songwriting team unraveling at the seams. What next?

For the group, 1968 began as 1966 had ended, with the Beatles pursuing separate projects; this was now the norm for intervals between their remaining group recordings. Ringo acted in the film *Candy* (begun in December 1967); Paul produced Cilla Black's recording of his song "Step Inside Love"; and George recorded in India for both his soundtrack to the film *Wonderwall* and the instrumental track to the Beatles' next B-side, "The Inner Light." John laid low for a time (vacationing in northern Africa in January), but he emerged quite noisily in mid-May, when he recorded Mellotron experiments with his new paramour as well as artistic advisor Yoko Ono, tracks that were released later that year in unedited form, with a defiant nude cover, as *Unfinished Music No. 1: Two Virgins*.

Harrison felt taken for granted, so he pursued more creative outlets than the others through 1968; surrounding the *Wonderwall* soundtrack release in October and November, he produced album sessions for Jackie Lomax in Los Angeles (where he first worked with a Moog synthesizer, later to grace *Abbey Road*) and visited Bob Dylan in the Catskills of New York, where the two wrote "I'd Have You Anytime" (which would appear on George's epic solo triple album of 1970, *All Things Must Pass*).

As critics delighted in taking down the biggest band of all time for the ill-considered *Magical Mystery Tour* project, *Pepper* left enough generosity, goodwill, and credibility in the Beatles' account to make a 1968 comeback seem likely, even imminent. Undaunted as usual, they used their lofty status to deflect concern. To make all the hyperventilating around *Magical Mystery Tour* seem like bad faith, they tossed an offhand single to the market, recorded in February, reasserting their mastery with a punchy throwaway, Paul's "Lady Madonna." Its boogie-woogie piano and soft-shoe reserve all but renounced hallucinogenic pretense. An agonizing gap persisted throughout the summer of 1968 as they worked on thirty-plus tracks for their next release. The public silence raised hopes and made the anticipation acute until it finally found exquisite release in McCartney's mid-tempo anthem "Hey Jude." It was a beautiful song, and innovative despite its complete lack of electronic gimmickry, and it became the Beatles' biggest hit since the days of Beatlemania.

Reversing course from 1967 psychedelia, the Beatles returned to earthier rock 'n' roll styles throughout 1968, following "Lady Madonna" with such tracks as "Back in the U.S.S.R." and "Birthday" from the double-album project *The Beatles*, which appeared in November, commonly called the *White Album*. This back-to-the-roots direction culminated in the January 1969 "Get Back" project, through which they made a return to cover material from the Presley era of their youth—Elvis, Little Richard, Chuck Berry, and Buddy Holly.

Before discussion of these larger efforts, one tangential project deserves mention. It began in 1967, saw continued work in 1968, and was released only in 1969: the animated feature film *Yellow Submarine*. The Beatles viewed it as a contractual headache. Although the band's involvement with the film was otherwise restricted to a scripted live-action cameo appearance tacked onto the film's ending, the movie did include four previously unreleased Beatle recordings (the oldest, "Only a Northern Song," a *Pepper* outtake from February 1967, the last, "Hey Bulldog," from February 1968) and a dozen already classic songs spanning from 1965's "Nowhere Man" to 1967's "All You Need Is Love." Created with the highest technical standards, the stylish cartoon resulted in a monument to two-dimensional pop art, first released in UK theatres in July 1968. A handful of its songs would be packaged alongside George Martin's orchestral score and released as an LP in January 1969. Photo 8.2 shows the Beatles in a production shot for the film.

In early February '68 the Beatles produced four tracks, with two designated as their next single: McCartney's "Lady Madonna" and Harrison's "The Inner Light." "Hey, Bulldog" was thrown over for the *Yellow Submarine* soundtrack, and "Across the Universe" got shelved. On February 15, the group kept their promise to themselves from the previous fall and traveled to Rishikesh, in the Himalayan foothills of northern India, to learn meditation techniques from the Maharishi Mahesh Yogi. The trip combined a spiritual quest with their first extended vacation together since the earliest days of Beatlemania. The entourage included spouses Cynthia Lennon, Maureen Starkey, and Pattie Harrison; Paul's fiancée, Jane Asher; and friends and assistants Mal Evans, Neil Aspinall, Peter Brown, and Alex Mardas.

At the ashram, they met up with an international coterie of anti-materialist celebrities, including Mike Love of the Beach Boys, folk-turned-pop-singer Donovan, and the Farrow sisters (movie star Mia, who had just left husband Frank Sinatra, and Prudence). Ringo and then Paul returned home within a month, but John and George stayed until April 12.

In addition to their spiritual growth (and the disavowal of recreational drugs), their musical productivity flourished in seclusion, leading to about thirty new songs. George Harrison, especially, began to blossom as a writer. Donovan helped the Beatles with various styles of fingerpicking (they had brought with them a new set of Martin guitars, John's first seen in a video for "Hello Goodbye"), highlighted best in John's "Julia" and Paul's "Blackbird." Love helped them write "Back in the U.S.S.R." Because of her epic meditation jags and generally reclusive nature, Prudence Farrow became the subject of a Lennon song ("Dear Prudence"), as did the Maharishi himself (disguised as "Sexy Sadie"). The Beatles' Transcendental Meditation experience signaled a peak of hippie idealism, shattered when they discovered that the Maharishi was only human; Lennon believed rumors about the guru's acting on his earthly passions and brought the relationship and visit to abrupt end. After the death of Epstein and the drop in the Maharishi's status, John sought a new companion / life coach in Yoko Ono, who

PHOTO 8.2. The Beatles in late January 1968, "Yellow Submarine" / "Eleanor Rigby" 45 (as reissued in the UK on its twentieth anniversary, August 4, 1986).

had visited the "Hey Bulldog" session on February 11 and who filled that void soon after his return to England on April 12. The others reported feeling Lennon had overreacted regarding the sweet but benign Maharishi, who nevertheless had sponged off the Beatles' status to win media fame.

APPLE AND SOLO EXCURSIONS

Following their episode of Transcendental Meditation, the Beatles announced the formation of a new multi-media company, Apple, with a publicity tour by Paul and John with a New York press conference and appearance on *The Tonight Show* in mid-May. Apple invited unknown, struggling performers and filmmakers to submit projects for funding. They took out ads asking musicians to send them tapes, so as to fast-track the audition process. On May 14, John told the *Tonight Show* audience,

> We decided to play businessmen for a bit, because we've got to run our own affairs now, so we've got this thing called Apple which is going to be records, films, and electronics, which all tie up, and to make a sort of an umbrella so's people who want to make films . . . don't have to go on their knees in an office begging for a break.

Largely due to the Beatles' own artistic wisdom and their direct involvement with the composition of a few new songs, instrumental contributions, and production help, Apple Records debuted with great fanfare. The company strove to harness all the creative energies already in motion, such as Paul's producing Cilla Black, John's new inspiration from Yoko, George's recording in Bombay, and Ringo's fledgling acting career. The most successful artists on its early roster—James Taylor, Mary Hopkin, Badfinger, and Billy Preston—came through direct contacts instead of the audition tapes that poured into their office; the filmmaking never got off the ground; and the electronics division fueled Lennon's fascination with sci-fi gadgets and led to a disastrous mess of a basement recording studio built by the slippery "Magic Alex" Mardas that required extensive outside expertise to make it serviceable. Without the steady hand of a Brian Epstein, Apple's epic ambitions, mixed success, and competing priorities fed the Beatles' own dissolution.

With their musical heroes holed up in the studios throughout the summer, the world looked toward new Beatles material almost as fervently as it had before *Sgt. Pepper*, and with greater unease. A new single, the first on their own Apple label, came only at the end of August, with McCartney's "answer" song to Lennon's "Revolution": McCartney conceived "Hey Jude" to console John's son Julian over the messy breakup of his parents' marriage and Yoko's intrusion into his life. In walking out on his wife Cynthia and four-year-old son, Lennon disrupted the band's entire social scene. Ono began accompanying Lennon everywhere, instigating special resentment when she set up camp in the studio for Beatles sessions. Paul seemed to be the only one with the nerve to visit Cynthia and Julian in their Weymouth home, where many Lennon-McCartney songwriting sessions had taken place, and where he brought "Hey Jules" (the song's working title) as a note of support to the confused, seemingly fatherless boy.

With one of Paul's gentlest, most beautiful melodies and humblest harmonic schemes, the song calls back an earlier time, one phrase taken from the Drifters' 1960 hit "Save the Last Dance for Me." "Hey Jude" became the new single, and the band booked an appearance on the *David Frost Show* to debut the song in early September. (Its B-side, John's "Revolution," was performed by the group for a promotional video; see Photo 8.3.) This soaring, surging ballad climaxed with a redemptive, sing-along coda that eclipsed the song proper, breaking all formal rules in triumph for the career comeback for which fans had waited for since "All You Need Is Love," if not "Yellow Submarine." As tear gas poisoned the Chicago Democratic Convention, the song conquered pop radio as an adult statement on how to sustain hope during periods of utter loss. The chanted "nah, nah, nah, nah-nah-nah-nah" solution stretched out into some better world as McCartney scatted his way through ecstatic repetition, the late-career echo of a younger singer's "yeah, yeah, yeah."

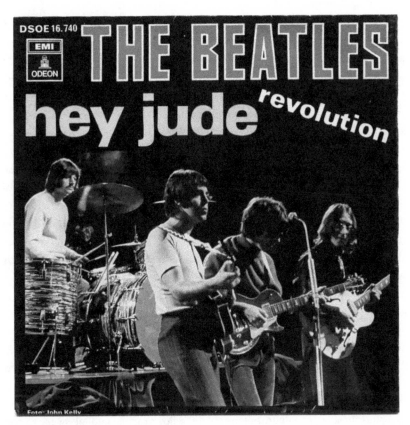

PHOTO 8.3. The Beatles performing "Revolution" for video at Twickenham Film Studios on September 4, 1968, photographed by John Kelly. "Hey Jude" / "Revolution" 45 (as released in Spain, October 15, 1968). Paul plays his Höfner bass; George plays "Lucy," the Les Paul guitar given him by Eric Clapton; John has stripped his Epiphone Casino down to bare wood.

THE *WHITE ALBUM*

In the context of the turmoil of the times, the Beatles' corporate woes, and the universality of the infinite refrain to "Hey Jude," the band's status as youth heroes took on radically new meanings. If the band had perfected their role as barometers of culture, both reflecting and amplifying their audience's thoughts and moods, how best to respond to the world's unrest? How best to harness the chaos that curtailed the utopian values they sparked with joy rockets like "She Loves You," "I'll Get You," and "Eight Days a Week," except to extend the idea of *Pepper*'s cover collage into untested realms?

On the *White Album*, these patchwork themes broaden toward pure noise, genre parody, conflicting stances, and the disregard of their own rock-star status to stretch the band's persona into a collection of individual voices with less and less vocal interaction, the group support they had always been able to rally splintering apart at times from their own negative stress and centrifugal energies. With its far-flung styles represented across a myriad of thirty new songs on two discs, the *White Album* maps the band's competing sensibilities and turns cohesion into a quaint, nostalgic idea. Rock would never again seem as unified and purposeful as when *Pepper* appeared (despite its own plethora of styles); the undertones of the *White Album* foretold of continuing splits and specializations, with heavy metal (Paul's "Helter Skelter") sitting next to chaste *Animal Farm* sarcasm (George's "Piggies") as if introduced from separate careers. Still, inspired kinship among members persists: John's "Glass Onion" could never have been written by Paul, but Paul does show brilliant inspiration in adding the perfect touch, accompanying the abrasive track with the jagged fingerprint of the Fender Jazz Bass.

In the new recordings, the electric guitar came to the forefront ("Birthday," "Savoy Truffle"), alongside acoustic guitars ("Rocky Raccoon," "Long, Long, Long") given the spotlight as never before. Having explored small independent recording studios for a year or so in addition to working in their Abbey Road mainstay, EMI Studios, the Beatles encountered eight-track tape for the first time, leading to improved fidelity with fewer generations of tape required for overdubs (in addition to a new flexibility in arranging that would sparkle throughout the following year's *Abbey Road*). All the revitalized sounds proved intriguing: if no longer day-glo psychedelic, the beautifully recorded sonics were multihued and vivid nonetheless.

The Beatles sounded as masterful as ever, advancing their ensemble virtuosity on meter-changing numbers like "Happiness Is a Warm Gun," and in many acrobatic tightrope walks through "Glass Onion," "Martha My Dear," "The Continuing Story of Bungalow Bill," and "Everybody's Got Something to Hide Except Me and My Monkey." Tracks like "Birthday," "Helter Skelter," and "Savoy Truffle" featured a band at the height of its group dynamics, reeling off new standards that FM radio eventually embraced as key "classic rock" album tracks, including Harrison's prototype for Led Zeppelin's "Stairway to Heaven" in the subtle-becoming-massive "While My Guitar Gently Weeps." Over its four sides, the album's many ebbs and flows carried enough sweep to create covert pleasures, buried riches, and hidden corridors, such as McCartney's raving "Why Don't We Do It in the Road?," the reverse image of Lennon's "Yer Blues" and no less thrilling; or "Cry Baby Cry," a midnight creep; or a pair of ballads like "I Will" adjoining "Julia" at the end of side 2, each devotional, each inimitably personal.

On one level, the Beatles played catch-up with Bob Dylan, whose four-sided *Blonde on Blonde* (1966) had challenged both rock's conceptual conceits and the very idea of linear song narrative. When Lennon addresses him directly in "Yer Blues," he acknowledges Dylan's far-reaching influence and has the last word on how their swords once crossed with "Norwegian Wood" and "4th Time Around," in which Dylan had recast Lennon's 12/8 meter and mystical melody as vaguely ambivalent eroticism.

The band sounded impossibly tight but also, for many listeners, like soloists with a backing unit more than close collaborators. The paradox would widen in 1969, as the Beatles continued to grow further apart—despite their improved ensemble resurrected from the abyss of the 1965–1966 tours—as their creative interests diverged. The poetic irony hovering over this and subsequent Beatle releases lies in how fluent and locked-in their groove remains even as their individual vantages shifted apart. This new LP marks the beginning of late-period Beatles, where songs would be introduced and recorded with reluctant secondary forces or none at all; Paul's "Ob-La-Di, Ob-La-Da" only jelled when an impatient, piano-pounding John sped up the tempo for the chosen take—after missing its bullseye for two weeks. Paul's fragment, "Can you take me back where I came from," ad-libbed between takes of "I Will," is a mere untitled palate cleanser for "Revolution 9." John and Paul together expressed ambivalence when George demonstrated "While My Guitar

Gently Weeps," and his "Long, Long, Long" (itself a response to *Blonde on Blonde*, its tune inspired by Dylan's "Sad Eyed Lady of the Lowlands") sat on some remote island far from the others' concerns. On this album, vocal duets become almost nonexistent, and where they do appear ("Julia"), they're slight, mechanically double-tracked solos by one individual singer. "I Will" features McCartney overdubbing his own voice as the bass line ("Dum-dum-dum"). A new trend begins: many original ideas would be rejected in group projects of 1968–1969, only to be revived in their solo careers: McCartney's Rishikesh leftovers "Teddy Boy" and "Junk" appear first on the 1970 LP *McCartney*. Lennon later reworked his own India-written "Child of Nature" as "Jealous Guy," which appears on his second post-Beatles album, *Imagine*, in 1971. Harrison's "Not Guilty," recorded and mixed but among the last of several castoffs on the *White Album*'s scrapheap, was dusted off for the composer's eponymous album of 1979.

In late May, as protests exploded in Paris, the Beatles gathered at George's home, Kinfauns, in Esher, to share new songs composed in India. Several tapes survive of the Beatles' demos recorded for each other, singing with acoustic guitar, sometimes double-tracked, playing along with their own homemade and sometimes charming backup effects. While the production of the album proved strenuous, this opening session lets the eavesdropper believe there was plenty of goodwill among band members who still enjoyed one another's company and melodies. (Harrison's "Sour Milk Sea," given over to Jackie Lomax, remains one of the great lost Beatle tracks from this tape.) Nearly all of these songs plus a few more appeared on the 1968 album, bulging at the seams even across two discs. Called simply *The Beatles* (no more hiding behind alter-egos), the LP sported packaging by the pop artist and London acquaintance Richard Hamilton that also toyed with form the way *Pepper* had, but with just as strong a return to basics as the rock 'n' roll behind its opening song: the front and back were pure white, with the small legend "The Beatles" embossed off-center and crookedly on the front, along with a unique stamped serial number on each set (see Photo 8.4), suggesting the reproduction of a fine (but blank) lithograph. Inside, the package contained an overtly formal set of posed individual portraits and a collage poster that traced the Beatles' entire career back to Hamburg, and even snippets of Ringo dancing with Elizabeth Taylor (as though her old-school star power could in any way compete). The cover's litotic empty frame cued its overall concept as *Pepper*'s negative image: an album as sweeping, cantankerous, and disheveled as its predecessor was tidy, ornate, and pop. The work renounced conceptual frameworks to address both a chaotic culture and a career conundrum: how to follow up the greatest concept album of all time without comparisons to its triumphs. Released on November 22, exactly five years after *With the Beatles*, it soon became known colloquially as the *White Album*.

Musically, Lennon veered furthest away from his mates. As with "A Day in the Life," John had found inspiration from the papers, which he turned obliquely into a daunting example of cold postmodernity. For the initial recordings for the *White Album*, news stories flooded his imagery in more direct fashion, provoking the Beatle's critiques of revolutionaries' unstated goals, threats of violence, and choice of Mao for a mascot. With both *Revolver* and *Pepper*, John's first contributions proved the weightiest of each project, and so "Tomorrow Never Knows" and "A Day in the Life" concluded each respective album. So once again, on the new LP, what was to emerge as the Revolution series marks the new album's first set of recordings, begun at the end of May. As if playing out its violent subject—the deadly uprisings in Paris, London, and the United States, unbridgeable differences and inequalities, Vietnam War atrocities, and the King assassination— the song itself would fragment into a number of separate tracks. The original recording trailed off

PHOTO 8.4. *The Beatles*, aka The *White Album* (released in US November 25, 1968).

into a netherworld of indeterminacy, the ending of which was separated from the song proper, to receive its own superimpositions of dozens of seemingly unrelated layered sources, for a version dubbed "Revolution 9," an experimental tape piece so violent, ugly, abstract and inchoate—the '60's *Guernica*—that Paul and George Martin argued for its exclusion from the album. Martin had found the widely misunderstood "I Am the Walrus" to be "organized chaos"; this next step seemed, to him, too far.

But contextualized chaos had always been a guiding principle for the Beatles, as in Ringo's crazed drumming through the last chorus of "Long Tall Sally," barely held together by a twelve-bar structure. Everyone felt this; the truly hip appreciated the content and message of "Walrus," but very few, only the cognoscenti and very free thinkers, would accept the freakishness of "Revolution 9" as music, let alone artistic brilliance. Just one further step toward mayhem, but still with strong organizing principles, "Revolution 9" regularly ranks as the least favorite Beatle recording in polls of fans. (John would not hesitate to go further out artistically, goaded on by his new collaborator, Yoko Ono, who had extensive avant-garde credentials with the Fluxus group. Paul, on the other hand, toyed with experimental ideas but shelved a project he would have called *Paul McCartney Goes Too Far*.) Lennon wanted the original "Revolution" released as a single to join a critical global discussion. The band insisted it was too slow, so they cut a faster version with angry, heavily distorted guitars and keyboard. This newly uptempo "Revolution" was slotted as their next A-side until McCartney came in with "Hey Jude," which pierced John's heart as only Paul could.

As recording sessions dragged on through the summer, George Martin and his engineers grew weary of how band members preferred working apart from one another and often sat out one another's tracks completely. The inaugural Kinfauns demo session had held extraordinary promise, but work thereafter followed a downward spiral, to the point where engineer Geoff Emerick quit, calling the proceedings "poisonous." When Martin stuck to his original vacation plans and also left, a young engineer named Chris Thomas had to step in and match wits with the world's greatest musicians (doing so brilliantly, especially with his elegant drawing-room harpsichord on George's "Piggies"). The Beatles even endured a walkout from drummer Ringo Starr, who had played one too many card games through too many disrespectful, self-indulgent delays. As if to rub his nose in it, an unfazed McCartney sat in on drums for two tracks cut in Starr's absence: "Back in the U.S.S.R." and "Dear Prudence," the last verse of which features his sublime drum flourishes.

Begged to return, Ringo came back and was welcomed with flowers. His exit never made the press, but his unprecedented departure shows just how strained the band's internal politics had become. Harrison found ways to have a soothing influence: when his mates reacted badly to "While My Guitar Gently Weeps," he invited his friend the blues guitar god Eric Clapton to play on the session, and the others put on their best behavior. (Lennon would have a live-performance epiphany in December 1968, playing "Yer Blues" along with Clapton and Keith Richard for the film *The Rolling Stones Rock and Roll Circus*, pulled from broadcast and rarely seen before 1996. This was the beginning of the Plastic Ono Band, a vehicle that would end up giving John more pleasure than the Beatles could—his alter-ego answer to Paul's *Sgt. Pepper*.) Despite the obvious bile, the Beatles also showed cooperative and friendly humors; recordings of the group and George Martin as they make decisions about arrangement reveal that John gently overruled their producer in advocating that Paul maintain the formal simplicity of "Blackbird" rather than adding to its structure, and he surely doomed to irrelevance his own tender "Child of Nature" by helping Paul find just the right instrumentation for "Mother Nature's Son," suggesting the sort of brass band he'd heard on a recent Harry Nilsson record (a cover of Paul's "She's Leaving Home").

At the end of October, Lennon, McCartney, Martin, and Thomas gathered in the control room for an epic mixing, mastering, and sequencing session lasting more than twenty-four hours, concocting the unruly, format-busting maze of tracks splayed across four sides. Martin argued strenuously for a single disc, without knowing the band wished to release two largely to fulfill a clause in their EMI contract. "Revolution 9" delighted few, but it was clear how Lennon's experimental impulse had led him from backward tapes in "I'm Only Sleeping" and "Rain" to formal experiments like "Tomorrow Never Knows," "A Day in the Life," and "I Am the Walrus." Capping this epic stretch with his most avant-garde gesture yet only strengthened the idea of Lennon as bold and uncompromising, whereas McCartney persisted in genre worksheets like "Ob-La-Di, Ob-La-Da," "Honey Pie," and "Rocky Raccoon." Everybody else voted against "Revolution 9," but Lennon insisted on it, and in the end, as usual, he got his way. Instead of closing the album, however, they cushioned side 4's layout with a dreamy closer, a Lennon lullaby sung by Starr. "Good Night" was lifted by sentimentally nostalgic strings, flutes, and soaring choir to bring baffled listeners in for a gentle landing. Following through on the trend of ending album track sequences with Lennon epics, the *White Album* doubles up, angling his defiant abstraction against rock's great sin, goopy sincerity.

Far from detaching them from a world that exploded with political conflict all around them, the booming cultural flux set up new paradoxes that mark the Beatles' new release: while peaking as an ensemble with tricky maneuvers of every imaginable sort, they were clearly writing more separately and about vastly different imaginative subjects. The unprecedented retreat in Rishikesh had led to a surfeit of material and their most epic work yet. If anything, the *White Album* captures the sound of the Beatles breaking up while clinging together.

"Dear Prudence"

Recorded August 28–29, 1968, for *The Beatles*

—Lennon's affectionate request that a friend "look around," with a goal of personal growth, is layered with multiple soothing and enlightening guitar and backing-vocal parts.

With rock 'n' roll surveying the teenage landscape, it's curious we don't have more songs about losing your virginity, a standard coming-of-age theme in fiction and film. In rock's early era, a song like the Drifters' "Save the Last Dance for Me" (1960) (Pomus-Shuman) made the dancing metaphor almost explicit through a Ben E. King lead vocal that soared enough to inspire the melody of "Hey Jude" eight years later. In 1964's "Chapel of Love," songwriters Ellie Greenwich and Jeff Barry wove a nifty metaphor for the Dixie Cups about going all the way, and by the 1970s, the Raspberries turned the cliché into a hit with "Go All the Way," which pleaded with its subject to give him a chance, no metaphors required. Others include songs by the Kinks ("Tired of Waiting for You"), the Byrds ("Chestnut Mare"), and Neil Diamond ("Girl, You'll Be a Woman Soon"). In "Cautious Man," Bruce Springsteen sings as Horton, a surefooted yet shy man who remains "faithful to his code," who suddenly lets his "cautiousness slip away."

"Dear Prudence" has a well-known historical backdrop: during the February–March meditational, Prudence Farrow became known as the group's introvert; she kept to her room, trying to "out-meditate" the others. But this only tells you so much about the track, which transcends its era as a subtle Lennon romance. The minimal, fragile lyric achieves a knowing confidence through simplicity: a simple plea for friendship blossoms into a fragrant, all-consuming texture, and a metaphorical sexual awakening takes shape through an uncommonly controlled slow buildup through the last verse.

The Beatles achieve a rare celestial effect through spare rock instrumentation: increasingly layered guitars, bass, piano, and drums. Lennon's elegant Travis-style fingerpicked guitar gets accented gently by tambourine and bass alternating with bass alone in the first verse (0:19 and 0:32), joined by descending bass counterpoint in the second verse (1:03), which resembles a similar line in the bridge to "Don't Let Me Down." Answering the roar of the opening track, it poses an Edenic calm as a retreat from the jet set suggested by "Back in the U.S.S.R."

The Beatles don't elaborate so much as build on an economy of scale and refine, refine, refine, creating a slowly ripening intensity. Instead of adding mere backup vocals (easy to imagine on this pastoral theme), they add counter-harmonies in many overdubbed guitars and let the drums loose on the final verse (2:56) for a satisfying welling up of sound, with high-register piano tinkling its approval (3:03). (McCartney actually plays this drum track; it's such a good Ringo imitation that many assumed it was Starr until the late 1980s, when Lewisohn consulted session logs to correct the record in *The Beatles: Recording Sessions*.)

"Dear Prudence" presents a new layer of Lennon's persona, through which he once raged at perceived betrayal ("You Can't Do That"), threatened betrayers with murder ("Run for Your Life"), or conveyed intimidation by women only in private ("Norwegian Wood"). This track nestles in an infinitely confident, slow-building desire that emphasizes affection above persuasion. "Prudence" avoids the insecurity, anxiety, and conflict that normally cloud his ballads, and forms a new "soft male" narrative that leads to solo songs like "Look at Me" and "Jealous Guy," narrated by a more contrite macho jerk.

The tenderness at play in this undulating groove harkens back to the Buddy Holly lyrics Lennon quotes ("The sun is out, the sky is blue," lifted from "Raining in My Heart," a posthumous B-side to 1959's "It Doesn't Matter Anymore"), the simplest lines elevating the most elegant texture. The Holly recording comes from a demo he made alone in his New York City apartment, to which Dick Jacobs added strings. But you can hear the essential Holly sentiment beneath its lush frame: a teary heartbreak at remembered sweetness. (Lennon did invert one aspect of the apparent model: Holly's song, written by Bryant and Bryant, features a rising chromatic line in an inner voice, whereas "Prudence" is based on the same descending mostly chromatic line heard in "Lucy in the Sky with Diamonds" and numerous other Beatle tracks.) By the final verse of "Dear Prudence," the persona behind "I'll Get You" and "You Can't Do That" has been obscured, left behind for a more settled expression of love's bounty.

CUE	SECTION	HARMONY	DETAIL
0:00	Introductory tattoo	I	Chromatically descending guitar line
0:18	Verse 1: S–R	I	Third-beat accents in bass, tambourine
0:44	Verse 1: D–C	I→VII–IV–I	
0:56	Tattoo		
1:03	Verse 2: SRDC		Bkg vocals enter before D
1:41	Tattoo		Tamboura-like arpeggiating electric-guitar drone added
1:47	Bridge	I–IV–V–IV–I–♭III→V–IV–I	
2:05	Tattoo		
2:11	Verse 3: SRDC		Lead guitar commentary
2:55	Verse 1: SRDC		Guitar countermelody, piano, drums
3:39	Coda		Descending diatonic guitar line into fadeout

"While My Guitar Gently Weeps"

Recorded September 5–6, 1968, for *The Beatles*

—a Guitar god graces his friends with one of the most stunning instrumental parts of their career, as George Harrison remixes the Beatle standbys of modal contrast and the descending chord progression to imaginative new heights.

It's an old blues trope—the crying guitar. B. B. King, famous for making the Gibson that he named "Lucille" weep with heavy wrist vibrato and subtle string bends, did so right from his 1956 debut album's "Crying Won't Help You Woman." But George Harrison trademarked the idea, with his 1961 bent-string duet with John Lennon, "Cry for a Shadow," his 1975 slide-guitar solo track, "This Guitar (Can't Keep from Crying)," and—smack between the two—the iconic 1968 gem "While My Guitar Gently Weeps." A guitar's tone is often associated with liquid; it can be creamy or saturated. When played with sustaining distortion, especially if the pitch or timbre is malleable, it can positively flow with molten spirits. When this effect is applied with wrist vibrato to a bluesy minor-pentatonic language, or even in a straight minor mode, sobbing will often be brought to mind. When you add all of this to a song built on the descending lament bass line, played with a solo guitar primed with a dose of wobbly tape-derived flanging, the results are permeated with sorrow and gloom. Still, the track carries the hope of redemption; Harrison's double-tracked verses, sung in simple parallel thirds, beg with uncommon grace.

Like the lament bass that John Lennon took from "Runaway" for "I'll Be Back," "While My Guitar Gently Weeps" is supported by an adaptation of the slow, depressing descent in A minor (A–G–F–E), but juxtaposes the A-minor tonal center with the parallel A major for extreme contrast. In "I'll Be Back," the A minor / A major switches connote changes from broken heart to verse-ending promises of return.[2] In "Weeps," the A-minor verses are set against bridges that, although they open in a shining A major, continue by dwelling on the early-Beatles standby, minor triads on iii, vi, a returning iii and then ii (all dampening the spirits to portray the singer's existential loss—"I don't know why . . ., I don't know how"), before landing on the pleading half-cadential V. There's something about the key of A that draws this bass line out of the Beatles: like "I'll Be Back," both "Lucy in the Sky with Diamonds" and "I Am the Walrus" are A-major songs based on a lament bass, and both of these fill in the bass descents with one chromatic tone (drooping down from A through G–F♯–F to E). The verse of "Weeps" does the same, although it twice inserts three chords before the arrival of the cadential E: first the double-plagal i→VII–IV, and then i→VII→III. The second pass (i→VII→III) lightly tonicizes C major, and so this song not only looks back

---

2. If "I'll Be Back" is given a vaguely Spanish flavor through classical nylon-string guitar, "Weeps" breathes some of that air by virtue of a castanet part added by Ringo.

to earlier Beatle models as noted above, but also breaks ground for the following year's "Something," with its contrast of A major, A minor, and C major. (In addition, much of this chord work also recalls McCartney's *Magical Mystery Tour* song "Your Mother Should Know" and points ahead to Lennon's *Abbey Road* centerpiece, "I Want You (She's So Heavy)," both of which pass from the tonic A minor through a tonicized C major to half cadences on E.) The minor setting gives the verse's major ♭VII, IV, and ♭VI chords a tragic quality, and the bridge's major mode is immediately undercut with its minor iii, vi and ii chords. The triads in the bridge are not only predominantly minor, but—especially with the iii that appears and then reappears—lie very distant from the goal tonic in terms of motion that would be traced by falling fifths, iii–vi–ii–V, but these fifths do find the retransitional V, which calls for the return of A minor. The singer is flailing away, lost with only the slimmest, never-realized major-mode hopes of rising out of despair. Attention is drawn to the depths by McCartney's sassy Fender Jazz Bass, which thickens the murkiness with double-stops through all verses after the first one, and with a doubling at the unison by a Fender Bass VI (named for its six-string configuration) through the bridges, the bass line of which drips with large wistful leaps doomed to drop right away, many pitches dragged down by descending slides that drench the entire proceedings in pessimism. For his part, Ringo snaps his hi-hat shut on all of the third beats of the intro and first verse with the sober finality of a death sentence.

"Weeps" never resolves into tonic at all, not even a sad minor one, but endlessly repeats the lament that reaches a crying dominant chord, fated to retrace its steps once again. Having Eric Clapton add finesse to this song was a touch of genius not only for his consummate artistry but also for the way the three improvised verse structures have the guitar speak in place of the singer (who shows that he can't do so himself by breaking down and dropping half of his lyrics in the last verse). It's especially trenchant that Clapton was brought to the studio as a balm when tensions were running high between band members; his performance, rich with the 025 blues trichord, replaced Harrison's attempt to wail through the song in a backward-recorded guitar part.

> Clapton makes this a monumental track. His technique—a left hand supple enough for a wide range of vibrato and fluid position shifts, a sense of rhythmic placement, phrasing, and ornamentation unequaled among his peers—is remarkable. Notice the increasing lengths of the thrice-heard first scale degrees at 0:17–0:19, the restraint in the many bars of rests punctuated by brief unexpected appearances (as at 0:28–0:29), the command exhibited in his turnaround phrases (0:31–0:34), the expressive string bends unheard in any other Beatles track (0:47–0:53, especially marking the structural change of mode with c♮ rising to c♯), the sense of power in a retransition (1:21–1:24), the sobbingest vibrato possible (2:01–2:07). And the phrases of his solo (1:55–2:31) are, as usual, composed with the surest and most measured rise in intensity, rhythmic activity, tonal drive, and registral climb, so that its final culmination is nothing short of majestic. It is largely this majesty, revisited at times in the wobbling coda, that rescues the song from its otherwise pathetic air. (Everett 1999, 202)

CUE	SECTION	HARMONY	DETAIL
0:00	Intro	a: i–4/2–IV/6→VIM7–i→VII–IV–V	PM's repeated note on piano
0:16	Verse1: antecedent	a: i–4/2–IV/6→VIM7–i→VII–IV–V	
0:33	Verse 1: consequent	a: i–4/2–IV/6→VIM7–i→VII→III–V	
0:50	Bridge 1	A: I–iii–vi/1–iii–ii–V (repeated)	GH vocal double-tracked at unison
1:24	Verse 2		
1:57	Guitar solo	(based on verse)	Eric Clapton on Les Paul with ADT
2:30	Bridge 2		
3:03	Verse 1: antecedent		
0:33	Verse 1: consequent		vocals cut out partway through
3:37	Coda	(twice through verse structure)	Clapton solo through fadeout

"Martha My Dear"

Recorded October 5–6, 1968, for *The Beatles*

—metric surprises and unexpected modulations bring a springy buoyancy to this odd ode to a dog.

In McCartney's string of soft-shoe trifles ("When I'm Sixty-Four," "Honey Pie," "Maxwell's Silver Hammer," and later solo turns like "You Gave Me the Answer" on *Venus and Mars*), "Martha My Dear"—named for a pet sheepdog—emerges as the sturdiest, most sardonic number, and one that matches its charm with craft. It poses as another unassuming, innocent curio, but its tart flavor holds up better, lingers with more sting, than the others. Alongside "Savoy Truffle," it almost sounds like George Harrison trying his hand at a McCartney number. (Harrison's "Sour Milk Sea" would have made the perfect B-side to "Martha"; they sound of a piece.) The formal structure of "Martha" (as diagrammed below) is original, pliant, and fragmentary. As such, it could not have been achieved without "Lovely Rita" and "Walrus" before it.

As Lennon proves adept at manipulating simple harmonic sequences into clever puzzles, McCartney spikes an otherwise fey attack with metric booby traps, making an irregular meter (a bar of five beats tripping each verse into quadruple time) seem perfectly natural next to a key scheme that mixes tender affection with wry bemusement. Strings-laden verses begin and end in E♭ (I) but tonicize iii (G minor) and then V (B♭) along the way. Oompah bridges weighed down by low brass start on D-minor chords (vi of II) before landing squarely on a tonicized F major (II) and return to D minor for a distracted opening to the retransition (triggered by a flugelhorn scampering in silliness), which follows two bars of 6/4 with three of 4/4 and another of 6/4. This phrase, rocking with strong snare backbeat fighting the guitar chords that slash the strong beats, pivots as if looking toward home with a sustained B♭ (V), suddenly augmented by violins, that gives much of the overbearing coyness some bite. That V is undercut with minor chords that lose their way, the silly flugelhorn now returning to be interrupted by tonic, which appears with sudden peekaboo hammerstrokes, Just Like That! (1:18–1:19). This opens the door for a brass interlude based on the verse structure, rescuing McCartney's camp with its own acerbic irregularities.

CUE	SECTION	HARMONY	DETAIL
0:00	Intro: antecedent	I–(V of)–iii–(V7 of)–(V of) V	Piano solo
0:09	Intro: cadence	V7–IVM7–V7	
0:18	Verse 1: phrase 1	(same as Intro)	Strings added
0:28	Verse 1: refrain	V7–IV7–V7	
0:38	Bridge 1	(vi7–ii9 of) II–(V–V7 of–vi–iii)	
0:59	Retransition	(vi–II9–V of II)–VM7–(vi–iii)	
1:18	Tonic announcement	I	last two beats of 6/4 bar
1:20	Brass interlude	(structure of both verse phrases)	
1:39	Bridge 2		
2:01	Retransition 2	(cuts all between flugelhorn statements)	
2:02	Verse 2: antecedent	I–(V of)–iii–(V7 of)–(V of) V	
2:13	Verse 2: refrain	V7–IV7–V7–I	bass solo for final cadence

"I'm So Tired"

Recorded October 8, 1968, for *The Beatles*

—carrying on with the sorts of contradictions heard within "Things We Said Today," "We Can Work It Out," and "A Day in the Life," this track builds without warning from complacent sigh to cross aggression.

Lennon traces several major story arcs across the Beatles catalog: the first might be his dreamscapes, with ever increasing layers of experimental intrigue ("Tomorrow Never Knows" to "Strawberry Fields Forever" to "I Am the Walrus" to "Revolution 9"). Another long arc might be dubbed "songs of fatigue": "I'm Only Sleeping"; the tragic story implied between two words "oh boy" in "A Day in the Life"; his paean to fame's relentlessness in "I'm So Tired"; and ultimately one of his last completed compositions, "Watching the Wheels."

"I'm So Tired" seeps right out from the falling interval between "oh" and "boy" in "A Day in the Life," as if the song siphons off the mood of that lingering *Pepper* coda. There's more grief in the way he drops between those two words than even the track's final crashingly empty chord (in Beatles terms, "oh boy" becomes the opposite of "yeah, yeah, yeah"). Those "oh boy" sighs capture the detachment it takes to withhold your emotional response as you read about the world's random savagery, the sensitivity McCartney's chipper businessman ("Woke up, fell out of bed") shrugs off with indifference. "I'm So Tired" would have sounded out of place if it had come anywhere before "A Day in the Life," even though songs like "I'm Only Sleeping" and "Nowhere Man" indirectly shoulder philosophical worry and cultural anxiety.

Lennon's experimentalism grew so extravagant throughout 1966 ("Tomorrow Never Knows") and 1967 ("I Am the Walrus") that by the time he backshifts into "roots" mode in 1968 (at first with "Hey Bulldog" and then "Revolution"), his metaphors distill into perfectly pitched literalisms. He was known both for his candor and double-edged humor, but when he sings "I'm So Tired," you can really hear the plain weariness in his voice, which springs from the same jaded attitude as "Sexy Sadie." Where that vocal captures a withering, implacable anger, "Tired" sounds limp, drained, and dispirited. It's the opposite of the high morale in "I Should Have Known Better" and roams the desolate emotional space outlined in "A Day in the Life," where death erases meaning and modernity drains hope.

Like other Lennon songs we've dug into here, he phrases his verses so they rise to angry stop-time breaks (after "peace of mind" at 1:04, and again at 1:45, where they stutter with one-more-time repetition), only now the pauses drop the mood into renewed sluggishness, and Lennon mumbles his way out of it. Guitar chords slice at the second halves of verses with sharp accents cueing dread, grief, and misanthropy. Except for the bridges (at 0:47 and 1:29), the track follows a slightly modified blues sequence in its bar-form *a a' b* structure, its diatonic basis tipping only on the key word "tired," which slips down to an unusually inflected major VII chord, before straightening out into IV and then V; the hackneyed second phrase (0:08–0:15), along with bits of the contemporaneous "Happiness Is a Warm Gun," sponges off doo-wop lines through Lennon's ambivalent falsetto.

The song's tension emerges from contempt and bitterness and the quirky, show-off melody: it's a musical paradox, an aria about disaffection that oozes virtuosity. The ensemble also reaches a nadir of medium-tempo sludge: Starr sounds like he wants to take an even slower tempo, and constantly drags the others back into his lugubrious feel. Any musician will confirm: sustaining slow tempos doubles the demands on an ensemble, and such grooves prove far more difficult to sustain than faster ones; it's one sign of virtuosity when a band that zigzags its way through rhythmic labyrinths like "Happiness Is a Warm Gun" and "Everybody's Got Something to Hide Except Me and My Monkey" ups the ante by drooping so successfully into sheer indolence.

CUE	SECTION	HARMONY	DETAIL
0:00	Verse 1: *a*	I–VII7–IV–V	
0:08	Verse 1: *a'*	I–vi–IV–V	Doo-wop progression
0:15	Verse 1: *b*	I–V+–vi–iv	Backbeat "chick" gtr chords
0:24	Verse 2: *a–a'–b*		Organ enters to prepare bridge
0:46	Bridge	I–V–IV–I	PM adds descant for cadence
1:06	Verse 3: *a–a'–b*		
1:28	Bridge		
1:48	Coda	IV–I	"one more time" cadence
1:51			Drum fills
1:57			Mumble into fadeout

"Everybody's Got Something to Hide Except Me and My Monkey"

Recorded June 27 and July 23, 1968, for *The Beatles*

—maniacal music accompanying one-man repartee.

As Lennon moves from mid-period development to late-period compression, his songwriting follows two threads typified by the recording of "Revolution." Originally a medium-tempo Chuck Berry–like boogie, "Revolution" morphed into a long, wild-eyed sound collage by the end of the 10'47" master (take 20), and Lennon broke it into two separate tracks. The first remained a straight, medium-tempo rock 'n' roll number; the second became his most experimental gesture. "Revolution 9" makes more sense when considered as part of a continuum extending from the overt tape manipulation of "I'm Only Sleeping," "Rain," and "Tomorrow Never Knows" to "Strawberry Fields Forever," "Being for the Benefit of Mr. Kite," and "I Am the Walrus."

Another set of tracks tries to mash these two impulses together: where "Dig a Pony" sets gibberish loose atop a Möbius-strip chord sequence, "Everybody's Got Something to Hide Except Me and My Monkey" combines self-negating wordplay with rhythmic quandaries for overcomplicated elation. Like "Glass Onion," "Everybody" mocks pretention and neatly inverts the argument: the lyric may be about nothing or everything, but it's a simple appendage to the music, which taunts and scalds with distorted offbeat guitar strokes and manic cowbell. Instead of rambling on as in his books (*A Spaniard in the Works* and *In His Own Write*), Lennon's lyric more resembles Bob Dylan's "Million Dollar Bash," then making the rounds on bootleg tapes, where Dylan proclaims "The harder they come, the bigger they crack." "The deeper you go, the higher you fly," may be Lennon's rejoinder, but his hard-rock frame wallops Dylan's rural feel. "Everybody" carries this off with kinetic virtuosity: the ensemble digs into the material exuberantly; the lyrics puncture vanity.

The song adds artifice to grit. "Everybody" is a tart, mangled, screwball farce, harnessing virtuoso control over wayward poetry. Where lyrics trace scatological abstraction, the music has a prolix glee right from the offbeat guitar chords that recall the opening of "She's a Woman"; it could be the reverse image of "Happiness Is a Warm Gun," more sex than drugs, with rhythmic traps that spring upon release instead of remaining coiled up with anxiety. As a companion piece to McCartney's "Birthday," "Everybody" has an intensity of attack that balances out the slowest batch of Lennon numbers on any album: "Dear Prudence," "I'm So Tired," "Sexy Sadie," and "Cry Baby Cry."

CUE	SECTION	HARMONY	DETAIL
0:00	Intro	I–IV	Guitar chords on offbeats
0:07	Chorus 1: *a*	I	In 4/4; cowbell on beat subdivisions
0:20	Chorus 1: *b*	IV→VII	
0:28	Chorus 1: *c*	V7–I	Refrain line (title)
0:32	Chorus 1: tag	I→VII→III–I→III→VII	Minor-pentatonic lead guitar in 7/4
0:39	Verse 1		Cowbell out
0:48	Chorus 2 and tag		
1:19	Verse 2		Cowbell returns
1:27	Chorus 3 and tag		Cowbell out
1:59	Coda	I→VII–I	Cowbell returns; guitar chords fadeout

"Sexy Sadie"

Recorded August 13 and 21, 1968, for *The Beatles*

—*slithering harmony portrays deceit in Lennon's revenge on one of his series of father figures.*

The Beatles' retreat to Rishikesh, India, in the spring of 1968 has become a blurry pop metaphor for daft hippies seeking enlightenment from the East. In reality, the venture had more complicated political intrigue. Harrison seems to have been sincerely interested in meditation and its spiritual context; the others found themselves drawn by the promise of peace of mind. Lennon, by this point, had pretty much irritated everybody in his circle with his daily drug intake, which had already harmed his marriage and promised to forestall productivity even further if it continued. So the others had a vested interest in getting him away from his usual haunts for some drying out, just as his time on the set of *How I Won the War* seems to have coaxed "Strawberry Fields Forever" from a setting far removed from early-hours clubbing and hard drugs.

It has grown familiar as an outré character in Beatles lore, but calling a song "Sexy Sadie" in 1968 marked the height of incredulity, especially coming from a band as popular as the Beatles. The "establishment" record labels and commercial radio wanted to act as if all of rock's sex and drug references didn't exist. The BBC banned "A Day in the Life" for its line "I'd love to turn you on," which survives more as poetic abstraction than an endorsement of intoxication. When Lennon first penned "Sadie," he used "Maharishi" as the working title lyric, and Harrison urged him to use a pseudonym. The other Beatles didn't feel as duped by the meditation guru nearly as much as Lennon did (he always felt betrayed after seeming to idealistically invest his personal authorities with the depths his real father had not shared) and knew that such outbursts could come back to bite them. Musical revenge has the weakest of motives: taking down someone else can wind up emphasizing how much you've been conned.

Although he obscures his target, "Sexy Sadie" wears its vengeance on its sleeve; there's no subtext. Lennon simply riffs on what he saw as the Maharishi's snake-oil transcendence, without extending its metaphorical fraud. It plays off rants like Dylan's bitterly conversational "Positively 4th Street" or the Rolling Stones' "Get Off of My Cloud," where dumping a lover or friend becomes an act of defiant self-aggrandizement. Notably, most of these songs are addressed to an unsympathetic "you," where listeners generally hear themselves being targeted. At this medium tempo, Lennon's resolve takes on a dark hue, poring over his subject's faults obsessively without realizing how this tone circles back against him. It's enough to make you wish you never knew the back story; it intrudes too much on the track's attributes and limits its possibilities.

CUE	SECTION	HARMONY	DETAIL
0:00	Intro	IV–V–I–VII7!–♭VII–V7	piano w/echo
0:08			Drums enter
0:09	Verse 1	I–VII7–iii–IV–V–I–VII7–IV–V–I–VII7→VII–V	
0:25			Bkg vocals: "woh-woh"
0:31	Verse 2		
0:47			"see-see-see-see"
0:54	Bridge 1	I–ii7–iii7–IVM7 II7→♭II7	♭II7 = jazzy tritone substitute for V7
1:09	Verse 3		
1:31	Verse 4		
1:37			Piano protest
1:54	Bridge 2		
2:10	Coda	based on verse	Falsetto; out of phase (iii then IV are now downbeats of phrases)

"Revolution 9"

Recorded May 30–31 and June 3, 4, 6, 10, 11, 20, 21, and 25, 1968, for *The Beatles*

—this time, the improvisatory chaos is that of Lennon's external world, instead of his inner disorder, the more usual inspiration. Brilliant, visionary, and the Beatles' most challenging experience. Don't give up on it too easily!

Many Beatles tracks explore fadeouts as trick mirrors that veer into alternative soundscapes. Even early on, many songs continue inventing themselves into the silence: the way Lennon's double-tracked vocal splits apart near the end of "Not a Second Time," or how backward guitars come unspooled on "I'm Only Sleeping." Others tracks prolong interest in material that seems to have ended (the leap-frogging chorale at the end of "Good Day Sunshine," the false endings to "Helter Skelter" and "Get Back," or the muted lead vocal in the final lap of "Yer Blues"). Sometimes these experiments lead to twisted non-endings, like those of "Doctor Robert," which cadences on the "wrong" II harmony just as the fadeout ends, or "Long, Long, Long," which flickers and fades like a dying ember. When he toyed with backward tapes on "I'm Only Sleeping" and "Rain," Lennon chased the hallucinogenic effects straight into some silent tunnel, as if a black hole had sucked the song into nothingness.

By the time they reached "Strawberry Fields Forever," a mere fadeout couldn't tame the song's emotional furies—so a *fade back-in* returned the chaos, as if the void disgorged the song back in triumph, melted and distended beyond recognition, with "lyrics" curdled into gibberish ("Cranberry sauce") and instruments melting like time itself. The brief string coda to "Glass Onion" reiterates this molten dissolve. "A Day in the Life," their grandest orchestral finale, had too much pretension to rely on its inconclusive E major chord, so it drifted off into artificial decay, synthetically holding back silence through compression and gain amplification, until the void yawned and an inaudible dog whistle on the run-out groove—meant to wake awestruck stoners from their daze—further punctuated the mood. A cackling inner groove of a manic looped snippet of conversation mocked this tragic overhang, as if the Frankenstein track had spooked even the Beatles into mannered gibberish. It's like Harrison's nervous laughter serving as a palate cleanser after the humorless "Within You Without You."

So if a fadeout symbolized an alternate world, what might such a world sound like? What if entering a fadeout became the track's core idea, its gravity, its subject? What if the racket that swarms around "All You Need Is Love," which includes snatches from Bach, "She Loves You," and "In the Mood," echoing *Pepper*'s celebrity collage in a parade of recognizable hooks, worked out to be the raw material itself? Could a randomized quilt of noise and found sound suggest the underside of the Beatles' utopian melodies?

"Revolution 9" began with "Revolution," another Lennon newspaper narrative, which addressed shifting realities; throughout the summer of 1968, each day brought new disruption. Lennon drafted it that May, as Paris and the heart of Europe erupted in a sweeping class revolt. A student protest about dorm conditions mushroomed into a broader working-class protest against the mistreatment of workers, and millions marched in the streets carrying situationist slogans. Business came to a halt; the government shut down. That summer, as the Beatles recorded the *White Album*, more protests erupted, and the world seemed to reel in reaction to the assassinations of Martin Luther King, Jr., and Robert Kennedy; the 1968 Democratic Convention in Chicago showcased police brutality beyond its typical racial outlines, and President Alexander Dubček mounted a series of reforms in Czechoslovakia—freedoms in the press and the economy—that baited the Soviet overlords. The American literary critic David Wyatt subtitled his 2015 history of the period *When America Turned: Reckoning with 1968*, and few doubted that the season brought defining incidents. It all made the stunned reaction to John F. Kennedy's death just five years earlier seem mild.

Among rock's youth audience, the mood on the ground grew anxious: a revolutionary spirit felt palpable, especially against totalitarian forces, but elections in late June returned de Gaulle's government in France, and by August Russian tanks invaded Prague. Lennon could be flippant about politics and cultural conflict ("more popular than Jesus"), but his response this time around held out ambivalence as a mark of sanity or caution. His spirit went with change, but tactics, heated rhetoric about "any means necessary," and street violence, even against the most fearsome repression, filled him with doubt.

Lennon famously recorded two versions of "Revolution," but not before writing two answers within the song: if "revolution" in the political sense meant "destruction" or violence, he sang "Count me out . . . in," with obvious ambivalence. The first version (recorded on May 30) clocked in at over ten minutes, with a fadeout that trumped everything that came before. (This song-form anticipates McCartney's "Hey Jude" trick, where the "Nah-nah-nah-nah" tail eats the song's body.) This track would be Lennon's comet, and its tail questioned the stability of meaning beyond "I Am the Walrus": trailing off into increasing chaos, the last six minutes of "Revolution," take 20, simulated a reflecting pool of the era's clashing ideologies, the noise of the streets caught and metamorphosed in sound. The result captured a slow-burn psychedelia seared by roaming guitar feedback and repeated shouts of "aaaaaaall right" and "riiiiiiiiight!" that drifted off into a dreamscape, an extended sound collage that could never be mistaken for a mere fadeout. Instead, the fadeout itself became the bed for a new song, as if every song the Beatles had ever faded into returned in zombified abstraction, between two deaths. Some passages resemble the amorphous transitions in "A Day in the Life," where ominous glissandos threaten to shake the needle from its groove, time from its meter, and the listener from the protagonist's newspaper narrative. Indeed, a snatch from "A Day in the Life" orchestra rehearsals is sampled in "Revolution 9." Lennon responded to rebellious energy with wary optimism: he sided with the protestors while picking apart their rhetoric. "Revolution 9" plants doubt in the weirdly upbeat inconsistency of "Revolution."

Naturally, all ten minutes became unwieldy, even for Lennon. So he cut it in two: the first segment became "Revolution 1," which we now know as the opening track of side 4. (When this track got vetoed for the new single, Lennon picked up the tempo to create "Revolution" for the B-side of "Hey Jude." That faster performance gleefully cops its opening cannonade guitar from a 1954 Pee Wee Crayton side, "Do unto Others.") The remainder of this original tape got much more treatment, extension, and manipulation to become "Revolution 9," which opens with Yoko Ono's plaintive piano waltz draping a sound engineer's test script ("number nine, number nine") for a maniacally calm recurring loop. (This anonymous voice long got mistaken for Lennon's own, even though he deliberately chose the speech of a random engineer to ricochet across the stereo channels.) This oracular voice became the only narrative thread as a tableau of street sounds, private conversations, trilling strings from the "A Day in the Life" session (0:24–0:29), a backward piano phrase from Schumann (0:29–0:43), choral singing with brass and cymbals, forwards and backwards, from Vaughan Williams (0:53–0:59), a symphonic cadence from Sibelius (2:18+), a BBC broadcast of Farid El Atrache's "Awal Hamsa" (7:12+), and much more—at least forty-five different sources, many found in EMI's tape library—all surfaced and submerged again, with various recordings played backwards and at double speed. Lennon and his uncredited co-composer Ono, with some help from Harrison, worked on it over numerous sessions in June, taking over the entire shop (Studios One, Two, and Three) on the twentieth of that month, urging engineers and staffers to hold up tape loops with pencils from across various rooms as Lennon worked the mixing board, fading noises in and out. The method resembled some of the processes used on "Tomorrow Never Knows," using the six-minute vamp of the original recording of "Revolution" as the backing track: the musical undulations stem from Lennon's spontaneous responses to sounds as they floated in and out of earshot, playing the recording console like an electronic instrument.

Apparently at first a random assemblage of loops (as was the calliope mélange of "Being for the Benefit of Mr. Kite"), the track makes little pretense of structure or organization; mapping it out proves useful only as a diagram of convulsion. But listen closely and often enough, and contours emerge, anticipations build to uncertain release, and, paradoxically, seemingly random gestures begin to acquire preordained certainty, like a dance into the unconscious joining chance with fate. After years of growing familiarity with the track's bold, erratic shapes, it begins to reveal how naked tape machines might be invested with souls, how fantastic technical trickery can yield an indelible human personality.

The cultural context of "Revolution 9" struck contemporaneous listeners like so much background noise. But the piece survives as a surprisingly adroit example of musique concrète, which McCartney enjoyed dabbling in, particularly in his legendary "Carnival of Light" of January 1967, recorded—but never released, even on bootleg—for a psychedelic light show in a London night club. With its impudence and length (which tests pop attention spans), the eight-minute track, the group's longest, prompts more debates about its merits than any other Beatles song. If the reader has difficulty appreciating the incoherent nature of "Revolution 9," as many do, consider Picasso's painting *Guernica*. Portraying Franco's use in 1937 of Nazi bombers to rain havoc and death on the Spanish citizens of Guernica, the huge canvas shows nothing but ugly atrocity—a woman holding her dead baby, a disemboweled horse—but its monochrome composition (particularly in suggesting the hope of light against the darkness of despair), as well as its authoritative command of emotions, is guided by an aesthetic beauty. So can the singular beauty of "Revolution 9" be approached, all of Picasso's severity and rigorous parallelisms deeply felt in Lennon/Ono's aural annihilation.

Perhaps this is where, even as the other Beatles tried to talk Lennon down off this particular ledge, the band revealed how much it frequently preordained the digital era, where sounds might be manipulated with ease, and an aural collage could someday be assembled with audio-processing software like Pro Tools, Logic Pro, or Audacity. Lennon held his ground: on a double album, he sensed, people would forgive a touch of excess. And if it pissed fans off, all the better: the Beatles had exposed a mainstream audience of music lovers to the most experimental electronic ideas in academia through composers like Pierre Schaeffer, Edgard Varèse, and Karlheinz Stockhausen (who appears on *Pepper's* cover). If it didn't enchant the curious, it might just signal how far the Beatles meant to stretch form, and how artists chase new ideas beyond what their audiences can comprehend.

In a quixotic reversal of content creating its own accidental form, several experimental groups began performing the number: in 1992, Kurt Hoffman's Band of Weeds put it on their album *Live at the Knitting Factory: Downtown Does the Beatles* (Knitting Factory Records), and the jam band Phish included it when they mounted the entire *White Album* onstage for a 1994 Halloween concert, released in 2002 as *Live Phish Volume 13*. More recently, the chamber orchestra Alarm Will Sound has programmed the piece, and "Revolution 9" anchors the Fab Faux's many stage performances of the *White Album*. The cohesion of the piece might be measured in the distance between your expectations of how it might sound live and the performed versions' proscribed variations—the distance between one's memory of a dream and its artificial re-enactment. If spliced tape loops and a mixing board could or even should be reproduced as performance material, "Revolution 9" has the kind of cultural significance to deliver expressive power, even as inverted philosophy, or, as critic Greil Marcus called it, "an aural litmus of unfocused paranoia" (http://www.rollingstone.com/music/news/lennons-music-a-range-of-genius-20101207).[3]

It's also impossible to separate "Revolution 9" from its successor, "Good Night," a tender lullaby awash in strings that brings a hush to the album's four sides. Lennon had Ringo sing it, as if it were far too sentimental for the man who sang "Glass Onion" and "Yer Blues." And just as when McCartney had tossed the drummer a "Yellow Submarine," Ringo carries "Good Night" past the finish line with unflinching sincerity.

---

3. In *The Beatles Complete Scores,* a generally good but sometimes weak attempt at transcription, the presentation of "Revolution 9" (814–823) resembles a black-and-white stick drawing of a rainbow.

As if to slam the case shut, the same month the *White Album* came out, Lennon and Ono released their first "solo" album, *Unfinished Music No. 1: Two Virgins*, with the couple posing nude on the cover. That obscenity firestorm upstaged whatever dismay might have shrouded "Revolution 9" as a cultural affront. Ironically, nothing on *Two Virgins*, an oddly coquettish venture, contests "Revolution 9" for sheer sound-twisting audacity and composerly authority.

POINTS FOR DISCUSSION

1. What sort of anxiety did *Pepper* induce in the Beatles of 1968?
2. Describe in musical terms how the Beatles' breakup can be heard across the four sides of the *White Album*. How did the Beatles' changing individual interests manifest themselves otherwise in 1968? What evidence is there of personal rancor?
3. Name some songs written in 1968 that were held back for various later recording projects.
4. George Harrison's songwriting famously leaps forward in this period. Discuss what he learned from Lennon and McCartney and how his writing voice remains distinctive. Could either Lennon or McCartney have written "While My Guitar Gently Weeps," "Savoy Truffle," or "Piggies"?
5. What were the original inspirations for some 1968 recordings? See if you can find online Paul McCartney talking with guitarist Carlos Bonell; what do they demonstrate?
6. Why was the Vietnam War, in faraway Southeast Asia, of such global significance?
7. How and why did the civil rights legislation of 1964–1965 offer weak consolation in 1968?
8. Can you discover examples aside from the Beatles in which politics, strife, and popular music converged in the late 1960s?
9. What were the goals of Apple? In what ways was the company a success and a failure?
10. Describe why Lennon refers to Bob Dylan's "Ballad of a Thin Man" in the middle of "Yer Blues" and its overall effect.
11. Much of the *White Album* was composed in India on guitars, and yet a number of keyboard instruments are heard in the resulting recordings. Discuss which eventual guitar parts might have survived as played in India and which might have been created after the return to London. The long-bootlegged and now (2018) officially released Esher demos may provide some hints.
12. If Lennon fails to appear on "Martha My Dear," "I Will," and "Blackbird" and McCartney remains absent from "Julia," how can these tracks be considered Beatles tracks? Does this expand the idea of the band or reduce it?
13. Play producer and narrow down the thirty songs on the *White Album* to a fifteen-song single disc. How best to sequence the tracks you choose? What tracks are the hardest to leave behind, and why? What new ideas emerge from your new track sequence?
14. In what way is the bridge of "Hey Jude" a throwback to 1963 stylings?

FURTHER READING

Branch, Taylor. *At Canaan's Edge: America in the King Years 1965–68*. New York: Simon & Schuster, 2006.

DeGroot, Gerard D. *The Sixties Unplugged: A Kaleidoscopic History of a Disorderly Decade*. Cambridge, MA: Harvard University Press, 2008.

DiLello, Richard. *The Longest Cocktail Party: An Insider's Diary of the Beatles, Their Million-Dollar Apple Empire, and Its Wild Rise and Fall*. Edinburgh: Canongate, 2005.

Doggett, Peter. *There's a Riot Goin' On: Revolution in the Sixties*. London: Canongate, 2008.

Doggett, Peter. *You Never Give Me Your Money: The Battle for the Soul of the Beatles*. New York: Harperstudio, 2010.

Gitlin, Todd. *The Sixties: Years of Hope, Days of Rage*. New York: Bantam, 1987.

Gould, Jonathan. *Can't Buy Me Love: The Beatles in the Sixties*. New York: Harmony, 2007.

Haskell, Barbara, and John G. Hanhardt. *Yoko Ono: Arias and Objects*. Salt Lake City: Peregrine Smith, 1991.

Hopkins, Jerry. *Yoko Ono*. New York: Macmillan, 1986.

Lapham, Lewis H. *With the Beatles*. Hoboken: Melville House, 2005.

MacDonald, Ian. *Revolution in the Head: The Beatles' Records and the Sixties*. New York: Henry Holt, 1994.

McCabe, Peter, and Robert D. Schonfeld. *Apple to the Core: The Unmaking of the Beatles*. New York: Pocket Books, 1972.

Osteen, Mark. *The Beatles through a Glass Onion: Reconsidering the White Album*. Ann Arbor: University of Michigan Press, 2019.

Wenner, Jann. *Lennon Remembers: The Rolling Stone Interviews*. San Francisco: Straight Arrow, 1971.

Wyatt, David. *When America Turned: Reckoning with 1968*. Amherst: University of Massachusetts, 2014.

CHAPTER 9

THEY MAY BE PARTED (1969–1970)

Hindsight casts a bittersweet light on the remainder of the Beatles' career. Unlike listeners of the 1960s, we now know how close the band came to breaking up during production of the final two albums over the first nine months of 1969. We also know that McCartney upset the other three by timing the April 1970 release of his first solo album right alongside the group's *Let It Be* and its documentary feature film. But the music they made together during this period transcends such complications; many critics maintain they reached their collective peak during their last work together, the *Abbey Road* sessions.

Many factors contributed to the band's breakup, including those already mentioned: Lennon's increasing obsession with Yoko Ono, his growing distance from McCartney as a songwriting partner, Harrison's creative ascendancy, the natural evolution over a dozen years of four distinct human beings, and the myriad disagreements about how to oversee their joint ownership rights and the Apple concern. But the Beatles myth proved so potent, so compellingly driving everybody's pop expectations, that fans wanted to believe the band's troubles to be minor and relished each new release as though the group's idealized spirit remained intact. The Beatles' dilemmas already forced serious creative and aesthetic negotiations, but their most recent work going into 1969 ("Back in the U.S.S.R.," "Revolution") still brimmed with utopian optimism.

As the new year approached, reviewers praised the *White Album* while noting its unusual contours, and despite the fact that none of its bounty found release as a single, fans happily plunked down for the larger package, while "Ob-La-Di, Ob-La-Da" became a late-1968 no. 1 hit in the United Kingdom for Marmalade. A decade later, Jerry Garcia of the Grateful Dead would begin making "Dear Prudence" a centerpiece of hundreds of his live sets, but regardless of these and the many other varied and notable covers of *White Album* material, and despite the LP's huge dog's breakfast of styles, the Beatles' own versions of every single track remain the most popular. Across their career and the many thousands of performances of their compositions, rare is the song for which the Beatles' recorded version isn't universally acclaimed as definitive.

The public's mood after the social upheavals of 1968 veered between hangover and tenuous expectancy: after all, July and August of the new year would bring a man landing on the moon and the Woodstock rock festival, respectively. But it also brought August's Charles Manson Family murders in Los Angeles, a consequence of his deranged fantasy of an impending race war (during which one of his followers notoriously wrote the Beatles' song title "Helter Skelter" on a refrigerator in one of the victim's blood) and December's white-on-black racial murder in the front row of a December Rolling Stones concert at Altamont (captured in the terrifying rock documentary *Gimme Shelter*). State violence persisted in the form of a New York City police raid in June on a Greenwich Village gay bar that kicked off the Stonewall rebellion and, with it, the gay liberation movement. The year ended with the murders of members of the Black Panther Party (all unarmed, some sleeping) by the Chicago police, following months of shootouts in the streets. Almost unnoticed, ARPANET was established in September, inaugurating the protocol of future supercomputer connections that became today's internet.

Perhaps because of the enormous contradictions in their culture, the Beatles avoided topical references in their last projects, aside from an unusual autobiographical narrative from John and Yoko. The Beatles stayed relevant mostly as symbols of endurance in the rock pantheon: few dared challenge their status, and many, such as Joe Cocker, paid them the highest respects simply by honoring their material through ingenious renovations, as in his bluesy rendition of "With a Little Help from My Friends," a Woodstock standout. As the Rolling Stones expressed the magnificent decadence of *Let It Bleed*, Bob Dylan began a long look backward with country and western (with *Nashville Skyline*), the Who took the idea of an album-length story to a new peak with *Tommy*, and the world was given a farewell album by Cream and a debut by Led Zeppelin, the Beatles weighed conceptual ambitions against craft in a tense combination of their peerless talents. Churning out product became almost secondary to keeping the band afloat.

1969–1970 British Releases:

LP: *Yellow Submarine* (rel. Jan. 17, 1969)

Side 1:	Side 2:
"Yellow Submarine"	["Pepperland"]
"Only a Northern Song"	[Medley: "Sea of Time" and "Sea of Holes"]
"All Together Now"	["Sea of Monsters"]
"Hey Bulldog"	["March of the Meanies"]
"It's All Too Much"	["Pepperland Laid Waste"]
"All You Need Is Love"	["Yellow Submarine in Pepperland"]

Single: "Get Back" / "Don't Let Me Down" (rel. Apr. 11, 1969)
Single: "The Ballad of John and Yoko" / "Old Brown Shoe" (rel. May 30, 1969)
LP: *Abbey Road* (rel. Sep. 26, 1969)

Side 1:
"Come Together"
"Something"
"Maxwell's Silver Hammer"
"Oh! Darling"
"Octopus's Garden"
"I Want You (She's So Heavy)"

Side 2:
"Here Comes the Sun"
"Because"
"You Never Give Me Your Money"
"Sun King"
"Mean Mr. Mustard"
"Polythene Pam"
"She Came In through the Bathroom Window"
"Golden Slumbers"
"Carry That Weight"
"The End"
"Her Majesty"

Single: "Something" / "Come Together" (rel. Oct. 31, 1969)
Single: "Let It Be" / "You Know My Name (Look Up the Number)" (rel. Mar. 6, 1970)
LP: *Let It Be* (rel. May 8, 1970)

Side 1:
"Two of Us"
"Dig a Pony"
"Across the Universe"
"I Me Mine"
"Dig It"
"Let It Be"
"Maggie Mae"

Side 2:
"I've Got a Feeling"
"One after 909"
"The Long and Winding Road"
"For You Blue"
"Get Back"

THE "GET BACK" PROJECT

Paul McCartney wanted to retake the concert stage. The Beatles started 1969 with grandiose hopes—they talked about playing at the pyramids of Giza, or aboard a ship in the Mediterranean. But George objected to anything that invited Beatlemania complications, and any hopes for a publicized concert disappeared when he quit for more than a week on the seventh day of filming. The January plan, spearheaded by Paul, was to rehearse and perform the oldies from their early career, one of many "getting back" gestures. Cameras captured weeks' worth of full-day practice sessions in hopes of a made-for-TV film (an antidote to *Magical Mystery Tour*?) of the group progressing toward a performance before a live audience.

John insisted any new recording contain no overdubs and be released as is, "warts and all." Oldies repertoire lent itself well to such live treatment. Turning away from the extreme psychedelic pretentions the band had championed with *Pepper*, he said in September 1968 that he was "trying to be more natural, less 'newspaper taxis,' say . . . Really, I just like rock & roll. . . . I'm still trying to reproduce 'Some Other Guy' sometimes or 'Be-Bop-A-Lula'" (Cott 1968). Ultimately, the TV format would be scrapped and replaced by a feature-film documentary, and the cover versions were quickly overtaken by new songs that would be recorded with editing as well as a few overdubs. Even as the *White Album* monopolized the top of the album charts, they gathered in the enormous Twickenham soundstage around space heaters on a union schedule throughout January, attending bleary-eyed morning sessions for the first time in years. The project's working title, "Get Back," described their post-psychedelic, roots-bound approach.

Like a couple trying to save its marriage by having a baby, the Beatles had all but disintegrated, and much of the time was spent propping up weary morale. McCartney had enough motivation and work ethic for the other three combined—watching *Let It Be*, you get the sense that if he didn't steer this project, nobody would. Film outtakes capture about eighty hours of lackluster rehearsal, the most recorded from any Beatles project. Unfortunately, the mood had not improved from the previous summer and fall, and McCartney's enthusiasm typically met with yawning ambivalence. However, since it comprises the only filmed sessions we have, and because of the thoroughness of this documentation, scholars pore over this material for clues about everything from musical influences to how Beatle compositions and arrangements take shape.

The push to complete the extra-difficult double album had been exhausting, and in the interim, Yoko suffered a miscarriage in December. There were some new songs—John's "Don't Let Me Down," "Dig a Pony," "I've Got a Feeling," "Child of Nature," and "Sun King"; Paul's "Two of Us" and "Maxwell's Silver Hammer"; and George's "All Things Must Pass" and "Let It Down" were the first ones attempted—but oldies were the charge: Chuck Berry's "Brown-Eyed Handsome Man," Buddy Holly's "Mailman, Bring Me No More Blues" and "Well, Alright," Jerry Lee Lewis's "Whole Lotta Shakin' Goin' On," Bo Diddley's "Crackin' Up," Elvis Presley's "All Shook Up," Carl Perkins's "Your True Love" and "Blue Suede Shoes," the Coasters' "Three Cool Cats," and Little Richard's "Lucille" all received run-throughs in the first days of rehearsal, and seemed to be the glue that would hold the band to a common purpose. One of these "oldies" was their own "One after 909," a bubbling Lennon-McCartney duet that buoyed the band beyond their circumstances. The charm of reviving one of their unpublished songs, rescued from oblivion after it was scrapped in March 1963, seemed to shift their ensemble back into friendly gear.

Filming the entirety of very raw and largely aimless rehearsals, however, brought added tensions alongside recurring ones. With his new offerings pushed aside by an openly insulting John Lennon, and with Paul ignoring his disdain for live performance, George walked out. He rejoined the band on the conditions that they move from the cavernous sound stage to the cozy new recording studio being installed in the basement of their Apple headquarters and drop any plans for a concert. Just as he'd done with Eric Clapton the previous year, George returned with a guest, Billy Preston, the keyboardist they had met back in Hamburg when he played for Little Richard. Preston brought mutual respect back to the studio, and his continuous involvement added major contributions to the "Get Back" project and then to several tracks on *Abbey Road*.

The Beatles devoted quite a bit of energy to running through numbers from their early club years, performing at least parts of 249 identifiable songs in the course of the month, but they also introduced fifty-two new compositions. Instead of climaxing aboard a cruise ship, or even a local stage, they simply recycled an old idea (lunchtime gigs at the Cavern) and went atop the roof of their central London offices on January 30 and played a forty-minute set for the film's finale. The rooftop concert, aided by Billy Preston on the trendy Fender Rhodes electric piano, featured only unheard originals: "One after 909" and four others—"Get Back," "Don't Let Me Down," "I've Got a Feeling," and "Dig a Pony." An additional three acoustic numbers, "Let It Be," "The Long and Winding Road," and "Two of Us" were completed in the basement studio on January 31 before Ringo was obligated to begin a film shoot of his own in February.

George Martin wanted nothing to do with the January recordings, which struck his ears as indulgent and sloppy. After filming came to a halt, the voluminous audio tapes were examined for months, picked over, and shelved again and again. Only after recording their entire next album, *Abbey Road*, did the Beatles return to the "Get Back" material. George's triple-meter song "I Me Mine" was to appear in the film, with John and Yoko mock-waltzing. No suitable recording existed for a soundtrack LP, so George, Paul, and Ringo came back to the studio for a final January 3, 1970, recording session. Tellingly, John, in Denmark, failed to appear for what was to be the group's final job. Engineer Glyn Johns whittled down his list of performances and mixed a rough draft, finishing on January 8. His proposed album of sixteen selections including mostly studio numbers, one of the rooftop performances ("909"), plus a couple of oldies—"Save the Last Dance for Me" and the Liverpool folk song once recorded by the Vipers Skiffle Group, respelled as "Maggie Mae"—took a back seat once again in early 1970 as plans for the TV show morphed into a film that would complete the Beatles' obligation to United Artists.

Unhappy with the Johns master and holding their own performance in low regard, the Beatles felt only a wizard could work the magic necessary to salvage the tapes. On the heels of his producing John's January 1970 recording "Instant Karma (We All Shine On)," Phil Spector, the American girl-group mastermind and composer of "To Know Him Is to Love Him" (a Beatles standby in 1960–1963 performances), was hired to put the album together. Known for his "wall of sound," Spector added syrupy orchestra and women's chorus to "Across the Universe," "I Me Mine," "Let It Be," and "The Long and Winding Road." The off-the-cuff improvisation "Dig It" was mastered for the album because it was to be included in the film. Spector would go on to produce George's triple-album debut, *All Things Must Pass*.

McCartney was outraged at the additions Spector made to his work without his approval, and his entreaties to remove them were ignored.[1] Despite the overdubbed varnishing, Lennon felt more sympathetic with the results on "Across the Universe" and some helpful editing improving "Dig a Pony"; he thought Spector "was given the shittiest load of badly recorded shit with a lousy feeling to it ever, and he made something out of it. . . . When I heard it I didn't puke" (Wenner 1971, 120–122). Much of the January 1969 recordings rewards serious listening and remains confident, at times even purposeful, despite how they felt about it. Their own personal attitudes, and the pressures of producing music while running a major new business concern, blurred their perceptions of how they sounded together. Although mostly recorded before *Abbey Road*, the album and movie—both ultimately entitled *Let It Be*—finally appeared together in May 1970 (see the album cover, Photo 9.1), in the wake of a stunning announcement from Paul McCartney: he was leaving the Beatles.

1. McCartney was finally vindicated in 2003 with the release of *Let It Be . . . Naked*, which presented the original January 1969 live-recorded tapes of eleven tracks with their familiar edits but without overdubs: "Get Back," "Dig a Pony," "For You Blue," "The Long and Winding Road," "Two of Us," "I've Got a Feeling," "One after 909," "Don't Let Me Down," "I Me Mine," "Across the Universe," and "Let It Be."

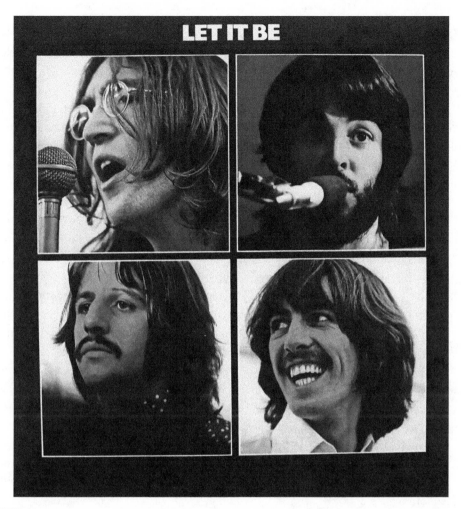

PHOTO 9.1. The Beatles photographed by Ethan Russell in January 1969 for the *Let It Be* LP (released in UK May 18, 1970).

"Two of Us"

Recorded January 31, 1969, for *Let It Be*

—*Paul and John with a duet by turns both modest and penetrating.*

At the beginning of the Lennon-McCartney partnership, their vocal harmonies emblemized brotherhood: sometimes forged from the same emotional conceit ("If I Fell"), sometimes bantering and wrestling for control ("We Can Work It Out"). In their late period, several numbers leap out as twilight duets that express a fond remembrance of salad days, abiding friendship, and a tacit acknowledgement of a partnership at sunset. Just as plainly, many of the generalizations about their sensibilities seem to fall away: Lennon wrote some of the Beatles' most sentimental songs (not just "This Boy," "Nowhere Man," and "In My Life" but even "Good Night"); McCartney stole Little Richard's tiara ("I'm Down") and made blistering rock in "Helter Skelter," "Why Don't We Do It in the Road?," and "Oh! Darling."

McCartney also specialized in another brand of looking-glass pop: the nurse in "Penny Lane" who knows she's an absurdist prop in a suburban idyll, or the man on the double-decker bus of "A Day in the Life" who's just awoken inside Lennon's nightmare. "Two of Us" joins this special category of whimsical enigmas, puzzles that deliver a thoughtful charm.

Running away with your fiancée crops up in several McCartney songs as he courted and married Linda Eastman: his solo debut's "That Would Be Something" and "Man We Was Lonely," *Ram*'s "Back Seat of My Car" and "Long-Haired Lady." In "Two of Us," Paul turns this modest precept into an elegy for the Lennon-McCartney partnership. The folksy tone belies an undertow of fond regret and resembles Lennon's writing style in the way it closes each stanza with a pause, sometimes for the recurring acoustic guitar breaks (at 0:10, 0:49, and finally, after a suspenseful silence, at 3:05), twice for the faraway bridges (in ♭III at 1:31 and 2:18, which winds through vi–i7–ii7–V; compare the bridge of "Here, There and Everywhere," and "To Know Her Is to Love Her" before that). These bridges visit the song from a distant horizon ("out ahead"), the future insinuating its way into some immanent past. Once these "memories" get released into the air, they color every new adventure the singer describes, the same way old friendships give way to new, and old stories fold into new experiences. This track's humble tone makes palpable its subtext that a late Lennon-McCartney duet could revive lost hopes. Lennon whistles aimlessly into the fadeout as the music falls away (mocking the Maori finale of "Hello Goodbye"?), and the picture goes dark.

CUE	SECTION	HARMONY	DETAIL
0:09	Tattoo	I	Acoustic guitar/bass trio
0:18	Verse 1: *a - a*	I–IV–ii7 (repeated for bar form)	PM/JL duet
0:39	Verse 1: *b* (refrain)	I–V–IV–I	
0:49	Tattoo		Guitar/bass trio
0:58	Verse 2: *a - a*		(repeated for bar form)
1:17	Verse 2: *b* (refrain)		Drums Transition
1:30	Bridge 1	(I–iii–vi7 of ♭III)–ii7–V7	Bass Retransition
1:44	Verse 3: *a - a*		
2:04	Verse 3: *b* (refrain)		Drums Transition
2:17	Bridge 2		
2:30	Verse 3: *a - a*		
2:52	Verse 3: *b* (refrain)		
3:04	Outro	I	Guitar/bass trio into fadeout, whistling

"Dig a Pony"

Recorded January 30, 1969, for *Let It Be*

—deceptive harmonic twists underlie tip-of-the-tongue and roundabout attempts at articulation that collapse into absolutely direct expressions of desire and a submission to clarity.

Lennon's stylistic development traces two distinct but congruent arcs. The first follows traditional, Chuck Berry–like narratives that tweak familiar patterns ("I Call Your Name," "Revolution"); the other extends further and further outward into experimental realms ("Tomorrow Never Knows" and "I Am the Walrus" toward "Revolution 9"). Paradoxically, John pivoted away from extremities just as he took Yoko as his second wife, on March 20, 1969. "Dig a Pony" combines these two threads: it's a clever combination of errant lyrics on top of old-school patterns, with arpeggiated riffs supplanting offbeat chords (it's a broken-chord cousin to "Everybody's Got Something to Hide Except Me and My Monkey").

Anybody who's read *A Spaniard in the Works* or *In His Own Write* recognizes Lennon's lyrical strategy: a run-on of irrational hipster argot, describing the indescribable, culminating in a hook that pledges commitment. If love is the slippery subject, Lennon's misdirection and oblique wordplay manifest its pleasures. Like many Lennon songs ("I'm So Tired," "Don't Let Me Down," "I Want You (She's So Heavy)"), the verses spiral up slowly to uncoil into a caesura, a brief silence where Lennon and McCartney gently bounce on the word "Be-cause" (at 1:13, 2:09, and 3:25), before tantalizing drum fills that either transition to the next verse (at 1:15–1:16 and 2:11–2:12) or rewind into the opening arpeggios (3:27–3:28). (Even these arpeggios echo earlier Beatles tattoos heard in "I Feel Fine," "Day Tripper," and "Birthday.")

Because the circular harmonic sequence begins on the deceptive ♭VII (*Let It Be* cues: 0:09), the double-plagal harmonies tickle the ear the way the lyrics tickle reason. We don't confirm the tonal center of the verse until Lennon starts singing, at which points it might sound like a surprising II, when it's simply a "deceptive" I (0:21). (Because the intro does not begin on a tonic chord, the double-plagal progression may be a bit deceptive at first, but the tonal center is asserted by its long duration.) By starting on such a remote harmony (as did, say, Wilson Pickett's "In the Midnight Hour"), verses make surprise landings, partly from Phil Spector's sly omission of the "All I want is you" retransitions (sung from the top in original performance, as seen in the rooftop footage). Depending on how you feel about some of Lennon's more peculiar eccentricities, the song raises interesting questions: Does Lennon's preconscious nonsense work better draped in muscular playing? Can you imagine the reverse: a wayward harmonic vessel carrying ultra-logical lyrics? This combination of the surreal with the earthy, a scatological blues in gibberish, delivers a mock pretension belied by the gritty performance. Can you imagine another way to make the verb "syndicate" sound vaguely flirtatious? Think of it as Lennon's take on Dylanesque irony: nonsense flirting with the tangible.

CUE	SECTION	HARMONY	DETAIL
0:08	Tattoo	♭VII–IV–I (repeated)	Guitars, bass unison
0:19	Verse 1: *a*	I–vi–ii→VII7–ii→VII7 –V	
0:40	Verse 1: *a*	I–vi–ii→VII7–ii→VII7 –V	
1:00	Verse 1: *b* (Refrain)	♭VII–IV–I	"Because" duet
1:12	Retransition	I	"Because" duet–drum fill
1:16	Verse 2	(as above)	
2:08	Retransition		
2:11	Guitar solo	(based on verse's *a* phrase)	
2:31	Verse 3	(as above)	
3:24	Retransition		
3:27	Tattoo	♭VII–IV–I	

"I've Got a Feeling"

Recorded January 30, 1969, for *Let It Be*

—*Paul and John find yet another way to combine their contributions.*

The *Let It Be* shoot was a chore from the start. Like *Yellow Submarine*, which was conceived and delivered by animators, the project began with forced cheer to fulfill a leftover contract obligation, combined with a last-ditch effort by McCartney to revive their flagging motivation. The first two-thirds of the movie show the Beatles in dog-tired rehearsal, working up arrangements from fragments and lapsing into oldies when they simply can't be bothered to spruce up their own original ideas. Some moments glow with pure joy: once Billy Preston joins in, they find shards of pleasures, at least in their own ensemble. One of the final jams erupts into "Shake, Rattle and Roll," wild and cacophonous, but it never drops anchor or lands anywhere; it's a wayward frame on slop. Many other songs betray a growing dread: blank faces that have looked at each other far too long, heard the same patter, and begrudge the routine. "Mailman, Bring Me No More Blues" (released on *Anthology 3*), Lennon's gloomy take on a Buddy Holly number, glimpses the rot at the end of the Beatles' tunnel. (The Roberts-Katz-Clayton track came from the B-Side of Buddy Holly's "Words of Love," their only other released Holly cover out of many they performed.)

An early sequence in the film shows them working on McCartney's bridge to "I've Got a Feeling," with Harrison playing the retransitional guitar break as his partner urges him not to reveal any discrete chromatic intervals in the microtonally falling lead guitar line (at 1:25–1:30). Harrison obliges for the camera several times, with resignation. But when they perform the number in the final rooftop sequence, the song springs to life as a fully finished arrangement: somewhere off-camera, they've pieced together a marvel. In the movie's final third, the "rooftop set," numbers that failed, going limp during rehearsal, suddenly rise up and breathe life back into their ensemble. Scholars and fans have traded raw tapes of this live performance—and of the many other hours of scuttled film soundtrack—since it transpired, and even its technical flaws give it snap (compared to Phil Spector's final polished production).

"I've Got a Feeling" comprises a farewell collaboration sung in tandem, a relay until the end when both sections pile on top of one another for an unlikely superimposition (on the final performance at 2:46). Unlike previous joint efforts, this track lays two melodies on top of each other, like the quodlibet of "Paperback Writer" / "Frère Jacques," two lenses sharpening an otherwise blurred view neither could bring into focus individually. The materials of each section—we'll call them verse A and verse B—work separately, like the vocal lines in "If I Fell," but each part also works as an unlikely fit for the other, a synecdoche for the Lennon-McCartney partnership itself. Atypically, McCartney's verses address his inner life, climaxing in a bridge with his fists in the air over romantic frustration ebbing through a double-plagal cadence (1:16–1:25, V→VII7–IV7–I7); in the B verses, Lennon, also atypically, pans back to chill out while describing what a hard year it's been (at 2:05, immediately repeated at 2:22). (His audience would have known that Ono suffered a miscarriage less than two months previously.) Listen to each section alone and you don't feel anything is missing; listen to them combined and you hear something larger than two parts blended together.

That final stanza (2:46) rings out with a palpable sense of return and arrival, as if the entire arrangement builds to a triumphant sigh of inexplicable synergy. Instead of a floating duet ("Two of Us," "Don't Let Me Down"), which seemed to reappear just as their songwriting partnership frayed, they turn in an exquisitely poised seesaw that ends on a hanging question mark (3:27). Alongside the hard-won harmony shared by McCartney and Lennon, Harrison feels only a headache, suppressed until the release of his solo "Wah Wah" (*All Things Must Past*, 1970), the intro to which distorts the "I've Got a Feeling" tattoo.

CUE	SECTION	HARMONY	instrumentation
0:00	Introductory tattoo	I–IV–I–IV	
0:06	Verse A1: *a*	I–IV–I–IV	PM solo
0:17	Verse A1: *a'*	I–IV–I–IV	
0:29	Verse A1: *b* (cadence)	I7–V→VII–IV–I	Lead guitar scale
0:41	Verse A2	(as above)	JL adds vocal harmony
1:16	Bridge	V→VII7–IV7–I7	PM shouts
1:25	Retransition	(microtonal)	Lead guitar
1:30	Verse A3		
2:05	Verse B1	I–IV–I–IV	JL solo
2:22	Verse B2	I–IV–I–IV	
2:46	Verse A/B		PM/JL superimposed

"One after 909"

Recorded January 30, 1969, for Let It Be

—the kernel of the "Get Back" spirit, a 1960 Lennon-McCartney original steeped in Chuck Berry.

This early ditty from the Lennon-McCartney scrapheap—they never liked the lyrics—rings out as the imaginary early hit they never had. It captures a nostalgia for teen fantasy itself, the glory days of Elvis, hula hoops and the steam trains of skiffle, a celebration of the heights of their musical feeling before fame. On the way to "She Loves You" and "I Want to Hold Your Hand," they wrote a story about a star-crossed lover who misses his train and curses fate as if dancing on dread. Every young rocker needed to have a train song, whether reviving a traditional folk song like the Animals did with "House of the Rising Sun," (a highly influential British Invasion hit of 1964), borrowing Lead Belly's "Rock Island Line" (which swarmed Merseyside and all of England via Lonnie Donegan's skiffle cover), or fashioning an original like Chuck Berry did with "Johnny B. Goode" (wherein the chug-a-chug locomotive inspires the guitarist's boogie figurations). You can even trace this theme back to Robert Johnson's "Love in Vain," which the Stones would cover on 1969's *Let It Bleed*, where a train's headlights symbolize the singer's frayed hopes: "The blue light was my baby, the red light was my mind."

And "909" emerged as a happenstance plot twist amid the dragging *Let It Be* sessions that proved so dispiriting in January 1969—it roared back to restore their hobbling ensemble. Most of the early tricks still inhabit the latter-day performance: the suspenseful stop-time pauses at the ends of verses (at 0:19 and 0:40, and 2:26), the uncanny repetitions, bent-string whistle-blowing Doppler effects, the climactic shaggy-dog punch line ("I got the number wrong!"). The singer's fate turns on the title of the song: the "One after 909," is actually the *wrong* train number, the cause of his distress.

And what giddy distress! Where the lyric describes disappointment, the music glides along the dizziest of grooves. Like "All My Loving" or "Ticket to Ride," the distance between what the singer describes and his clearly overjoyed sensations make you wonder about his sincerity: if missing the train spells disaster, why does he sound so elated? Why do his partners squeal when the guitar hits those same stop-time breaks during the solo (1:44–1:46)?

CUE	SECTION	HARMONY	DETAIL
0:00	Intro	I7	
0:08	Verse 1	I7–IV7–I7–V7–I7	JL lead vocal, PM descant
0:29	Verse 2		
0:50	Bridge 1	IV7–I7–II7–V7	JL solo
1:12	Verse 1	I7–IV7–I7–V7–I7	Guitar lead responses
1:32	Guitar solo	(based on verse)	Guitar solo
1:53	Bridge 2		PM with JL
2:14	Verse 1		
2:31	Coda	I7–V7–I7	"One more time" ending

"Don't Let Me Down"

Recorded January 28, 1969, for B-side of "Get Back"

—John revisits the uncertainty of "If I Fell," but Paul's counterpoint now comes more from his bass line than his descant vocal.

Ever since they became self-conscious musicians (by *A Hard Day's Night*), McCartney began taking (very brief) bass solos in Lennon's songs: at the ends of stanzas in "I'll Cry Instead" (1:34–1:36) and "I'm Only Sleeping" (0:33 and 2:00, over John's sarcastic yawn); setting him loose throughout "Rain," "Nowhere Man," and "Hey Bulldog"; spotlighting him in "Everybody's Got Something to Hide" (2:03); and allowing him a lead melodic role in "Come Together." (McCartney climaxes this virtuoso stream by attempting to steal the whole production away from Harrison's "Something" when he leaps up on top of the guitar solo [at 2:03–2:10] to take an immodest bow.) In "Don't Let Me Down," McCartney's bass underpins Lennon's bridge with descending steps, which elaborate exquisitely on the lower counterpoint in "Dear Prudence." But combined with his upper vocal harmony, McCartney coddles Lennon's blues wailing from above and below.

It's impossible to separate "Don't Let Me Down" from all the business wrangling brewing offstage, as Lennon was about to throw his lot in with would-be manager Allen Klein and declare war on McCartney's future father-in-law, John Eastman, in the battle for control over the group members' financial future. Two years after the death of Brian Epstein, Lennon convinced Harrison and Starr to join him in seeking the managerial services of New Jersey's crude and shady Klein (who had recently secured hefty back-royalty earnings for the Rolling Stones), but McCartney could not agree. Paul had begun a romance with a New York photographer, Linda Eastman, whose father John ran a successful entertainment law practice. Standing on the Apple rooftop, the Lennon-McCartney partnership is perched on disaster, only they didn't know it yet. In a few months' time, Dick James would sell his shares of Northern Songs behind their backs, delivering their publishing catalog to a bunch of bankers. This superior sundown Lennon-McCartney duet finds them sounding more like brothers than they have since "If I Fell" and summarizes a series of musical farewells they offer up in their final months together, alongside "Two of Us," "I've Got a Feeling," and "Dig a Pony." Amid so many great late Lennon vocals, this exhortation still rings out as farewell, at least as much as "You Never Give Me Your Money" becomes McCartney's and "The End" literalizes the band's finish. Lennon leaps headlong into his second marriage with hoarse outcries offset by piercing falsettos, so much so that McCartney's upper part floats invisibly (on each title line, at 0:17 and 0:56); most don't even hear it as a duet.

Each verse opens with Lennon alone, trailing off from any regular meter to linger on his affection ("Nobody ever loved me like she does"), a wavering, free-fall effect right as the song wants to rebound from its chorus. By withholding the verse for a moment of anticipation, Lennon conveys the risk and the fear he sings about. That gibberish verse Lennon sings on the roof in *Let It Be* only heightens the camaraderie (and exposes the *Let It Be . . . Naked* scam, where they marketed an elaborately edited master as an untouched "live" set). Long after all these poetic effects linger in the mind, questions remain about who it is that Lennon addresses in this first-person narrative: Yoko Ono? Paul McCartney? The band responding to his pleas? The Apple firm they run, whose rooftop he stands upon? The rest of us? In the weeks after his assassination in 1980, this track became as hard to listen to as that line in "The Ballad of John and Yoko": "The way things are going / They're gonna crucify me."

CUE	SECTION	HARMONY	INSTRUMENTATION
0:00	Tattoo	I–IV–I	Lead guitar
0:04	Chorus 1	ii7–V13–I	JL solo vocal
0:17	Chorus 1	ii7–V13–I	PM adds descant
0:32	Verse 1	ii7–IM7	PM/JL duet (repeated)
0:57	Chorus 2		duet
1:22	Bridge	I–V7–I	Bass counterpoint
1:41	Tattoo as retransition	I–IV–I	Lead guitar
1:47	Chorus 3		
2:13	Verse 2		JL solo vocal
2:40	Chorus 4		Emotional release
3:04	Coda		JL falsetto, piano vamping

THE SPRING OF 1969

Many happy events occurred between the sour *Let It Be* recordings and the band's demise. Photo 9.2 shows the group as they appeared in April 1969. That spring brought individual projects, with McCartney playing bass on James Taylor's "Carolina in My Mind" and twelve-string acoustic on Mary Hopkin's "Goodbye" and Starr co-starring with Peter Sellers in the movie of Terry Southern's absurdist 1959 novel *The Magic Christian*. John had divorced Cynthia and married Yoko in Gibraltar in March 1969. Their honeymoon was a whirlwind tour: a few days in Paris, a week-long bed-in for world peace in Amsterdam, and a quixotic stage performance in Vienna with Yoko caterwauling inside a large bag. The "bed-in" was their parody of worldwide campus sit-in and teach-in demonstrations of recent years; delighted by the constant attention of the world's press, John and Yoko made a statement for peace as performance art. All of their antics were documented in the newspaper-story-like lyrics to "The Ballad of John and Yoko," which John and Paul recorded as a duo and released as a Beatles single, and the newlyweds' *Wedding Album*. John and Yoko carried their "commercial for peace" to Montreal in September, where they held a second bed-in, culminating with the hotel-room recording of "Give Peace a Chance," John's anthem chanted with the help of a roomful of visitors. In a break from normal Beatles procedure, this became a single credited to the Plastic Ono Band, although the tradition of granting Paul McCartney joint writer's credit continued. (McCartney, Harrison, and Starr do not contribute to the single.) The two Beatles records that did appear that spring were "Get Back" / "Don't Let

カム・トゥゲザー
COME TOGETHER

サムシング
SOMETHING

◆ ビートルズ
THE BEATLES

AR-2400
←STEREO→

Apple
RECORDS

¥ 400

PHOTO 9.2. The Beatles along the Thames, April 9, 1969. "Something" / "Come Together" 45 (as released in Japan). Paul McCartney wears the Quarry Men uniform in which he was photographed in 1958.

Me Down" in April and "The Ballad of John and Yoko" / "Old Brown Shoe," this last a sprightly Harrison track, at the end of May.

"The Ballad of John and Yoko"

Recorded April 14, 1969, for A-side

—John's spur-of-the-moment elopement captured in a camp rockabilly one-off.

Few showbiz feuds took on the scale and furor of the Lennon-McCartney battle during the spring of 1969, when most fans assumed everything was going along swell.

The January "Get Back" sessions had left such a sour note in everybody's ears they mothballed the tapes for weeks and then gave them to engineer Glyn Johns to produce. (Following his abandonment of the group to Chris Thomas, who produced many of the *White Album* sessions, George Martin's role in *Let It Be* would always be at some remove.) That season's singles helped patch over any breakup rifts the press began reporting: "Get Back" / "Don't Let Me Down" appeared in April, with a press release quip from McCartney that ran in the trade ads ("We made it into a song to roller coast by. PS John adds, It's John playing the fab live guitar solo"; see Miles 2001, 339).

But at the end of May, they put out "The Ballad of John and Yoko" backed with "Old Brown Shoe," a tart Harrison number recorded two days after "Ballad." Lennon's flippant, as-it-happens tale of his celebrity wedding only gets more complicated and unlikely the more historical details emerge.

For starters, Lennon's second marriage had impulsive beginnings. Within a week after McCartney's wedding to Linda Eastman in London, Lennon goaded an assistant into finding a romantic spot where he could marry Yoko without too much paperwork. The Rock of Gibraltar at the southern tip of Spain was still a UK overseas territory, so they quickly hopped on a plane and had an official preside over a hasty legal ceremony, the couple dressed in white.

Within a few days, Lennon had penned a quickie narrative for his quickie elopement and went knocking on McCartney's door for collaboration. Together, the two of them (Harrison was out of the country; Starr was still filming *The Magic Christian*) played, sang, overdubbed, and mixed the neo-rockabilly track in under eight hours on April 14, with Lennon on guitars and McCartney on piano, bass, maracas, and drums. Engineer Geoff Emerick remembers the session as friendly and convivial, which set the band on split tracks: in their business offices they pursued mutually exclusive goals, contracting with separate managers and lawyers and squabbling over Apple. But in the studio, the Beatles' muse kept them prolific through the summer, and it measures their belief in their ensemble that they worked steadily to create *Abbey Road* even as their legal conflicts mounted.

For the most part, they concealed their business disputes from the public. As you listen to "Ballad," you could never predict McCartney and Ono would become epic foes or that the Beatles' core songwriting team members had anything but affection for one another. "Ballad" casts Lennon as the lead figure in a series of media cartoons where his character has as much fun seducing the world's press into farcical "happenings" as the media does straining to make sense of his emerging post-Beatle persona.

Just as "One after 909" eagerly attempts a "train" song, a genre exercise that became a pillar of rock style, "The Ballad of John and Yoko" echoes another vaguely Spanish Berry number ("You Never Can Tell") about a "teenage wedding" where "the old folks wished 'em well," which has as much knowing skepticism as elderly affection. (It echoes the Spanish overtones of a couple of songs McCartney covered for the BBC: "The Honeymoon Song," from director Michael Powell's Golden Palm–winning 1959 film, and Consuelo Velázquez's 1940 Mexican bolero "Besame Mucho," and the Latin sound emulated in the first Beatle B-sides.) Finally, it inverts the tone of "A Day in the Life," a "newspaper" song culled from the morning papers, without the tragic overhang.

CUE	SECTION	HARMONY	DETAIL
0:00	Intro	I	
0:03	Verse 1	I–I7–IV–I–V7–I	JL lead vocal
0:31	Verse 2		
0:59	Verse 3		
1:28	Bridge	IV–V7	PM/JL duet
1:43	Retransition		Stop-time for snare on extra two beats
1:44	Verse 4		Maracas, PM descant added
2:12	Verse 5		Guitar answers vocals
2:38	Coda	V7–I–V7–I	"One more time" ending

ABBEY ROAD

From inside the Beatles' camp in the spring of 1969, the future looked dim. Apple's ambitions had far outpaced anybody's grasp on management, expenses outpaced revenues, and business consultants began to worry at how easily such a venture might run aground. Lennon and McCartney had long since stopped writing together, the "Get Back" tapes languished, and no further full-group session plans emerged until the summer, when George Martin got a call from McCartney asking him to produce again, assuring the reluctant master it would get back to being "like the old days."

Martin's role had been secondary in the "Get Back" project, as the Beatles meant their roots project to be a live straight-to-tape recording, without any production sheen. Martin felt sidelined, and he seriously questioned the band's commitment to making a full-fledged group effort. McCartney promised him they would "behave." So there were occasional February-through-May sessions devoted to "I Want You (She's So Heavy)," "Something," "Old Brown Shoe," "Oh! Darling," "Octopus's Garden," and "You Never Give Me Your Money," and they picked up the pace in July as they gathered for more work to be overseen by Martin, at EMI's Studio Two on Abbey Road.

McCartney had some leftovers from January (including "Maxwell's Silver Hammer"), and Lennon brought in several bold new pieces ("Come Together") alongside patches of unfinished work going back to India ("Mean Mr. Mustard," "Polythene Pam"). Harrison impressed everybody with some of his strongest contributions yet: "Something," an idea he'd been kicking around for a year before it became the lush ballad with strings and magnificent McCartney bass line, and "Here Comes the Sun," a gentle, meter-shifting ode to new beginnings. Harrison also helped Ringo with chord choices to beef up his own composition, the vocal ditty "Octopus's Garden," for a sequel to "Yellow Submarine." (The songwriting lesson makes for one of the more convivial sequences in the otherwise dreary Let It Be footage.)

Abbey Road appeared that September (just after Woodstock), affirming everybody's best hopes for the band and rock's future. Their use of a new electronic instrument, the Moog synthesizer, in particular as a lead on "Here Comes the Sun," sounded both boldly original and organic. But at the time, it's important to remember, even with *Let It Be* material in their back pocket, that they recorded *Abbey Road* as a finale, a farewell to one another and their place in music history. *Let It Be* appeared the following year but comprised material recorded earlier, and it remains an anomaly, out of step with how the band conceived this material. Most serious treatments of these records take note of this and consider *Abbey Road* as the more unified, self-conscious swan song.

Abbey Road, whose cover is shown in Photo 9.3, shows unprecedented collaboration born in a mist of tension. The album coheres in a compromise between Paul's song sequence on side 2 and John's preference for songs presented as individual components—*not* part of what he heard as Paul's "pop-opera"—on side 1. Lost in this balance, though, comes steady song-writing growth from George Harrison. We have had many opportunities in these chapters to comment on George's work as a guitarist and to note his songwriting contributions, but his presence on *Abbey Road* ushers in new depth. Many hold his *Abbey Road* songs "Something" and "Here Comes the Sun" as among the band's best. But the greatness of "Something" goes far beyond that. For one thing, it brings out some of McCartney's best melodic writing on bass; he is not simply creating imaginative ostinato ideas repeated in varied contexts but writing a

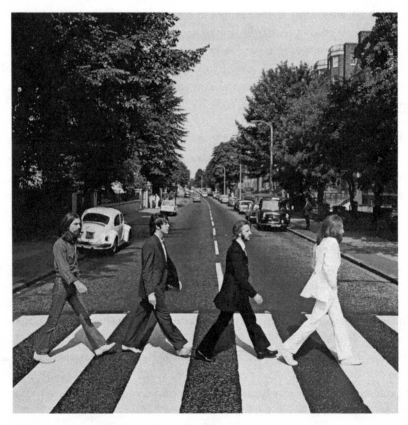

PHOTO 9.3. The Beatles as photographed by Iain Macmillan on August 8, 1969, for the *Abbey Road* LP (released US October 1, 1969). While EMI insisted that The *White Album* be identified with a front-cover legend (its title thereon embossed), the photo here was enough to identify the band.

soaring, large-scale through-composed melody given ever-more creative embellishments that continually commands attention, vying with vocals and lead guitar in the Beatles' strongest show of sustained contrapuntal interest. Paul showed similar support for George's "While My Guitar Gently Weeps" and "Old Brown Shoe," as if habitually gunning to steal the solo spotlight away from the lead guitarist. Even more importantly, "Something" shapes the tonal structure of the entire album's core key areas, C and A, and shows the Beatles' collaborative spirit at its highest levels. The notion of interactive ensemble receives renewed attention, in a context where McCartney desired great interconnectedness while Lennon complained, "By the time the Beatles were at their peak, we were cutting each other down to size, we were limiting our capacity to write and perform by having to fit it into some kind of format and that's why it caused trouble" (interview of October 25, 1971, in Wigg 1976). George's "Something" lies at the center of this renewed synergy rooted in independence.

Harrison began writing "Something" in 1968; he was captured on tape bringing the song along in the *Let It Be* sessions of January 1969, and he recorded a demo on February 25 that he gave to Joe Cocker. He then attempted basic tracks with Paul, Ringo, and George Martin on April 16 and recorded an entirely new performance on May 2 that resulted in the master's foundation. Meanwhile, work proceeded on the rest of the album: "I Want You (She's So Heavy)" began on February 22, "Oh! Darling" on April 20, and "Octopus's Garden" on April 26. All of these songs plus the later "Come Together" and "Maxwell's Silver Hammer" ended up as independent entities on side 1 of the LP to please John, whereas most songs of side 2 (tracks 7–17 of the CD) were joined together as a larger medley that fed McCartney's large-scale ambitions. Wasn't it always that way? John's inspiration came in spurts with fantastic single songs (and was turning in 1969 to topical one-offs like "The Ballad of John and Yoko" and "Give Peace a Chance"), while Paul wanted to frame the big picture, setting the stage for *Pepper* and *Magical Mystery Tour*. John's large-scale thoughts were poetic, Paul's practical, each visionary in his own way. After April 26, the next recording for *Abbey Road*, Paul's "You Never Give Me Your Money" (begun in sessions on May 6 and July 1), continued building upon a new idea created in "Something" that determined the tonal structure of side 2: the conflict between key centers of C and A.

This conflict played out in the series of songs recorded for side 2 in July: Paul's "Golden Slumbers" / "Carry That Weight" (begun July 2), George's "Here Comes the Sun" (July 7), Paul's "The End" (July 23), John's "Sun King" / "Mean Mr. Mustard" (July 24), and John's "Polythene Pam" / Paul's "She Came In through the Bathroom Window" (July 25). The medley coheres through conflicting tonal centers thus: "You Never Give Me Your Money" begins in A minor, moves to C major for the "Out of college" section (at 1:09), returns to the home key through a complex guitar-duet retransition featuring remarkable ensemble playing from John and George (2:09+), but now as A major instead of A minor for the "One sweet dream" section (2:28+), and then concludes by repeatedly shifting between C major and A major for the coda (2:48+). "Sun King," "Mean Mr. Mustard," and "Polythene Pam" are all in E major, the dominant of A, to which they return through a deliberate stepwise guitar-doubled bass descent (scale degrees 5–4–3–2–1) to the A that introduces "She Came In through the Bathroom Window." "Golden Slumbers" begins in A Minor, like "You Never Give Me Your Money," but moves to C major (from 0:21) at "home" (fittingly) and stays there to the end. "Carry That Weight" continues in C major and passes through A minor for the recapitulation of the "You Never Give Me Your Money" theme, to end back home in C major, only to transition to A major for "The End." This, the medley's final song, follows alternating solos from Paul, George, and John, three each, in A major, with a final modulation at the word "equal" to C major for the broad conclusion.

The entire medley thus alternates between the home key of C and digressions in A, rendered both as A minor and A major. This is exactly the model that "Something" laid out: the song as a whole is in C major, has passages in A minor ("I don't want to leave you now"), but its bridges ("You're asking me") are set in the contrasting A major. The song ends with a feint from the home key of C back to A major (at 2:46), only to reject this to end squarely in C. George's stand-alone side 2 song, "Here Comes the Sun," is played with a D-major fingering but capoed so it sounds a fifth higher, in A major. It could have been capoed elsewhere—George could have sung and played it just as easily to sound in G major or B♭major, but the song sounds in A with significant expressions of C: the long repeated passage in the triple-time guitar break (beginning at 1:30) begins with a C-major chord, and so the whole "sun, sun, sun, here it comes" passage alternates between C major and A major, just as Paul would later compose the "One two three four five six seven, all good children go to heaven" coda of "You Never Give Me Your Money."

Many other melodic, harmonic, and rhythmic ideas unite *Abbey Road*: the "sun, sun, sun, sun, here it comes" phrase in "Here Comes the Sun" is based on the same syncopated rhythm that had been performed in octaves in the descending grand piano riff that divides phrases in the bridge of "Something." The initial pitches played there, A–G♯–G–F♯, are reversed in octaves in the same rhythm (F♯–G–G♯–A) to usher in the "One sweet dream" section of "You Never Give Me Your Money." The chord progression that underlies that "One Sweet Dream" passage, I–II♯–♭III–V–I, is softened (as I–II♯–♭III–IV–I) to become the final slow-tempo plagal cadence of "The End."

John's "Because," recorded in August and also heard on side 2, seems to violate the A/C framework, as it's in C♯ minor, but it ends on a dissonant sonority that resolves into the A-minor opening of "You Never Give Me Your Money" so it can be considered as a lengthy slow introduction to the medley. McCartney cut the fragmentary "Her Majesty," in D major, from the middle of the medley, asked for it to be thrown out, and so an engineer removed it but, not wishing to destroy it, spliced it to a long piece of silent leader at the end of the reel. McCartney liked the way this worked out and ordered the master to retain the odd edit, making for rock history's first "hidden" track (initially, the title of "Her Majesty" was not listed on the album cover). Although "Her Majesty" lies in D major, the edit cuts off the final chord and so the fragment ends on the pitch A, an off-balance nod to the medley's tonal digression point. No large-scale tonal structure in any of the 1970s' "progressive" rock epics such as Jethro Tull's *Thick as a Brick* or Yes's *Tales from Topographic Oceans* achieves such coherence. *Abbey Road* was released in September to universal acclaim and with no hint that it was the group's last work together.

Because *Abbey Road* is the Beatles' only album to have been recorded entirely in eight tracks, we present here a tally of the second-generation contents of the final working tape of "Something," which was mixed to stereo for the master. Given are the Track number, panned location in the stereo mix, forces captured with relevant engineers' colorings, and dates of original recording:

Track 1 (heard center):
  GH lead guitar, played on Gibson Les Paul, given ADT (recorded May 5)
  JL Challen piano (muted except for two chromatic descents in octaves in bridge) (May 2)
  GH second bass part[2] (played from bridge to end, very low in mix) (August 15)

---

2. This is the final part overdubbed by George, incorrectly reported elsewhere to have been the "guitar solo."

Track 2 (heard center):
  RS Ludwig Hollywood drum set (May 2)
  RS suspended cymbal (July 16)
  Handclaps, tom-toms, and hi-hat subdivisions in A-major bridge (July 16)

Track 3 (heard left-center):
  4 cellos, string bass arco (low in mix, with reverb) (August 15)

Track 4 (heard right-center):
  12 violins, 4 violas arco (low in mix, with reverb) in verses; offbeat pizzicato chords (no reverb) in bridge (August 15)

Track 5 (heard right):
  PM Rickenbacker bass (May 5)

Track 6 (heard left):
  GH rhythm guitar, played on Fender Telecaster through Leslie cabinet (May 2)

Track 7 (heard center):
  GH lead vocal (double-tracked in refrains, given ADT in bridge, with reverb) (July 16)
  PM descant vocal (in bridge and third verse, with reverb; his busking along with the guitar solo is muted out of mix) (July 16)

Track 8 (heard left):
  Billy Preston's Lowrey Heritage DSO-1 organ (with reverb) (May 2)

"Oh! Darling"

Recorded April 20–July 23, 1969, for *Abbey Road*

—once again, Paul gets back to the 1950s.

Ever since the early Beatles pumped up their Hamburg show with extended blowouts of "What'd I Say," Ray Charles's 1959 fusion of secular lust with gospel feel, Paul McCartney has repeatedly taken on his great vocal mentor through imitation. Among his better wailing workouts ("I'm Down," "She's a Woman," "Got to Get You into My Life") and piano-based R&B grooves ("Lady Madonna," "Why Don't We Do It in the Road"), the late-period track "Oh! Darling" promises to be an R&B standard but fizzles somewhat into cool imitation. As with "Hey Jude" before it, the song does work as a sidebar to McCartney's singing, instead of the other way around. But as McCartney streaks through his final lap, his vocal performance begins to suggest a cartoonish apotheosis, one particularly discredited by a falsetto shriek at 3:08 that remains incongruous in its mistimed formal placement, a pretense at passion seemingly giving way to desperation.

"Oh! Darling" suggests many possible '50s-era African American influences, among them Fats Domino (especially for the piano's left-hand bass line) as well as Ray Charles. Slim Harpo's "Rainin' in My Heart" and Charles Brown's "Please Come Home for Christmas" are reasonably cited as possible forebears. Author Jonathan Gould points out similarities to the Platters' "The Great Pretender," James Brown's "Please, Please, Please," and Little Richard's "Send Me Some Lovin'"; "The displaced exclamation point in McCartney's title," Gould points out, "is taken from Richard's 'Ooh! My Soul.'" Such debts have been multiply repaid: listeners to a brand-new *Abbey Road* remembered Wilson Pickett's cover of "Hey Jude," released at the beginning of 1969, and the rock era's finest African American pop vocalists would continue to record McCartney material as high tributes: Aretha Franklin's take on "Eleanor Rigby" and Stevie Wonder's rendition of "We Can Work It Out" would both reach the top 5 in *Billboard*'s soul charts within the coming two years. These and other performances testify to the Beatles' universal appeal across all audiences, with renditions of Beatle songs later to come in styles ranging from jazz to baroque.

If *White Album* numbers from McCartney like "Honey Pie" and "Why Don't We Do It in the Road?" delivered charm and thrills while lampooning their genres, this *Abbey Road* showcase positively anchors side 1, otherwise solidly bookended by Lennon's blues number "Come Together" and his own vocal epic, "I Want You (She's So Heavy)." Lennon once revealed how badly he had wanted to sing "Oh! Darling": in 1980, he said the song "was a great one of Paul's that he didn't sing too well. I always thought that I could've done it better—it was more my style than his. He wrote it, so what the hell, he's going to sing it. If he'd had any sense he should have let me sing it." Especially for partisan Lennon fans, this must stand as one of the great missed opportunities in the catalog; nonetheless, several early reviewers actually mistakenly credited the vocal to the frequently raucous Lennon.

Geoff Emerick remembers McCartney spending several days tearing up his voice, practicing to find just the right effect.

> It was around this time that Paul started getting in the habit of coming in early every afternoon, before the others arrived, to have a go at singing the lead vocal to 'Oh Darling.' Not only did he have me record it with fifties-style tape echo, he even monitored the backing track over speakers instead of headphones because he wanted to feel as though he were singing to a live audience. Every day we'd be treated to a hell of a performance as McCartney put his all into singing the song all the way through once and once only, nearly ripping his vocal cords to shreds in the process. (Emerick 2006, 283)

While rehearsing his vocal part, an echo-inspired McCartney would lapse into humorous pseudo-Latin cathedral chants and Alpine yodels. In the final mix, echo is most pronounced at the song's stop-time retransition points, at "I nearly broke down and *di-i-i-ied*," rhyming with the six-year-old stop-time "cry-hy-hy" of the "This Boy" retransition.

Instrumentally, ironies pile on top of one another through ensemble expertise: the track starts off with swagger and daring, Lennon's single augmented-chord arpeggio introducing his piano-based lament. The individual play of chord members in that opening piano gesture reverberates in both bridges where grand cascades shine from Harrison's highly compressed and Leslie-colored guitar—as if any lead player could steal attention from McCartney's vocal attack—and lingers in the track's final moment with a unique tremolo-rich, behind-the-bridge aura shining from each of Harrison's individually plucked six strings. Ringo brings his own passion to transitional fills as John channels Jerry Lee Lewis's right-hand stammering on the piano. Paul's bass line sways gently throughout, hooking from beneath with a line similar to one he would play alongside similarly stabbing backbeat guitar chords in "Let Me Roll It" (*Band on the Run*). Discreetly smooth vocal harmonies color the final verse. It's difficult to take "Oh! Darling" seriously, but it's just as hard to write off as a mere style-aping exercise.

On one level, McCartney pays respect to the luminaries with whom he grew up. In another sense, the song serves as a sweet-yet-tart kind of "Get Back" homage to the forever-broken Lennon-McCartney partnership. If *Abbey Road*'s side 2 draws the band's final curtain with a concluding drum solo and three-way guitar battle, the individual numbers on side 1 compress four expansive sensibilities into tight-fisted miniatures, conferring on "Oh! Darling" its raw yet disciplined power.

CUE	SECTION	HARMONY	DETAIL
0:00	Introduction	V+	Piano arpeggio
0:01	Verse 1	I–V–vi	Solo vocal break
0:16		IV–ii–V–ii–V–I–IV–I–V+	Background vocals, left
0:35	Verse 2		Repeat solo vocal break; background vocals continue above
1:01	Transition a	I–IV–I–V7/IV	Drum fills build tension
1:08	Bridge 1	IV→VI–I	Guitar arpeggio backdrop
		II–V→VI–V+	
1:37	Transition b		Solo vocal break
1:41	Verse 3		Background vocals second half only
2:07	Transition c		Spoken (threat?) "Believe me, darling"
2:14	Bridge 2		
2:43	Transition b		Guitar arpeggio backdrop
2:47	Verse 4		Background vocals throughout
3:13	Transition d	I–IV–I	
3:18	Final cadence	♭II7–I	Final electric guitar arpeggio

THE EX-BEATLES

The day before *Abbey Road*'s release, John Lennon and Yoko Ono made a "solo" appearance at the Toronto Rock and Roll Revival festival billed as the Plastic Ono Band, singing "Yer Blues" (from the *White Album*), "Cold Turkey" (an as-yet unrecorded number declined by the Beatles), "Give Peace a Chance" (the single recorded at June's Montreal bed-in), and a number of oldies such as "Money (That's What I Want)," "Dizzy Miss Lizzie," and "Blue Suede Shoes." To finish, Yoko let fly two long provocative pieces, "Don't Worry Kyoko (Mummy's Only Looking for Her Hand in the Snow)" and a twelve-minute tirade, "John John (Let's Hope for Peace)," which upset fans even more than "Revolution 9" had. No matter how far the idea of the Beatles stretched, it couldn't quite fit Ono's spectral screams. Confounding his fans by joining rock 'n' roll with the avant-garde tickled Lennon's sense of aesthetic outrage. His self-consciousness as a solo act emerged quickly after his *Abbey Road* zenith as a Beatle.

John Lennon and George Harrison both performed onstage in 1969: In addition to John's gig in Toronto that September, George played slide guitar for a number of R&B-fueled shows across Britain and Denmark with friends Delaney and Bonnie Bramlet in December. (Members of this band formed the core for Eric Clapton's eponymous first solo album, his "Derek and the Dominoes"–credited *Layla*, and George's own *All Things Must Pass*, among other important releases.) Together, both John and George played for a year-end UNICEF benefit concert in London. Recall that it was Paul who'd wanted to get back onstage as early as late 1968, and who, since the breakup of the Beatles, has performed 771 shows through 2018. Still, as a group, the Beatles managed just that one unannounced rooftop performance on January 30, 1969, their only public appearance after the calamitous 1966 tour. Their final day of publicity photos is represented by the cover of *Hey Jude* (see Photo 9.4), which collected recordings going back as far as 1964 that had never appeared on an EMI LP.

With *Abbey Road* in the can by the end of August 1969, Lennon offered the Beatles his brand-new "Cold Turkey," a frightful number about heroin withdrawal, but they refused. This spurred Lennon to release his second solo single ("Give Peace a Chance" was released in July, "Cold Turkey" in October) even before the Beatles officially called it quits: he recorded the track as the ever-changing Plastic Ono Band, this time with Klaus Voormann on bass and Alan White on drums. After this single, an album featuring John and Yoko's performance at the Toronto fest of September 1969 (*Live Peace in Toronto 1969*) hit the market in December, advancing rumors about the Beatles' demise. John and Yoko had also put together a swiftly recorded series of duets in the *Two Virgins* vein capturing a number of travails they'd endured the previous year called *Unfinished Music No. 2: Life With the Lions*. This and George's *Electronic Sound* both came out in May 1969 on the Zapple label, an Apple subsidiary meant for a line of "experimental" (meaning sloppy) recordings. (The Zapple line stopped with these two; a third album of poetry readings called *Listening to Richard Brautigan* was mastered but scrapped by Allen Klein; it would be released by EMI Harvest in the United States.) The year 1970 brought solo albums by all four ex-Beatles, and two of them—*John Lennon / Plastic Ono Band* and George's *All Things Must Pass*—had monumental ambitions, setting marks that many feel were never again hit by a solo Beatle. Even with the greatness of *Abbey Road*, the ex-Beatles clearly felt most productive on their own, free to follow preferred directions not acceptable to their bandmates: Lennon the raw and uncomfortable, McCartney the pretty and

PHOTO 9.4. The Beatles as photographed by Ethan Russell at John Lennon and Yoko Ono's home, Tittenhurst Park, August 22, 1969. *Hey Jude* LP (released in US February 26, 1970).

grandiose, Harrison the spiritual and soaring, and Starr (with *Sentimental Journey*) the crooning and casual.

But some didn't accept that *Abbey Road*, or any other product after 1966, had truly been a group project: beginning with reviews of the new album in student newspapers at Drake University and the University of Michigan, and fueled by DJ Russ Gibb of WKNR in Detroit, rumors quickly began to circulate that Paul McCartney had been killed in a November 1966 car crash and replaced by a double, and that by conspiracy, clues to this event had been planted in every subsequent Beatle release. Naturally, the Beatles' penchant for dropping mysterious bits into their recordings fanned the flames: a new ghoulish wave of Beatlemania emerged. The "Paul Is Dead" story gained world-wide traction, with fans going over every detail of the catalog—both records and their covers—to find clues planted everywhere: John's reference to "cranberry sauce" at the end of "Strawberry Fields" was heard as "I buried Paul"; the *Pepper* montage could be taken as a funeral for the band, with Mussolini's hand over Paul's head supposedly being a symbol of death; on the back of the album, George points to the lyric "Wednesday morning at five o'clock," supposedly fixing the time of Paul's passing. The walrus on the *Magical Mystery Tour* cover supposedly symbolizes death in certain obscure faiths; in "Revolution 9," "number nine" backward sounds like "Turn me on, dead man." Played in reverse, John's gibberish before "Blackbird" can be heard as "Paul is dead now; miss him, miss him, miss him." The license plate on the local piano tuner's Volkswagen that happened to be captured on the *Abbey Road* cover declares "28 IF"—purportedly the age Paul would be had he lived (in June 1969, McCartney actually turned 27). Dozens of such "discoveries" created a freakish storm taken so seriously that Paul had to dispute his demise over and over again.

McCartney's artistic break with John, George, and Ringo over Phil Spector's handling of *Let It Be* ran parallel to his business differences with the other three, principally related to the unresolved decision as to whether it would be Allen Klein or John Eastman representing the Beatles in legal and managerial matters. Eastman began advising his future son-in-law, and he and Klein became proxy figures in the resulting Lennon-McCartney feud. Ringo had quit and returned in August 1968, George did the same in January 1969, and in September 1969 John made plain his intentions to seek a "divorce" from the Beatles. John never did further work with them after September. Klein and the others asked Lennon to keep quiet about the split, as they were in the middle of delicate contract negotiations; he obliged. Finally, on April 10, 1970, as he courted press for his first solo album, McCartney announced to the world that he was leaving the Beatles.

John would say that he'd worried over inviting Paul to join the Quarry Men right from the start—he wrestled through the summer of 1957 with the prospect of losing his domination over the group, suspecting that Paul was the more talented musician. As strong as Lennon's hold on the band was, McCartney upstaged him in many ways: Paul showed John that they could both write songs; Paul was the early musical director, the one to direct the ensemble with count-ins most often onstage; Paul began the quest for adding non-pop sources to their sound (blues through his Casino, music-hall, classical, even barbershop); Paul took John's 1966–1967 masterpieces "Strawberry Fields Forever" and "Lucy in the Sky with Diamonds" and added introductory parts for exotic keyboards that raised their value immeasurably; Paul drove the overarching concepts behind *Sgt. Pepper's Lonely Hearts Club Band* and *Magical Mystery Tour*; Paul flipped John's "I Am the Walrus" and "Revolution" by creating respective A-sides "Hello Goodbye" (which John rued) and "Hey Jude" (which John had to admit was the better song); Paul outshone George as lead guitarist in his own songs "While My Guitar Gently Weeps" and "Something" with his bass and his tonal imagination; Paul bossypantsed Ringo and George with his detailed head arrangements for where the cymbal needed to be struck or how George was to fill in gaps with microtones ("I can hear myself annoying you," Paul admitted during rehearsal as seen in the film *Let It Be*); Paul took John's song "Everybody Had a Hard Year" and recast it as "I've Got a Feeling" (led off, of course, by Paul); Paul insisted on the large-scale format of *Abbey Road*; Paul took sides in business matters against the three others in choice of management and in buying shares of their publishing company behind the others' backs. Whereas his mates had each quit the band privately, it was Paul who first let on that he was breaking with the Beatles by announcing it irrevocably to the world. John, George, and Ringo put up with a lot because of Paul's overwhelming musical facility. Yoko did not break up the Beatles; she just gave John the strength to walk away from the wreck.

John, Paul, George, and Ringo produced quite successful solo albums and singles through the remainders of their careers, occasionally appearing on each other's work. John Lennon's life was cut short in December 1980, and George's as well in November 2001, but Ringo Starr and particularly Paul McCartney continue to tour and record steadily to this day. The most significant of their many acclaimed solo releases include:

McCartney (McCartney, 1970)

All Things Must Pass (Harrison, 1970)

John Lennon / Plastic Ono Band (Lennon, 1970)

Imagine (Lennon, 1971)

Ram (McCartney, 1971)

Band on the Run (McCartney with Wings, 1973)

Ringo (Starr, 1973)

Rock 'n' Roll (Lennon, 1975)

Thirty-Three & 1/3 (Harrison, 1976)

Back to the Egg (McCartney with Wings, 1979)

Double Fantasy (Lennon and Ono, 1980)

Tug of War (McCartney, 1982)

Cloud Nine (Harrison, 1987)

Paul McCartney's Liverpool Oratorio (McCartney, 1991)

Time Takes Time (Starr, 1992)

Run Devil Run (McCartney, 1999)

Memory Almost Full (McCartney, 2007)

Egypt Station (McCartney, 2018)

In 1994–1995, Paul, George, and Ringo gathered a few times to record new parts written for unfinished songs that John had composed and for which he had recorded home demo tapes. Jeff Lynne of both the Electric Light Orchestra and George's guitar-heavy late-1980s group with Bob Dylan, Roy Orbison, and Tom Petty, the Traveling Wilburys, polished the tapes and prepared them for the "Threetles" overdubs that graced "Free as a Bird" and "Real Love." Each song, reaching for more than it could deliver, became a hit single supported by a new video (the one for "Free" loaded with visual references to dozens of Beatle songs) and anchored the *Anthology* project. The *Beatles Anthology* was a documentary told through a six-hour, three-night television broadcast subsequently marketed in multiple video formats and a large book, their own definitive telling of their own story, as overseen by one-time road manager Neil Aspinall. The series contains many outtakes and live performances of value for musical archaeologists, even as much of the first-person testimony plows fact under myth. Despite and because of the inclusion of a number of recorded interviews with him, the loss of Lennon's hovers over the project, a conspicuous absence.

THE BEATLES' LEGACY

Early in their career, the Beatles framed rock style in such a commanding fashion that they revived hits for Chuck Berry ("Rock and Roll Music") and Little Richard ("Long Tall Sally"), touched on country and rockabilly influences through Carl Perkins and Buck Owens ("Everybody's Trying to Be My Baby" and "Act Naturally"), and even embraced and created mainstream pop standards to appeal to older listeners ("Till There Was You," "Yesterday"). By the end of their career, they had invested so much in rock; their music launched many substyles, which in many ways led to the thousands of niches we enjoy on the internet today. Rap, emo, and dubstep may not have direct links to their catalog, but the Beatles' expansive reach inspired every songwriter and record producer that followed, and the pop music of the 1970s through the early twenty-first century remains unimaginable without them.

Imitation of the Beatles that began with other Liverpool beat bands copying the Beatles' success has been continuous. In the early 1970s, Apple Records launched power pop's Badfinger with an early McCartney smash ("Come and Get It," from the *Magic Christian* soundtrack), and George Harrison helped produce their third album, *Straight Up* (1971). The Raspberries and Billy Joel recorded aggressively derivative hits like the former's "Go All the Way" (1971) and the latter's "Movin' Out" (1977) and "Scandinavian Skies" (1982), music through which a shared appreciation of sources drove the sound. Moving into the 1980s, the Clash resolutely decried 1960s mythology as "phony Beatlemania" in "London Calling" (1979), Dream Academy paid explicit tribute in "Life in a Northern Town" (1985), and XTC produced overtly imitative tracks like "Mayor of Simpleton" (1989) and "I'd Like That" (1999). In the 1990s, Nirvana and Radiohead both seemed to channel aspects of the *White Album*. Since 2000, the Fountains of Wayne have echoed the punch of "Day Tripper" and "Ticket to Ride," and especially the aural surprises of *Revolver* with their album *Traffic and Weather* (2007). Danger Mouse even produced a full-length mash-up of Jay-Z's *Black Album* with the *White Album* to create *The Grey Album* (2004), a tour de force that positions the Beatles as prototypes for hip-hop (as they were for sampling, in their found lyrics and their tapes stolen for "Revolution 9"). Hundreds of other artists have recorded songs written by the Beatles, and hundreds more have been influenced by them; musicians cannot help but measure themselves against the earlier group's achievements. The Beatles' catalog has been the subject of countless radio series, Cirque de Soleil's perennial Las Vegas show *Love*, and the megahit Rock Band video game. *Pepper* and the *White Album* topped *Billboard*'s album charts fifty years after their respective premieres, in 2017–2018, with Apple's production of deluxe celebratory box-set rereleases.

Today's listeners keep returning to Beatle records as the definitive voice of the 1960s, extolling the impossibly varied career of the biggest-selling and most critically acclaimed rock band in history. As the most stimulating popular music of the tonal era (spanning four hundred years), their catalog survives as a rich source of pleasure, meaning, and human interaction. If the Beatles catalog transcends its era, it's also the best emotional map of the period, with coming-of-age themes resonating far into our own time. Their ever-changing music made them sound new at every turn. Each record unleashed an enchanting stream of ideas, life- and love-affirming views, always-eccentric appearance, top-of-the-world nonchalance, and global leadership in every social and cultural domain they touched to make them indelible masters in pop's realm of surface flash and short fuses. They created a new world inside rock 'n' roll, as if it had secret galaxies to explore all along, and suggested new openings for performers who never experienced Chuck Berry's caprice or Buddy Holly's joy. In gestures as different as "I'll Get You" and "Hey Jude," the Beatles achieved sublimity of spirit, offhanded profundity, strength through humor, and an abiding solidarity with each other and their audience. Their music spans serene majesty ("Golden Slumbers") and deep sadness ("For No One"), warm romance ("In My Life") and capricious joking ("You Know My Name (Look up the Number)"), childlike silliness ("Ob-La-Di, Ob-La-Da") and wild experimentation ("Tomorrow Never Knows"), deceptive ease

("Yesterday") and charismatic virtuosity ("Happiness Is A Warm Gun"); their themes stretch rock from teenage experience ("I Saw Her Standing There") into young adulthood ("Carry That Weight") and later years ("Eleanor Rigby," "When I'm Sixty-Four"). Their range defies most imaginations, and yet on every track they remain inimitable, a band with a thousand selves. If history wants to proclaim the next great American art form after jazz, it should look to the Beatles, Brits who universalized distinctly American styles divided by race and class to transform rock 'n' roll into the universal medium of rock.

POINTS FOR DISCUSSION

1. Describe how late-Beatles material compares to that of earlier periods. In what ways does the later music seem like a backlash against that of 1966–1967?
2. When do you think they hit their creative peak? Why? How do echoes from their early work ("One after 909") influence the way we hear late tracks such as "Come Together"?
3. Why do you think the Beatles dropped their interest in complex production techniques so deliberately after *Pepper* and the *White Album*? Does their material seem better suited to scaled-back enhancements, or have their creative interests merely changed? Discuss how differently the Beatles sound when produced by Phil Spector (*Let It Be*) versus George Martin (*Abbey Road*).
4. In what ways did John Lennon and Paul McCartney differ musically in 1969? In what ways did Lennon succeed in making his music more "authentic" than that of McCartney? In what ways did Harrison make musical strides in 1969? Describe how the sound of four Beatles as solo artists begins to appear in late Beatles recordings.
5. What difficulties led to the band's breakup? What can you discover about their differing goals and ambitions in 1969?
6. How did topics in the Beatles' lyrics expand after 1965? Discuss some ways in which their music changed alongside the lyrics by discussing several post-1965 songs.
7. Name a Beatle song released in 1969–1970 that has unusual metric relationships and explain briefly what is unusual about it in this regard.
8. Discuss at least four different pathbreaking techniques using magnetic recording tape used by the Beatles in the period 1965–1969; cite specific songs as examples of each.
9. Name one instrument played by George Harrison, one by John Lennon, and one by Paul McCartney in 1965–1969 with which they had not recorded before 1965.
10. Name a Beatles song recorded after 1965 with two or more strongly contrasting tonal centers. What keys are involved?
11. Choose a few songs from the years 1966–1970 through which you can discuss ways in which the Beatles brought new rhythmic, melodic, harmonic, formal, and timbral ideas into rock music.
12. What can you learn about the ways that *Abbey Road* coheres musically?
13. Choose some examples of popular music of the past five or ten years and compare it to that of the Beatles.

FURTHER READING

Christgau, Robert. *Any Old Way You Choose It: Rock and Other Music, 1967–1973*. Rev. ed. New York: Cooper Square, 2000.

Cott, Jonathan. Interview with John Lennon. *Rolling Stone*, November 23, 1968.

Doggett, Peter. *Abbey Road / Let It Be: The Beatles*. Classic Rock Albums Series. New York: Schirmer, 1998.

Doggett, Peter. *You Never Give Me Your Money: The Battle for the Soul of the Beatles*. New York: Harperstudio, 2010.

Emerick, Geoff. *Here, There and Everywhere: My Life Recording the Music of the Beatles*. London: Gotham Books, 2006.

Gould, Jonathan. *Can't Buy Me Love: The Beatles, Britain, and America*. New York: Three Rivers, 2007.

Kozinn, Allan, 1995. *The Beatles*. 20th-Century Composers. London: Phaidon, 1995.

Madinger, Chip, and Mark Easter. *Eight Arms to Hold You: The Solo Beatles Compendium*. Chesterfield, MO: 44.1 Productions, 2000.

Matteo, Steve. *Let It Be*. New York: Continuum, 2004.

McCabe, Peter, and Robert D. Schonfeld. *Apple to the Core: The Unmaking of the Beatles*. New York: Pocket Books, 1972.

McKinney, Devin. *Magic Circles: The Beatles in Dream and History*. Cambridge, MA: Harvard University Press, 2003.

Miles, Barry. *The Beatles Diary*, vol. 1, *The Beatles Years*. London: Omnibus, 2001.

O'Brien, Geoffrey. *Dream Time: Chapters from the Sixties*. New York: Counterpoint, 1988.

Southall, Brian. *Northern Songs: The True Story of the Beatles Song Publishing Empire*. With Rupert Perry. London: Omnibus Press, 2006.

Wenner, Jann. *Lennon Remembers: The Rolling Stone Interviews*. San Francisco: Straight Arrow, 1971.

Wigg, David. *The Beatles Tapes from the David Wigg Interviews*. [London]: Polydor 2683068, 1976.

APPENDIX 1

Recordings That Influenced the Early Beatles

All chart information is taken directly from *Billboard* (US) and the *New Musical Express* (UK) unless stated otherwise.

Song Title	Artist	US chart date and peak position	UK chart date and peak position
The World Is Waiting for the Sunrise	Les Paul and Mary Ford	18 Aug 1951, no. 2	
Hey, Good Lookin'	Hank Williams	15 Sep 1951, no. 29	—
The Little White Cloud That Cried	Johnnie Ray	24 Nov 1951, no. 2	1951, no. 2
Whistle My Love	Elton Hayes	—	Apr 1952, —
Walkin' My Baby Back Home	Johnnie Ray	24 May 1952, no. 4	15 Nov 1952, no. 12
High Noon (Do Not Forsake Me)	Frankie Laine	12 Jul 1952, no. 5	15 Nov 1952, no. 7
Three Coins in the Fountain	Frank Sinatra	29 May 1954, no. 4	17 July 1954, no. 1
Digging My Potatoes	Lonnie Donegan	—	1954, —
That's Alright (Mama)	Elvis Presley	1954, —	—
Ain't That a Shame	Fats Domino	16 Jul 1955, no. 10	26 Jan 1957, no. 23
Maybelline	Chuck Berry	20 Aug 1955, no. 5	—
Sixteen Tons	Tennessee Ernie Ford	12 Nov 1955, no. 1	7 Jan 1956, no. 1
Tryin' to Get to You	Elvis Presley	1955, —	2 Nov 1957, no. 16
Baby Let's Play House	Elvis Presley	1955, —	18 Jan 1958, —
I Forgot to Remember to Forget	Elvis Presley	1955, —	1957, no. 25

Song Title	Artist	US chart date and peak position	UK chart date and peak position
Rock Island Line	Lonnie Donegan	24 Mar 1956, no. 8	7 Jan 1956, no. 8
Tutti Frutti	Little Richard	14 Jan 1956, no. 17	23 Feb 1957, no. 29
Blue Suede Shoes	Carl Perkins	3 Mar 1956, no. 2	19 May 1956, no. 10
Main Title Theme, *The Man With the Golden Arm*	Billy May and His Orchestra	24 Mar 1956, no. 49	28 Apr 1956, no. 9
Long Tall Sally	Little Richard	7 Apr 1956, no. 6	9 Feb 1957, no. 3
The Saints Rock n Roll	Bill Haley and His Comets	7 Apr 1956, no. 18	26 May 56, no. 5
Blue Suede Shoes	Elvis Presley	7 Apr 1956, no. 20	26 May 1956, no. 9
Moonglow and Theme from *Picnic*	Morris Stoloff	14 Apr 1956, no. 1	2 Jun 1956, no. 7
Slippin' and Slidin' (Peepin' and Hidin')	Little Richard	21 Apr 1956, no. 33	—
Lost John	Lonnie Donegan	9 Jun 1956, no. 58	28 Apr 1956, no. 2
Be-Bop-a-Lula	Gene Vincent and His Blue Caps	16 Jun 1956, no. 7	14 Jul 1956, no. 16
Roll Over Beethoven	Chuck Berry	30 Jun 1956, no. 29	—
Rip It Up	Little Richard	7 Jul 1956, no. 17	15 Dec 1956, no. 30
Railroad Bill	Lonnie Donegan	—	7 Jul 1956, no. 20
Bad Penny Blues	The Humphrey Lyttelton Band	—	14 Jul 1956, no. 21
Hound Dog	Elvis Presley	4 Aug 1956, no. 1	22 Sep 1956, no. 2
Love Me Tender	Elvis Presley	20 Oct 1956, no. 1	8 Dec 1956, no. 11
Bluejean Bop	Gene Vincent	1956, —	20 Oct 1956, no. 16
Too Much Monkey Business	Chuck Berry	1956, —	—
You Can't Catch Me	Chuck Berry	1956, —	—
Lonesome Tears in My Eyes	Johnny Burnette	1956, —	—
Clarabella	The Jodimars	1956, —	—
Everybody's Trying to Be My Baby	Carl Perkins	1956, —	—
Honey Don't	Carl Perkins	1956, —	—
Sure to Fall (In Love With You)	Carl Perkins	1956, —	—
Tennessee	Carl Perkins	1956, —	—
I Got a Woman	Elvis Presley	1956, —	—
I'm Gonna Sit Right Down and Cry (over You)	Elvis Presley	1956, —	—
Ain't She Sweet	Gene Vincent	1956, —	—
Come Go With Me	The Dell-Vikings	16 Feb 1957, no. 4	—
Just Because	Lloyd Price	2 Mar 1957, no. 29	—
Lucille	Little Richard	23 Mar 1957, no. 21	29 Jun 1957, no. 10
Your True Love	Carl Perkins	23 Mar 57, no. 67	—
Cumberland Gap	The Vipers Skiffle Group	—	30 Mar 1957, no. 10

Song Title	Artist	US chart date and peak position	UK chart date and peak position
All Shook Up	Elvis Presley	6 Apr 1957, no. 1	15 Jul 1957, no. 1
That's When Your Heartaches Begin	Elvis Presley	13 Apr 1957, no. 58	—
Young Blood	The Coasters	6 May 1957, no. 8	—
Fabulous	Charlie Gracie	6 May 1957, no. 16	15 Jun 1957, no. 8
Searchin'	The Coasters	13 May 1957, no. 3	28 Sep 1957, no. 30
Bye Bye Love	The Everly Brothers	20 May 1957, no. 2	13 Jul 1957, no. 6
Jenny, Jenny	Little Richard	17 Jun 1957, no. 10	21 Sep 1957, no. 11
Puttin' On the Style	Lonnie Donegan	—	22 Jun 1957, no. 1
Whole Lotta Shakin' Goin' On	Jerry Lee Lewis	24 Jun 1957, no. 3	28 Sep 1957, no. 8
Miss Ann	Little Richard	24 Jun 1957, no. 56	—
That'll Be the Day	The Crickets	12 Aug 1957, no. 1	28 Sep 1957, no. 1
Party	Elvis Presley	—	5 Oct 57, no. 15
Jailhouse Rock	Elvis Presley	14 Oct 1957, no. 1	25 Jan 1958, no. 1
Peggy Sue	Buddy Holly	11 Nov 1957, no. 3	7 Dec 1957, no. 6
Rock and Roll Music	Chuck Berry	11 Nov 1957, no. 8	—
Bony Moronie	Larry Williams	11 Nov 1957, no. 14	18 Jan 1958, no. 11
Raunchy	Bill Justis	18 Nov 1957, no. 2	11 Jan 1958, no. 11
Great Balls of Fire	Jerry Lee Lewis	25 Nov 1957, no. 2	21 Dec 1957, no. 1
Twenty Flight Rock	Eddie Cochran	1957, —	—
Words of Love	Buddy Holly	1957, —	—
Glad All Over	Carl Perkins	1957, —	—
Lend Me Your Comb	Carl Perkins	1957, —	—
Matchbox	Carl Perkins	1957, —	—
Mean Woman Blues	Elvis Presley	1957, —	—
Maggie May	Vipers Skiffle Group	—	1957, —
Sweet Little Sixteen	Chuck Berry	17 Feb 1958, no. 2	26 Apr 1958, no. 16
Maybe Baby	The Crickets	3 Mar 1958, no. 17	15 Mar 1958, no. 4
Movin' and Groovin'	Duane Eddy	17 Mar 1958, no. 72	—
Dizzy, Miss Lizzy	Larry Williams	1958, —	14 Apr 1958, no. 69
Slow Down	Larry Williams	14 Apr 1958, —	—
All I Have to Do Is Dream	The Everly Brothers	21 Apr 1958, no. 1	24 May 1958, no. 1
Johnny B. Goode	Chuck Berry	28 Apr 1958, no. 8	—
High School Confidential	Jerry Lee Lewis	2 Jun 1958, no. 21	24 Jan 1959, no. 12
Ooh! My Soul	Little Richard	9 Jun 1958, no. 31	12 Jul 1958, no. 22
Rebel-'Rouser	Duane Eddy	30 Jun 1958, no. 6	6 Sep 1958, no. 19
Carol	Chuck Berry	25 Aug 1958, no. 18	—
Move It	Cliff Richard and the Drifters	1958, —	13 Sep 1958, no. 2
To Know Him Is to Love Him	The Teddy Bears	22 Sep 1958, no. 1	20 Dec 1958, no. 2

Song Title	Artist	US chart date and peak position	UK chart date and peak position
Nothin' Shakin' (but the Leaves on the Trees)	Eddie Fontaine	22 Sep 1958, no. 64	—
C'mon Everybody	Eddie Cochran	24 Nov 1958, no. 35	14 Mar 1959, no. 6
I'll Always Be in Love with You	Fats Domino	1958, —	—
Midnight Special	Lonnie Donegan	—	1958, —
Dance in the Street	Gene Vincent	1958, —	—
Alright, Okay, You Win	Peggy Lee	26 Jan 1959, no. 68	—
Three Cool Cats	The Coasters	2 Feb 1959, —	—
Almost Grown	Chuck Berry	30 Mar 1959, no. 32	—
Raining in My Heart	Buddy Holly	30 Mar 1959, no. 88	—
Little Queenie	Chuck Berry	13 Apr 1959, no. 80	—
Kansas City / Hey-Hey-Hey-Hey!	Little Richard	11 May 1959, no. 95	6 Jun 1959, no. 26
Memphis, Tennessee	Chuck Berry	22 Jun 1959, —	1963, —
What'd I Say	Ray Charles	6 Jul 1959, no. 6	—
Crackin' Up	Bo Diddley	6 Jul 1959, no. 62	—
Leave My Kitten Alone	Little Willie John	3 Aug 1959, no. 60	—
Shout!	The Isley Brothers	21 Sep 1959, no. 47	—
Red Hot	Ronnie Hawkins	1959, —	—
Crying, Waiting, Hoping	Buddy Holly	1959, —	—
The Honeymoon Song (Bound by Love)	Marino Marini	1959, —	—
(Baby) Hully Gully	The Olympics	1959, —	—
Take Out Some Insurance on Me Baby	Jimmy Reed	1959, —	—
Hippy Hippy Shake	Chan Romero	1959, —	—
Bad Boy	Larry Williams	1959, —	—
Wild Cat	Gene Vincent	1960, —	16 Jan 1960, no. 39
Hallelujah, I Love Her So	Eddie Cochran	1960, —	23 Jan 1960, no. 22
Money (That's What I Want)	Barrett Strong	1 Feb 1960, no. 23	—
Road Runner	Bo Diddley	29 Feb 1960, no. 75	—
Shazam!	Duane Eddy	21 Mar 1960, no. 45	30 Apr 1960, no. 4
Cathy's Clown	The Everly Brothers	18 Apr 1960, no. 1	16 Apr 1960, no. 1
Besame Mucho	The Coasters	2 May 1960, no. 70	—
Alley-Oop	The Hollywood Argyles	30 May 1960, no. 1	23 Jul 1960, no. 24
Shakin' All Over	Johnny Kidd and the Pirates	—	18 Jun 1960, no. 1
Apache	The Shadows	—	23 Jul 1960, no. 1
You Don't Understand Me	Bobby Freeman	15 Aug 1960, —	—
Save the Last Dance for Me	The Drifters	5 Sep 1960, no. 1	5 Nov 1960, no. 2
I Wish I Could Shimmy Like My Sister Kate	The Olympics	12 Sep 1960, no. 42	21 Jan 1961, no. 40

Song Title	Artist	US chart date and peak position	UK chart date and peak position
You're Sixteen	Johnny Burnette	31 Oct 1960, no. 8	14 Jan 1961, no. 3
Boys	The Shirelles	21 Nov 1960, —	—
Angel Baby	Rosie and the Originals	12 Dec 1960, no. 5	—
I Got to Find My Baby	Chuck Berry	1960, —	—
So How Come (No One Loves Me)	The Everly Brothers	1960, —	—
Red Sails in the Sunset	Emile Ford	—	1960, —
A Taste of Honey	Lenny Welch	1960, —	—
Will You Love Me Tomorrow	The Shirelles	20 Nov 1961, no. 1	11 Feb 1961, no. 4
If You Gotta Make a Fool of Somebody	James Ray	20 Nov 1961, no. 22	—
Chariot	Rhet Stoller	—	14 Jan 1961, no. 26
More Than I Can Say	Bobby Vee	27 Feb 1961, no. 61	15 Apr 1961, no. 4
Theme for a Dream	Cliff Richard and the Shadows	—	4 Mar 1961, no. 3
Runaway	Del Shannon	6 Mar 1961, no. 1	29 Apr 1961, no. 48
Wooden Heart	Elvis Presley	5 Dec 1964, no. 107	11 Mar 1961, no. 1
Till There Was You	Peggy Lee	—	25 Mar 1961, no. 30
Mama Said	The Shirelles	17 Apr 1961, no. 4	—
Buzz Buzz-a-Diddle-It	Freddy Cannon	1 May 1961, no. 51	—
Stand by Me	Ben E. King	8 May 1961, no. 4	24 Jun 1961, no. 27
The Frightened City	The Shadows	—	13 May 1961, no. 3
Quarter to Three	Gary U. S. Bonds	22 May 1961, no. 1	22 Jul 1961, no. 7
Watch Your Step	Bobby Parker	12 Jun 1961, no. 51	—
Time	Craig Douglas	—	1 Jul 1961, no. 9
I Just Don't Understand	Ann-Margret	24 Jul 1961, no. 17	—
Take Good Care of My Baby	Bobby Vee	7 Aug 1961, no. 1	28 Oct 1961, no. 3
(Marie's the Name) His Latest Flame	Elvis Presley	28 Aug 1961, no. 4	4 Nov 1961, no. 1
Please Mr. Postman	The Marvelettes	4 Sep 1961, no. 1	—
Hit the Road Jack	Ray Charles	11 Sep 1961, no. 1	21 Oct 1961, no. 6
September in the Rain	Dinah Washington	16 Oct 1961, no. 23	2 Dec 1961, no. 35
I'm a Moody Guy	Shane Fenton and the Fentones	—	28 Oct 1961, no. 22
Peppermint Twist	Joey Dee and the Starliters	20 Nov 1961, no. 1	10 Feb 1962, no. 33
Baby It's You	The Shirelles	18 Dec 1961, no. 8	—
The Sheik of Araby	Fats Domino	1961, —	—
Trambone	The Remo Four	—	1961, —
What a Crazy World We're Living In	Joe Brown	—	13 Jan 1962, no. 37
Hey! Baby	Bruce Channel	27 Jan 1962, no. 1	24 Mar 1962, no. 2
What's Your Name	Don and Juan	10 Feb 1962, no. 7	—

Song Title	Artist	US chart date and peak position	UK chart date and peak position
Dream Baby (How Long Must I Dream)	Roy Orbison	17 Feb 1962, no. 4	3 Oct 1962, no. 2
You Better Move On	Arthur Alexander	24 Feb 1962, no. 24	—
A Shot of Rhythm and Blues	Arthur Alexander	24 Feb 1962, —	—
It's All Over Now	Shane Fenton and the Fentones	—	7 Apr 1962, no. 29
Love Is a Swingin' Thing	The Shirelles	7 Apr 1962, no. 109	—
Mister Moonlight	Dr. Feelgood and the Interns	21 Apr 1962, —	—
Fortune Teller	Benny Spellman	5 May 1962, —	—
A Picture of You	Joe Brown	—	19 May 1962, no. 2
Sharing You	Bobby Vee	19 May 1962, no. 15	9 Jun 1962, no. 10
Where Have You Been (All My Life)	Arthur Alexander	26 May 1962, no. 58	—
Soldier of Love (Lay Down Your Arms)	Arthur Alexander	26 May 1962, —	—
Twist and Shout	The Isley Brothers	2 Jun 1962, no. 17	1963, no. 42
Don't Ever Change	The Crickets	1962, —	23 Jun 1962, no. 5
Bring It On Home to Me	Sam Cooke	23 Jun 1962, no. 13	—
The Loco-Motion	Little Eva	30 Jun 1962, no. 1	8 Sep 1962, no. 2
I Remember You	Frank Ifield	8 Sep 1962, no. 5	7 Jul 1962, no. 1
Cindy's Birthday	Shane Fenton and the Fentones	—	14 Jul 1962, no. 19
Sheila	Tommy Roe	28 Jul 1962, no. 1	8 Sep 1962, no. 3
Reminiscing	Buddy Holly	—	15 Sep 1962, no. 17
Anna (Go to Him)	Arthur Alexander	27 Oct 1962, no. 68	—
Keep Your Hands Off My Baby	Little Eva	3 Nov 1962, no. 12	5 Jan 1963, no. 30
Chains	The Cookies	10 Nov 1962, no. 17	1963, no. 50
You've Really Got a Hold On Me	The Miracles	8 Dec 1962, no. 8	—
He's Sure the Boy I Love	The Crystals	29 Dec. 1962, no. 11	—
Some Other Guy	Richie Barrett	1962, —	—
I'm Talking about You	Chuck Berry	1962, —	—
Devil in His Heart	The Donays	1962, —	—
Open (Your Lovin' Arms)	Buddy Knox	1962, —	—
Diamonds	Jet Harris and Tony Meehan	—	12 Jan 1963, no. 1
Let's Stomp	Bobby Comstock	16 Feb 1963, no. 57	—
Act Naturally	Buck Owens	1963, —	—
Forget Him	Bobby Rydell	9 Nov. 1963, no. 4	25 May 1963, no. 13
No Particular Place to Go	Chuck Berry	23 May 1964, no. 10	9 May 1964, no. 3

APPENDIX 2

Timeline

MONTH-YEAR	UK EVENTS	US EVENTS	WORLD EVENTS
Apr-20			Ravi Shankar born (7th)
Oct-23			Bert Kaempfert born (16th)
Jan-26	George Martin born (3rd)		
Oct-26		Chuck Berry born (18th)	
Apr-32		Carl Perkins born (9th)	
Dec-32		Richard Penniman ("Little Richard") born (5th)	
Feb-33			Yoko Ono born (18th)
Sep-34	Brian Epstein born (19th)		
Jan-35		Elvis Presley born (8th)	
Apr-36		Roy Orbison born (23rd)	
Sep-36		Buddy Holly born (7th)	
Feb-37		Don Everly born (1st)	
Dec-37		Premiere of Walt Disney's *Snow White and the Seven Dwarfs*	
Jan-39		Phil Everly born (19th)	
Sep-39	Cynthia Lennon born (10th)		
Dec-39		Phil Spector born (26th)	
Jan-40	Food rationing begins		

MONTH-YEAR	UK EVENTS	US EVENTS	WORLD EVENTS
Feb-40		Smokey Robinson born (19th); Glenn Miller's "In the Mood" no. 1	
Mar-40			Germany and Italy allied against UK and France
Apr-40			Germany invades Denmark, Norway
May-40	Tony Sheridan born (21st); Winston Churchill becomes prime minister		Germany invades France; Netherlands, begins sending Jews to concentration camps
Jun-40	Stu Sutcliffe born (23rd)		Soviet Union annexes Baltic states
Jul-40	Ringo Starr born (7th); Germans begin aerial bombing of Britain	Bugs Bunny makes cartoon debut	
Sep-40			Japan invades French Indochina, forms Axis with Germany and Italy
Oct-40	John Lennon born (9th); Cliff Richard born (14th)		Italy invades Greece
Nov-40		F. D. Roosevelt elected to third term as US president	UK bombs Hamburg, Germany
Dec-40		First synthesis of plutonium	
Feb-41	First penicillin treatment		
Mar-41		First FM radio station operates in Nashville	
May-41	Joe Brown born (13th)	Premiere of *Citizen Kane*; Bob Dylan born (24th)	
Jun-41			Italy and Romania declare war against Soviet Union
Jul-41		First commercial television broadcast	
Aug-41		David Crosby born (14th)	
Sep-41		Linda Eastman born (24th)	Germany begins siege of Leningrad (lifted Jan. '44)
Nov-41	Pete Best born (24th)		
Dec-41		Japan attacks US; US and allies declare war on Japan	Germany and Italy declare war on US
Jan-42		Muhammad Ali born as Cassius Clay (17th)	
Feb-42		Carole King born (9th)	
May-42		Tommy Roe born (9th)	
Jun-42	Paul McCartney born (18th)	Brian Wilson born (20th)	
Jul-42		Roger McGuinn born (13th)	

MONTH-YEAR	UK EVENTS	US EVENTS	WORLD EVENTS
Aug-42			US Marines and Navy land at Guadalcanal; Mohandas Gandhi arrested by British (begins hunger strike in Feb. '43, released May '44)
Oct-42			Germans fire rocket into outer space
Nov-42		Premiere of *Casablanca*; Jimi Hendrix born (27th)	US and UK forces land in northern Africa
Dec-42		Gasoline rationing begins in US; first sustained nuclear chain reaction in Chicago	
Jan-43		Duke Ellington plays Carnegie Hall; George Washington Carver dies (5th); Chris Montez born (17th)	First US bombing of Germany
Feb-43	George Harrison born (25th)		
Mar-43	Vivian Stanshall born (21st)	Integrated musical *Oklahoma!* opens	
Apr-43			Effects of LSD studied in Switzerland
Jul-43	Mick Jagger born (26th)		
Aug-43			Allies invade Italy (Italy surrenders to Allies in Sep.)
Dec-43	Keith Richards born as Keith Richard (18th)		
Jan-44	Jimmy Page born (9th)		
Mar-44	Pattie Boyd born (17)	Jimmy Dorsey's "Besame Mucho" no. 1	
Apr-44		United Negro College Fund inaugurated	
May-44	Joe Cocker born (20th)		
Jun-44			D-Day: US lands in Normandy, liberating France
Jul-44		Jackie Robinson arrested for refusing to move to the back of segregated army bus	
Aug-44			Anne Frank discovered hiding in Amsterdam (dies Mar. '45)
Oct-44			US forces invade Germany
Nov-44		F. D. Roosevelt elected to fourth term	
Mar-45	Eric Clapton born (30th)		
Apr-45		F. D. Roosevelt dies; Harry Truman becomes president	
May-45	Pete Townshend born (19th)		Germany surrenders to Allies

MONTH-YEAR	UK EVENTS	US EVENTS	WORLD EVENTS
Aug-45	Orwell's *Animal Farm* published		Atomic bombs fall on Japan, which surrenders to Allies
Oct-45		United Nations founded	
Nov-45		First electronic computer, ENIAC, assembled in Philadelphia; first issue of *Ebony* published	
Apr-46	Jane Asher born (5th)		
May-46	Donovan Leitch born (10th)		
Aug-46	Maureen Cox born (4th)		
Sep-46	Helen Shapiro born (28th)	Billy Preston born (9th)	
Jan-47			Communists take power in Poland
Feb-47			Christian Dior launches line in Paris
Apr-47		Jackie Robinson signs, plays, with the Brooklyn Dodgers	
May-47		Truman Doctrine begins the Cold War	
Jun-47		Marshall Plan begins European reconstruction	
Aug-47			India breaks from British Empire; Pakistan breaks from India
Dec-47	Women first awarded bachelor's degrees from University of Cambridge	Transistor created	
Jan-48			Mahatma Gandhi assassinated
		James Taylor born (12th)	
Jun-48		Columbia Records introduces the LP record	
Jun-49	Orwell's *1984* published; dock workers strike		
Aug-49			Soviet Union tests atomic bomb
Oct-49			People's Republic of China proclaimed
Dec-49		Lead Belly dies (6th)	
May-50		Stevie Wonder born (13th)	
Jun-50			Korean War begins (ends July '53)
Oct-50		Comic strip "Peanuts" published	
Jan-52		University of Tennessee admits its first black student	
Feb-52	Elizabeth II proclaimed queen of UK		Premiere of Beckett's *Waiting for Godot*
Jan-53		Hank Williams dies (1st)	

MONTH-YEAR	UK EVENTS	US EVENTS	WORLD EVENTS
Mar-53		Salk's polio vaccine announced	
May-53	Frankie Laine's "I Believe" no. 1		
Aug-53			Soviet Union announces it has nuclear bomb
Sep-53	Rationing of sugar ends		
Apr-54		Army-McCarthy hearings begin	
May-54		US Supreme rules in *Brown v. Board of Ed.* that racially segregated public schools are unconstitutional	
Sep-54	Frank Sinatra's "Three Coins in the Fountain" no. 1		
Jan-55	Bill Haley and His Comets' "Shake, Rattle and Roll" no. 4	Marian Anderson performs at Metropolitan Opera	
Mar-55		Premiere of *Blackboard Jungle*	
Jul-55		Bill Haley and His Comets' "Rock Around the Clock" no. 1; Elvis Presley's "Baby Let's Play House" no. 5	
Nov-55	Bill Haley and His Comets' "Rock Around the Clock" no. 1		Vietnam War begins
Dec-55		Rosa Parks refuses to give up her seat on Montgomery, AL, bus	
Feb-56	Lonnie Donegan's "Rock Island Line" no. 8; Dick James's "Robin Hood," on Parlophone, no. 14		
Mar-56		Elvis Presley's eponymous first album released	
Apr-56		Elvis Presley's "Heartbreak Hotel" no. 1	
May-56		Little Richard's "Long Tall Sally" no. 4	
Jun-56	Lonnie Donegan's "Lost John" no. 2; Elvis Presley's "Heartbreak Hotel" no. 2; Carl Perkins's "Blue Suede Shoes" no. 10	Elvis Presley performs "Hound Dog" on *Milton Berle Show*; Chuck Berry's "Roll Over Beethoven" no. 29	
Jul-56	Humphrey Lyttelton's "Bad Penny Blues" no. 19; the Goons, "I'm Walking Backward for Christmas" no. 4	Elvis Presley's "I Want You, I Need You, I Love You" no. 1; Gene Vincent's "Be-Bop-a-Lula" no. 7	

MONTH-YEAR	UK EVENTS	US EVENTS	WORLD EVENTS
Aug-56	Gene Vincent's "Be-Bop-a-Lula" no. 16	Elvis Presley's "Hound Dog" / "Don't Be Cruel" no. 1	
Oct-56	Paul McCartney's mother, Mary, dies (30)		UK and France bomb Egypt to force reopening of Suez Canal
Nov-56		US Supreme Court rules segregated bus laws to be unconstitutional; Ginsberg's *Howl and Other Poems* published; Elvis Presley's "Love Me Tender" no. 1	Soviets troops crush Hungarian Revolution
Dec-56		*The Girl Can't Help It* and *Don't Knock the Rock* released	
Jan-57	Cavern Club opens as jazz venue in Liverpool		
Feb-57	Bing Crosby and Grace Kelly's "True Love" no. 4	Elvis Presley's "Too Much" no. 1	
Mar-57	Little Richard's "Long Tall Sally" no. 3		
Apr-57	Lonnie Donegan's "Cumberland Gap" no. 1	Elvis Presley's "All Shook Up" no. 1; Little Richard's "Lucille" no. 21	
May-57	Charlie Gracie's "Butterfly" no. 12	Dell-Vikings' "Come Go with Me" no. 4	
Jun-57	Quarry Men audition unsuccessfully for *TV Star Search* at Empire Theatre, Liverpool (9th); Lonnie Donegan's "Puttin' On the Style" no. 1		
Jul-57	John Lennon and Paul McCartney meet at Quarry Men performance at St. Peter's Church festival (6th); Elvis Presley's "All Shook Up" no. 1	Elvis Presley's "(Let Me Be Your) Teddy Bear" no. 1; Coasters' "Searchin'" / "Young Blood" no. 3	
Aug-57	Paul Anka's "Diana" no. 1; Everly Brothers' "Bye Bye Love" no. 6; Little Richard's "Lucille" no. 10		
Sep-57		The Crickets' "That'll Be the Day" no. 1	
Oct-57	Paul McCartney first performs with the Quarry Men (18th)	Elvis Presley's "Jailhouse Rock" no. 1	

MONTH-YEAR	UK EVENTS	US EVENTS	WORLD EVENTS
Nov-57	Crickets' "That'll Be the Day" no. 1; Jerry Lee Lewis's "Whole Lotta Shakin' Goin' On" no. 8; Elvis Presley's "Tryin' to Get to You" no. 16; Coasters' "Searchin'" no. 30		Launch of Sputnik 1
Dec-57	Everly Brothers' "Wake Up Little Susie" no. 2	Bill Justis's "Raunchy" no. 2; Buddy Holly's "Peggy Sue" no. 3; Chuck Berry's "Rock and Roll Music" no. 8; *The Music Man* debuts on Broadway	
Jan-58	Buddy Holly's "Peggy Sue" no. 6		
Feb-58	George Harrison joins the Quarry Men; Bill Justis's "Raunchy" no. 11	Elvis Presley's "Don't" no. 1	
Mar-58		Elvis Presley inducted into US Army (discharged Mar. '60); Chuck Berry's "Sweet Little Sixteen" no. 2; Little Richard's "Good Golly Miss Molly" no. 10; the Crickets' "Maybe Baby" no. 18; Duane Eddy's "Movin' and Groovin'" no. 72	
May-58	Chuck Berry's "Sweet Little Sixteen" no. 16		
Jun-58		Little Richard's "Ooh! My Soul" no. 31	
Jul-58	Quarry Men record two songs in Liverpool studio (12th); Julia Lennon dies (15th)	Elvis Presley's "Hard Headed Woman" no. 1	
Aug-58	Quarry Men open the Casbah Club (29th, play many dates there through Oct.); Little Richard's "Ooh! My Soul" no. 22		
Sep-58	Peggy Lee's "Fever" no. 5; Duane Eddy's "Rebel-'Rouser" no. 19	Chuck Berry's "Carol" no. 18	
Oct-58	Cliff Richard's "Move It" no. 2; women permitted as representatives in House of Lords		
Jan-59	Teddy Bears' "To Know Him Is to Love Him" no. 2	Berry Gordy founds Motown Records in Detroit	
Feb-59		Buddy Holly dies (3rd)	

MONTH-YEAR	UK EVENTS	US EVENTS	WORLD EVENTS
Apr-59	Eddie Cochran's "C'mon Everybody" no. 6	Barrett Strong's "Money" no. 23	
May-59		Chuck Berry's "Little Queenie" no. 80; Little Richard's "Kansas City" / "Hey-Hey-Hey-Hey!" no. 95	
Jun-59	Stu Sutcliffe joins the Quarry Men; Little Richard's "Kansas City" no. 26		
Jul-59		Chuck Berry's "Back in the USA" / "Memphis, Tennessee" no. 37	
Aug-59		Little Willie John's "Leave My Kitten Alone" no. 60	
Nov-59	Quarry Men audition in nearby Manchester but return to Liverpool before judging (15th)		
Jan-60	Gene Vincent's "Wild Cat" no. 21		
Feb-60	Eddie Cochran's "Hallelujah I Love Her So" no. 22		
Mar-60		Bo Diddley's "Road Runner" no. 75	US sends 3,500 troops to Vietnam
Apr-60	John and Paul perform as the Nerk Twins in Caversham pub (23rd–24th); Silver Beetles make Forthlin Road recordings; Eddie Cochran dies (17th)		
May-60	Silver Beetles tour northern Scotland with Johnny Gentle (20th–28th); Everly Brothers' "Cathy's Clown" no. 1	Coasters' "Besame Mucho" no. 70; 1960 Civil Rights Law signed; FDA approves contraceptive pill	
Jun-60	Silver Beatles appear on Saturday nights throughout June and July at Grosvenor Ballroom, Wallasey; Jim Reeves's "He'll Have to Go" no. 7		
Jul-60		Hollywood Argyles' "Alley-Oop" no. 1; Greensboro, NC, Woolworth's lunch counter serves first meal to an African American	World's first female head of government elected in Ceylon

MONTH-YEAR	UK EVENTS	US EVENTS	WORLD EVENTS
Aug-60	Pete Best joins Beatles; Johnny Kidd and the Pirates' "Shakin' All Over" no. 1; Shadows' "Apache" no. 1		Beatles begin residency in Indra Club, Hamburg, West Germany (17th through 3 Oct.)
Sep-60	Chubby Checker's "The Twist" no. 44	Chubby Checker's "The Twist" no. 1	
Oct-60	Roy Orbison's "Only the Lonely" no. 1	The Drifters' "Save the Last Dance for Me" no. 1; Isley Brothers' "Shout" no. 47; Elvis Presley's *G.I. Blues* released	Beatles play Kaiserkeller, Hamburg (4th through 30 Nov.)
Nov-60		J. F. Kennedy defeats R. Nixon to be youngest man elected to US presidency	Beatles continue at Kaiserkeller, Hamburg
Dec-60	Beatles perform at Litherland Town Hall (27th); Drifters' "Save the Last Dance for Me" no. 2		
Jan-61	Beatles continue numerous performances in north Liverpool dance halls through March; Ventures' "Perfida" no. 4; Rhet Stoller's "Chariot" no. 26	Shirelles' "Will You Love Me Tomorrow" no. 1	
Feb-61	Beatles begin their residency at the Cavern (9th), alternating appearances there with the Casbah and various dance halls through March; Shadows' "F.B.I." no. 6		
Mar-61	Elvis Presley's "Wooden Heart" no. 1; Shirelles' "Will You Love Me Tomorrow" no. 4; George Formby dies (6th)	J. F. Kennedy establishes the Peace Corps	
Apr-61	Peggy Lee's "Till There Was You" no. 30		Beatles in residence at Top Ten Club, Hamburg (1st through 1 July)
May-61	Temperance Seven's "You're Driving Me Crazy," on Parlophone, no. 1	Alan Shepard is first American in outer space; Freedom Riders bus is bombed in AL; Freedom Riders arrested in MS	
Jun-61	Shadows' "The Frightened City" no. 3	Ben E. King's "Stand by Me" no. 4	Beatles record with Tony Sheridan in Hamburg (22nd–23rd)

MONTH-YEAR	UK EVENTS	US EVENTS	WORLD EVENTS
Jul-61	Beatles return to Liverpool engagements (13th through all of 1961); Del Shannon's "Runaway" no. 1; Roy Orbison's "Running Scared" no. 9; *Mersey Beat* first published		
Aug-61	Gary U. S. Bonds's "Quarter to Three" no. 7; Ben E. King's "Stand by Me" no. 27		Construction of the Berlin Wall begins
Sep-61		Elvis Presley's "(Marie's the Name) His Latest Flame" no. 4	
Oct-61	John and Paul spend two weeks in Paris and receive first Beatle haircut; Helen Shapiro's "Walking Back to Happiness" no. 1		"My Bonnie" / "The Saints" released in West Germany
Nov-61	Beatles meet Brian Epstein (9th), play for 3,000 at "Operation Big Beat" in New Brighton; Shane Fenton and the Fentones' "I'm a Moody Guy," on Parlophone, no. 22		US sends 18,000 troops to Vietnam; war official in Dec.
Dec-61	Beatles' disastrous date in Aldershot (9th); Bobby Vee's "Take Good Care of My Baby" no. 3; Dinah Washington's "September in the Rain" no. 35	The Marvelettes' "Please Mr. Postman" no. 1; Martin Luther King, Jr., arrested in Albany, GA (15th)	
Jan-62	Beatles audition unsuccessfully for Decca Records (1st), continue daily performances at Cavern and throughout Liverpool (through 8 Apr.); *Mersey Beat* names Beatles Liverpool's top group; "My Bonnie" / "The Saints" released in UK (5th); Beatles audition successfully for BBC (12th); Chubby Checker's "The Twist" re-charts at no. 14; Joe Brown's "What a Crazy World We're Living In" no. 37	Chubby Checker's "The Twist" regains no. 1 position more than a year after first run	

MONTH-YEAR	UK EVENTS	US EVENTS	WORLD EVENTS
Feb-62	Elvis Presley's "Can't Help Falling in Love" no. 1		Tony Sheridan and the Beat Brothers' "My Bonnie" no. 33 in West Germany; US begins embargo of Cuba
Mar-62	Beatles' first BBC Radio appearance, in Manchester (7th)	Roy Orbison's "Dream Baby (How Long Must I Dream" no. 4; Bob Dylan's eponymous first album released	
Apr-62	Stu Sutcliffe dies (10th); Roy Orbison's "Dream Baby (How Long Must I Dream)" no. 2; Bruce Channel's "Hey Baby" no. 2	"My Bonnie" / "The Saints" released (23rd); Arthur Alexander's "You Better Move On" / "A Shot of Rhythm and Blues" no. 24	Beatles' first residency at the Star-Club, Hamburg (13th through 31 May), record with Tony Sheridan in Hamburg
Jun-62	Beatles record material at EMI unreleased until 1995 (6th), return to Cavern Club and other mostly local venues (9th through Oct.); Joe Brown's "A Picture of You" no. 2; Shirelles' "Soldier Boy" no. 23	Arthur Alexander's "Where Have You Been All My Life" / "Soldier of Love" no. 58; SDS delivers the Port Huron Statement	
Jul-62	Frank Ifield's "I Remember You" no. 1; Rolling Stones make their debut in London	Martin Luther King, Jr., arrested in Albany, GA, jailed, leading to coalition of SNCC and NAACP forming Albany Movement; Andy Warhol exhibits *Campbell's Soup Cans*; Telstar launched	
Aug-62	Ringo Starr replaces Pete Best in the Beatles (18th), Beatles filmed at Cavern for television (22nd); John Lennon marries Cynthia Powell (23rd); Crickets' "Don't Ever Change" no. 5	Little Eva's "The Loco-Motion" no. 1; Isley Brothers' "Twist and Shout" no. 17	
Sep-62	Beatles record first A-side, "Love Me Do" (4th) and B-side, "P.S. I Love You" (11th), for Ron Richards and George Martin at EMI	Rachel Carson's *Silent Spring* published	Soviet missiles found in Cuba, precipitating US blockade (Cuban Missile Crisis)
Oct-62	"Love Me Do" / "P.S. I Love You" released (5th; no. 17 in Dec.); Beatles play second to Little Richard at both Tower Ballroom (12th) and Empire Theatre (28th); Tommy Roe's "Sheila" no. 3; Buddy Holly's "Reminiscing" no. 17	*Peter, Paul and Mary* LP no. 1; James Meredith registers at University of Mississippi (1st) following intervention of US Attorney General Robert F. Kennedy	

MONTH-YEAR	UK EVENTS	US EVENTS	WORLD EVENTS
Nov-62	Beatles record "Please Please Me" / "Ask Me Why" at EMI (26th), perform across England and Wales including radio and television dates (through 17 Dec.)	Little Eva's "Keep Your Hands Off My Baby" no. 12; Cookies' "Chains" no. 17; Arthur Alexander's "Anna (Go to Him)" no. 68	Beatles and Little Richard onstage at the Star-Club, Hamburg (1st–14th); UN condemns South Africa's apartheid
Dec-62	The Miracles' "You've Really Got a Hold on Me" no. 87; UK installs American nuclear missiles	Helen Gurley Brown's *Sex and the Single Girl* published	Beatles' last residency at Star-Club (18th–31st), recorded there (24th–31st)
Jan-63	Beatles perform in Scotland (2nd–8th); "Please Please Me" / "Ask Me Why" released (11th; no. 2 in Feb.); Beatles appear on TV's "Thank Your Lucky Stars" (13th); Little Eva's "Keep Your Hands Off My Baby" no. 30; Johnny Kidd and the Pirates' "A Shot of Rhythm and Blues" no. 48; Cookies' "Chains" no. 50; Gerry and the Pacemakers record "How Do You Do It" (22nd, no. 1 in Apr.); Bob Dylan performs in London coffee houses	George Wallace becomes governor of Alabama	
Feb-63	Beatles begin Helen Shapiro tour (2nd–9th); Beatles record *Please Please Me* (11th); Beatles resume Shapiro tour (23rd through Mar. 3); Harold Wilson elected leader of Britain's Labour Party (14th)	Betty Friedan's *The Feminine Mystique* published; the Miracles' "You've Really Got a Hold on Me" no. 8	
Mar-63	Beatles record third single (5th); Beatles top bill with Tommy Roe and Chris Montez (9th–31st); *Please Please Me* released (22nd)		

MONTH-YEAR	UK EVENTS	US EVENTS	WORLD EVENTS
Apr-63	Julian Lennon born (8th); "From Me to You" / "Thank You Girl" released (11th; no. 1 in May); Andrew Loog Oldham signs management contract with the Rolling Stones; 50,000 "Ban the Bomb" anti-nuclear protesters rally in London's Hyde Park (15th) (movement co-opted by Partial Test-Ban Treaty)	Martin Luther King, Jr., arrested in Birmingham, AL	
May-63	Beatles tour with Roy Orbison (18th through June 9th)	"From Me to You" / "Thank You Girl" released (27th; no. 41 in Apr. '64); Bob Dylan's *The Freewheelin' Bob Dylan* released; Bob Dylan refuses to appear on Ed Sullivan Show after network censors do not allow him to perform "Talkin' John Birch Paranoid Blues" (12th)	
Jun-63	Beatles continue with ballroom gigs and BBC broadcasts; John Profumo resigns in scandal (5th)	AL gov. George Wallace refuses black students at the University of Alabama (11th); civil rights activist Medgar Evers assassinated in MS (12th)	US President Kennedy delivers "Ich bin ein Berliner" speech (26th) in solidarity with country divided by Iron Curtain
Jul-63	Beatles record "She Loves You" / "I'll Get You" (1st); recordings for second LP (18th and 30th)	Vee Jay releases *Introducing the Beatles* (22nd?); First geosynchronous satellite, Syncom 2, launched	
Aug-63	"She Loves You" / "I'll Get You" released (23rd; no. 1 in Sep.); Billy J. Kramer and the Dakotas' "Bad to Me" no. 1	Peter, Paul and Mary's "Blowin' in the Wind" no. 2; Martin Luther King, Jr., delivers "I Have a Dream" speech to 250,000 civil rights marchers in Washington, DC (28th)	US, UK, and Soviets sign partial test ban treaty
Sep-63	Beatles continue recording second album at EMI (11th and 12th)	"She Loves You" / "I'll Get You" released (16th; no. 1 Mar. '64)	
Oct-63	Beatles' London Palladium appearance (13th); Beatles record fifth single (17th) and complete LP recordings (3rd, 17th and 23rd); Prime Minister Harold Macmillan resigns over Profumo scandal (18th)	Ronettes' "Be My Baby" no. 2; Sam Cooke arrested trying to register at "whites only" motel in Shreveport, LA	Beatles tour Sweden (23rd–31st)

MONTH-YEAR	UK EVENTS	US EVENTS	WORLD EVENTS
Nov-63	*With the Beatles* released (22nd); "I Want to Hold Your Hand" / "This Boy" released (29th; no. 1 in Dec.); Rolling Stones' "I Wanna Be Your Man" released (1st)	Capitol Records signs Beatles; John F. Kennedy assassinated (22nd)	
Nov-64	Royal Command Performance at Prince of Wales Theatre, London (4th)		South Vietnam's first president, Ngo Dinh Diem, overthrown in coup (1st) and assassinated (2nd)
Dec-63	Beatles' London Christmas concerts (24th through Jan. 11 '64)		Beatles' "Roll Over Beethoven" / "Please Mr. Postman" released in Canada (9th; no. 68 in US in Apr. '64)
Jan-64	Beatles continue London Christmas Show (through 11th), play London Palladium (12th); Peter and Gordon record "A World Without Love" (21st; no. 1 in Apr.)	Vee Jay re-releases *Introducing the Beatles* (10th; no. 2 in Feb.); Capitol releases "I Want to Hold Your Hand" / "I Saw Her Standing There" (13th; no. 1 in Feb); *Meet the Beatles* released (20th; no. 1 in Feb.); MGM re-releases "My Bonnie" / "The Saints" (27th; no. 26 in Mar.); Vee Jay re-releases "Please Please Me" / "From Me to You" (30th; no. 3 in Mar.); Surgeon General reports that smoking may be hazardous to health	Beatles perform (15th through 4 Feb.) and record (29th) in Paris; Soviets shoot down US Air Force jet over East Germany
Feb-64	Beatles record at EMI (25th–27th)	Beatles arrive in US (7th) for Ed Sullivan Show appearances (9th, 16th) and concerts in Washington, DC (11th) and New York's Carnegie Hall (12th); Cassius Clay becomes heavyweight champion by defeating Sonny Liston (25th)	"All My Loving" / "This Boy" released in Canada (17th; no. 45 in US in Apr.)
Mar-64	Beatles record at EMI (1st), shooting for first film (2nd through 24 Apr.); "Can't Buy Me Love" / "You Can't Do That" released (20th; no. 1 in Apr.); John Lennon's *In His Own Write* published (23rd); Radio Caroline becomes first pirate radio station	"Twist and Shout" / "There's a Place" released (2nd; no. 2 in Apr.); "Can't Buy Me Love" / "You Can't Do That" released (16th; no. 1 in Apr.); Do You Want to Know a Secret" / "Thank You Girl" released (23rd; no. 2 in May); Malcolm X forms a black nationalist party; Ford Motors introduces the Mustang	"Komm Gib Mir Deine Hand" / "Sie Liebt Dich" released in West Germany (5th)

MONTH-YEAR	UK EVENTS	US EVENTS	WORLD EVENTS
Apr-64	Beatles continue shooting first film (through 24th), record at EMI (16th), perform *NME* Poll Winners' concert (26th), tape *Around the Beatles* television special (28th), play Scotland (29th and 30th); Rolling Stones' eponymous first album released (16th)	Beatles hold top five places in the *Billboard* "Hot 100" singles chart (4th); Capitol releases *The Beatles' Second Album* (10th; no. 1 in May); Tollie releases "Love Me Do" / "P.S. I Love You" (27th; no. 1 in May); Sidney Poitier is first African American to win Best Actor Academy Award	Nelson Mandela delivers "I Am Prepared to Die" speech (sentenced to life in prison in June)
May-64	Beatles' "Ain't She Sweet" / "If You Love Me Baby" released (29th)	"Sie Liebt Dich" / "I'll Get You" released (21st; no. 97 in June); BASIC program run for first time; students march against Vietnam War in major cities	
Jun-64	Beatles record at EMI (1st–2nd); *Long Tall Sally* EP released (19th)	"Sweet Georgia Brown" / "Take Out Some Insurance On Me, Baby" released (1st); *A Hard Day's Night* soundtrack released (26th; no. 1 in July); Ku Klux Klan murders three civil rights workers in MS	Beatles play Denmark and Netherlands (4th–6th), Hong Kong and Oceania (9th–30th)
Jul-64	Premiere of *A Hard Day's Night* (6th); "A Hard Day's Night" / "Things We Said Today" released (10th; no. 1 in Jul.); *A Hard Day's Night* LP released (10th); Beatles perform on British stage, radio, and television (7th–26th)	"Ain't She Sweet" / "Nobody's Child" released (6th; no. 19 in Aug.); "A Hard Day's Night" / "I Should Have Known Better" released (13th; no. 1 in Aug.); *Something New* released (20th; no. 2 in Aug.); Racial segregation outlawed by Civil Rights Act; race riots in Rochester, New York	Beatles perform in Sweden (28th and 29th); US sends 5,000 military advisers to Vietnam
Aug-64	Beatles record at EMI (11th, 14th), perform in UK (2nd, 9th, 16th)	Beatles tour US (19th through Sep. 20th); "Matchbox" / "Slow Down" released (24th; no. 17 in Oct.); Gulf of Tonkin incident leads congress to grant L. B. Johnson war powers; race riots in Philadelphia; publication of Timothy Leary, Ralph Metzner and Richard Alpert's *The Psychedelic Experience: A Manual Based on the Tibetan Book of the Dead*	
Sep-64	Beatles record at EMI (29th–30th), perform in London (27th); Pete Townshend of the Who smashes first guitar	John Lennon announces that the Beatles will not play to segregated audience in FL (11th)	

MONTH-YEAR	UK EVENTS	US EVENTS	WORLD EVENTS
Oct-64	Beatles perform throughout Britain and No. Ireland on stage, radio, and TV (9th–25th, 28th through 29 Nov.), record at EMI (6th, 8th, 18th, 26th); The Kinks' eponymous first album released; Harold Wilson of Labour Party becomes prime minister	Moog synthesizer is demonstrated; Martin Luther King, Jr., awarded Nobel Peace Prize	People's Republic of China tests atomic bomb
Nov-64	Beatles continue UK performances (through 29th); "I Feel Fine" / "She's a Woman" released (27th; no. 1 in Dec.)	"I Feel Fine" / "She's a Woman" released (23rd; no. 1 in Dec.); Brian Wilson stops touring	France tests atomic bomb
Dec-64	*Beatles for Sale* released (4th); Beatles begin London Christmas concerts (22nd through Jan. 16th, '65); top 40 broadcasting begun by offshore pirate station	*Beatles '65* released (15th; no. 1 in Jan. '65); 800 students at University of California arrested in sit-in; Comedian Lenny Bruce imprisoned for obscenity; Sam Cooke killed in Los Angeles (11th)	Martin Luther King, Jr., delivers acceptance speech for Nobel Peace Prize, Oslo (10th)
Jan-65	Continuation of Christmas concerts (1st through 16th); Winston Churchill dies (24th)		
Feb-65	Beatles record at EMI (15th–20th)	"Eight Days a Week" / "I Don't Want to Spoil the Party" released (15th; no. 1 in Mar.); Malcolm X assassinated (21st)	Beatles shooting for second feature film in the Bahamas (23rd through 9 Mar.)
Mar-65	Beatles record at EMI (30th), unreleased; shooting for film in London (24th through 11 May); TV appearance on *Thank Your Lucky Stars* (28th)	*The Early Beatles* released (22nd; no. 43 in June); Dylan's *Bringing It All Back Home* released; first American combat troops sent to Vietnam; murder and police beatings in AL lead L. B. Johnson to ask Congress to pass Voting Rights Act (signed Aug. 6th); M. L. King, Jr., marches from Selma to Montgomery, AL	US begins three years of bombing in South Vietnam, "Operation Rolling Thunder" (2nd)

MONTH-YEAR	UK EVENTS	US EVENTS	WORLD EVENTS
Apr-65	"Ticket to Ride" / "Yes It Is" released (9th; no. 1 in Apr.); continued shooting for feature film; videos for new single shot (10th); *NME* Poll Winners' concert (11th); Beatles record at EMI (13th); Bob Dylan tours UK (30th through May 10th) as filmed for *Don't Look Back* documentary	"Ticket to Ride" / "Yes It Is" released (19th; no. 1 in May); SDS leads 25,000 protesters against Vietnam War in Washington, DC	
May-65	continued shooting of feature film (through 11th); Beatles record two Larry Williams songs at EMI (10th); overdubbing speech for film (18 May and 16 June); final taping for BBC Radio (26th)	30,000 demonstrate against Vietnam War in Berkeley, CA	
Jun-65	Beatles awarded MBE; Beatles record at EMI (14th, 15th, and 17th); John Lennon's *A Spaniard in the Works* published (24th)	*Beatles VI* released (14th; no. 1 in July)	Beatles tour France, Italy, and Spain (20th through July 3rd)
Jul-65	"Help!" / "I'm Down" released (23rd; no. 1 in Aug.)	"Help!" / "I'm Down" released (19th; no. 1 in Sep.); Bob Dylan goes electric at Newport Folk Festival (25th); Johnson announces increase to 35,000 monthly of men drafted; Martin Luther King, Jr., calls for end to Vietnam war	
Aug-65	Beatles perform live on television for *Blackpool Night Out* (1st); *Help!* LP released (6th)	*Help!* soundtrack released (13th; no. 1 in Sep.); Beatles tour US (15th through 31st), taping sequence for broadcast on Sullivan show (14th), filming concert played for 56,000 at Shea Stadium in New York (15th), recording at Hollywood Bowl (29th and 30th); Bob Dylan's *Highway 61 Revisited* released; race riots in Los Angeles.	
Sep-65		"Yesterday" / "Act Naturally" released (13th; no. 1 in Oct.); race riots in Watts, Los Angeles (11th–15th); Dylan's "Like a Rolling Stone" released	

MONTH-YEAR	UK EVENTS	US EVENTS	WORLD EVENTS
Oct-65	Beatles record at EMI (12th, 13th, 16th, 18th, 20th–22nd, 24th, 29th); Beatles awarded MBE medals at Buckingham Palace (26th)		
Nov-65	Beatles tape TV special, *The Music of Lennon and McCartney* (1st and 2nd), record at EMI (3rd, 4th, 6th, 8th–11th), tape videos to accompany five songs (23rd)	*The Sound of Music* soundtrack LP reaches no. 1 in 35th week on album charts; New York Blackout: 30 million left without power for half day in US Northeast and Ontario (9th)	
Dec-65	Beatles tour UK (3rd–12th); "We Can Work It Out" / "Day Tripper" released (3rd; no. 1 in Dec.); *Rubber Soul* released (3rd)	*Rubber Soul* released (3rd; no. 1 in Jan. '66); "We Can Work It Out" / "Day Tripper" released (6th; no. 1 in Jan. '66)	
Jan-66	Beatles dub new parts onto Shea film (5th)	San Francisco Trips Festival (21st–23rd): Ken Kesey's first Acid Test	Indira Gandhi PM India (19th)
Feb-66		"Nowhere Man" / "What Goes On" released (21st; no. 3 in Mar.)	
Mar-66	John Lennon says "Beatles more popular than Jesus" in press interview; Beatles shoot "Butcher" photos with Robert Whitaker (25th)		
Apr-66	Beatles record at EMI (on 33 dates from 6th through 21 June)	US now has 250,000 troops in Vietnam	
May-66	Beatles perform for *NME* Poll Winners' concert, Wembley (1st); continued recording at EMI (5th–26th); film promo clips for new single (19th–20th); Lennon-Dylan car ride (27th)	"Paperback Writer" / "Rain" released (30th; no. 1 in June); Beach Boys' *Pet Sounds* released; Bob Dylan's *Blonde on Blonde* released; 8,000 march to the Pentagon, outside Washington, DC, to protest the Vietnam War (15th)	
Jun-66	Continued recording at EMI (1st–21st); "Paperback Writer" / "Rain" released (10th; no. 1 in June); live television performance on *Top of the Pops* (16th)	*"Yesterday" ... and Today* released (15th; no. 1 in July); Frank Zappa's *Freak Out!* released; National Organization for Women founded; Division Street race riots in Chicago (12th–19th)	Beatles perform in West Germany, Tokyo, and Manila (24th through July 4th)

MONTH-YEAR	UK EVENTS	US EVENTS	WORLD EVENTS
Jul-66	Violence mars protest against Vietnam War in London, 31 arrests; England defeats Germany 4-2 to win FIFA World Cup (30th)	Beach Boys' LP *Pet Sounds* no. 10; Bob Dylan severely injured in motorcycle accident in Woodstock, NY (26th); Hough race riots in Cleveland, Ohio (18th–23rd); race riots in Chicago (23rd)	
Aug-66	*Revolver* released (5th), "Yellow Submarine" / "Eleanor Rigby" released (5th; no. 1 in Aug.)	*Revolver* released (8th; no. 1 in Sep.); "Yellow Submarine" / "Eleanor Rigby" released (8th; no. 2 in Sep.); Beatles tour US (12th–29th), opening with press conference in Chicago (11th); Beatles' final concert for paying crowd in San Francisco (29th); Watts race riots in Los Angeles (11th–17th); Charles Whitman murder spree, Austin (1st)	
Sep-66			John Lennon shooting *How I Won the War* in West Germany and Spain (6th–6 Nov.); George Harrison studying sitar in India (14th–22 Oct.)
Oct-66	Johnny Kidd dies (7th)	Black Panther Party founded; LSD criminalized	
Nov-66	John Lennon meets Yoko Ono at Indica Gallery (9th); Beatles record "Strawberry Fields Forever" / "Penny Lane" at EMI (on 17 dates from 24th through 17 Jan. '67); Mary Quant, designer of mini skirt, appointed Order of the British Empire (15th)		
Dec-66	Paul McCartney's "Love in the Open Air" released (23rd); Beatles begin recording for *Sgt. Pepper's Lonely Hearts Club Band* (on 40 dates from 6th through 21 Apr. '67)		500,000 US troops in Vietnam
Jan-67	Beatles continue recording "Penny Lane" at EMI (4th–17th); continue recording for *Sgt. Pepper's Lonely Hearts Club Band* at EMI (19th through 21 Apr.); location shooting of promo films for new single (30th through 7 Feb.); Paul McCartney's *The Family Way* soundtrack released (6th)	Paul McCartney's *The Family Way* soundtrack released (12th); Human Be-In in San Francisco (14th)	

MONTH-YEAR	UK EVENTS	US EVENTS	WORLD EVENTS
Feb-67	Beatles continue recording for *Sgt. Pepper's Lonely Hearts Club Band* at EMI and Regent Sound; Beatles recording for *Yellow Submarine* soundtrack at EMI (13th–June 2nd); "Strawberry Fields Forever" / "Penny Lane" released (17th; no. 2 in Feb.)	"Penny Lane" / "Strawberry Fields Forever" released (17th; no. 1 in Mar.)	Rolling Stones Mick Jagger and Keith Richards arrested in West Sussex, UK, drug raid (12th)
Mar-67	Beatles continue recording for *Sgt. Pepper's Lonely Hearts Club Band* at EMI		
Apr-67	Beatles continue recording for *Sgt. Pepper's Lonely Hearts Club Band* at EMI (through 21st); record title song for "Magical Mystery Tour" soundtrack at EMI (25th–27th); *The 14-Hour Technicolor Dream* staged (29th)	Martin Luther King, Benjamin Spock, and Harry Belafonte lead up to 400,000 peaceful antiwar protesters to United Nations headquarters in New York (15th); 10,000 protest Vietnam War in San Francisco; Muhammad Ali refuses army induction, is stripped of boxing title	
May-67	Beatles record B-sides and songs for *Yellow Submarine* soundtrack at Olympic, EMI, De Lane Lea (11th, 12th, 17th, 25th, 31st)		
Jun-67	*Sgt. Pepper's Lonely Hearts Club Band* released (1st); Beatles record for A- and B-side, *Yellow Submarine* soundtrack at De Lane Lea, EMI, and Olympic (2nd, 7th–9th, 14th–26th), perform "All You Need Is Love" for *Our World* television special (25th)	*Sgt. Pepper's Lonely Hearts Club Band* released (2nd; no. 1 in July); Monterey Pop Festival (16th–18th); race riots in Tampa, Buffalo; Supreme Court finds prohibition of interracial marriage unconstitutional	Six-Day War between Israel and three neighboring Arab states
Jul-67	"All You Need Is Love" / "Baby You're a Rich Man" released (7th; no. 1 in July); homosexuality decriminalized	"All You Need Is Love" / "Baby You're a Rich Man" released (17th; no. 1 in Aug.); race riots in Newark, NJ, leave 26 dead; 43 dead in race riots in Detroit	
Aug-67	Beatles recording for *Magical Mystery Tour* soundtrack at Chappell (22nd–23rd); Brian Epstein dies (27th); Pink Floyd's *Piper at the Gates of Dawn* released	George Harrison visits Haight-Ashbury (7th); race riots in Washington, DC; Thurgood Marshall confirmed as first African American on US Supreme Court	Pirate radio stations outlawed in UK; Belgian surrealist René Magritte dies (15th)

MONTH-YEAR	UK EVENTS	US EVENTS	WORLD EVENTS
Sep-67	Beatles recording for *Magical Mystery Tour* soundtrack at EMI (5th–8th, 16th, 25th–29th), location shooting for television special (11th through 31 Oct.); BBC Radio inaugurates pop-music format on Radio 1 (30th)		
Oct-67	Beatles record "Hello Goodbye" (2nd and 19th) and more work for *Magical Mystery Tour* at EMI and De Lane Lea (6th, 12th, 25th); location shooting for television special (1st, 29th)	Joan Baez and 38 others arrested in protest of Vietnam War; 76 injured in Univ. of Wisconsin-Madison protest against Dow Chemical (maker of napalm); tens of thousands protest the war in the Pentagon outside of Washington, DC (21st)	Shooting for *Magical Mystery Tour* in Nice (30th–31st)
Nov-67	Beatles record "Hello Goodbye" overdub at EMI (2nd); "Hello Goodbye" / "I Am the Walrus" released (24th; no. 1 in Dec.); shooting for *Magical Mystery Tour* (3rd); shooting promo film for "Hello Goodbye" (10th); record for fan club's Christmas record at EMI (28th); George Harrison recording *Wonderwall* soundtrack (22nd–Jan. 30th '68)	*Magical Mystery Tour* released (27th; no. 1 in Jan. '68); "Hello Goodbye" / "I Am the Walrus" released (27th; no. 1 in Dec.); Carl Stokes elected mayor of Cleveland, first major US city with African American mayor	
Dec-67	Apple boutique opens in London (7th); *Magical Mystery Tour* EP set released (8th); *Magical Mystery Tour* televised (26th)	Jimi Hendrix Experience's *Axis: Bold As Love* released; Yippies call for New Nation	Ringo shooting cameo role for *Candy* in Rome (7th–16th)
Jan-68	George Harrison continues recording *Wonderwall* soundtrack in London (5th and 30th); Harold Wilson endorses the "I'm Backing Britain" campaign	Prominent and revered child psychologist Dr. Benjamin Spock indicted for encouraging draft resistance (5th)	George Harrison recording *Wonderwall* soundtrack and "The Inner Light" in Bombay (9th–13th); North Vietnam begins Tet Offensive (30th)
Feb-68	Beatles record new single, "Across the Universe," and Hey Bulldog" at EMI (3rd–4th, 6th, 8th, 11th)	Three college students killed in civil rights protest in SC; other protests in WI and NC	Beatles retreat in Rishikesh (15th through Apr. 12th)

MONTH-YEAR	UK EVENTS	US EVENTS	WORLD EVENTS
Mar-68	"Lady Madonna" / "The Inner Light" released (15th; no. 1 in Mar.); 91 injured in protest of Vietnam War in London	"Lady Madonna" / "The Inner Light" released (18th; no. 4 in Apr.); students shut down Howard University in protest of Vietnam War and lack of African studies	Student protests in Poland; My Lai Massacre (16th)
Apr-68	Enoch Powell makes "Rivers of Blood" speech	M. L. King, Jr., assassinated in Memphis (4th); *Hair* opens on Broadway; Columbia University shut down by students protesting Vietnam War	Pierre Trudeau becomes prime minister of Canada
May-68	Beatles record "Kinfauns" demos (last wk of May); record the *White Album* at EMI (30th through Oct. 17th); John Lennon and Yoko Ono record *Two Virgins* at Kenwood (19th?)	Beatles announce creation of Apple in New York (11th–15th)	Students spark protest by one million in Paris; Tariq Ali publishes *The Black Dwarf*
Jun-68	Beatles continue recording for the *White Album* at EMI (4th–28th)	Robert F. Kennedy assassinated in Los Angeles (5th)	First free Hyde Park concert (29th), with Pink Floyd and Jethro Tull
Jul-68	Beatles continue recording for the *White Album* at EMI (1st–25th), record "Hey Jude" at Trident (31st–2 Aug.); premiere of *Yellow Submarine* (17th)		
Aug-68	Beatles continue recording "Hey Jude" at Trident (1st–2nd), continue recording for the *White Album* at EMI and Trident (7th–29th); Ringo Starr quits band (22nd); "Hey Jude" / "Revolution" released (30th; no. 1 in Sep.)	"Hey Jude" / "Revolution" released (26th; no. 1 in Sep.); brutal arrests of Vietnam War protesters outside Democratic National Convention in Chicago	Invasion of Czechoslovakia
Sep-68	Ringo Starr rejoins the Beatles (3rd); Beatles continue recording the *White Album* at EMI (5th–26th); shooting of videos for new single (4th)	Miss America pageant protested in Atlantic City as exploitative of women	
Oct-68	Beatles continue recording the *White Album* at Trident, EMI (1st–17th); first appearance by Led Zeppelin; police brutality in Derry, Northern Ireland, protests	Lennon arrested for possession of marijuana (18)	Student protest ends violently in Mexico City; Olympics there see black power salute from African American medalists

MONTH-YEAR	UK EVENTS	US EVENTS	WORLD EVENTS
Nov-68	*The Beatles* (aka the *White Album*) released (22nd); John Lennon and Yoko Ono's *Unfinished Music No. 1: Two Virgins* released (29th)	*The Beatles* (aka the *White Album*) released (25th; no. 1 in Dec.); George Harrison introduced to Moog synthesizer in LA (15th), George Harrison's *Wonderwall* soundtrack released (1st; no. 49 in Mar. '69); John Lennon and Yoko Ono's *Unfinished Music No. 1: Two Virgins* released (11th; no. 124 in Mar. '69); Yoko Ono miscarries (21st); Yale to begin admitting women; Richard Nixon elected president	US begins bombing Laos
Dec-68	John Lennon shooting for *Rolling Stones Rock and Roll Circus* (11th)	Comeback performance of Elvis Presley (3rd)	
Jan-69	Beatles shooting for film (2nd–31st), perform "Rooftop" concert, London (30th); *Yellow Submarine* soundtrack released (17th); Led Zeppelin releases eponymous first album; Rupert Murdoch buys *News of the World*	*Yellow Submarine* soundtrack released (13th; no. 2 in Mar.)	
Feb-69	Beatles record for *Abbey Road* at Trident and EMI (22nd through Aug. 25th); John Lennon, George Harrison, and Ringo Starr hire Allen Klein as manager (3rd); Ringo Starr shooting *The Magic Christian* (3rd through 2 May)		
Mar-69	John Lennon and Yoko Ono perform at Cambridge University (2nd); Paul McCartney marries Linda Eastman in London (12th)		John Lennon marries Yoko Ono in Gibraltar (20th), stage bed-in in Amsterdam (25th–31st)

MONTH-YEAR	UK EVENTS	US EVENTS	WORLD EVENTS
Apr-69	"Get Back" / "Don't Let Me Down" released (11th; no. 1 in Apr.); Beatles record "The Ballad of John and Yoko" / "Old Brown Shoe" at EMI (14th–18th), continue recording for *Abbey Road* at EMI (20th, 26th, 29th), guitar overdub for "Let It Be" (30th); John Lennon and Yoko Ono record *Wedding Album* at EMI (22nd, 27th)	SDS take over Harvard University	
May-69	Beatles continue recording for *Abbey Road* at EMI, Olympic (2nd, 5th); "The Ballad of John and Yoko" / "Old Brown Shoe" released (30th; no. 1 in June); John Lennon and Yoko Ono's *Unfinished Music No. 2: Life with the Lions* released (9th), George Harrison's *Electronic Sounds* released (9th)	"Get Back" / "Don't Let Me Down" released (5th; no. 1 in May); John Lennon and Yoko Ono's *Unfinished Music No. 2: Life with the Lions* released (26th; no. 174 in Aug.); George Harrison's *Electronic Sounds* released (26th; no. 191 in July)	John Lennon and Yoko Ono stage bed-in in Montreal (26th through June 2nd)
Jun-69		"The Ballad of John and Yoko" / "Old Brown Shoe" released (4th; no. 8 in July); Stonewall Riots in New York (28th)	John Lennon records "Give Peace a Chance" in Montreal (1st)
Jul-69	Beatles continue recording for *Abbey Road* at EMI (1st–31st); John Lennon hospitalized in Scotland following car accident (1st–6th); Plastic Ono Band's "Give Peace a Chance" / "Remember Love" released (4th; no. 2 in July); Brian Jones dies (3rd)	Plastic Ono Band's "Give Peace a Chance" / "Remember Love" released (7th; no. 14 in Sep.); *Easy Rider* released (14th); poet and White Panther John Sinclair sentenced to jail for possession of two joints (25th)	First withdrawals of US troops from Vietnam; landing of Apollo 11 astronauts on the moon (20th)
Aug-69	Beatles continue recording for *Abbey Road* at EMI (1st–25th); British troops sent to Northern Ireland	Woodstock Music and Arts Festival, Bethel, NY (15th–18th); Manson murders (9th)	Bob Dylan heads first Isle of Wight festival (29th)
Sep-69	*Abbey Road* released (26th); Plastic Ono Bands records "Cold Turkey" at EMI, Trident (25th–26th, 5 Oct.)		Plastic Ono Band performs at University of Toronto (13th)

MONTH-YEAR	UK EVENTS	US EVENTS	WORLD EVENTS
Oct-69	"Something" / "Come Together" released (31st; no. 4 in Nov.); Plastic Ono Band records "Don't Worry Kyoko" at Lansdowne (3rd); their "Cold Turkey" / "Don't Worry Kyoko (Mummy's Only Looking for a Hand in the Snow)" released (24th; no. 14 in Nov.); Ringo Starr recording *Sentimental Journey* at EMI, Wessex and Trident (27th through Mar. 6th, '70); Paul McCartney interviewed at Scottish home to quash death rumors (24th); *Led Zeppelin II* released (22nd); premiere of "Monty Python's Flying Circus"	*Abbey Road* released (1st; no. 1 in Nov.); "Something" / "Come Together" released (6th; no. 1 in Nov.); Plastic Ono Band's "Cold Turkey" / "Don't Worry Kyoko (Mummy's Only Looking for a Hand in the Snow)" released (20th; no. 30 in Jan. '70); John Lennon and Yoko Ono's *Wedding Album* released (20th); ARPANET established	
Nov-69	John Lennon returns his MBE in protest; John Lennon and Yoko Ono's *Wedding Album* released (7th)	Native Americans take Alcatraz Island; Moratorium Day: 250,000 protest Vietnam War in Washington, DC (15th)	
Dec-69	McCartney records eponymous first solo LP (through Mar. 23rd, '70); Plastic Ono Band's *Live Peace in Toronto—1969* released (12th); George Harrison performs at Albert Hall and other UK dates with Delaney and Bonnie (2nd–7th); John Lennon and George Harrison perform UNICEF concert in London (15th)	Plastic Ono Band's *Live Peace in Toronto—1969* released (12th; no. 10 in Feb. '70); Chicago police murder Black Panther Party members in their sleep; Altamont Free Concert (6th)	George Harrison tours Scandinavia with Delaney and Bonnie (10th–14th)
Jan-70	Beatles record "I Me Mine" and dubs for "Let It Be" at EMI (3rd–4th); John Lennon records "Instant Karma" at EMI (27th); Ringo Starr continues recordings for *Sentimental Journey* at EMI (14th)		

MONTH-YEAR	UK EVENTS	US EVENTS	WORLD EVENTS
Feb-70	Plastic Ono Band's "Instant Karma" / "Who Has Seen the Wind" released (6th; no. 5 in Feb.); Ringo Starr continues recording for *Sentimental Journey* at EMI and De Lane Lea (2nd–19th, 25th), records "It Don't Come Easy" / "Early 1970" at EMI and Trident (18th–19th, Mar. and Oct.); John Lennon shoots "Instant Karma" videos (11th); Paul McCartney recording eponymous solo LP at Morgan and EMI	Plastic Ono Band's "Instant Karma" / "Who Has Seen the Wind" released (20th; no. 3 in Mar.)	
Mar-70	"Let It Be" / "You Know My Name (Look Up the Number" released (6th; no. 2 in Mar.); Ringo Starr's *Sentimental Journey* released (27th)	"Let It Be" / "You Know My Name (Look Up the Number" released (11th; no. 1 in Apr.)	
Apr-70	Ringo Starr completes recording of *Sentimental Journey* at Morgan (5th–6th), continues work on "It Don't Come Easy" at Trident (8th, 11th); Paul McCartney announces breakup of the Beatles (10th); *McCartney* released (17th)	*McCartney* released (20th; no. 1 in May); Ringo Starr's *Sentimental Journey* released (24th; no. 22 in June)	
May-70	*Let It Be* released (8th)	"The Long and Winding Road" / "For You Blue" released (11th; no. 1 in June); *Let It Be* released (18th; no. 1 in June); premiere of *Let It Be* (12th)	
Sep-70	Ringo Starr's *Beaucoups of Blues* released (25th)	Ringo Starr's *Beaucoups of Blues* released (28th; no. 65 in Nov.)	
Nov-70	George Harrison's *All Things Must Pass* released (27th)	George Harrison's *All Things Must Pass* released (30th; no. 1 in Jan. '71)	
Dec-70	John Lennon's *Plastic Ono Band* released (11th)	John Lennon's *Plastic Ono Band* released (11th; no. 6 in Jan. '71)	
Dec-80		John Lennon murdered in New York by delusional fan (8th)	

MONTH-YEAR	UK EVENTS	US EVENTS	WORLD EVENTS
Jan-94	Yoko Ono gives three John Lennon demos to Paul McCartney for dubbing for *Anthology* project		
Feb-94	Paul McCartney, George Harrison, and Ringo Starr dub onto "Free As a Bird" (into Mar.)		
Feb-95	Paul McCartney, George Harrison, and Ringo Starr dub onto "Real Love"		
Nov-95	"Anthology" broadcast (19th, 22nd, and 23rd)	"Anthology" broadcast (19th, 22nd, and 23rd)	
Dec-95	"Free As a Bird" released (4th) no. 2	"Free As a Bird" released (12th) no. 6	
Mar-96	"Real Love" released (5th) no. 4	"Real Love" released (5th) no. 11	
Dec-99	George Harrison suffers severe knifing at home requiring hospitalization (29th)		
Nov-01		George Harrison dies of lung cancer in Los Angeles (29th)	
Mar-16		George Martin dies (8th)	

SELECTED BIBLIOGRAPHY

PRINT SOURCES

Aldridge, Alan, ed. 1969. *The Beatles Illustrated Lyrics*. New York: Delacorte.

Ali, Tariq. 2005. *Street Fighting Years: An Autobiography of the Sixties*. New York: Verso.

Anjoorian, Jason. 1994. *The Beatles Japanese Record Guide*. Shrewsbury, MA: Jason.

Appy, Christian G. 2015. *American Reckoning: The Vietnam War and Our National Identity*. New York: Viking.

Babiuk, Andy. 2015. *Beatles Gear: All the Fab Four's Instruments, From Stage to Studio; The Ultimate Edition*. San Francisco: Backbeat.

Badman, Keith. 1999. *The Beatles: After the Break-Up, 1970–2000; A Day-By-Day Diary*. New York: Omnibus.

Badman, Keith. 2000. *The Beatles: Off the Record*. New York: Omnibus.

Baird, Julia. 1988. *John Lennon, My Brother*. With Geoffrey Giuliano. New York: Henry Holt.

Baird, Julia. 1989. *John Lennon My Brother: Memories of Growing Up Together*. With Geoffrey Giuliano. London: Jove.

Baird, Julia. 2007. *Imagine This: Growing Up with My Brother John Lennon*. London: Hodder & Stoughton.

Baker, Nicholson. 2008. *Human Smoke: The Beginnings of World War II, the End of Civilization*. New York: Simon & Schuster.

Bangs, Lester. 1988. *Psychotic Reactions and Carburetor Dung*. Greil Marcus, ed. New York: Alfred A. Knopf.

Barbard, Stephen. 1989. *On the Radio: Music Radio in Britain*. Milron Keynes, UK: Open University Press.

Barrow, Tony. 2005. *John, Paul, George, Ringo and Me: The Real Beatles Story*. New York: Thunder's Mouth.

Beatles. 1993. *The Beatles Complete Scores*. Chicago: Hal Leonard.

Beatles. 2000. *The Beatles Anthology*. San Francisco: Chronicle Books.

Belchem, John, ed. 2006. *Liverpool 800: Culture, Character and History*. Liverpool: Liverpool University Press.

Belchem, John. 2007. *Irish, Catholic and Scouse: The History of the Liverpool-Irish, 1800–1939*. Liverpool: Liverpool University Press.

Bennett, Andy, and Jon Stratton, eds. 2010. *Britpop and the English Music Tradition*. London: Ashgate.

Benson, Harry. 2000. *Harry Benson: Fifty Years in Pictures*. New York: Abrams.

Best, Pete, and Patrick Doncaster. 1985. *Beatle! The Pete Best Story*. London: Plexus.

Best, Roag. 2003. *The Beatles: The True Beginnings*. With Pete Best and Rory Best. New York: St. Martin's.

Blaney, John. 2005. *Listen to This Book*. Guildford: Paper Jukebox.

Bowman, Rob. 1997. *Soulsville, U.S.A.: The Story of Stax Records*. New York: Schirmer.

Boyd, Pattie. 2007. *Wonderful Tonight: George Harrison, Eric Clapton and Me*. With Penny Junor. New York: Harmony.

Bracewell, Michael. 2008. *Re-make/Re-model: Becoming Roxy Music*. New York: Da Capo.

Brackett, David. 1995. *Interpreting Popular Music*. Berkeley: University of California Press.

Bradley, Dick. 1992. *Understanding Rock 'n' Roll: Popular Music in Britain, 1955–1964*. Buckingham, UK: Open University Press.

Bramwell, Tony, and Rosemary Kingsland. 2005. *Magical Mystery Tours: My Life with the Beatles*. New York: St. Martin's.

Branch, Taylor. 1998. *Parting the Waters: America in the King Years, 1954–63*. New York: Simon & Schuster.

Branch, Taylor. 1998. *Pillar of Fire: America in the King Years, 1963–65*. New York: Simon & Schuster.

Branch, Taylor. 2006. *At Canaan's Edge: America in the King Years, 1965–68*. New York: Simon & Schuster.

Braun, Michael. 1964. *Love Me Do: The Beatles' Progress*. London: Penguin.

Brocken, Michael. 2010. *Other Voices: Hidden Histories of Liverpool's Popular Music Scenes, 1930s–1970s*. Surrey: Ashgate.

Bromell, Nick. 2000. *Tomorrow Never Knows: Rock and Psychedelics in the 1960s*. Chicago: University of Chicago Press.

Brown, Peter, and Steven Gaines, 1983. *The Love You Make—An Insider's Story of the Beatles*. New York: McGraw-Hill.

Cannon, Lou. 1991. *President Reagan: The Role of a Lifetime*. New York: Simon & Schuster.

Carlin, Peter. 2009. *Paul McCartney: A Life*. New York: Touchstone.

Carr, Roy, and Tony Tyler. 1995. *The Beatles: An Illustrated Record*. New York: Harmony.

Castleman, Harry, and Walter Podrazik. 1976. *All Together Now: The First Complete Beatles Discography, 1961–1975*. Ann Arbor, MI: Pierian Press.

Christgau, Robert. 2000. *Any Old Way You Choose It: Rock and Other Music, 1967–1973*. Rev. ed. New York: Cooper Square.

Clapton, Eric. 2007. *Clapton: The Autobiography*. New York: Broadway Books.

Clayson, Alan. 1996. *Beat Merchants: The Origins, History, Impact and Rock Legacy of the 1960s British Pop Groups*. London: Blandford.

Clayson, Alan. 1998. *Hamburg: The Cradle of British Rock*. London: Sanctuary.

Clayson, Alan. 2003. *John Lennon*. London: Sanctuary.

Clayson, Alan. 2004. *Woman: the Incredible Life of Yoko Ono*. With Barb Jungr and Robb Johnson. New Malden, UK: Chrome Dreams.

Clayson, Alan, and Spencer Leigh. 2003. *The Walrus Was Ringo*. New Malden, UK: Chrome Dreams.

Clayson, Alan, and Pauline Sutcliffe. 1994. *Backbeat: Stuart Sutcliffe; The Lost Beatle*. Philadelphia: Trans-Atlantic.

Coleman, Ray. 1986. *John Lennon*. New York: McGraw-Hill.

Coleman, Ray. 1989. *The Man Who Made the Beatles: An Intimate Biography of Brian Epstein*. New York: McGraw-Hill.

Cording, Robert, ed.. 1998. *In My Life: Encounters with the Beatles*. With Shelli Jankowski-Smith and E. J. Miller Laino. New York: Fromm International.

Cott, Jonathan. 1968. Interview with John Lennon. *Rolling Stone*, November 23.

Cotterill, Dave, and Ian Lysaght, dirs. 2007. *Liverpool's Cunard Yanks*. DVD: Souled Out Films.

Coupe, Laurence. 2007. *Beat Sound, Beat Vision: The Beat Spirit in Popular Song*. Manchester: Manchester University Press.

Covach, John. 1990. "The Rutles and the Use of Specific Models in Musical Satire." *Indiana Theory Review* 11:199–44.

Covach, John, and Andy Flory. 2015. *What's That Sound?: An Introduction to Rock and Its History*. 4th ed. New York: W. W. Norton.

Cross, Charles. 2006. *A Room Full of Mirrors*. New York: Hyperion.

Davies, Hunter. 1968. *The Beatles: The Authorized Biography*. New York: McGraw-Hill.

Davies, Hunter. 2001. *The Quarrymen*. London: Omnibus.

Davies, Huner, ed. 2012. *The John Lennon Letters*. New York: Little, Brown.

Davies, Hunter. 2014. *The Beatles Lyrics*. New York: Little, Brown.

DeGroot, Gerard D. 2008. *The Sixties Unplugged: A Kaleidoscopic History of a Disorderly Decade*. Cambridge, MA: Harvard University Press.

Dickstein, Morris. 1977. *Gates of Eden: American Culture in the Sixties*. New York: Basic Books.

DiLello, Richard. (1972) 2005. *The Longest Cocktail Party: An Insider's Diary of the Beatles, Their Million-Dollar Apple Empire, and Its Wild Rise and Fall*. Edinburgh: Canongate.

Doggett, Peter. 1998. *Abbey Road / Let It Be: The Beatles*. Classic Rock Albums Series. New York: Schirmer.

Doggett, Peter. 2005. *The Art and Music of John Lennon*. New York: Wise.

Doggett, Peter. 2008. *There's a Riot Goin' On: Revolution in the Sixties*. London: Canongate.

Doggett, Peter. 2010. *You Never Give Me Your Money: The Battle for the Soul of the Beatles*. New York: Harperstudio.

Du Noyer, Paul. 2002. *Liverpool: Wondrous Place; Music from Cavern to Cream*. London: Virgin.

Dyer, Geoff. 2007. *The Ongoing Moment*. New York: Vintage. 2007.

Edwards, Henry, and May Pang. 1983. *Loving John*. New York: Warner.

Elliott, Anthony. 1999. *The Mourning of John Lennon*. Berkeley: University of California Press.

Emerick, Geoff, and Howard Massey. 2007. *Here, There and Everywhere: My Life Recording the Music of the Beatles*. New York: Gotham.

Emerson, Ken. 2006. *Always Magic in the Air: The Bomp and Brilliance of the Brill Building Era*. Boston: Penguin.

Epstein, Brian. 1964. *A Cellarful Of Noise*. New York: Doubleday.

Everett, Walter. 1986. "Fantastic Remembrance in John Lennon's 'Strawberry Fields Forever' and 'Julia.'" *Musical Quarterly* 72, no. 3: 360–393.

Everett, Walter. 1987. "Text-Painting in the Foreground and Middleground of Paul McCartney's Beatle Song, 'She's Leaving Home.'" *In Theory Only* 9, no. 7: 5–21.

Everett, Walter. 1992. "Voice Leading and Harmony as Expressive Devices in the Early Music of the Beatles: 'She Loves You.'" *College Music Symposium* 32:19–37.

Everett, Walter. 1995. "The Beatles as Composers: The Genesis of *Abbey Road*, Side Two." In *Concert Music, Rock, and Jazz since 1945*, ed. Elizabeth West Marvin and Richard Hermann, 172–228. Rochester, NY: University of Rochester.

Everett, Walter. 1999. *The Beatles as Musicians: Revolver through the Anthology*. New York: Oxford University Press.

Everett, Walter. 2001. *The Beatles As Musicians: The Quarry Men through* Rubber Soul. New York: Oxford University Press.

Everett, Walter. 2006. "Painting Their Room in a Colorful Way." In *Reading the Beatles,* ed. K. Womack and T. F. Davis, 71–94. Albany: State University of New York Press.

Everett, Walter. 2008. *The Foundations of Rock: From "Blue Suede Shoes" to "Suite: Judy Blue Eyes."* New York: Oxford University Press.

Everett, Walter. 2009. "Any Time at All: The Beatles' Free Phrase Rhythms." In *The Cambridge Companion to the Beatles,* ed. K. Womack, 183–199. Cambridge: Cambridge University Press.

Everett, Walter. 2014. "High Art Born of Deep Crisis: 'Strawberry Fields Forever.' " In *Beatles Special Edition,* ed. Ben Nussbaum. Irvine, CA: i–5 Publishing.

Everett, Walter. 2019. "Children of Nature: Origins of the Beatles' Tabula Rasa." In *The Beatles through a Glass Onion: Reconsidering the White Album,* ed. Mark Osteen. Ann Arbor: University of Michigan Press.

Faithfull, Marianne. 2000. *Faithfull: An Autobiography.* New York: Cooper Square.

Farrow, Mia. 1997. *What Falls Away.* New York: Nan A. Talese.

Fawcett, Anthony. 1976. *John Lennon One Day at a Time.* New York: Grove.

Fields, Danny. 2000. *Linda McCartney.* Boston: Little, Brown.

Firminger, John, and Spencer Leigh. 1996. *Halfway to Paradise: British Pop Music, 1955–1962.* Liverpool: Finbarr International.

Fletcher, Tony. 1999. *Moon: The Life and Death of a Rock Legend.* New York: Avon.

Flippo, Chet. 1988. *Yesterday: The Unauthorized Biography of Paul McCartney.* New York: Doubleday/Dell.

Frame, Pete. 1997. *The Beatles and Some Other Guys: Rock Family Trees of the Early 1960s.* London: Omnibus.

Freeman, Robert. 1983. *Yesterday: The Beatles, 1963–1965.* New York: Holt Rinehart & Winston.

Frith, Simon, and Howard Horne. 1987. *Art into Pop.* London: Methuen.

Frith, Simon, et al. 2013. *The History of Live Music in Britain,* vol. 1, *1950–1967: From Dance Hall to the 100 Club.* London: Ashgate.

Frontani, Michael R. 2007. *The Beatles: Image and the Media.* Jackson: University Press of Mississippi.

Garofalo, Steve, and Reebee Chapple. 1977. *Rock 'n' Roll Is Here to Pay: The History and Politics of the Music Industry.* Chicago: Nelson Hall.

Garry, Len. 1997. John, *Paul and Me: Before the Beatles: The True Story of the Very Early Days.* Toronto: CG.

Geller, Debbie. 2000. *In My Life: The Brian Epstein Story.* New York: St. Martin's.

Gentle, Johnny, and Ian Forsyth. 1998. *Johnny Gentle and the Beatles: First Ever Tour, Scotland, 1960.* Runcom, UK: Merseyrock.

Gilmore, Mikal. 2008. *Stories Done: Writings on the 1960s and Its Discontents.* New York City: Free Press.

Gitlin, Todd. 1987. *The Sixties: Years of Hope, Days of Rage.* New York: Bantam.

Gladwell, Malcolm. 2008. *Outliers: The Story of Success.* New York: Little, Brown.

Goldman, Albert. 1988. *The Lives of John Lennon.* New York: Morrow.

Goldrosen, John, and John Beecher. 1996. *Remembering Buddy: The Definitive Biography of Buddy Holly.* New York: Da Capo.

Gottfridsson, Hans Olof. 1997. *The Beatles from Cavern to Star-Club: The Illustrated Chronicle, Discography and Price Guide, 1957–1962.* Stockholm: Premium Publishing.

Gould, Jonathan. 2007. *Can't Buy Me Love: The Beatles in the Sixties.* New York: Harmony.

Gracyzk, Theodore. 1996. *Rhythm and Noise: An Aesthetics of Rock.* Durham, NC: Duke University Press.

Green, John. 1983. *Dakota Days: The True Story of John Lennon's Final Days.* New York: St. Martin's.

Green, Jonathon. 1988. *Days in the Life: Voices from the English Underground, 1961–1971.* London: Minerva.

Grossman, Henry. 2008. *Kaleidoscope Eyes*. Houston: Curvebender.

Gunderson, Chuck. 2014. *Some Fun Tonight! The Backstage Story of How the Beatles Rocked America: The Historic Tours of 1964–1966*. San Diego: self-published.

Guralnick, Peter. 1986. *Sweet Soul Music: Rhythm and Blues and the Southern Dream of Freedom*. New York: Harper & Row.

Guralnick, Peter. 1994. *Last Train to Memphis: The Rise of Elvis Presley*. New York: Little, Brown.

Guralnick, Peter. 2000. *Careless Love*. New York: Little, Brown.

Halberstam, David, 1994. *The Fifties*. New York: Ballantine.

Harris, David. 1982. *Dreams Die Hard: Three Men's Journey through the '60s*. New York: St. Martin's.

Harrison, George. 1980. *I Me Mine*. New York: Simon & Schuster.

Harrison, Olivia. 2011, *George Harrison: Living in the Material World*. New York: Abrams.

Harrisson, Tom. 1975. *Living through the Blitz*. New York: Harpercollins.

Harry, Bill. 1977. *Mersey Beat: The Beginnings of the Beatles*. London: Quick Fox.

Harry, Billy. 2001. *The John Lennon Encyclopedia*. London: Virgin.

Haskell, Barbara, and John G. Hanhardt. 1991. *Yoko Ono: Arias and Objects*. Salt Lake City: Peregrine Smith.

Hayden, Tom. 2005. *The Port Huron Statement: The Visionary Call of the 1960s Revolution*. New York: Perseus.

Hayes, Harold. 1969. *Smiling through the Apocalypse: Esquire's History of the Sixties*. New York: McCall.

Hemmingsen, Piers A. 2003. *The Beatles Canadian Discography, 1962–1970*. [Toronto]: Beatlology.

Henke, James. 2000. *Lennon: His Life and Work*. Cleveland: Rock and Roll Hall of Fame and Museum.

Henke, James. 2003. *Lennon Legend: An Illustrated Life of John Lennon*. San Francisco: Chronicle Books.

Hennessy, Peter. 2006. *Having It So Good: Britain in the Fifties*. London: Allen Lane.

Heylin, Clinton. 2005. *All Yesterdays' Parties: The Velvet Underground in Print, 1966–1971*. New York: Da Capo.

Hieronimus, Robert R. 2002. *Inside the Yellow Submarine: The Making of the Beatles' Animated Classic*. Iola, WI: Krause.

Hoberman, J. 2003. *The Dream Life: Movies, Media, and the Mythology of the Sixties*. New York: New Press.

Hoffman, Dezo. 1984. *The Beatles Conquer America: The Photographic Record of Their First Tour*. New York: Avon.

Holm-Hudson, Kevin. 2002. *Progressive Rock Reconsidered*. New York: Routledge.

Hopkins, Jerry. 1986. *Yoko Ono*. New York: Macmillan.

Howlett, Kevin. 2013. *The Beatles: The BBC Archives, 1962–1970*. New York: Harper Design.

Hyde, Francis E. 1971. *Liverpool and the Mersey: An Economic History of a Port, 1700–1970*. Newton Abbot, UK: David & Charles.

Ingham, Chris. 2009. *The Rough Guide to the Beatles*. London: Rough Guides.

Jorgensen, Ernst. 1998. *Elvis Presley, A Life in Music: The Complete Recording Sessions*. New York: St. Martin's.

Kane, Larry. 2003. *Ticket to Ride: Inside The Beatles' 1964 and 1965 Tours that Changed the World*. Philadelphia: Running Press.

Keeler, Christine. 2002. *The Truth at Last*. New York: Picador.

Kehew, Brian, and Kevin Ryan. 2006. *Recording the Beatles: The Studio Equipment and Techniques Used to Create Their Classic Albums*. Houston: Curvebender.

Kessler, Jude Southerland. 2013. *She Loves You* John Lennon Series 3. Monroe, LA: On the Rock.

Kirchherr, Astrid, and Max Scheller. 2007. *Yesterday: The Beatles Once Upon a Time*. New York: Vendome.

Kozinn, Allan. 1995. *The Beatles*. 20th-Century Composers. London: Phaidon.

Kozinn, Allan. 2014. *Got That Something: How the Beatles' "I Want to Hold Your Hand" Changed Everything*. Amazon Digital Services.

Laing, Dave. 1972. *Buddy Holly.* New York: Collier.

Lapham, Lewis H. 2005. *With the Beatles.* Hoboken, UK: Melville House.

Lawrence, Alistair. 2012. *Abbey Road Studios: The Best Studio in the World.* London: Bloomsbury.

Leach, Sam. 1992. *Follow the Merseybeat Road.* Liverpool: Eden.

Leach, Sam. 1999. *The Birth of the Beatles.* Gwynedd, UK: Pharaoh.

Leaf, David, dir. 2006. *The U.S. vs. John Lennon.* Lions Gate. DVD.

Leary, Timothy, Ralph Metzner, and Richard Alpert. (1964) 1995. *The Psychedelic Experience: A Manual Based on the Tibetan Book of the Dead.* New York: Citadel.

Leigh, Spencer. 2002. *The Best of Fellas: The Story of Bob Wooler, Liverpool's First DJ, the Man Who Introduced the Beatles.* Liverpool: Drivegreen.

Leigh, Spencer. 2011. *The Beatles in Hamburg: The Stories, the Scene and How It All Began.* Chicago: Chicago Review Press.

Leigh, Spencer. 2012. *The Beatles in Liverpool: The Stories, the Scene and the Path to Stardom.* Chicago: Chicago Review Press.

Lemann, Nicholas. 1991. *The Promised Land: The Great Migration and How It Changed America.* New York: Alfred A. Knopf.

Lennon, Cynthia. 1980. *A Twist of Lennon.* New York: Avon.

Lennon, Cynthia. 2005. *John.* New York: Random House.

Lennon, John. 1981a. *The Last Lennon Tapes: John Lennon and Yoko Ono in Conversation with Andy Peebles, 6 December 1980.* London: British Broadcasting Corporation.

Lennon, John. 1981b. *The Writings of John Lennon: In His Own Write / A Spaniard in the Works.* New York: Simon & Schuster.

Lennon, John. 1992. *Ai: Japan Through John Lennon's Eyes; A Personal Sketchbook.* Redwood, CA: Cadence.

Lennon, John, Yoko Ono, and David Sheff. 1981. *The Playboy Interviews with John Lennon and Yoko Ono.* New York: Putnam.

Lennon, Pauline. 1990. *Daddy, Come Home: The True Story of John Lennon and His Father.* London: Angus & Robertson.

Lewisohn, Mark. 1986. *The Beatles Live!* New York: Henry Holt.

Lewisohn, Mark. 1988. *The Beatles: Recording Sessions; The Official Abbey Road Studio Session Notes, 1962–1970.* London: Harmony.

Lewisohn, Mark. 1990. *The Beatles Day By Day: A Chronology, 1962–1989.* New York: Harmony.

Lewisohn, Mark. 1992. *The Complete Beatles Chronicle.* New York: Harmony.

Lewisohn, Mark. 2013. *Tune In: All These Years,* vol. 1. New York: Crown Archetype.

Liverpool Post and Echo Ltd. 1983. *Bombers over Merseyside: The Authoritative Record of the Blitz, 1940–1941.* Liverpool: Scouse.

MacDonald, Ian. 1994. *Revolution in the Head: The Beatles' Records and the Sixties.* New York: Henry Holt.

Madinger, Chip, and Mark Easter. 2000. *Eight Arms to Hold You: The Solo Beatles Compendium.* Chesterfield, MO: 44.1.

Mailer, Norman. 1968. *The Armies of the Night: The History as Novel, the Novel as History.* New York: New American Library.

Manchester, William. 1988. *Last of the Lions: William Spencer Churchill Alone, 1932–1940.* Boston: Little, Brown.

Mansfield, Ken. 2007. *The White Book: The Beatles, the Bands, the Biz; An Insider's Look at an Era.* Nashville: Thomas Nelson.

Marqusee, Mike. 1999. *Redemption Song: Muhammed Ali and the Spirit of the Sixties.* New York: Verso.

Marqusee, Mike. 2005. *Wicked Messenger: Bob Dylan and the 1960s*. New York: Seven Stories.

Marsh, Dave. 2007. *The Beatles' Second Album*. Rock of Ages. Emmaus, PA: Rodale.

Martin, George. 1979. *All You Need Is Ears*. With Jeremy Hornsby. New York: St. Martin's.

Martin, George, exec. prod. 1992. *The Making of Sgt. Pepper*. Aired June 14, 1992, on ITV and September 27, 1992, on the Disney Channel.

Martin, George, and William Pearson. 1994. *The Summer of Love: The Making of Sgt. Pepper*. London: Macmillan.

Matteo, Steve. 2004. *Let It Be*. New York: Continuum.

McCabe, Peter, and Robert D. Schonfeld. 1972. *Apple to the Core: The Unmaking of the Beatles*. New York: Pocket Books.

McCartney, Michael. 1981. *The Macs: Mike McCartney's Family Album*. New York: Delilah Communications.

McCartney, Paul. 1989. *The McCartney World Tour*. (98-page booklet)

McCullin, Don. 2010. *A Day in the Life of the Beatles*. New York: Rizzoli.

McDermott, John. 2009. *Ultimate Hendrix: An Illustrated Encyclopedia of Live Concerts and Sessions*. New York: BackBeat.

McKinney, Devin. 2003. *Magic Circles: The Beatles in Dream and History*. Cambridge, MA: Harvard University Press.

McLuhan, Marshall. 2001. *Understanding Media: The Extensions of Man*. New York: Routledge.

McNab, Ken. 2012. *The Beatles in Scotland*. Edinburgh: Polygon.

Mellers, Wilfrid. 1973. *Twilight of the Gods: The Music of the Beatles*. New York: Schirmer.

Melly, George. 2013. *Revolt into Style: The Pop Arts in Britain*. London: Faber & Faber.

Meltzer, Richard. 1988. *The Aesthetics of Rock*. New York: Da Capo.

Miles, Barry. 1997. *Paul McCartney: Many Years from Now*. New York: Henry Holt.

Miles, Barry. 2001. *The Beatles Diary*, vol. 1, *The Beatles Years*. London: Omnibus.

Millard, André. 2012. *Beatlemania: Technology, Business, and Teen Culture in Cold War America*. Baltimore: Johns Hopkins University Press.

Miller, Jim, ed. 1976. *The Rolling Stone Illustrated History of Rock and Roll*. New York: Rolling Stone Press.

Moltmaker, Azing, and Samuel Coomans. 2003. *Beatles Singles and Sleeves from Europe: Illustrated Discography*, vol. 1, *1961–1971*. Alkmaar, Netherlands: SB4.

Moltmaker, Azing, and Samuel Coomans. 2004. *Beatles Singles and Sleeves from Around the World: Illustrated Discography*, vol. 2, *1962–1970*. Alkmaar, Netherlands: SB4.

Moltmaker, Azing, and Samuel Coomans. 2005. *The Beatles EP's from Europe: Illustrated Discography*, vol. 3, *1962–1970*. Alkmaar, Netherlands: SB4.

Moltmaker, Azing, and Samuel Coomans. 2008. *Beatles EP's and Sleeves from Around the World: Illustrated Discography*, vol. 4, *1961–1971*. Alkmaa, Netherlands: SB4.

Montieth, Sharon. 2008. *American Culture in the 1960s*. Edinburgh: Edinburgh University Press.

Moore, Allan, ed. 2002. *The Cambridge Companion to Blues and Gospel Music*. Cambridge: Cambridge University Press.

Moore, Allan. 2003. *Rock: The Primary Text*. London: Ashgate.

Mulhern, Tom. 1990. Interview with Paul McCartney. *Guitar Player*, July.

Munroe, Alexandra. 2000. *Yes Yoko Ono*. With Jon Hendricks. New York: Japan Society and Harry N. Abrams.

Napier-Bell, Simon. 1998. *You Don't Have to Say You Love Me*. London: Ebury.

Nobile, D. F. 2011. "Form and Voice Leading in Early Beatles Songs." *Music Theory Online* 17, no 3, http://www.mtosmt.org/issues/mto.11.17.3/mto.11.17.3.nobile.html.

Norman, Philip. 1981. *Shout!: The Beatles in Their Generation*. New York: Simon & Schuster.

Norman, Philip. 2008. *Lennon: The Life*. New York: Ecco.

O'Brien, Geoffrey. 1988. *Dream Time: Chapters from the Sixties*. New York: Counterpoint.

Oldham, Andrew Loog. 2001. *Stoned: A Memoir of London in the 1960s*. New York: St. Martin's.

Oldham, Andrew Loog. 2003. *2Stoned*. London: Vintage Rand.

Ono, Yoko. (1964) 1970. *Grapefruit: Works and Drawings by Yoko Ono*. New York: Simon & Schuster.

Ono, Yoko. 2000. *Lennon: His Life and Work*. Cleveland: Rock and Roll Hall of Fame.

Ono, Yoko. 2006. *Memories of John Lennon*. Brattleboro, VT: Harper.

Osteen, Mark. 2019. *The Beatles through a Glass Onion: Reconsidering the White Album*. Ann Arbor: University of Michigan Press.

Pang, May. 2008. *Instamatic Karma: Photographs of John Lennon*. New York: St. Martin's.

Parker, Alan, and Phil Strongman. 2003. *John Lennon and the FBI Files*. London: Sanctuary.

Pawlowski, Gareth L. 1989, *How They Became the Beatles: A Definitive History of the Early Years, 1960–1964*. New York: E. P. Dutton.

Pedler, Dominic. 2003. *The Songwriting Secrets of the Beatles*. London: Omnibus.

Perone, James. 2009. *Mods, Rockers, and the Music of the British Invasion*. London: Praeger.

Pritchard, David, and Alan Lysaght. 1998. *The Beatles: An Oral History*. Toronto: Stoddard.

Reising, Russell, ed. 2002. *Every Sound There Is: The Beatles'* Revolver *and the Transformation of Rock and Roll*. London: Ashgate.

Ribowsky, Mark. 1989. *He's a Rebel: The Truth about Phil Spector, Rock and Roll's Legendary Mad Man*. New York: Dutton.

Riley, Tim. 1988. *Tell Me Why: The Beatles: Album by Album, Song by Song, the Sixties and After*. New York: Alfred A. Knopf.

Riley, Tim. 1992a. *Hard Rain: A Dylan Commentary*. New York: Alfred A. Knopf.

Riley, Tim. 1992b. *Madonna Illustrated*. New York: Hyperion.

Riley, Tim. 2004. *Fever: How Rock 'n' Roll Transformed Gender in America*. New York: St. Martin's.

Riley, Tim. 2011. *Lennon: The Man, the Myth, the Music; The Definitive Life*. New York: Hyperion.

Robertson, John, 1990. *The Art and Life of John Lennon*. New York: Birch Lane.

Rolling Stone. 1982. *The Ballad of John and Yoko*. Garden City, NY: Doubleday Dolphin.

Ross, Danny. 1996. *A Bluecoat Boy in the 1920's*. Gunnison, CO: Pharaoh.

Rumpf, Wolfgang. 2007. *Music in the Air: AFN, BFBS, Ö3, Radio Luxembourg und die Radiokultur in Deutschland*. Berlin: Lit.

Sale, Kirkpatrick. 1973. *SDS*. New York: Vintage.

Salewicz, Chris. 1986. *McCartney: The Definitive Biography*. New York: St. Martin's.

Salewicz, Chris. 2002. *Mick and Keith*. London: Orion.

Saltzman, Paul. 2000. *The Beatles in Rishikesh*. New York: Penguin.

Sandbrook, Dominic. 2005. *Never Had It So Good: A History of Britain from Suez to the Beatles*. New York: Little, Brown.

Sarris, Andrew, 2006. "Bravo Beatles!" In *Read the Beatles*, ed. June Skinner Sawyers. New York: Penguin.

Sauceda, James. 1983. *The Literary Lennon: A Comedy of Letters*. Ann Arbor, MI: Pierian Press.

Sawyer, June Skinner, ed. 2006. *Read the Beatles: Classic and New Writings on the Beatles, Their Legacy, and Why They Still Matter*. New York: Penguin.

Schaffner, Nicholas. 1978. *The Beatles Forever*. New York: McGraw-Hill.

Schaffner, Nicholas. 1980. *The Boys from Liverpool: John, Paul, George, Ringo*. London: Routledge Kegan & Paul.

Schultheiss, Tom. 1982. *The Beatles—A Day in the Life: The Day-by-Day Diary, 1960–1970*. New York: Perigee.

Schwarz, David. 1997. "Scatting, the Acoustic Mirror, and the Real in the Beatles' "I Want You (She's So Heavy).'" In *Listening Subjects: Music, Psychoanalysis, Culture*, ed. D. Schwarz. Durham, NC: Duke University Press.

Schwartz, Roberta Freund. 2007. *How Britain Got the Blues: The Transmission and Reception of American Blues Style in the United Kingdom*. London: Ashgate.

Scott, Ken. 2012. *Abbey Road NW8 to Ziggy Stardust W1*. Los Angeles: Alfred Music.

Seaman, Frederic. 1991. *The Last Days of John Lennon: A Personal Memoir*. New York: Birch Lane.

Sheff, David. 1981. "Interview: John Lennon and Yoko Ono." *Playboy*, January.

Sheffield, Rob. 2017. *Dreaming the Beatles: The Love Story of One Band and the Whole World*. New York: HarperCollins.

Shelton, Robert. 1986. *No Direction Home: The Life and Music of Bob Dylan*. New York: Ballantine.

Shotton, Pete. 1983. *John Lennon in My Life*. With Nicholas Schaffner. New York: Stein & Day.

Solt, Andrew, dir. 1988. *Imagine (Deluxe Edition)*. Warner Home Video, DVD.

Southall, Brian. 1982. *Abbey Road: The Story of the World's Most Famous Recording Studios*. Cambridge: Patrick Stephens.

Southall, Brian. 2006. *Northern Songs: The True Story of the Beatles Song Publishing Empire*. With Rupert Perry. London: Omnibus.

Southall, Brian. 2010. *Beatles Memorabilia: The Julian Lennon Collection*. With Julian Lennon. London: Goodman.

Spector, Ronnie. 1990. *Be My Baby: How I Survived Mascara, Miniskirts, and Madness, or My Life as a Fabulous Ronette*. With Vince Waldron. New York: Harper Perennial.

Spicer, Mark. 2009. "Strategic Intertextuality in Three of John Lennon's Late Beatles Songs." *Gamut* 2:347–375.

Spicer, Mark, ed. 2011. *Rock Music*. London: Ashgate.

Spicer, Mark, and John Covach, eds. 2010. *Sounding Out Pop*. Ann Arbor: University of Michigan Press.

Spinetti, Victor, and Peter Rankin. 2006. *Up Front . . . His Strictly Confidential Autobiography*. London: Anova.

Spitz, Bob. 2005. *The Beatles: A Biography*. New York: Little, Brown.

Spizer, Bruce. 1998. *Beatles Records on Vee-Jay*. New Orleans: 498 Productions.

Spizer, Bruce, 2000a. *The Beatles' Story on Capitol Records, Part One: Beatlemania and the Singles*. New Orleans: 498 Productions.

Spizer, Bruce, 2000b. *The Beatles Story on Capitol Records, Part Two: The Albums*. New York: 498 Productions.

Spizer, Bruce, 2003a. *The Beatles Are Coming: The Birth of Beatlemania in America*. New Orleans: 498 Productions.

Spizer, Bruce, 2003b. *The Beatles on Apple Records*. New Orleans: 498 Productions.

Spizer, Bruce. 2007. *The Beatles Swan Song*. New Orleans: 498 Productions.

Spizer, Bruce. 2011. *Beatles for Sale on Parlophone Records*. New Orleans: 498 Productions.

Spizer, Bruce. 2018. *The Beatles White Album and the Launch of Apple*. New Orleans: 498 Productions.

Stark, Steve D. 2005. *Meet the Beatles: A Cultural History of the Band That Shook Youth, Gender, and the World*. New York: HarperCollins.

Starr, Ringo. 2004. *Postcards from the Boys*. Britain: Cassell Illustrated.

Stein, Jean, and George Plimpton. 1982. *Edie: An American Biography*. New York: Alfred A. Knopf.

Stokes, Geoffrey. 1980. *The Beatles*. New York: Times Books.

Stolting, Elke. 1975. *Deutsche Schlager und englische Popmusik in Deutschland: Ideologiekritische Untersuchung Zweier Textstile Während der Jahre, 1960–1970*. Bonn: Bouvier.

Sulpy, Doug, and Ray Schweighardt. 1994. *Drugs, Divorce and a Slipping Image*. Princeton Junction, NJ: 910.

Sulpy, Doug, and Ray Schweighardt. 1997. *Get Back: The Unauthorized Chronicle of the Beatles'* Let it Be *Disaster.* New York: St. Martin's.

Sussman, Al. 2013. *Changin' Times: November 22, 1963–March 1, 1964; 101 Days That Shaped a Generation.* Chicago: Parading Press.

Sutcliffe, Pauline. 2001. *Stuart Sutcliffe: The Beatles' Shadow and His Lonely Hearts Club.* With Douglas Thompson. London: Sidgwick & Jackson.

Sutcliffe, Pauline, and Kay Williams. 1996. *Stuart:The Life and Art of Stuart Sutcliffe.* London: Genesis.

Szatmary, David P. 2010. *Rockin' in Time: A Social History of Rock-and-Roll.* 7th ed. Upper Saddle River, NJ: Prentice-Hall.

Tashian, Barry. 1997. *Ticket to Ride: The Extraordinary Diary of The Beatles Last Tour.* New York: Dowling.

Taylor, Alistair. 1988. *Yesterday: The Beatles Remembered.* London: Sidgwick & Jackson Limited.

Taylor, Alistair. 2003. *With the Beatles.* London: John Blake.

Taylor, Derek. 1973. *As Time Goes By.* London: Davis-Poynter.

Taylor, Derek. 1988. *It Was 20 Years Ago Today.* New York: Fireside.

Thompson, Gordon. 2008. *Please Please Me: Sixties British Pop, Inside Out.* New York: Oxford University Press.

Thomson, Elizabeth, and Daivd Gutman. *The Lennon Companion: Twenty-Five Years of Comment.* New York: Da Capo.

Wagner, Naphtali. 2002. "Tonal Family Resemblance in *Revolver.*" In *Every Sound There Is: The Beatles'* Revolver *and the Transformation of Rock and Roll,* ed. R. Reising, 109–120. London: Ashgate.

Wagner, Naphtali. 2003. "'Domestication' of Blue Notes in the Beatles' Songs." *Music Theory Spectrum* 25, no. 2: 353–365.

Wagner, Naphtali. 2004. "Fixing a Hole in the Scale: Suppressed Notes in the Beatles' Songs." *Popular Music* 23, no. 3: 257–269.

Wagner, Naphtali. 2008. "The Beatles' Psycheclassical Synthesis: Psyechedelic Classicism and Classical Psychedelia in *Sgt. Pepper.*" In *Sgt. Pepper and the Beatles,* ed. Olivier Julien. London: Ashgate.

Walker, Christopher, dir. 2004. *John Lennon's Jukebox.* Sydney: ABC.

Warwick, Jacqueline. 2001. "You're Going to Lose That Girl: The Beatles and the Girl Groups." *Beatlestudies* 3:161–167.

Warwick, Jacqueline. 2007. *Girl Groups, Girl Culture: Popular Music and Identity in the 1960s.* New York: Routledge.

Warwick, Neil. 2004. *The Complete Book of the British Charts: Singles and Albums.* With John Kutner and Tony Brown. 3rd. ed. London: Omnibus.

Wenner, Jann. 1971. *Lennon Remembers: The Rolling Stone Interviews.* San Francisco: Straight Arrow.

Whitaker, Bob. 1991. *The Unseen Beatles: Photographs by Bob Whitaker.* San Francisco: Harper Collins.

Wiener, Jon. (1984) 1991. *Come Together: John Lennon in His Time.* Urbana: University of Illinois Press.

Wigg, David. 1976. *The Beatles Tapes from the David Wigg Interviews.* London: Polydor 2683068.

Williams, Allan. 1975. *The Man Who Gave the Beatles Away.* With William Marshall. London: Elm Tree.

Williams, Richard. 1972. *Out of His Head: The Sound of Phil Spector.* New York: E. P. Dutton.

Winn. John C. 2003. *That Magic Feeling: The Beatles' Recorded Legacy,* vol. 2, *1966–1970.* Sharon, VT: Multiplus.

Winn, John C. 2005. *Lifting Latches: The Beatles' Recorded Legacy,* vol. 2, *Inside the Beatles Vaults.* Sharon, VT: Multiplus.

Winn, John C. 2006. *Beatlegmania,* vol. 1. Sharon, VT: Multiplus.

Winn, John C. 2008. *Way Beyond Compare: The Beatles' Recorded Legacy,* vol. 1, *1957–1965.* New York: Three Rivers.

Wolfe, Tom. 1968. *The Electric Kool-Aid Acid Test.* New York: Farrar, Straus & Giroux.

Womack, Kenneth. 2007. *Long and Winding Roads: The Evolving Artistry of the Beatles*. New York: Continuum.

Womack, Kenneth, ed. 2009. *The Cambridge Companion to the Beatles*. Cambridge: Cambridge University Press.

Womack, Kenneth. 2017. *Maximum Volume: The Life of Beatles Producer George Martin; The Early Years, 1926–1966*. Chicago: Chicago Review Press.

Womack, Kenneth. 2018. *Sound Pictures: The Life of Beatles Producer George Martin; The Later Years, 1966–2016*. Chicago: Chicago Review Press.

Womack, Kenneth, and Kathryn B. Cox. 2017. *The Beatles, Sgt. Pepper, and the Summer of Love*. [Lanham, MD]: Lexington.

Womack, Kenneth, and Todd F. Davis, eds. 2006. *Reading the Beatles: Cultural Studies, Literary Criticism, and the Fab Four* Albany: State University of New York Press.

Womack, Kenneth, and Katie Kapurch. 2016. *New Critical Perspectives on the Beatles: Things We Said Today*. London: Palgrave Macmillan.

Wyatt, David. 2014. *When America Turned: Reckoning with 1968*. Amherst: University of Massachusetts Press.

Wynn, Neil A., ed. 2007. *Cross the Water Blues: African American Music in Europe*. Jackson: University Press of Mississippi.

Yogananda, Paramahansa. (1946) 1977. *Autobiography of a Yogi*. Los Angeles: Self-Realization Fellowship.

Zain, C. C. 1936. *Brotherhood of Light: The Sacred Tarot*. Los Angeles: Church of Light.

Zak, Albin. 2001. *The Poetics of Rock*. Berkeley: University of California Press.

INTERNET SOURCES

Alan Pollack "Notes on" Series: http://www.icce.rug.nl/~soundscapes/DATABASES/AWP/awp-notes_on.shtml.

Ashton, David. "The Time Capsule: Stories—Age Concern England." *Home | Care Services for Elderly People: Health, Home, Pension & Insurance Cover for Over 50s | Age Concern England*. Web: http://www.thetimecapsule.org.uk/TimeCapsule/1960s_D55D7B9D222E4780A856A8F10B4CBAD9.htm.

Bagism: http://www.bagism.com/.

Beathoven: Studying the Beatles: http://www.oocities.org/sunsetstrip/arena/9943/beathoven/index.htm.

Beatlefan: http://www.beatlefan.com.

Beatlegs Podcast: http://dinsdalep.podomatic.com/.

Beatle Money: http://www.beatlemoney.com.

Beatle Photo Blog: http://beatlephotoblog.com/.

Beatles Bible: http://www.beatlesbible.com.

Beatles Internet Album: http://www.beatlesagain.com.

Beatles Interviews: http://www.beatlesinterviews.org/.

Beatles Links: http://www.beatlelinks.net/links/.

Beatles (Official): http://www.beatles.com.

Child of Nature's Beatle Photo Blog: http://childofnaturebeatles.blogspot.com/.

Fest For Beatle Fans: http://www.thefest.com/.

Imagine Peace: http://imaginepeace.com/.

George Martin: http://pcug.org.au/~jhenry.

John Lennon: http://www.johnlennon.com/html/news.aspx.

John Lennon FBI Files: http://www.lennonfbifiles.com/.

Lennon Family: http://www.lennon.net/.

Live: Peace In Toronto: http://beatles.ncf.ca/live_peace_in_toronto_p1.html.

Paul McCartney: www.mplcommunications.com/mccartney.

Paul McCartney Central: www.macca-central.com.

Quarry Men: http://www.originalquarrymen.co.uk/.

Rare Beatles: http://www.rarebeatles.com.

Soundscapes: Beabliography: http://www.icce.rug.nl/~soundscapes/BEAB/index.shtml.

Yoko Ono: http://www.yoko-ono.com/.

INDEX

Iron Curtain (*see* cold war, Soviet Union)
irony (in lyrics and/or music), 72–73, 86, 90–91,
    103–4, 116, 121–23, 124, 142, 145, 147,
    171, 213
Isley Brothers, The, 15–16, 46, 62, 238, 240, 249, 251
Israel, 150, 178–79
"It Won't Be Long," 56, 71, 139, 143
"It's All Too Much," 207
"It's Only Love," 101

Jagger, Mick (*see also* Rolling Stones, The), 15, 64,
    149, 152–53, 180
Jan [Berry] and Dean [Torrence], 81–82
Japage 3, 26–27
jazz, 22–23, 34–35, 40, 43, 50, 51, 60–61, 81–82, 89,
    101–2, 126, 173, 199, 226, 232–33
"Jealous Guy," 186–87, 189, 191, 209
Jefferson Airplane, 152, 156
Jodimars, The, 15, 34
Joe Brown and His Bruvvers, 45
"John John (Let's Hope for Peace)," 228
John Lennon / Plastic Ono Band, 144, 228–29,
    231, 267
"Johnny B. Goode," 6, 15, 60, 216, 237
Johns, Glyn, 210, 219–20
Johnson, President Lyndon B., 81, 95–96, 101–2,
    134, 150–51, 176–77, 178, 179
Johnson, Robert, 138, 216
"Julia," 24, 89, 125, 147, 180, 182–83, 186–87
"Junk," 186–87
"(Just Like) Starting Over," 66, 103n1
Justis, Bill, 26, 237, 247

Kaempfert, Bert, 41–43, 46, 49–50
Kaiserkeller, The (Hamburg), 35–36
Kansas City, MO, 95, 96–97, 178
"Kansas City" (*see also* "Hey-Hey-Hey-Hey!"), 34,
    46, 83, 95, 96–97, 100, 113–14
"Keep Your Hands off My Baby," 14–15, 41, 57, 240,
    252
Kennedy, President John F., 55, 71, 80–81, 141,
    178, 200–1
Kennedy, Senator Robert F., 176, 178–79, 180, 200–1
Kennedy Airport (New York), 78–80
Kesey, Ken, 155–56, 168
keyboard
    celeste, 58, 70
    Challen upright piano, 165, 224
    clavichord, 131
    Fender Rhodes electric piano, 209–10
    Hammond RT-3 electronioc organ, 122
    harmonium, 116, 167

harpsichord, 122, 189
Hohner Pianet electric piano, 108, 110, 173–74
keyboard generally, xiii, 58, 108, 167, 209, 230
Lowrey Heritage Deluxe DSO-1 electronic organ,
    160, 161, 162, 164–65, 225
Mellotron, 134, 147, 160, 181
Moog synthesizer, 181, 221–22, 256, 263
organ, 142, 197
piano, xi, 20, 25, 27–28, 58, 69, 70, 97, 122,
    122n9, 131, 167, 171, 186, 190–91, 194–95,
    199, 202, 217–18, 220, 224, 225–26, 227
Ramsden upright piano, 76
Steinway grand piano, 163, 164
Steinway upright piano, 181
Vox Continental electronic organ, 108, 160,
    161, 163
Wurlitzer electric piano, 188
King, Ben E., 41, 108, 190
King, Carole (*see also* Goffin-King), x, 11, 13,
    14–15, 41
King, Rev. Dr. Martin Luther, Jr. (*see also* civil rights),
    4, 55, 81, 95–96, 101, 102, 134, 151–52, 176,
    178, 187–88, 200–1
King-Size Taylor and the Dominoes, 34–35, 43
Kinks, The, 64, 82, 103, 106, 190, 256
Kirchherr, Astrid, 35–36
Klein, Allen, 217, 228–29, 230
"Komm, Gib Mir Deine Hand," 82, 89n1
Koschmider, Bruno, 35–36

"Lady Madonna," 171, 180, 181–82, 225
Lancashire, England, 20, 166–67
Langham, Richard, 58
Laos (*see* Vietnam War)
Leach, Sam, 43, 44–45
Lead Belly [né Huddie Ledbetter], 22–23, 216
Leary, Timothy, 136, 158
"Leave My Kitten Alone," 41, 238, 248
Led Zeppelin, 15, 60, 118, 186, 207, 262, 265
"Lend Me Your Comb," 93, 237
Lennon, Alfred, 20, 24, 146
Lennon, Cynthia (née Powell), 35, 182, 184, 198,
    218–19, 251
Lennon, Julia (née Stanley), 5, 20, 24–25, 27, 146,
    147, 247
Lennon, Julian, 24, 158, 160, 253
Lester, Richard, 84
"Let It Be" (song), 25, 208, 209–10, 210n1, 265, 266
Let It Be (album), 32, 206, 208–20, 221–22, 223, 230, 266
Let It Be (film), 182, 206, 208–18, 230
Let It Be . . . Naked, 210n1, 217–18
Let It Bleed, 180, 207, 216

Lewis, Jerry Lee, 5–6, 7–8, 9, 12–13, 22–23, 31, 34, 81–82, 108, 112, 209, 227, 237, 247

Lewisohn, Mark, 26–27, 190–91

LGBTQ sexuality and gay liberation, 8–9, 14–15, 43, 102, 152, 207

Lieber, Jerry (*see also* Lieber-Stoller), 41

Lieber-Stoller, 16

"Like a Rolling Stone," 99–100, 257

"Like Dreamers Do," 45, 48–49

Litherland Town Hall (Liverpool), 35–36, 40, 249

"Little Child," 56, 86

Little Eva (Boyd), 14–15, 41

"Little Queenie," 34, 60, 238, 248

Little Richard (Penniman), x, 1–3, 5–6, 7–9, 12–14, 15, 22–23, 25, 31, 34, 46, 55, 64, 80–82, 96–97, 109, 114, 182, 209, 211–12, 226, 231–32

Live at the BBC, 11–14, 16 (*see also* British Broadcasting Corporation)

Live Peace in Toronto 1969, 228–29

Liverpool, England, xiii, 1, 4–5, 15, 19–20, 22–25, 26–27, 33–36, 39, 40, 43, 44, 45–46, 47–48, 56–57, 58, 59, 63–64, 75–77, 84, 85, 106, 120, 120–21n8, 126, 145–46, 210, 232

Liverpool Cathedral, 24–25

Liverpool College of Art, 26–27, 32–33

Lomax, Jackie, 181, 187

London, England, 15, 19, 31, 35–36, 43, 45, 54, 64, 75, 76, 78–80, 103, 105n3, 107, 114–15, 132, 134, 136, 155–56, 172, 173, 180, 187–88, 202, 209–10, 220, 228

"Lonesome Tears in My Eyes," 85, 236

"Long and Winding Road, The," 173, 208, 209–10, 210n1

"Long, Long, Long," 180, 186–87, 200

"Long Tall Sally" (song), 1, 8–9, 15, 24–25, 34, 80–81, 82, 94, 95, 96–97, 109, 113–14, 188, 231–32, 236, 245, 255

Long Tall Sally (EP), 82

Los Angeles, CA (*see also* Hollywood), 95, 101, 136, 178–79, 181, 207

Love (album), 74n1, 162n1, 232

Love, Mike (*see also* Beach Boys, The), 182–83

"Love Me Do," 11, 39, 40, 46–47, 48, 50, 51, 55, 56–57, 62, 71, 131–32, 251, 255

"Love Me Tender," 5, 113

"Love of the Loved," 51, 108, 137n3

"Love You To," 16, 130–32, 134–35

"Lovely Rita," 149, 158

Lowe, John "Duff" (*see also* Quarry Men, The), 26–29

LSD, 134–36, 139–40, 141, 152–53, 155–56, 158, 160, 166, 172, 243, 259

"Lucille," 15, 209, 236, 246

"Lucy in the Sky with Diamonds," xiv–xv, 24, 118, 139, 141, 149, 158, 159–64, 173–74, 191, 192–93, 230

Ludwig drums (*see* percussion)

Lynch, Kenny, 57

lyrics (poetic aspects of) (*see also* found lyrics, irony, persona), 49, 55, 68, 84, 92, 123, 134–35, 135n1, 136, 140, 146–47, 158–59, 172, 197–98, 213, 216

"Maggie Mae" / "Maggie May," 24–25, 208, 210, 237

Magic Christian, The, 209–10, 218–19, 220, 232

"Magical Mystery Tour" (song), 150, 170

Magical Mystery Tour (EP set), 150, 158, 168–74, 175, 181, 229–30, 260–61

Magical Mystery Tour (film), 168–69, 181, 208, 223, 230

Maharishi Mahesh Yogi, The, 139–40, 152, 181, 182–83, 199

"Mailman, Bring Me No More Blues," 209, 214

Manchester, England, 19, 26–27, 64

Mandela, Nelson (*see also* civil rights, South Africa), 81

maracas (*see* percussion)

Marcus, Greil, 145, 203

Mardas, Alex, 182, 184

mariachi, 81–82, 108

"(Marie's the Name) His Latest Flame," 41, 239, 250

marijuana, 82, 102, 103, 121, 141, 152–53, 154–55, 166

Marrion, Albert, 44–45

"Marseillaise, La," 152, 179

Martha [Reeves] and the Vandellas, 81–82, 110

"Martha My Dear," 180, 186, 194–95

Martin, George, xiv–xv, 39, 45–48, 49–51, 58, 60–61, 67–68, 69, 70, 76, 85, 108, 112, 113, 122, 145, 147, 158, 162n1, 163, 173–74, 182, 187–88, 189, 200–1, 210, 219–20, 221, 223, 241, 251, 267

Martin guitars (*see* guitar)

Marvelettes, The, 46, 49, 239, 250

Marvin, Hank (*see also* Shadows, The), 31, 104–5n2

"Matchbox," 32, 82, 237, 255

Matthew, Brian, 56–58

"Maxwell's Silver Hammer," 171, 194, 208, 209, 221, 223

"Maybelline," 6, 60

MBE (Member of the British Empire), 103, 122–23

McCartney, 186–87, 206, 230, 231, 267

McCartney, James ("Jim"), 20, 25, 32, 145

McCartney, Linda (née Eastman), 212, 217, 220

McCartney, Mary (née Mohin), 20, 25

McCartney, Mike, 26–27, 32

McGuinn, Roger (*see also* Byrds, The), 84

"Mean Mr. Mustard," 208, 221, 223–24

Meet the Beatles!, 78–80

melisma, 30–31, 87–88, 93, 106, 118–19, Video 2.6

Mellotron (*see* keyboard)

Memory Almost Full, 231

Memphis, TN, 4, 5, 6, 27, 31, 122, 131–32, 133–34, 178

"Memphis, Tennessee," 46, 60, 238, 248, 262

Menlove Avenue (Liverpool), 24, 120–21n8

Mersey Beat, 33, 43, 45, 75, 250

Mersey River, 19, 43, 120–21n8

Mersey Sound, The, 75

Merseybeat, 81–82

meter, 42–43, 116–17, 134–35, 160, 161–62, 163–64, 186, 194–95, 198, 199, 201, 210, 217–18, 220–21, 224, Video 1.2

Miami, FL, 81, 84

"Michelle," 101, 121, 125–26, 139, 141

middle eight (formal unit) (*see* bridge)

Mike Sammes Singers, The, 45–46, 173, 189

Miles, Barry, 136, 156, 172

Miracles, The, 49, 106n6

"Misery," 55, 57, 58, 62, 70

mixing (*see* recording procedure)

mode mixture (*see* tonal conflict and contrast)

modulation (*see* tonal conflict and contrast)

"Money (That's What I Want)," 56, 62, 67, 69, 92, 181, 228, 238, 248

Monterey Pop Festival, 152

Montreal, Canada, 94–95, 218–19, 228

Moore, Scotty (*see also* Presley, Elvis), 13, 27–29, 30–31

Moore, Tommy, 33–34

mordent, 42–43, 125, Video 2.6

Moretti, Joe (*see also* Johnny Kidd and the Pirates), 45

"Mother," 24

"Mother Nature's Son," 180, 189

Motown (Records/Studios), 11, 49, 67, 81–82, 99–100, 109n7, 121, 122, 129, 247

motto (formal unit), 65–66, 111, 143–44

"Move It," 104–5n2

"Movin' 'n' Groovin'," 32, 237, 247

"Mr. Moonlight," 83, 96–97, 240

"Mr. Tambourine Man," 84, 99–100

multiphonics, Video 2.6

music hall (*see also* Tin Pan Alley), 16, 20, 25, 32, 136–37, 230

Music Man, The, 80, 136–37, 247

"My Bonnie (Lies Over the Ocean)," 40, 42–43, 44–45, 250–51, 254

My Bonnie (EP), 40

NEMS (*see* North End Music Stores)

New Brighton, Liverpool, 43

New Musical Express, The (NME), 21–22, 58, 63–64

New York, NY, 78–80, 82, 84, 101, 141, 146, 183–84, 207

New Zealand and Maori, 94, 170, 212

Newark, NJ, 101, 151–52

Newby, Chas, 35–36, 40–41

Newport Folk Festival, RI, 82

Nicol, Jimmie, 94

"Night Before, The," 101, 108, 110–11

Nixon, President Richard M., 152–53, 179, 179n1

"No Particular Place to Go," 10–11, 60, 240

"No Reply," 68, 83, 97

North End Music Stores (NEMS), 43–44

North Vietnam (*see* Vietnam War)

"Norwegian Wood (This Bird Has Flown)," xiv–xv, 89, 101, 121, 122–23, 186, 191

"Not a Second Time," xxi, 56, 69–70, 71, 92, 110–11, 142, 200

"Not Guilty," 186–87

"Nowhere Man," 101, 121–22, 139, 143, 166–67, 182, 196, 211–12, 217

nuclear weapons (*see* atomic bomb)

"Ob-La-Di, Ob-La-Da," 180, 186–87, 189, 207, 232–33

oboe, 46, 76

"Octopus's Garden," 208, 221, 223

offbeat, 72, 104–5, 139, 198, 213, Video 1.2

offset doo-wop, 64–65, 72–73, 87–88, 171

"Oh! Darling," 110, 208, 211–12, 221, 223, 225–27

"Old Brown Shoe," 208, 218–19, 220, 221, 222–23

Oldham, Andrew Loog, 57, 76–77, 253

On Air: Live at the BBC Volume 2, 11–13 (*see also* British Broadcasting Corporation)

"One after 909," xiv–xv, 32, 34, 59, 86, 208, 209–10, 210n1, 216, 220–21

"Only a Northern Song," 16, 182, 207

Ono, Yoko, x, 113, 136, 146, 147, 158–59, 176–77, 181, 182–83, 184, 188, 202–4, 206–7, 209, 210, 213, 215, 217–21, 228–29, 230, 241, 259, 262, 264, 265, 266, 267

open phrase group, Video 1.3

"Operation Big Beat," 43, 44

Orbison, Roy, 6, 46, 48, 51, 54, 59, 231, 240, 241, 249, 250, 251, 253 orchestra, 137–38, 156, 157–59, 165, 166–67, 174, 182, 189, 200, 201–2, 210

ostinato, 61, 104–6, 107, 118, 119–20, 121–22, 222–23

outro (formal unit) (*see* coda)

overdubbing (*see* recording procedure)

"P.S. I Love You," 40, 46–47, 48, 55, 113, 220–21, 251, 255

pacifism, 95–96, 102, 121, 134, 150–52, 166, 176, 218–19

"Paperback Writer," xxi, 130, 143–44, 215

Paris, France, 74n1, 78–80, 82, 97, 179, 187–88, 200–1, 218–19

Parlophone Records, 45–46, 245, 250

Parnes, Larry, 33–34, 35

Paul McCartney's Liverpool Oratorio, 231

pedal point (*see also* drone), 97, 114, 119, 125

"Peggy Sue," 7–8, 237, 247

Penny Lane (Liverpool), 25–26, 120, 121, 145

"Penny Lane," xxi, 76, 89, 111, 141, 145–46, 149, 154–55, 157–58, 160, 169, 171, 212, 259, 260

percussion, Video 1.2, Video 2.3, Video 3.1
  alarm clock, 166
  bass and drums duet, 97
  bass drum, 34–35, 41–42, 56, 160, 162, Video 1.2, Video 2.3
  bongos, 67
  claves, 108
  cowbell, 93, 197–98
  cymbals, 41–42, 47–48, 70, 106, 107, 131–32, 139, 160, 161, 162–63, 164, 202, 225, 230, Video 3.1
  drummer/drumming, xiv, xx, 7, 16–18, 31–32, 33–34, 35, 47–48, 50, 58, 122, 188–89, 203
  drum(s), generally, xiii, 7, 11, 16–17, 22–23, 24, 27–28, 31–32, 34–35, 47, 58, 80, 104, 105, 228, Video 1.2
  floor tom-tom, 65, 162–63, Video 3.1
  guiro, 108
  handclaps, 67, 72, 74, 74n1, 163, 225
  hi-hat, 41–42, 65, 139, 161, 162–64, 193, 225, Video 1.2
  Ludwig Downbeat kits, 22, 41, 56, 58, 65, 66, 67–68, 69, 70, 74, 91, 104–5, 107, 114, 119–20, 121, 131, 143, 160, 161–63, 170, 189, 190–91, 199, Video 1.2, Video 2.3, Video 3.1
  Ludwig Hollywood kit, 212, 220–21, 225, 227
  maracas, 48, 111, 114, 163, 165, 220–21
  Premier kit, 48, 52, 56

snare drum, 41–42, 47–48, 107, 162–63, 194–95, 221, Video 1.2, Video 2.3, Video 3.1

tabla, 158

tambourine, 48, 104–5, 107, 119–20, 190, 191

timpani, 97

tom-tom (including fills), 17, 41–42, 47–48, 51–52, 55, 65, 104–5, 119–20, 160, 189, 197, 213–14, 225, 227, Video 2.3, Video 3.1

washboard, 23–24

period (formal unit), 93, 107, 193, Video 1.3

Perkins, Carl, x, 5–6, 7–9, 12–14, 22–23, 27, 31, 32, 34, 45, 51, 62, 93, 96–97, 209, 231–32, 236, 237, 241, 245

persona and authorial voice, 68, 82, 87, 89–91, 92, 106n5, 110–11, 113, 116–17, 118, 119–20, 122, 124, 138, 139, 141–42, 144, 145–47, 156, 157–59, 165–66, 167, 171, 185–86, 187, 191, 193, 199, 200, 212, 215, 216

Pet Sounds, 155

Peter and Gordon, 76, 254

Peter, Paul, and Mary, 81–82, 251, 254

Philippines, The, 130, 132

Phillips, Percy, 27

Phillips, Sam (*see also* Sun Records/Studios), 6, 9, 27, 96–97

phrase rhythm, 48–49, 72–73, 111, 117, 118–20, 122, 123–24, 161, 167, 172–73, 174, Video 1.2

piano (*see* keyboard)

Pickett, Wilson, 95–96, 213, 226

"Picture of You, A," 16, 46

"Piggies," 180, 185–86, 189

Pink Floyd, 122n9, 155–56, 158–59

Plastic Ono Band, 189, 218–19, 228–29, 264, 265, 266

"Please Mr. Postman," 46, 56, 67, 69, 239, 250, 254

"Please Please Me" (song), 48, 50–52, 55, 56, 58, 62, 67, 71, 75–76, 81, 139, 158–59, 254

Please Please Me (album), 48, 54, 55, 58, 62, 67, 92, 158–59, 252

politics (national and international), 41, 95–96, 102, 132, 139–40, 150–51, 152–53, 176–79, 181, 184, 189–90, 200–1

Polydor Records (Germany), 41–42, 44–45

"Polythene Pam," 206, 221, 223–24

Pomus, Doc, 16, 41, 190

Pop Go the Beatles, 41, 59, 190

pop art and postmodernism, 156–57, 165, 166–67, 187–88, 196

power chord (and other thirdless chords), 72, 73, 74, 106–7, 108, 119, 125, 126, Video 1.5

pre-chorus (formal unit), 159, 160, 161–64

rock ('n' roll), x, 1–2, 3–4, 5, 6, 8–9, 11, 12, 14–15, 16, 17–18, 20–21, 22–23, 33, 34–35, 40, 41, 45, 49–50, 60, 62, 71, 78, 80, 81–82, 84–85, 95–96, 99, 107, 108, 113–14, 136–37, 152–53, 158, 179, 182, 187, 190, 197, 228, 232–33

"Rock and Roll Music," 6, 83, 96–97, 113–14, 231–32, 237, 247

Rock Band, 74n1, 162n1, 232

"Rock Island Line," 22–23, 216, 236, 245

rockabilly, 6, 11, 16, 27–29, 64, 85, 111, 121–22, 219, 220, 231–32

"Rocky Raccoon," 171, 180, 186, 189

Rodgers, Richard, and Oscar Hammerstein, 101–2, 137

"Roll Over Beethoven," 6, 15, 16, 56, 60, 67, 69, 94, 95, 236, 245, 254

Rolling Stones, The, xv, 4, 15, 31, 57, 60, 64, 82, 99–100, 107, 122, 136–37, 149, 152–53, 155, 180, 189, 199, 207, 217, 251, 253, 254, 255, 260, 263

Rolling Stones Rock and Roll Circus, The, 189

"Rooftop" concert (London), 32, 115, 209–10, 213, 214–15, 217–18, 228

Rory Storm and the Hurricanes, 34–35, 40, 43

Royal Academy of Dramatic Art (London), 43

Royal Albert Hall (London), 56–57, 76

Rubber Soul, 17, 22, 101, 113–15, 120–26, 130, 132, 134–35, 149, 181, 258

"Run for Your Life," 87, 101, 191

Rydell, Bobby, 64–65

"Saints, The" (*see* "When the Saints Go Marching In")

San Francisco, CA, 134, 152, 155–56

"Satisfaction" (*see* "(I Can't Get No) Satisfaction")

Saturday Club, 11–12, 24, 56–57, 58

"Save the Last Dance for Me," 41, 184, 190, 210, 238, 249

Saville Theatre (London), 152, 154–55

"Savoy Truffle," 158, 180, 186, 194

scale(s) (chromatic, major, major pentatonic, microtonal, minor, minor pentatonic), 51, 65, 66, 68, 106, 107, 119–20, 162, 163–64, 174, 191, 192, 198, 214–15, 224, 230, Video 1.3, Video 1.4, Video 1.6

Schlager, 35, 41

Schumann, Robert, 123, 202

Scotland, 33–34, 85

Searchers, The, 63–64, 81

"Searchin'," 8–9, 41

Sellers, Peter, 46, 218–19

sentence (formal unit) (*see also* SRDC), 29, 48–49

sex and (typically heteronormative) sexuality (*see also* LGBTQ sexuality), 10–11, 15–16, 24–25, 30–31, 35, 52, 55, 57, 60, 70, 71–73, 91, 101–2, 121, 150, 180, 182–83, 190, 198, 199, 225

"Sexy Sadie," 180, 182–83, 196, 198–99

"Sgt. Pepper's Lonely Hearts Club Band" (song), 149, 154–55, 158

Sgt. Pepper's Lonely Hearts Club Band (album), xiii–xv, 17, 22, 123, 149, 150, 152–53, 154–67, 168–69, 170, 181, 182, 184, 185–86, 187–88, 189, 196, 200, 203, 208–9, 223, 229–30, 232, 259, 260

"Sgt. Pepper's Lonely Hearts Club Band (Reprise)," 149, 158, 159, 165

Shadows, The, 11, 31, 42–43, 45–46, 104–5n2, 238, 239, 249

Shakespeare, William, 136, 158–59, 173

"Shakin' All Over," 45, 238, 249

Shane Fenton and the Fentones, 45–46

Shankar, Ravi, 144

Shapiro, Helen, 57

"She Came In through the Bathroom Window," 208, 223–24

"She Loves You," xiv–xv, xxi, 13, 30–31, 51, 56, 61, 62–63, 64–66, 71, 78, 81, 87, 88, 92, 94, 95, 104–5, 109, 110–11, 117–19, 139, 142, 185, 200, 216, 253

"She Said She Said," xiv–xv, 130, 134–35, 136

"She's a Woman," 83, 97, 198, 225, 256

"She's Leaving Home," xi, 65–66, 122, 149, 151–52, 158, 189

Shea Stadium (New York), 103

"Sheik of Araby, The," 16, 41

Sheridan, Tony, 11, 35–36, 41–43, 46, 93, 242, 249, 251

"Shimmy Shimmy," 44

Shirelles, The, 14–15, 34–35, 41, 49, 58, 73, 239, 240, 250, 251

"Shot of Rhythm and Blues, A," 57

Shotton, Pete (*see also* Quarry Men, The), 24–25

shuffle, 27–29, 93, 162–63, Video 1.2

Shuman, Mort (*see also* Pomus, Doc), 41, 190

"Sie Liebt Dich," 82, 254, 255

Silver Beatles, The, 33

sitar (*see* guitar)

Six-Day War, 150, 178–79

skiffle, 22–23, 24–25, 40, 50, 216

slavery (*see* civil rights)

"Slow Down," 82

Smith, George, 24

Smith, Mimi (née Stanley), 24, 120–21n8, 146

Smith, Norman, 122n9
snare drum (*see* percussion)
"So How Come (No One Loves Me)," 13–14, 239
"Some Other Guy," 17, 46, 208–9, 240
"Something," 121, 126, 139, 160, 161, 192–93, 208,
    217, 221, 222–23, 224–25, 230
son clave rhythm, Video 3.1
soul music (*see also* rhythm and blues), 81–82, 110,
    121–22, 226
"Sour Milk Sea," 187, 194
South Africa (*see also* civil rights: apartheid),
    39–40, 81
Soviet Union (*see also* cold war)
    communism, 5–6, 35, 176–77, 179, 187–88
    generally, 5–6, 39–40
    Iron Curtain, 5–6, 35
    Soviet-bloc, 5–6, 179, 200–1
    Sputnik, 5–6
    spying, 55
Spain, 144, 145–46, 202–3, 220
Spaniard in the Works, A, 24, 197, 213
Spector, Phil, 4–5, 210, 213, 214–15, 230
Speke, Liverpool, 20, 25, 26
SRDC form, 29–30, 51–52, 67, 70, 91, 124, 191,
    Video 2.2
St. Peter's Church, Woolton, 24–25
"Stand By Me," 41, 108
Star-Club (Hamburg), 49
Starkey, Maureen (née Cox), 182
Stax Records, 95–96, 121, 122, 129
"Step Inside Love," 181
Stoller, Mike (*see also* Lieber-Stoller), 16, 41, 45
stop time, 27–29, 62, 106, 108, 110–11, 119–20,
    142, 143–44, 160, 162–63, 173, 196, 212, 216,
    220–21, 226–27, Video 1.2
"Strawberry Fields Forever," xi, 25, 72–73, 89, 121,
    142, 144–47, 149, 154–55, 156, 157–58, 160,
    161, 169, 173, 195, 197, 198, 200, 229–30,
    259, 260
string instruments (bass viol, dilruba, harp, viola,
    violin, violoncello) (*see also* orchestra), 108,
    113, 114, 130, 147, 151–52, 158, 162n1, 164,
    166, 172–73–, 191, 194–95, 200, 203–4,
    221, 225
strophic form, Video 1.3
Students for a Democratic Society, 102, 121, 151
Sullivan, Ed (*see Ed Sullivan Show, The*)
Sun (Records/Studios) (*see also* Phillips, Sam), 5, 6,
    24–25, 27, 30–31, 96–97
"Sun King," 208, 209, 223–24
Supremes, The, 95–96, 99–100, 109, 121–22
"Sure to Fall (In Love with You)," 13–14, 34, 93

surf backbeat (*see* backbeat)
surf music, 81–82
suspension (4-3), 114, 116–17, 122, 126, 139, 144
Sutcliffe, Stu, 32–33, 35–36, 40–41, 242, 248, 251
Swan Records, 80–81
"Sweet Georgia Brown," 40, 46, 82, 93, 255
"Sweet Little Sixteen," 60, 237, 247
Swinging Blue Jeans, The, 63–64, 81
syncopation, 17, 61, 65–66, 68, 71–72, 73, 93,
    103–5, 104–5n2, 139, 140, 141–42, 163–64,
    224, Video 1.2, Video 3.1

"Take Good Care of My Baby," 64–65, 137
"Take Out Some Insurance on Me, Baby," 82, 137,
    238, 255
tamboura, 104–5, 158, 160, 161, 163, 164
tambourine (*see* percussion)
tape manipulation (*see* recording procedure)
"Taste of Honey, A" 44, 46, 55, 58, 93, 136–37, 239
tattoo (formal unit), 48–49, 52, 65, 66, 91, 104–5,
    107, 118, 119–20, 139, 140, 143, 144, 173, 174,
    191, 212, 213, 215, 217–18, Video 1.7
"Taxman," 130, 131–32, 134–35
Taylor, James, 184, 218–19
tea-chest bass, 22–23, 24–25
teenagers (*see also* generation gap), 6, 11–13, 19, 31,
    35–36, 41, 55, 60, 71–72, 73, 75–76, 80, 81–82,
    91, 99, 103, 123, 132, 133–34, 147, 150–52,
    156, 190, 216, 220–21
"Tell Me What You See," 100–1, 108
"Tell Me Why," 82
Temperance Seven, The, 45–46
tempo, 27–29, 46–48, 51, 58, 60–61, 62, 80, 90–91,
    125, 160, 161–63, 181, 186–87, 188, 196, 197,
    198, 202, Video 1.2
"Thank You Girl," 17, 56, 59, 173, 253, 254
"That'll Be the Day," 27, 73
"That's All Right (Mama)," 4, 5, 13, 15, 34
"There's a Place," xxi, 55, 58, 62–63, 90–91,
    142, 254
"Things We Said Today," 68, 82–83, 92, 95, 113, 195,
    255
"Think for Yourself," 101, 121–22
"This Boy," 30–31, 56, 65–66, 73, 80, 92, 94, 108,
    173, 211–12, 226–27, 254
"This Guitar (Can't Keep from Crying)," 192
Thomas, Chris, 189, 219–20
"Three Cool Cats," 8–9, 16, 41, 209
"Ticket to Ride," xxi, 17, 98, 100, 101, 104–7, 114–15,
    119, 126, 216, 232, 257, 273, 278
"Till There Was You," 45–46, 56, 67, 69, 78, 80, 94,
    136–37, 137n2, 231–32, 239, 249